The Memphis Belle

NOTE

  During most of the time period covered by this book the branch of the U.S. military services known today as the "Air Force" was known as the "U.S. Army Air Corps." The various divisions of the Air Corps were known as "" such as the Eighth Air Force, the Fifteenth Air Force, etc.
  The term "Air Force," covering the various Air Forces collectively, did not come into official use until 1947. For purposes of simplicity and to avoid confusion, we have, in this book, simply used the term Air Force, or Air Forces.

First Edition

Copyright © 1987 by Menno Duerksen

Published by Castle Books Inc.
P.O. Box 17262
Memphis, Tenn. 38187

ISBN 0-916693-10-4
ISBN 0-916693-09-0

PRINTED IN THE UNITED STATES OF AMERICA

Foreword

General Ira C. Eaker was commanding general of the Eighth Air Force in the European Theater during World War II. Beginning with a handful of pioneering planes in 1942, fighting against tremendous odds, the Eighth eventually would unleash huge fleets of bombers which would play a decisive role in the defeat of Adolf Hitler's Third Reich.

It was on June 1, 1943, still during the early stages of that air war, when General Eaker issued the order that one B-17 Flying Fortress be detached from combat duty and sent back to the United States along with its crew, for a nationwide tour to publicize the War Bond sales effort.

The plane selected was the Memphis Belle.

On April 22, 1987, as the City of Memphis prepared to dedicate a new home for the historic old bomber, General Eaker, despite his 91 years and somewhat impaired health, wrote a letter to Colonel Robert K. Morgan, wartime pilot of the Belle, congratulating him and the citizens of Memphis on the occasion of that dedication.

The general graciously gave us permission to use that letter as a foreword to this book. Only a few months later, on August 6, 1987, General Eaker died.

Dear Colonel Morgan and Crew:

Vivid in my memory is the day, June 6, 1943, almost 44 years ago, when General Devers, Commander of the European Theater, and I bade you farewell at Bovingdon - the first 8th Air Force bomber and crew to be sent home upon the completion of 25 combat missions.

You took off that day on a 26th mission - to dramatize to Americans at home in those early, tense days of World War II what our heavy bombers were accomplishing in smashing Hitler's war machine. Your mission on the home front was in many respects as important as your exemplary performance on the war front. Aided by Major William Wyler's superb documentary *Memphis Belle* film, you gave a fine boost to civilian morale, helped the War Bond campaign and, not least, provided significant evidence of what air power could do.

Now your famous B-17, beautifully restored, is being dedicated in her final home in honor both of you and also those thousands of other airmen and ground crews who took the battle to the enemy. Let us in particular salute those airmen who gave their lives in carrying out this mission. The Memphis Belle shall remain a living memorial to their brave deeds four decades ago and a reminder to present and future generations of Americans of the need to remain vigilant and strong in the preservation of freedom.

Though I cannot be with you in person on this historic occasion, I am greatly honored by your invitation to participate in spirit. I send my congratulations to all who helped make the Memphis Belle preservation possible and in particular to Mayor Richard C. Hackett and the citizens of Memphis.

Sincerely,

Ira C. Eaker
General, USAF (Ret)
Former commander, U.S.
Eighth Air Force

Memphis Belle Memorial Association
Board of Directors

Credits

Whenever a writer attempts to write a book such as this one, there comes a time when it is his duty to acknowledge that he could never have done the job without help. A lot of help.

It's never possible to give adequate credit to everyone who helped, but the writer must try.

Primary acknowledgement will have to go to Frank Donofrio, president of the Memphis Belle Memorial Association, who has spent years learning about the historic old airplane and freely told us what he knew. To Dr. Harry Friedman, vice-president of the Association, who has spent years doing research on the plane and freely gave us access to everything he had.

We must thank the eight - or is it eleven - surviving members of the Belle's crew who patiently spent many hours talking to me about their memories. And thanks for much help from the family members of the two Memphis Belle crewmen who have died.

Special thanks would have to go to Colonel Robert K. Morgan, pilot of the Belle, who behind the scenes has done more than anyone will ever know and has graciously allowed us to use his love story, which may soon be celebrated in a motion picture.

We could never forget Margaret Polk, the real Memphis Belle, who spent hours talking to us. She opened up three huge scrapbooks which contained the intimate details and mementos of her romance with Colonel Morgan. Margaret is a gracious lady.

Then we must acknowledge the assistance of the U. S. Air Forces Museum at Wright-Patterson Air Force Base, Ohio, the U. S. Air Force Research Center at Maxwell Air Force Base, Alabama, and the National Archives Research Center at Suitland, Maryland.

Grateful thanks also to the Historical Services Section of the Boeing Company in Seattle, Washington, builders of the Memphis Belle, and to the Memphis Public Library, which opened its files.

I also remember my good friend, Robert Morris, who called me on a Sunday morning, July 6, 1986, to say he and his wife were driving out to the Memphis airport to see the Memphis Belle.

"Why don't you and Thea come along with us?"

The old bomber and several other World War II planes were on display at the airport as part of a campaign to raise funds for the Belle's restoration. Bob knew of my previous association with the plane, one going back to 1942 when I wrote the first news stories about the airplane, and the romance involving her pilot.

My wife and I went along. So I was standing in the shade of the Belle's broad wings that afternoon, chatting with Frank Donofrio, who also knew of my interest in the plane.

Suddenly Frank turned to me and said, "You should be the one to write a book about the Memphis Belle."

The Author

Menno Duerksen is an award-winning writer, who began his career with the Memphis Press-Scimitar in 1941. In 1945 he began covering Europe and the Middle East for United Press. He reported the Nuremberg war crimes trials. He was in Palestine when the state of Israel was formed.

For the past 23 years he has written magazine articles, dealing mostly with the automobile industry. In 1977 and again in 1984, he won the prestigious Benz Award, offered by the Society of Automotive Historians, for the best magazine series on General Motors.

In 1942, while a reporter with the Press-Scimitar, Duerksen wrote the first stories about the romance between Margaret Polk and the bomber pilot. He was at the Memphis Municipal Airport on June 19, 1943, together with Margaret Polk, the pilot's sweetheart, when the Belle and her crew came home to launch the triumphal national publicity tour.

His previous book, Dear God, I'm Only a Boy, published by Castle Books in 1986, tells of his boyhood in a Mennonite farm community in Oklahoma and of his adult years as a reporter in Europe and the Middle East.

The following paragraph was inadvertently dropped following paragraph two on page 30:

Later, in air battles, such tests would be even more severe. One of the classic examples came when Lieutenant Clark M. Garber Jr., took off from a base in England on a bombing mission. He had on board a full load of bombs and gasoline, plus the 10 men in his crew. As he flew through dense clouds, shortly after take-off, another B-17 suddenly loomed in front of him.

Dedication

This book must be dedicated, primarily, to the members of the crew which flew the Memphis Belle through the angry skies of German-held Europe in 1942 and 1943.

But it has been said that it took 100 men on the ground, the ground crew plus support personnel, to keep just one heavy bomber in the air. No dedication would be complete without including those men on the ground.

Nor would it be complete without including every man of the 91st Heavy Bombardment Group to which the Belle belonged. Other pilots and their crews flew on the Belle's wings, helping protect her - even as the Belle helped protect them. It was only through group efforts of the 91st, the 303rd, the 92nd, the 97th, the 301st, to name only the first groups to engage the enemy, that the Eighth Air Force was able to put enough planes in the air to make an air invasion of Europe possible. A single bomber, attacking Europe alone, was unthinkable.

Then there were the fighter pilots who, at least part of the time during those early months, bravely provided escort protection for the bombers.

To make it complete, we would simply have to say that while this book is largely the story of one plane and one crew, it must be dedicated to all the men of the Eighth Air Force, including the men who did not come back home.

Table of Contents

The Memphis Belle

Now the real story of World War II's most famous warplane.

by Menno Duerksen

CASTLE ⬛ BOOKS

The American Heroes Series

P. O. BOX 17262   MEMPHIS, TENN.   38187

The Memphis Belle Comes Home

The slim, glow-eyed girl in the flower print cotton dress stood waiting on the taxi apron of Memphis Airport, her eyes lifted to the distant sky, her heart pounding with anticipation.

The dashing young pilot who had named his B-17 bomber the Memphis Belle in her honor, was coming home to her from the bloody air battles over Europe.

The girl waited for the man who had held her in his arms, whispering words of love, asking her to marry him. He had promised that he would come home to her, only her, after the war.

Now he was coming. He was only moments away.

The time was June 19, 1943, and America was still at war. Millions of America's young sons were committed to battle. Tens of thousands would never return.

Since Japan had blasted America into the war on December 7, 1941, with her sneak attack on Pearl Harbor, America's part in the global war had been largely in the air, especially in Europe where Hitler's Nazi Germany was the main target. Planes like the Memphis Belle had borne the brunt of the battle. General Eisenhower's giant invasion of France on D-Day was still a year into the future.

The Memphis Belle had been a lucky plane. Twenty-five times she had plowed her way to her target through acres of flak and swarms of Germany's deadly fighter planes. The Belle had taken a beating. She had limped home with bullet holes and shell holes stitched in her sides, with engines shot out, gaping flak holes in her wings, her entire tail nearly shot off. Miraculously, her crew largely escaped injury at a time when the casualty rate for planes flying 25 missions was near 82 per cent.

But there, painted on her sides, were 25 bombs, each marking another dangerous bombing mission. Eight swastikas in a row said that her gunners had shot down eight German planes.

Because of her luck and her record, she had begun attracting the attention of top Air Force brass. News dispatches from the war front to newspapers back home had begun to mention the Memphis Belle.

Near the end of her combat tour she had been selected to star in a War Department film to be shown to the people on the home front to show what America's young fliers were doing.

When War Department officials thought of bringing one of the battle scarred planes back home for a national tour to boost War Bond sales, the Memphis Belle was a natural choice. Perhaps the name played a part in the choice of the Belle for such publicity. It was a tradition that when a pilot finished his training and was given a plane to fly into battle, he would have a christening and give his new plane a name.

There was the Lucky Lady. Old Bill. Ace High. Hell's Angels. A thousand others. The Memphis Belle was a lilting name, glittering with romance. It was a true romance that caught the nation's imagination and warmed the heart.

When Lieutenant Robert K. Morgan took command of his big Boeing B-17 bomber, he named her the Memphis Belle in honor of his fiancee, Margaret Polk, of Memphis, Tennessee. Morgan met her while in training near Seattle, Washington. Margaret had been there visiting her sister who was married to an Air Force officer stationed at the air base there.

Morgan wooed Margaret and obtained her promise to be his.

Memphis newspapers learned of the romance and began printing stories about it. The quick and effortless publicity won by their romance may have been part of the reason the War Department chose the Belle and her crew to come home and make a big publicity tour as the first of the battle-torn B-17s to fly home.

Memphis had been chosen as the very first stop on the tour because of the Memphis belle who waited eagerly now on the taxi apron of the Memphis runway for the first drumming sound in the distance of big bomber engines.

Waiting nearby were ranking military dignitaries, Mayor Walter Chandler of Memphis, and other top officials.

A contingent of P-40s and P-38s were sent out by the Air Force to meet the Memphis Belle and escort her in to the Memphis Airport.

And now they came.

The fast fighter planes came roaring into sight and then, in keeping with the gala occasion, the frisky young fighter pilots put on a show of aerial acrobatics. Rolls. Wing-overs. Dives. Loops. Chandelles.

For the group of proud Americans, watching below, it was a thrilling moment. Real war planes raced through the skies, showing what the new pilots could do on the eve of their departure for the war fronts. This was a rare sight for civilians.

There was more drama to come. The big, four-engine Memphis Belle roared into sight. Instead of landing promptly, as was expected, Robert Morgan, now a captain, saw what the fighter planes were doing and he decided to join their act.

Morgan began putting the bomber through nearly every maneuver that the flipping little fighter planes were doing.

The big bomber was not designed to act like a nimble fighter plane. Flying rules for the heavy bombers forbade flying in a way that would place one of the big, expensive planes and her crew in danger. But the Memphis Belle was doing just that - rolls, flips, wing-overs. The only maneuver Morgan did not try in his B-17 that day was the loop.

He did something which was just as daring, perhaps even more dangerous.

First, he climbed high into the sky over Memphis, then suddenly flipped the bomber over into a power dive. It was not just a steep swoop. It was a true power dive. The plane appeared from the ground to be standing on its nose.

Down, down it came in a screaming song of power like a dive bomber, four big Wright-Cyclone engines howling.

Down it came. Steadily. Faster and faster.

My God! What was that crazy pilot trying to do?

It lasted only a few seconds. The air was charged. Was the big plane going down - with the pilot's stunned fiancee watching? The tension brought choking lumps to the throats of every spectator.

Down and down it came. Closer and closer to the bare face of the concrete runway. The fighter pilots had not tried this.

Down it came.

Someone screamed, "Pull her up! Pull her up!"

One thing was certain. Only a most skilled pilot could now avoid disaster.

Then, in that last moment for decision, the nose of the Memphis Belle began slowly to rise toward the horizon.

With a screaming roar the bomber bottomed out and streaked across the runway so close that a man could have reached up and touched her metal belly.

The thing was crazy. Daring. A bit insane.

11

The big plane was shooting skyward, now, carried aloft by the furious momentum of the frightening dive. Giant propellers chopped off huge bites of air in its climb - and its pilot and crew were safe now.

As the Belle began to pull her nose toward the horizon, a ranking military officer in the welcoming committee said: "That crazy sonofabitch knows that we can't court-martial him."

Obviously, Captain Morgan knew they couldn't - not here in Memphis on the first stop of the bond tour with his fiancee here to meet him. That would be bad public relations for the Air Force. It would be very bad for public morale. Depressing for bond sales.

They decided to greet Captain Morgan, all smiles.

Americans may have needed something like this. Seeing the hottest pilots in the world could give them an uplifting sense of pride as they fought their murderous global war. It could make them proud of the young Americans who flew their war machines into the eye of death - and spat in that eye.

After all, should a young pilot be denied a bit of horseplay?

The crew, asked about that dive, only grinned and shrugged. They said that they trusted their captain.

He always brought them home, they said.

Captain Morgan let the Belle climb and claw for more altitude over the Memphis airport and then he was ready to let her land. A few minutes later he was down and rolling up to the taxi apron, stopping about 50 feet from the reception committee.

The engines throbbed to a halt.

Now one could see that impudent painting on the side of the nose of the plane. It was the picture of a curvy girl in a low-cut bathing suit. Below the picture was the name, Memphis Belle. And nearby on the concrete apron was the girl for whom the plane was named.

The door of the plane swung open and the tall, lanky Captain Morgan was loping across the apron. He had no eyes or hand-shakes for the distinguished cluster of men in the reception committee. His eyes were only on the slim figure of the girl who was rushing to meet him, her eyes shining with happiness and pride.

They hugged.

They kissed.

The young pilot lifted her off the ground and whirled her around in joyful exuberance. He and the Memphis Belle had come flying home at last - just as he had promised.

It was a storybook ending to a storybook tale. Something that lifted the heart and caught the breath.

But was it the real ending?
There was much more to the story which has never been truly told - until now.

The War
Why the Memphis Belle Flew

Most Americans of the World War II generation have always agreed that it was the war with which they felt most comfortable.

Most Americans would prefer peace to war but when U. S. territory was attacked, dramatically, tragically and treacherously as it was at Pearl Harbor, our people united in agreeing that it was a war that had to be fought and won.

For America, World War II began officially on the quiet Sunday morning when a swarm of Japanese warplanes took off from a carrier, swooped down out of blue morning skies over Hawaii, dropped a hail of deadly bombs and torpedos, sinking almost an entire fleet of American warships and killing hundreds of American sailors.

In a larger sense, the war had begun long before that. In the Pacific arena, Japan had begun grabbing territory from Manchuria and China in the 1930s. America sympathized with the Chinese but did not intervene - until after Pearl Harbor.

At about the same time in Europe, the Germans under Adolf Hitler embarked on a program of territorial conquest. Hitler, without bothering to declare war, took all of Austria and part of Czechoslovakia. He said that both territories were part of an old German empire. He was reclaiming them. Then, on September 1, 1939 Hitler attacked Poland and the war in Europe began officially. England and France had guaranteed Poland's integrity and so when the Germans invaded Poland, England and France declared war.

In 1940, in an awesome display of power, Germany crushed France and threatened to jump across the English Channel and invade England. The British were saved by the English Channel that separated England from Europe. And by badly outnumbered British fighter pilots who, in their heroic "Battle of Britain", stopped

14

a massive attempt by German flyers to crush England with bombs from the air.

Our country was not involved in the fighting but our sympathies were with England and we sent them support in the form of weapons and supplies.

On June 22, 1941, after Hitler gave up on his plan to invade England, he turned his attention to Russia and launched a giant invasion. He had been saying for years that he wanted a part of Soviet territory to use as agricultural land to feed Germans.

Despite the fact that most Americans had never been on friendly terms with the communist regime in Moscow, the invasion created a more sympathetic attitude toward the Soviet Union.

In the meantime, Germany formed a military alliance with Japan. Each nation agreed that if the other were attacked, or if either became involved in a war with the United States, the other nation would come to its assistance.

Therefore, when President Roosevelt declared war on Japan, after the brutal surprise attack on our Naval ships lying at anchor in Pearl Harbor, Germany immediately declared war on the United States. This made us allies of the Soviets who were fighting Hitler.

Germany scored enormous victories in the opening days of her invasion of Russia, defeating huge Russian armies and conquering vast territories. The Russians fought back desperately. Most of the world thought Russia would quickly fall before the onrushing victorious German armies.

As the Germans raced toward Moscow, Joseph Stalin, the premier of the Soviet Union, pleaded with American and British leaders to attack Germany from the west so that pressure on Moscow would be reduced. Stalin asked for an invasion of Europe.

America and its British ally now faced the same handicap the Germans had faced when they tried to crush England in 1940 and 1941. America was separated from Europe by the Atlantic Ocean and the English Channel - and invasions by sea are the most difficult operations of all.

The Anglo-American allies simply were not prepared, in 1942, for such an invasion. America had not had the time needed to recruit its armies and train them. It did not have the landing ships and all the other special equipment needed to take such a giant step across the ocean.

Despite their attack against Russia, the Germans had been able to keep strong military defenses posted on the coast of the Atlantic Ocean.

15

So there was only one way to attack the Germans and take pressure off the Russians - hit them through the air. Stalin was not satisfied with air attacks as a substitute for land invasion but there was no alternative.

We would try to smash the German factories and military installations from the air.

British bombers flew mostly at night when they went out to hit German targets. They had tried daylight bombing but had given it up after suffering heavy losses to German fighter planes. They flew heavy four-engine bombers - Stirlings and Lancasters - but these were not as heavily armed as bombers being built in America.

If we sent American bombers to England to help the British in their air campaign, the tables would be turned. We would face the same problem Hitler had faced in 1940 when he gave up on his plan to cross the English Channel and tried, instead, to crush the English with his own bombers.

German bombers had been repulsed by English flyers in their magnificent Spitfire and Hurricane fighters. Wouldn't German pilots, flying their famed Messerschmitt 109s and Focke Wulf 190s, now be able to stop the American bombers?

The answer was that the German bombers had been rather small, single-engine or twin-engine aircraft with very little defense equipment. However, the Americans had the new Boeing B-17, a four-engine bomber bristling with heavy machine guns able to fire in all directions. The Americans also were bringing over the big Consolidated B-24, its four engines and armament nearly as heavy as the B-17's.

The Germans had never seen such planes as these.

In the meantime, something else had changed, because of still another German weapon, the submarines. German submarines were strangling England by sinking ships that were bringing food and supplies to the beleaguered islands. Unless the Americans could stop those submarines, there would be no England from which to launch an attack on occupied Europe. An invasion certainly could not be launched from as far away as the United States.

Normally, the job of stopping submarines is a job for the Navy, but there was something the Air Forces could do about it, too. When the Germans had occupied France, they immediately began building submarine bases all along the Atlantic coast - at Brest, St. Nazaire, La Pallice, Lorient. If American bombers could smash those bases, they would help save the British isles.

16

That is why, when the Americans finally got into the act with their daylight bomb strikes, many of their missions were aimed at German submarine bases. Especially at St. Nazaire, one of the biggest and best equipped submarine bases on the coast. Our bombers flew over St. Nazaire so many times that it became known as the "Milk Run." A pretty hot milk run.

Even before the United States became involved in the war, while England was fighting her desperate battle for survival, we sent military observers to England to study the tactics and results of their air war. The British had tried daylight bombing but, by the summer of 1942, when the first American bombers began to arrive, they had largely given up on it and flew their bombing missions in darkness. British airmen gave the arriving Americans a word of advice: "Don't try daylight bombing. It won't work."

The stubborn Americans would try, anyway.

It was not just a matter of flying planes across the Atlantic. Before they could be sent, there had to be many waiting air bases and airfields - far more than the British had at that time. In fact, the British had to give the Yanks a few of their own Royal Air Force bases while rushing work on new bases.

The first American B-17 base in England would be at Polebrook. It was activated in July of 1942 with the 97th Heavy Bombardment Group moving in. This would be the first Yank group to go into air battle.

The 97th Heavy Bombardment Group consisted of four squadrons of three flights each, with three planes per flight. Usually, one of the squadrons was short one plane so that it had only eight planes, giving the group only 35 planes. And rarely would a squadron be able to put all of its planes in the air on any mission. Some of the planes usually would be on the ground for mechanical work or repairs of battle damag.

The Memphis Belle, in its 25 missions between November 7, 1942, and May 19, 1943, had its tail blasted on two different missions, had a gaping hole blown in a wing on one mission, and lost an engine on nine different outings - keeping ground repair crews busy, sometimes around the clock.

The Memphis Belle was one of the nine planes in the 324th Squadron, one of the four squadrons that formed the 91st Bomb Group. The Group arrived in England in September of 1942 and joined many formation practice flights over the countryside before being declared ready for combat on November 1, 1942.

17

The group was stationed at Bassingbourn, just 50 miles north of London.

Other groups arriving in England at about the same time were the 303rd, the 305th and the 306th. They were stationed at airfields near Bassingbourn. When the high command ordered a mission, they usually assigned planes from several groups to rendezvous at a given point in the air over England - then proceed toward the target, each group flying in an assigned position. Thus, a group might be assigned to fly low group, high group, tail group, lead group and so on.

The lead group and tail group usually got the heaviest attacks from enemy fighter planes.

In bad weather, or when crews had difficulties with radio communications, a group sometimes failed to rendezvous with the other groups on schedule and they might have to proceed to the target as a lone group. It was usual that casualties were heaviest on these strikes because the German fighter pilots always pounced on the smallest groups, or on any straggling plane which fell out of formation due to battle damage or engine failure.

In the early months of action, the attack formations that flew to bomb German targets were often composed of less than 30 or 40 planes. There were seldom more than 60 or 70 in the formation.

The Americans quickly learned that their best protection against the swarming German fighter planes was in numbers and in keeping tight formations. Since the numbers were so often short, they flew in such tight formations that, at times, the pilots swore that their wings overlapped and bumped. You got a bit of propeller turbulence, flying so close to one another, and the plane was hard to control, but it was better than being shot down.

Tight overlapping of planes gave the gunners on all the planes a chance to overlap their firepower. Each plane protected the other by throwing a literal wall of bullets against the attacking fighters. It took a lot of guts to fly an attacking fighter through such a metallic shower, but some of the Germans were gutsy enough to try it.

So, few in numbers, the pioneer bomber groups came to England and flew into the military storm, learning air tricks and surviving - or else, going down in flames or in parachutes. The crewmen who survived passed their experiences and tricks along to crewmen still in training. By late 1943 and in 1944 and 1945, the American attack formations would sometimes number into the hundreds of bombers, sometimes 500 or more.

Later crews would owe much to these early air pioneers. Back home, they were called heroes.

"I hated that word," said John "J.P." Quinlan, the Memphis Belle tail gunner credited with shooting down two German fighters. J. P. was the "spark plug," the morale booster of the whole crew, the only crew member on official record as having been wounded. He saved the plane a dozen times by his crafty spotting of flak and attacking fighters.

"I hated it," he said. "I was never a hero - only a survivor."

The Best Airplane

They were, said the men who flew them into battle, the best airplanes ever made, those Boeing B-17s.

It was a claim that set the sparks flying. That brought hot retorts from the partisans of other famous airplanes. How about the B-29? It could fly further, fly higher and carry bigger loads. How about the B-24? The B-26? The P-38? The P-47? Or the P-51, said by many to be the best fighter plane America made during World War II?

Stop and consider the claim of the B-17 against the background of history and the greatest global war ever fought. Consider the number of B-17s which fought those sky battles. Consider the scope of those battles. Consider the punishment they took and survived. If one considers all these things, then the B-17 may well have been the best of them all.

One thing is certain, the B-17 was capable of doing far more than her designers ever claimed for her. The pilots and the brave crews who flew her into battle proved that, again and again.

Colonel Bob Morgan was one such pilot. After flying his 25 combat missions over Europe, he brought the Memphis Belle back home in 1943 to tour the nation for the War Department, showing thousands of bug-eyed Americans in city after city that he could flip that big four-engine bomber around in the sky in a wild manner most people imagined only a nimble single-engine fighter was capable of doing.

Perhaps never quite so wildly as on that day, June 19, 1943, when he and his crew flew the Belle back home to Memphis and to the girl standing on the concrete apron below, watching the plane winging back to her with her fiance at the controls.

"The only thing you didn't do up there was the loop-the-loop," someone said that day.

"Oh, the Belle can do a loop, too," Morgan said. "I've seen B-17s do a complete loop.

"Oh, it wasn't done on purpose. It was in combat when a B-17 would be shot up and go tumbling toward the ground. I've

20

seen them sometimes do a complete loop without ripping the wings off. This is a tough airplane. The best I ever flew."

Morgan maintained that the Flying Fortress was the best thing in the air, even after he took the cockpit of the bigger and more sophisticated B-29, flying the lead plane of the first B-29 bombing raid over Tokyo.

Perhaps it is impossible to pinpoint the exact moment that a major weapon system is born. This is true in the case of the first true heavy bomber, the B-17.

Oh, there had been so-called heavy bombers as early as World War I. But even those that had more than one engine and sported three wings were not true heavies. Their contribution to the war, aside from creating a bit of terror and some minor damage from inaccurately dropped bombs, was negligible.

But there were men in the armed forces who could look beyond these poor results and see a new strategic weapon in the skies. The best known of these men in America was Brigadier General William "Billy" Mitchell, who had raised eyebrows and hackles immediately following World War I by suggesting that flying bombers could sink battleships.

Billy would be court-martialed, in time, for his obstinacy and for his advocacy of a new type of warfare. Yet, he was given a chance to prove that bombers could sink battleships - even a battleship that had been declared unsinkable.

The captured German battleship Ostfriesland was anchored dead in the water and refused to give up easily, but she finally sank under the rain of bombs. The attacking planes, carrying bombs weighing up to 1,100 pounds, were multi-engine Martins and Handley-Pages.

One of the earliest attempts at building a giant bomber led to the Barling in 1920, a huge tri-plane with six engines and a wing-span of 120 feet. But the giant could barely fly, even without a bomb load. It was soon forgotten.

Along came the Boeing story. The Seattle, Washington, company was established in 1916 as the Pacific Aero Products Company, a name which was quickly changed to the Boeing Airplane Company. Its first products were seaplanes. During World War I the company built trainer planes for the military.

After that war the company became known as one of the top builders of single-engine observation and fighter pursuits for the Army, the Navy and the Marines. Top military leadership turned thumbs down on anything suggesting bigness or bombers. Most planes made during the 1920s were biplanes made of fabric and light wood.

Civilian interest in aviation was limited to carrying passengers and some mail. Few could then visualize the impact that aviation was going to have on the future. The flight of Charles Lindberg, the "Lone Eagle" flying non-stop from New York to Paris in 1927, probably did more to stir interest in flying than anything else that happened in the 1920s.

In 1930, Boeing made a startling contribution to aviation, a new design called the Monomail. It was so revolutionary in design that it could almost be said to be the prototype for virtually all airplanes built, large or small, for generations to come. Nothing less than a low-wing aluminum monoplane that was so futuristic in design that, even looking at it today, one can see the famed war planes of World War II - whether it be the single-engine, twin-engine or four-engine. In essence, this was the plane of the future.

The Monomail was the first plane in a line of development that would lead to the B-17. The next step was the same plane, only stretched out to make room for six passengers and some cargo. It was a big step. They put an engine on each wing and it became the Boeing 247, one of the first in the coming generation of passenger and transport planes.

Although Boeing got little encouragement from the military, the firm built a bomber version called the Y1B-9A. It became known as the B-9 and flew so fast that it outran the Army's best single-engine fighter plane. The plane did have some bugs and Boeing lost out to Martin's B-10 in a bid to sell a bomber to the Army.

For the time being, Boeing had to be satisfied with making a success of its passenger version which carried ten passengers plus a pilot, co-pilot and stewardess.

In its final form, the 247-D with its newly developed Hamilton-Standard variable pitch propellers and rubber de-icer boots, had a top speed of 200 miles an hour. The age of modern air transport was on its way.

Although a far cry from the plane that would eventually make history as the B-17, it is certain that the B-17 could never have been built so well, and in the proper time frame, if it had not been for the engineering experience gained in the making of these earlier planes. In that respect they had been the true forerunners of the modern heavy bomber.

Behind the scenes, the times were not auspicious for developing a radical new weapons system - for use in the air or anywhere else. It was the time of the Great Depression of the 1930s. The Army and Navy had little money to spend on new weapons systems. Beyond that, the nation was at peace. Americans had little taste for military preparedness. After all, they had fought World War I to "make the world safe for democracy."

Billy Mitchell spoke so loudly and so long about the need for the development of a heavy bomber that he was court-martialed and banned from the armed forces for five years. He died before his vision was vindicated.

Not all his arguments had fallen on deaf ears. A new generation of young military officers was appearing on the scene, a bit more attuned to the future. Even a few of the older officers were beginning to recognize that air power was a force that had to be reckoned with. In 1933 the War Department ordered test maneuvers on the West Coast to determine the value of air power in helping repel a possible invasion. The results showed that air power could indeed play a role in any possible war of the future. It was also recognized that a heavy bomber was needed, one capable of carrying at least a ton of bombs 2,000 miles, possibly 5,000 miles.

Early in 1934, a military budget was created to develop a long range bomber. Based on the showing of the early B-9 and the B-247, Boeing was granted a contract to develop a single experimental model.

For once, Boeing engineers overshot their mark. The plane they turned out was the largest airplane ever built in the U.S. It had a wingspan of 149 feet. Its fuselage was 87 feet, 7 inches long. Using even the best and most powerful engines available, the plane was too big and heavy. Top speed was under 200 mph and fuel consumption was prohibitive. The plane, called the XB-15, would not do.

The next try was more realistic. The Army now asked for bids on a plane that would fly 250 mph at an altitude of 10,000 feet, carrying a useful load. It asked that the plane be able to climb to 35,000 feet and stay there up to 10 hours. It also had to stay in the air, carrying its useful load, with one of its engines dead.

The B-17 was coming closer now.

To build the first experimental model, Boeing now set up Project 299 and assigned to direct the project one of its youngest engineers, Edward Curtis Wells, 24, a graduate of Stanford University who had done design work on Boeing's 247.

Somehow, sensing the importance of what they were doing, Boeing assigned virtually its entire resources to the new project, with several engineers working on the various components such as the fuselage, wings, engines, landing gear, and so on. Working at top speed, Boeing was able to complete the first test machine by July of 1935.

Word of the projects, despite its cloak of secrecy, had leaked out. Newspapers began printing stories about a giant mystery plane being built in the Seattle plant.

When the big machine was rolled out through the hangar doors it was almost a spitting image of the earlier B-15, only a bit smaller. But it was still big enough to claim the title as the biggest land plane in America.

To get the desired speed, range and climbing ability, Boeing engineers had refined the experience they had gained from working on the B-15 and the earlier planes. Somehow, everything worked out.

The wingspan now was 103 feet and the fuselage 69 feet long. The Army's specifications had not called for four engines but Boeing engineers had felt that they must have four to meet the requirements. So there they were, two Pratt & Whitney radial engines on each side of the fuselage.

The big plane, with test pilot Leslie Tower at the controls, flew for the first time on July 28, 1935. When Tower came back in and landed, he reported that the new plane was perfect.

After several additional flights to check out all systems and smooth out any possible rough spots, the plane was ready to go to Wright Field for testing.

The 2,000 mile flight from Seattle to Dayton, Ohio, in itself answered many of the questions, such as its range, for one thing, and its speed. The plane averaged 232 mph on the nine-hour flight, breaking all records for that distance. The average altitude had been 22,000 feet.

In fact, the speed was so startling that when the pilot radioed the Wright Field tower of his arrival, the tower men did not believe it. They had not expected the plane for another two hours.

Everything was coming up roses. Or was it?

Tragedy lay in the future of the perfect plane.

With Army test pilot Lieutenant Donald Putt at the controls, the plane easily passed all its preliminary tests. Then, on October 30, Major Ployer Hill, the chief test pilot, was scheduled to take the plane up for one final evaluation. Putt would fly as his co-pilot,

24

with Tower going along as the observer. With all these experienced pilots in the cockpit, what was about to happen seems impossible.

Hill warmed up the engines and took off. It was a perfect take off. Then, just as the big plane began a graceful climbing turn, it suddenly flipped over and crashed, bursting into flames. Tower and Hill were killed. Putt and two other crew members managed to escape the blazing plane.

Almost everyone who saw that crash must have felt that the new plane was dead. But in the investigation of the crash, it was found that nothing on the plane had malfunctioned. It had been a human error.

In building the plane, Boeing had installed a locking tab on the control surfaces of the tail to keep them from being whipped around by the wind while they were parked. Before taking off, the pilot was supposed to push a button to unlock the tab. For some reason, not one of the three experienced pilots aboard the plane had remembered to unlock the tail tab.

This exonerated the plane itself, but Boeing had to face the fact that its only model of the new airplane was gone, crashed and burned. No matter how well the plane was cleared of blame, there remained a psychological problem. Critics could now say the machine was far too big and complicated to be handled safely.

When it was all threshed out, the Army, which had been on the verge of ordering 65 of the new YB-17s as they would be designated, reduced their order to only 13. Meanwhile, Douglas grabbed the big plum, a contract for 133 B-18s. The B-18 had only two engines. But the smaller plane was now more palatable to military leaders, who had been made quite nervous by the crash of the Boeing entry.

There was even more bad luck in the offing. Boeing made some improvements as they began production on their diminished order of 13 planes. For one thing, they switched from the Pratt & Whitney engine to a more powerful Wright Cyclone. There were also improvements made in the landing gear.

Then Boeing announced the first of the new YB-17s was ready for testing. The army sent one of its crack pilots to Seattle to fly the plane. On landing after his flight, he applied the brakes too hard. The brakes froze and locked up. The plane went into a violent skid and was heavily damaged.

This time, Congressional investigators asked more questions. Some of the investigators wanted to scrap the plane. In the end, it was finally decided to go ahead with the original production order, but both Boeing and Air Force officers knew that one more crash would cause the B-17 program to be scrapped.

If there was a silver lining in all this dismal series of events, it was that it all led to the creation of the famed routine pilot check list which pilots today are required to go through before taking off. There must be no more locked tail tabs.

By August of 1937, the first dozen of the B-17s were delivered to Langley Field, Virginia, and assigned to the 2nd Bombardment Group. The new Flying Fortress was operational.

That "Flying Fortress"s nickname had been coined by a news writer when the first of the new planes showed up, bristling with its five machine gun positions as defense against enemy fighter planes in case of actual combat.

If they thought of it as a fortress then, how much more could the name apply on later models, when twin tail guns were added, along with a belly turret with twin guns plus another turret on top of the plane. In later models, a chin turret was added to the front end, and crews sometimes flew with a waist panel open to expose even more .50 caliber machine guns ready for action.

One of the first demonstrations of the capabilities of the new B-17 came when the 2nd Bombardment Group got permission to fly six of the planes to Buenos Aires, Argentina, under the command of Lieutenant Colonel Robert C. Olds, group commander. It would be a goodwill mission.

The 12,000-mile flight was completed faster and with less trouble than any previous flight of that nature, setting another new record. The longest leg of the trip was the 2,695-mile leg from Miami to Lima, Peru. It was completed in 15 hours and 32 minutes.

One of the worst incidents of the flight came when one of the planes broke through a concrete runway while refueling and had to be hoisted out of the hole. It came out without damage, and the plane was able to continue the flight.

During the next few years, the B-17 continued to smash records, one of the most notable being on a flight from Seattle to New York, completed in 9 hours and 14 minutes. It averaged 265 mph, setting a new speed record for planes in its class.

It was on the political front that the new heavy bomber ran into its biggest problems. As war clouds loomed over Europe and there was a growing feeling in some that Americans would become involved, the nation's military leaders decided that emphasis must be put on small planes that could support ground operations. There would be no money in the 1939-1940 budget for heavy bombers.

26

Another stalemate came when Boeing and the War Department became embroiled in an argument over the price that would be paid for the 13 planes already on order. Boeing originally expected a large order and had made cost estimates on that basis. When only a small order was placed, Boeing found that the planes could not be built for the original estimate of $198,000 per plane. If they were paid less than $205,000 per plane, the company would lose money. The War Department refused to budge from the original estimate and Boeing came very close to cancelling its program. In the end, the program was saved when Boeing eliminated a few items of equipment from the planes, and the government squeezed a few more dollars into its offer, increasing it to $202,000.

A difference had been split. The B-17 was saved.

Meantime, the German army, under orders from Hitler, marched into Poland. World War II had begun.

But the B-17's first taste of combat would be less than glorious. As it turned out, it was British flyers who first exposed the Flying Fortress to enemy gunfire after President Roosevelt concluded the Lend Lease program designed to supply Britain with the weapons of war.

With Poland and France removed from the battle, Britain, in 1940 was fighting alone. It was desperately short of weapons. Britain asked for B-17s to be included in their Lend Lease orders. The Americans gave them 20 out of the current order of 38 planes.

Despite repeated warnings that the B-17 could not protect itself properly unless it flew missions as part of a group of other B-17s, providing all the bombers with overlapping fire power, the British sent them out on bombing attacks in groups of two and three. They tried bombing from a height which, considering the bomb sights available, was too high for accuracy. At high altitude, the bomber's guns froze and gunners could not fire back when German fighters attacked them. Within the first four months, the British lost eight of the first 20 planes sent to them.

The Germans dubbed them the "Flying Coffins."

The British gave up and assigned the remaining B-17s to submarine patrols and coastal duties. Daylight bombing was for the birds, they said.

But the Americans learned valuable lessons from the British experiment. The model delivered to the British had been the B-17C. It differed from the earlier models in that it had more armament, including a bathtub-type gun position under the fuselage to protect the tail and belly of the plane. The plane now carried a total of seven guns - six .50s and one .30 caliber, plus more armor protection around the gun positions.

Boeing had, in the meantime, gone through the B-17D series, which was little changed from the C series.

Then came the B-17E, and for the first time, the plane was equipped with armament to make it a truly offensive weapon, able to defend itself effectively. The B-17 now deserved the title of Flying Fortress.

So drastic were the design changes, the new B-17E could almost be called a new airplane when compared with the original model. From the wing back, the entire appearance of the plane had changed,. It now had a much thicker body and greatly increased tail surfaces, which would not only make the plane more stable in its bombing run but provide more safety from flak or machine gun damage.

The thicker body was necessary to make room for what would prove to be one of the most important protective devices yet built into the plane, a machine gun position in the tail with lethal twin .50 caliber blasters. This pair would virtually stop the enemy from attacking from the rear, which had been their favorite approach until now.

But that was only the beginning. The heavier plane body now had two more defense positions, both equipped with a pair of deadly 50 caliber machine guns. One was a power-operated turret located below the fuselage. The gunner in it was usually a small man, curled up in a fetal position behind his guns to protect the plane's belly. Then, virtually the same type power-operated turret on top of the plane, again with the twin .50s.

The first experience for American crews flying B-17s came in the Pacific as the Japanese attacked Pearl Harbor.

It was a tragi-comedy. America had known that war was threatening and had been reinforcing Pacific bases with more man-power and equipment.

There was a certain irony in the flight of 12 new B-17s, flying out as part of the Pacific reinforcement action. As they approached Pearl Harbor, the Japanese attacked. The B-17s were caught in the melee. Since the crew had no way of knowing about the attack, they were taken by surprise. Since it had been assumed they were flying in peace time, their guns were not even loaded.

Several of the unarmed planes were heavily damaged as they desperately attempted emergency landings. Others were destroyed or damaged on the ground. Several crewmen were killed, others wounded.

When the Japanese planes hit the Philippines, they caught more of the B-17s parked helplessly on the ground and blasted them to bits.

When they were sent out on attack, the B-17s were not very effective against moving sea targets. Part of the problem may have been the inexperience of the crews. It would remain for the European scene of battle to determine what a B-17 could do.

In the history of the development of almost any series of machines, taking motor cars as an example, there are always some models which stand out as happy combinations of perfection. These are the classic models. The great Cadillac V-16s of the 1930s. The great Chrysler Imperial Eights of the same period. The mighty and classic Duesenberg J. And there are others.

If the same can be said for airplanes, it seems that when Boeing engineers put the B-17 together, it became one of those happy combinations of near perfection. It was strong. It was tough. It was durable. It was highly maneuverable, an ability which saved many a Flying Fortress and her crews in the skies over Europe. It was, for its day, considering its weight, size and four engines, a fast airplane.

It had the greatest aggregation of fire power ever put on an airplane until that time. When flying in close formation, as the American flyers quickly learned to do, the amount of fire power it could concentrate on attacking fighter planes, was awesome.

One of the features most beloved by pilots was the ease with which it could be mastered. As some pilots put it, "The plane would almost fly itself." Yet, when called on, it responded almost like a fighter plane.

If you took a vote of the crews of the Flying Fortresses that clashed with the Germans over Europe, the single feature of the plane that would get the most votes - or prayers of thanksgiving - was the amazing toughness of the plane under fire from the ground or from the air.

One can only speak of miracles in describing some of the blasted Fortresses which, somehow, came home after being hit over and over again.

The miracles had begun long before the B-17 was bloodied in battle.

In the early stages of the development of the B-17, one of the first was set aside as a test plane. It was fitted out with special instruments, to test the plane's reaction to stress. Even before the tests began an act of God performed the test for them.

Lieutenant William Bentley was approaching Langley Field in the test plane and was preparing to land when he and the plane were struck by one of those violent and freakish storms which sometimes do unpredictable things. Pilots in later times would call the event a "wind shear." The shear flipped Bentley's B-17 over on its back, sending it into a spin down through the clouds.

When the plunging plane emerged from the belly of the clouds, Bentley was skillful enough to bring it under control and land it safely. No one was more surprised than he that the wings had not been ripped off the heavy plane. The wings were bent a bit, with a few of their rivets popped, but the plane was intact. The plane had been tested.

To avoid a collision, Lieutenant Garber yanked the nose up and kicked the plane into a sharp turn. With such a heavy load of bombs and gasoline, the plane went into a stall and slipped over into a dive.

Garber estimated that the plane was streaking down at a speed of more than 400 mph.

As Garber described it later: "According to the slide rules, there was no chance of pulling out of the dive. The strain would tear the wings off a loaded ship the size of ours. But there wasn't any other choice. We were goners if I didn't try. So I held my breath and started to pull out.

"There were tearing noises. The bombs ripped loose and went crashing out through the bottom of the ship. Then - the bomber came up level. The wings were still with us."

During the violent maneuver, the heads of the bombardier and navigator crashed through Plexiglas windows. Two gunners were almost thrown out and had to be yanked back into the plane by other crew members.

Lieutenant Garber not only landed the plane safely, but after a few minor repairs, the plane was back in service - with a new name. The crew voted to change the name from the original "Hellsappopin" to "Borrowed Time."

Another classic example came during a raid on Vegesack, Germany, when the formation of B-17s was jumped by a swarm of German fighters.

During the battle, one B-17 shuddered under six direct hits by 20 mm. cannon shells and more than 200 machine gun bullets, wounding three of the crew. But the plane got the crew home.

There was another B-17 that came home from an epic battle with more than 800 bullet holes in it.

There were a whole series of stories about B-17s shot up so badly they limped home on three, two or sometimes only one engine, so badly damaged they nearly collapsed on landing. The important thing being that they had come home. The list of such stories fills books.

And then there was the Memphis Belle.

On two of her missions she had a large portion of her tail shot off. On another mission a gaping hole was blasted in her right wing. She was scarred from end to end by machine gun and cannon holes. Sergeant John Quinlan, the tail gunner, used one of those bullet holes near the tail as his ash tray for his cigar butts. Nine engines were shot out of the Memphis Belle and had to be replaced.

All this was accomplished without injury to the crew except for one slight thigh wound suffered by Sergeant Quinlan. The Belle would come to be known as a very lucky ship.

The Memphis Belle, one of the F series B-17s, came off the assembly line at the Boeing plant in Seattle on July 2, 1942, bearing identification number B-17-F-10B0-3170. Her serial number, 42-24485. For log keeping purposes, the military adopted the practice of identifying war planes by the last three digits of their serial numbers and so this particular plane would become known as No. 485. She was turned over to the U. S. Government on July 15, 1942.

Boeing billed the government $314,109 as the cost of the Memphis Belle. Since modifications and equipment were being added constantly, Number 485 was sent to Wright Field at Dayton, Ohio, for its fitting out. Then, on August 31, it was flown to Dow Field, near Bangor, Maine, the last staging point before combat, where combat crews were assigned to planes. Final testing and shakedown flights were made at Dayton before taking off for "Bolero," the code name for England.

At last, on September 25, 1942, the Memphis Belle and her crew took off for the zone of combat.

The Pilot
He Always Brought Us Home

He was tall. He was slim. He had curly hair, the kind a girl might like to run her fingers through. Beyond all that he was a wartime pilot.

Everybody understood, in that hectic age when all the world seemed to be at war, that a certain aura of romance hung around these young men who hurled their planes through the skies in search of the enemy. If you didn't know it, they told you. With that air of bold impudence with which they walked, talked and flirted with the girls. The way they crushed their military caps and wore them that way, in defiance of the West Point tradition.

If they wore any cap at all. Military regulations said they did. Bob Morgan preferred not to and thus invited the wrath of the West Pointers counted among his commanding officers. It even cost him a promotion, in his advanced training days, when he ended up as the only flight leader who was still a second lieutenant. Not to speak of the reprimands he had to suffer Or did he really suffer?

But everyone had to agree, even if some did it grudgingly, when it came to flying a plane, he was one of the best. Even if he was hard on the brakes coming in, fast and hot. The kind of pilot who could talk to an airplane and make it do things the manufacturers did not tell you about in the specifications. The kind of pilot you didn't have to worry about when you gave him orders to fly his plane into enemy-held territory and there do what had to be done.

Even after he had proved all this by flying 25 missions, through skies filled with flak and swarms of gutsy German fighter pilots out for a kill, if you asked one of his crew members what they thought of Robert K. Morgan, the answer was always the same: "He's a damn good pilot. He always brought us home." They seldom talked about him as a person, only a pilot.

32

With the girls, it was different. Again, perhaps nobody could ever clearly define those things but somehow the charm and attraction were there. Some pretty bit of femininity was always ready to run those fingers through his hair.

From the very beginning, Bob Morgan had a lot of things going for him. Even if that cruel Depression did finally catch up with his family, mostly his dad, knocking him down, all the way from being the president of a successful furniture manufacturing company to being the watchman, who guarded the locked-up plant, for $50 a month. It was an experience Bob never forgot.

Losing his mother about the same time didn't help. One could always suggest that the psychological blow of seeing what was happening to her world, her way of life, her husband being crushed that way, might have contributed to her death. They say things do happen that way sometimes.

It was Bob himself who said, "I believe my mother dying was the biggest blow in my life. My mother was a beautiful and lovely woman. I looked up to her as if she were an angel. She and I had big plans for us. We were going to go on trips together and then, bang, all of it was blown out."

In the beginning, things had been different. "I grew up in a sort of protective society," Bob said. "You know, we had nurses to take care of me and all that sort of thing."

Which didn't prevent him from doing all the "he-boy" types of things that boys everywere like to do. Hunting. Fishing.

"You know, one of the Vanderbilt estates is located at Asheville. Through my family I got to know one of the wardens on the estate. He took me fishing and hunting, taught me to shoot."

All of which happened before that big crash hit his father. All of the kid stuff taking place in a time when all the skies were blue and the squirrels were jumping and mothers were beautiful.

It was a glorious time when a boy could think of a prank like pouring a kettle of hot water into a yellow jacket's nest.

"What I didn't know was that those yellow jackets had two entrances to their den and the next thing I knew, they were hitting me from behind. They bit me just about every place a boy can be bitten. I've been afraid of yellow jackets ever since."

Or like the time his mother was having a cocktail party on the lawn and he got the water hose, breaking up the party by squirting water on the maids.

33

"That was one time when Dad got out his razor strap and whipped me pretty good," Bob said. "I got by with a lot but Dad was no softie. He knew how to use that strap."

If Bob later acquired the reputation of being a little on the wild side as a pilot, there is that old cliche about the child being father of the man. We asked him about it.

"Sure I was wild as a kid," said Bob. "I had the world's speed record from Asheville, North Carolina, to Greenville, South Carolina. I used to see a girl down there, went almost every day. It was 60 miles and a mountain road but I drove it in 55 minutes in Dad's Buick. Everybody in town knew about and talked about it."

The boy's character went through a bit of tempering, too, by what happened to his dad, the wealthy, successful businessman who was completely flattened by the depression.

"He was completely broke," Bob said. "I mean busted - completely. We even had to sell our house.

It was Cornelia Vanderbilt, a close friend of Bob's mother, who came to the rescue after that.

"When we lost our house, she let us live in a house on her estate, rent free," Bob said. "Dad and I lived there by ourselves. Dad did the cooking and I had to do the house cleaning."

But perhaps there was also a lesson to a teen-age boy in the way his dad handled the situation.

"Dad still had some friends in Massachusetts, and when the depression eased up a bit, he borrowed some money from one of his friends, bought the factory back, opened it up and got it started again."

Before it was over, Bob's father owned three furniture factories.

Which meant, of course, that Bob was able to get his education, studying business administration at the University of Pennsylvania. His first job, after graduation, was with the Addressograph-Multigraph Corporation of Cleveland, Ohio, makers of office equipment.

"They put me through their school in Cleveland where I learned about their machines, and then I went on the road as a traveling service person," Bob said.

This was where the beginning of the war caught him.

Actually, Morgan was one of the early volunteers, getting into the service in 1940 before Pearl Harbor.

"I could see the war coming so I decided to get into the Air Force," he said. "I called Dad and told him what I wanted to do and he told me that if this was what I wanted, go ahead."

Once again Morgan would be one of those who almost got washed out before he got started. Like his fellow crew member on the Memphis Belle, Bill Winchell, Morgan had problems with the eyes.

"The flight surgeon told me that one of my eyes didn't quite come up to 20/20 and, in that time, it had to be 20/20 to get into pilot training," he said. "But for some reason, the flight surgeon took a liking to me and told me he was going to help me. He took me in a dark room and gave me some ice to hold on my eye. After five minutes, he came in and got me, gave me the test again and my eye passed, 20/20."

Then the man who would one day acquire that reputation as a wild pilot, almost washed himself out.

"When we started flying in primary training, I was scared to death," Bob said. "The first time my instructor took me out and did a loop with a slow roll, I said to myself, 'I'm not sure this is for me.' I sort of lost interest and wasn't really applying myself.

"We had civilian instructors in those days and I had a guy named Earl Friedel. I guess he sensed that something was wrong, so one day he said he wanted me to meet him down at the hangar in the evening. When I got there he pulled up a couple of chairs. We sat down and he told me I was about to wash out.

"But, like the flight surgeon, he took an interest in me and wanted to help me. He said, 'You've got the greatest opportunity in the world. The Government is spending $60,000 to make a pilot out of you and you just aren't taking it seriously. You've got this haphazard attitude.'

"He had a broom with him and he took the broomstick between his legs and said, 'When I was a kid I wanted to fly so bad that I'd hang around the airfield and watch everything the pilots did. I'd look inside the planes and see that stick. Then I'd go home, sit on the front porch with a broomstick between my legs and go through all the maneuvers for hours. That was 90 per cent of my flight training because I wanted to do it so badly. If you don't appreciate what I've done for you, just say so and I'll wash you out tomorrow.'

"Well, I guess that talk did me a lot of good because after that I got with it and passed my tests."

35

Then came the next episode of a near-washout with Morgan himself again doing the washing.

"They were sending me down to Augusta for basic training but then, at the last minute, somebody was checking the records and found out I lacked 40 minutes of having enough flying time to go to advanced training. They told me to take a plane and just fly around for 40 minutes. I got up there and had been flying about 35 minutes and was about to get ready to land when I got this crazy idea to buzz the field. Well, I buzzed it good and that was a no-no.

"When I got back on the ground I got called on the carpet by the commanding officer. He chewed me out good and he said: 'Morgan, if we hadn't already sent your papers to Augusta, you wouldn't be going. I'd wash you out right now. I'm letting you go but if you ever do that again you're through.'"

If that commander had only known how many times in the future Morgan would be buzzing airfields, he probably would have had a heart attack.

Next question: Was Morgan going to be a fighter pilot or a bomber pilot?

"Most people would have guessed that I would want to be a fighter pilot from the way I drove a car," Morgan said. "I was a maniac for speed. So, people would think I was crazy enough to be a fighter pilot. But I liked company. I didn't like the idea of being up there in the air by myself. If I went up in a B-17 I would have nine other guys up there with me and I liked that fine. That was the reason I picked bombers."

Which didn't stop him from flying the big planes as if they were fighters.

In fact, Morgan had barely made it into the four-engine planes at McDill Field in Florida when he started that buzzing business again. And once more landed in trouble.

"While we were stationed at McDill, they sometimes sent us out on submarine patrols in the Gulf. I don't remember ever seeing a submarine but one Sunday, when we were coming in, I spotted a big house with a beautiful lawn and somebody was having a lawn party. I decided to buzz that party. Man I almost set that plane down in the punch bowl. What I didn't know was that it was our commanding general who was having the lawn party. The next morning, I was called in by my commanding officer who chewed me out plenty and I was told that as long as I stayed under that general's command, I would never get a promotion."

After that, it seemed, Morgan's life was going to be a series of reprimands and chew-outs.

The next one came after pilots were told that, as part of their training, they could make a few discretionary flights, like landing at places near their home towns where they could see their parents. Morgan decided to land at Asheville, North Carolina, where his father lived. The only problem being that Asheville, at that time, didn't have a landing strip long enough for a B-17 to land on. He decided to do it anyway.

"I burned out the brakes on the plane, getting it stopped on that tiny airfield," Morgan said. "They had to send a crew of mechanics from McDill to put on new brakes."

This may have allowed Morgan a bit more time to visit his father, but it also earned him another of those chew-outs that now seemed to be a routine part of his training. As punishment for that landing at Asheville, as the group was being transferred from McDill to Walla Walla, Washington, for final advanced training before being sent overseas, other pilots got to make the transfer by air but Morgan had to make the trip by slow, hot train ride.

Which should have cured Morgan from riding the brakes so hard but it didn't.

"I became known as Floorboard Freddie because I wore out more brakes than any pilot in our group," said Morgan.

"I landed them hot. I always said I'd rather run out of runway at the other end than not make the runway on the touchdown. So, I always came in hotter than anyone else."

At Walla Walla, he would remain in hot water because of his insistance on going around bareheaded, refusing to wear the cap required by military regulations.

This time the rebuke came from Captain H. Smelser, the West Pointer and commander of the 324th Squadron who would take over the job of chewing out this young second lieutenant named Robert K. Morgan, day after day, for showing up minus his cap. Since Morgan had been appointed flight leader of his flight, he was due a promotion to first lieutenant, but Smelser put the word out that so long as a certain smart young shavetail insisted on defying cap regulations, there would be no promotion.

"Major Smelser was a West Pointer and he had been in the Pacific where he flew B-17s," said Morgan. "He was one of those spit-and-polish officers who carried a swagger stick and tried to enforce every regulation in the book. I never did get along with him. He resented all of us young pilots who had never been to West

Point but got to fly on an equal basis with the regular Army men. He assigned me to every dirty job on the base. When one of the planes went on a training mission and crashed in the mountains, killing every man on board, he assigned me to the job of going out to recover the bodies and all that."

The result of all this, said Morgan, was that when the 91st Bomb Group was sent overseas into combat, Morgan was still a second lieutenant. After Major Smelser was killed on his third mission, a raid over St. Nazaire on November 23, said Morgan, his promotion papers, still unacted on, were found in Smelser's desk drawer. They were taken out and acted on by his successor. Robert K. Morgan was a first lieutenant at last.

In the meantime, Morgan and his crew had met the Memphis Belle.

It was late in August of 1942 when the 91st Bomb Group, which had been in advanced training at Walla Walla, Washington, was declared ready for combat and ordered to proceed to England. It had been rumored that the Group would be sent to the Pacific, but now it was official that they were bound for England to do battle with the forces of Hitler.

Before being sent overseas, they were to turn in their old planes, pretty well battered by now, and be assigned new planes. They would proceed to Gowan Field, near Boise, Idaho, where they would be assigned their new planes, the new B-17-Fs, now equipped with new power-driven turrets in the belly and up on the top. The new planes would have more fire power and thus be more deadly in combat with fighter planes.

But when the Group arrived at Boise, they found that only six of the new B-17Fs had arrived there. They were still required to turn in their old planes. This meant that six crews, plus a certain number of non-crewmembers would fly to their next stop, Bangor, Maine, while the remainder would have to travel by train.

Morgan's crew did not receive a new plane at Boise, but he remembers that he flew to Bangor on another plane. In any case, on September 1 Morgan arrived at Bangor and met the new B-17F that was to play such a fateful part in his life - the Memphis Belle.

Oh, she had no name then, just another Flying Fortress. Almost every member of Morgan's crew, including Morgan himself, are a bit vague about their first impressions of the big bomber.

"I guess the most important thing I remember about her was that she was nice and clean," said Morgan. "Our old plane had been getting sort of messy. I remember the first time I flew her she seemed to feel a bit heavier than the planes we had been flying. But she handled real nice and responded well to the controls. It was a nice airplane."

Equipped with more turrets, the plane was heavier, indeed.

No matter that she might have felt a bit heavier, Morgan was going to prove that the new plane was nimble.

Morgan and his crew would have nearly a month to get used to their new plane, making at least a required 100 hours of shakedown flying to test new equipment, fuel consumption, etc. On at least one of those flights, Morgan managed to include his home town of Asheville, North Carolina, and Memphis, Tennessee, home of Margaret Polk, his fiancee.

In any case, it would be September 25, 1942, when No. 485, now sporting the name Memphis Belle, and a Petty girl painted on her nose, took off for the wars. Destination: Bolero. It could just as well have been Shangri-La, for Bolero was the code name for England.

Their first destination, a makeshift Royal Air Force base at Kimbolton, England. The 91st Bomb Group had made only a few test flights from Kimbolton before the runways, never built to support heavy B-17s, began to crumble.

Somebody in the command structure hinted that there was a better airfield located at Bassingbourn, about 50 miles north of London. It had been one of the RAF's permanent air bases and had just been evacuated by an RAF unit that had been sent to North Africa to do battle with the famed Afrika Korps under the command of the German general, Erwin Rommel.

The story usually told when veterans of the 91st Bomb Group get together is that a scouting party from the 91st, including Colonel Stanley Wray, Group commander, got permission to fly down to Bassignbourn and look it over. No official permission had been given to move in.

When Colonel Wray landed at Bassingbourn and saw all the beautiful permanent living quarters, the nice, smooth and apparently solid runways, he simply moved in and established squatters' rights. Even when the squatters were reminded by the high command that they had no official permission to be there, the squatters just dug in deeper and hung on.

Eventually, the story goes, even though it took weeks, the top command, somewhat grudgingly, finally made it official. Now Bassingbourn belonged to the 91st.

"Man, we were living high," Morgan recalls. "These were not barracks but homes, nice old British homes. It was great. Compared to Kimbolton it was heaven."

Now came several weeks of practice missions over England and the English Channel. Finally, on November 7, 1942, the big day, their first real combat mission.

Perhaps it is understandable, after so many years, but when you talk to the crew of the Memphis Belle, all of them, they have trouble remembering details of individual missions. There were 25 missions, some tougher than others, they can remember incidents but not an orderly sorting out of the missions.

Oh, they all remember that first mission. Mostly because it was their first, to bomb the harbor installations at Brest.

"We were tense, apprehensive," said Morgan, "wondering what it would be like. Then, when it was over, we were relieved because, well, not much had happened. We didn't meet the war on that mission. We were thinking, 'Gee, is it going to be this easy?'"

It wasn't.

They would have to wait only two days, for Novermber 9, to find that out. That second mission would be to bomb the submarine pens at St. Nazaire.

The Germans were sensitive as hell about those submarine pens. Submarines, at that time, were one of their main weapons, their major hope in preventing the Americans from coming to the rescue of their British allies. The strategy, sink their ships before they can get to England. Flying to St. Nazaire to drop bombs was to stir up the proverbial hornet's nest.

"We got the hell shot out of us," said Morgan. "Somebody in Hollywood must have dreamed up that mission."

The idea had been to go in low, to fool the German radar operators so that German fighter pilots wouldn't get a chance to take off. Then, just before reaching the target, to climb to about 9,000 feet, bomb and get away before the Germans could shoot back.

But even at 9,000 feet, anti-aircraft fire could be devastating and nobody fooled the German ack-ack crews. As somebody said, the German crews slept beside their guns and could go into action in a matter of minutes. Or less.

As the writer of the official history of the 91st Bomb Group put it: "Just before our aircraft released the bombs, they opened up with every conceivable type of anti-aircraft weapon."

At least one of the four groups in the attack lost threeB-17s. The 91st was luckier. It lost no planes but, as the official historian wrote: "Every plane in the formation was hit." The group came back home with one dead man and ten wounded.

As for the Memphis Belle, said Morgan: "We counted 62 holes in the plane when we got back." In fact, Morgan had to land the plane at Exeter, a closer RAF base. One engine was out and they were out of gas.

After refueling, they made emergency repairs and tried to start the dead engine. It wouldn't fire. Sergeant Levi Dillon, flight engineer, and his assistant, Sergeant Harold Loch, sweated over it for several hours - and finally gave up. That was when the pilot made one of those typical Morgan decisions.

He decided to try to take off on the three engines.

It was known that a B-17 could fly on three engines, possibly two if you threw out all excess weight and didn't have any bombs on board. If you were already airborne.

As time went on, many a B-17 would come home on three engines. Even two, after every scrap of excess weight, the guns, parachutes, everything, was dumped overboard. Eventually there would be stories of a plane limping back, the last few miles, losing altitude, on one engine. But taking off was something else.

The regulations said no. The manufacturer's instructions said no. But Morgan was going to try.

As he put it himself, also typical Morgan: "Both Evans and I had heavy dates that night and we were determined to get back, one way or another."

Gee, risking his plane and his life to see a girl?

The idea was to take off with only one man on board, aside from the pilot, to keep the plane as light as possible. He didn't say it but, well, that way the casualties would be low in case something went wrong. He needed one man on board with him to goose the engine controls on the sick engine, hoping that, once the plane got off the ground, the cranking action of windmilling the propeller would start the balky power plant.

"I called for volunteers," said Morgan.

It was Dillon, the flight engineer, who held up his hand. Morgan had hoped for that because Dillon knew his engines.

"When Morgan opened the throttles," said Dillon, "and the plane started down the runway, it kept yawing to one side, constantly. Morgan had to fight the controls to keep the plane on the runway. I thought we'd never make it. We damn near crashed. Somehow he kept the machine on the runway and got it into the air."

Sure enough, with Dillon goosing the controls, the wind began windmilling the propeller. Whooey, a puff of smoke and the dead engine exploded into life. Morgan circled back, landed and the rest of his crew jumped on board. They headed for Bassingbourn.

Heavy date, look out. Here comes Morgan.

But now that they had been educated, via mission number two, that war was hell, it was time to get on with their job. There were 23 more missions to come and some would be as tough, if not worse, than that second go.

As pilot, Morgan would have to learn that, if you hoped to survive you had to learn to duck. To dive fast in a four-engine plane never made for such tricks. To flip the big machine around in a manner that had crewmen and ammunition boxes flying around inside the plane like jumping jacks, or plastered to the roof or floor by centrifugal force, unable to move. The fast maneuvers also made it difficult for Morgan's wing men, pilots who positioned their bombers close to his wings, to stay in formation.

"Sometimes that left my wing men complaining that they couldn't keep up with me," said Morgan. "They had orders to stay on my wings but here I was, diving like crazy. But what was I going to do, with one of my crew, like Quinlan back there in the tail, yelling into the intercom that a fighter was coming right in on us. He'd yell": 'Dive, chief, dive quick. He's going to hit us.' So I dove."

But even such tactics didn't help much against the flak.

"I hated that stuff," said Morgan, echoing what almost every airman in the Eighth Air Force said. "You couldn't fight back."

On the way to the target, or coming home, planes could take evasive action to escape the flak, like changing directions or altitude to throw the gunners off. But there was always that deadly moment of truth, the bomb run, when the plane had to be held on an absolutely steady course while the bombardier tried to get his bomb sight aligned on the target.

"One of the favorite tricks of the Germans was to figure out our altitude and bombing run course and then they'd throw up a huge barrage of ack-ack at that point," said Morgan. "When we would go into our bombing run, that barrage would be right there waiting for us. They shot the hell out of us."

The American flyers did learn one trick that took at least part of the sting out of the flak.

"We'd travel all the way across France at an altitude about 2,000 feet higher than we planned to bomb at," said Morgan. "The

Germans would be getting our altitude and setting their ranges for that bombing run barrage but then, just before we went into the bomb run, we would drop 2,000 feet. That threw them off and all their shells would explode 2,000 feet above us."

There were times when the German flak would be tracking you from behind, following and gradually moving up. That was when the pilot had to team up with his tail gunner to trick the enemy.

"Quinlan, back there in the tail, would see a chain of bursts creeping up on us and then, just when it started getting close, he would call out and I'd change course. Then the Germans would have to start tracking all over again."

As Quinlan himself put it in a debriefing session following a mission in 1943," "The pilot would throw the plane out of position, I'd look back and see the flak bursting right where we had been. I think this little tactic saved us many times."

The Americans had hoped, when they built the B-17s with superchargers, that they would be able to fly high enough to be above the German flak, but the Germans kept building more powerful flak guns, said Morgan.

"We were over Wilhelmshaven on one mission at 29,000 feet and the flak was right up there with us," said Morgan. He remembered that once the British had sent their high flying Mosquito bombers over Essen, Germany, at 35,000 feet and eight of them were shot down.

The Americans had to learn many things, remembers Morgan. For example, there was a blind spot on the B-17F, despite all the guns and turrets. There was no gun shooting straight forward out of the nose, only two singles which couldn't quite cover the center position, straight ahead. So the German fighter pilots began coming in, straight on.

The only defense against this attack, said Morgan, was to position the lead planes in such a formation that they could protect each other by overlapping their angles of gunfire. Or, he said, sometimes he would dip the nose of his plane up or down, giving the top and belly turrets a chance to fire. Back home, the Boeing Company was working on a B-17G which would have a two-gun turret in the nose.

"Our intelligence people saved us a lot of times," said Morgan. "They would brief us on where the German flak batteries were located and that gave us a chance to fly a course that would stay out of their range."

Even when they had to venture into an area loaded with flak guns in order to reach a target, there were still a few tricks that could be pulled.

One such trick was used on the raid to hit the Focke Wulf fighter plane plant at Bremen.

"We always liked to hit a plant making fighter planes," said Morgan. "We figured it was one way of reducing the number of German fighters in the air, coming at us. On this occasion, the intelligence people told us the Germans had 178 flak guns in the Bremen area to turn on us. But we worked out a course, coming in on Bremen from the southwest to the northeast, on a heading so they would never be able to fire more than 72 of their flak guns on us at a time. We found the plant, bombed it, then turned to the right and made a complete turn and came out. That's the long way around but it was better than having the other 106 guns shooting at us, too."

Which probably left some frustrated German gunners on the ground, cussing.

Sometimes the Memphis Belle was simply lucky, in the right place at the right time. Various groups of American bombers making attacks would be staggered at various altitudes and positions, lead groups and tail groups.

"We were the high group that day," Morgan said. "The boys in the low group really caught hell. The Germans had set up a barrage and it really caught them. We lost 16 bombers that day, all in the low group.

Sometimes it was luck of another kind that saved the Belle, as on November 23, 1942, when the 91st was scheduled to hit St. Nazaire, one of the most hotly defended spots.

As the Memphis Belle took off, its number two engine conked. Morgan was forced to turn back and miss the raid.

It was crewman Bill Winchell who said it: "Maybe it was destiny that the Belle turned back that day. Only four of our planes reached the target and only two of them came back."

When it had all started, the formations of American bombers flew rather loose. They quickly learned to tighten it up.

"After a few missions," said Morgan, "we were flying so tight that our wings sometimes overlapped and planes would get bucked around by propeller turbulence."

"That way, the firepower we could throw at German fighters was awesome. It took a very brave German fighter pilot to come in at us through that hail of machine gun fire."

44

But some came through.

The American bag of tricks included such things as feints and diversions. On a feint, a formation would fly towards one target and then, as the Germans were getting ready to defend it, dispatching their squadrons of fighters in that direction, the attacking group would make a sharp turn and head for another target.

Sometimes a group would be sent out as a diversion towards a target. At the last moment, after attracting the attention of gunners and fighter groups on the ground, it would turn back. Meanwhile, the real attack force would be coming in from another direction.

"Sometimes these tricks worked," said Morgan. "Sometimes they didn't. The Germans were smart, too, and kept changing their defense tactics just as often was we changed attack plans."

When the fanatic Germans protected their submarine pens by building a roof eight feet thick, which even the heaviest 2,000-pound bombs could not smash, the Americans began aiming at the submarine landing slips and the workshop buildings surrounding the pens.

"Without the slips and the workshops the pens didn't do any good," said one crew member. "They couldn't put an eight-foot thick roof over everything."

Somehow, through luck, skill and all the evasive tactics they could dream up, through the guts and accuracy of the gunners aboard, the Memphis Belle and her pilot survived.

It had to be a great moment, that last mission for the crew on May 17, 1943, when they knew they would be going home. Now they could lay down their guns and go home. The war wasn't over, not by a far shot, but under the rules then in force, 25 missions were decreed to be enough hell for one man. They would have new assignments.

So here was the Memphis Belle, her crew jubilant because, as Quinlan would say, over and over, "We were survivors."

Was it any surprise that the pilot of that plane, Bob Morgan, would decide to celebrate by giving the field at Bassingbourn a proper buzzing?

"I came in so low that I was cutting the grass," said Morgan.

The story got out that he knocked the flagpole off the administration building. That part, he said, was not true. After all, he had the squadron commander, Major A. W. Aycock, on board as co-pilot. That, perhaps, might have prevented the buzz from being the ultimate wild one.

Back home, that triumphant tour which eventually turned sour because, as Morgan put it, "It was too much of a good thing. There was too much wine, women and song. And not necessarily in that order."

It would be when the tour took them to Wichita, Kansas, the home of Boeing's assembly plant, that Morgan found out there was a bomber bigger and more powerful, capable of flying higher and faster, carrying bigger loads. It was being assembled in Wichita and some were already flying the B-29. They were slated for duty in the Pacific. It would be a B-29 named the Enola Gay that would make history by carrying the first atom bomb to be dropped in war, on Hiroshima.

"They let me climb into one of those planes and sit in the pilot's seat," said Morgan.

"That did it. Here I was, surrounded by all that luxury in a pressurized cabin. That huge body. I just had to fly it."

That was when Morgan volunteered for a second tour of duty in the Pacific and began pulling strings to get into the seat of one of those B-29s. The only member of the Belle's crew who would go with him would be Vince Evans, the bombardier. Quinlan volunteered, thinking he would be flying with Morgan, but somehow things got snafued and he ended up on another B-29.

Morgan, now a major, would also make a bit of history when he became the pilot to lead the first B-29 bombing attack on Tokyo. His B-29 would be called the Dauntless Dottie, in honor of a girl he married, Dorothy. But that is another story.

There was a question that had to be asked. How did Bob Morgan, the man who had flown both the B-17 and the B-29, compare the two? Was the B-29 a better plane than the B-17?

Morgan didn't hesitate. "No. It wasn't near as good a plane as the B-17. Of course, the B-29 was built for a different purpose. It had more range, more carrying capacity and, because of its size, had more power-assisted controls. But when it came to sheer ruggedness, its ability to take punishment, its flyability, there just wasn't anything like the B-17. If we had needed to fly the B-29 in Europe, we would have been ruined."

Morgan probably realized when he had said that, he might have to duck a bit of ground flak from the partisans of the B-29, but he had his reasons.

He had been through a lot with a B-17 called the Memphis Belle and she would always occupy top spot in his heart - at least when it came to airplanes.

After the war, Morgan returned to his native Asheville. For a time, with his brother, he operated the furniture factories that had belonged to his father. For a time he was an automobile dealer, selling the VW Beatles so beloved by a certain generation of Americans. No matter that they had been made by his one-time enemies in Germany.

Here, in the beloved hills of his native state, he would rear his four children. Eventually, he and Dorothy came to a parting of the ways and he remarried. Now there is an Elizabeth in his life.

"We've been married eight years," said Morgan. The two of them work together in the real estate business. "It keeps us pretty busy and we have done quite well.

Does he still fly his own airplane?

"I still fly but not my own plane. The business I'm in doesn't call for a plane. But for many years I had a plane and, in fact, I probably came closer to getting killed in a private plane than I ever did flying combat in Europe.

"I was flying a twin Cessna and we were going duck hunting on the East Coast. The weather was just horrible. It was in December. We ran into ice, sleet, everything. I had two friends in the back seat and another friend of mine was in the co-pilot's seat. We were loaded. We took off and climbed to 6,000 feet. I thought we would break through it but we didn't. The ice was building up on the wings and then the carburetors began icing up.

"I pulled all the carburetor heat we had but it didn't help. Both engines quit. I knew we had to come down. We had been over the mountains and I didn't know where we were.

"Coming down, we finally broke out of the clouds at 500 feet with both engines dead. It had to be some kind of miracle. Right under me was a grass landing strip. I couldn't have flown any further because of the dead engines. It was Hendersonville, North Carolina. I made a dead stick landing with both engines dead. Somebody was really looking out for me that day."

Bob Morgan still has a copy of the film that was made by Billie Wyler, the Hollywood producer who flew five missions on the Memphis Belle and other planes to make a War Department film to be shown to the people back home while World War II was still being fought. To show people how it was over there in the skies filled with flak and fighters. The film was shown in theaters all over the country, making the Memphis Belle, perhaps, the most famous plane of World War II.

47

He will, if he is asked, still get the film out and show it to community clubs or school groups, Air Force reserves and so on.

"I still like to do this because the kids have no idea what it was really like over there in 1942 and 1943. Most of them get a bang out of the movie and enjoy it. But sometimes you get a different kind of reaction. One day, after I had shown it to a high school group, one of the students, a girl, came up to me and said, 'Mr. Morgan, that film is just a lot of propaganda.' I didn't know what to say."

It was clear, as Bob Morgan, in 1986, told that little story, that the man who piloted the Memphis Belle, consciously or otherwise, was a bit wounded by the girl's reaction. Perhaps the film had, indeed, been propaganda. Perhaps the War Department, as it sponsored the film, had even intended it that way. They had wanted to tell the American people, the parents and the wives of the boys flying those planes in combat, what those boys were going through. What it was like. What the airmen were doing for their country.

But to Bob Morgan, the man who flew the Memphis Belle, that film was a bit more than that. It was a part of his life. Something he had lived in that time so many years ago.

He could remember the Memphis Belle only with pride.

Over the years, this man Robert K. Morgan has reflected on other things as well. That luck thing, for example.

It had all begun back in England when Morgan, his crew and the Memphis Belle were flying their combat missions. As she came home, time after time, shot full of holes, pieces of her tail and her wings shot off, people began calling her a lucky plane. The pilot and crew, a lucky crew. Even Morgan himself, at the time, in speeches and press interviews, had used the word "luck." But as the years passed, the maturing one-time war pilot began having other thoughts about it.

In a moment of reflection, recently, Morgan said, "We talk about luck. People mention it to me but as I look back, it wasn't luck. It wasn't skill.

"As for myself, the good Lord had reasons for me to come back. My job here wasn't finished. Evidently, it is not finished yet. Combat in Europe. Combat in the Pacific. It wasn't my skill or luck.

"The good Lord had a purpose for me.

"He has a purpose for everyone."

48

Verinis
The Other Pilot

It was on the day when his engine failed, when he ran out of runway and flipped over, smashing his face into the gunsight, with the raw gasoline dripping down on him, threatening to burst into flames, that a certain fighter pilot named James Angelo Verinis decided he didn't want to be a fighter pilot any more.

Even before that eventful day, he had made a parachute jump from a plane with a conked engine and he had landed in a tree. Before that he had blown a tire on landing and the plane went slithering off the runway. Before that, he bounced a trainer plane off the runway and then circled the field eight times before he had enough nerve built up to try another landing.

If all that wasn't enough, there was the time when his roommate was killed in a crash and he was asked to escort the casket home. He had to tell the family not to open the casket.

"I decided I had enough," said Verinis.

The colonel asked him if he was through with flying.

"I told him I wouldn't mind flying if it was in something that had more fans up front," said Verinis.

That is how Verinis became the co-pilot of the Memphis Belle, a plane with four big fans up front. In fact, he did so well in the co-pilot's seat that he later qualified as a first pilot and was assigned a plane of his own to fly in combat.

"I'd say my career as a B-17 pilot was quite successful," he said.

Folks could have called him Jimmy the Greek but they didn't. In the days when he was a sparkling basketball player at Hillhouse High in New Haven, Connecticut, his buddies called him Angie.

Perhaps it is no surprise that some of his fondest memories come from his days on the basketball court as point man for a team that won the district championship. More great memories were made   at the University of Connecticut where his team beat the University of Rhode Island team for the conference championship.

Many wondered how he did it, standing only five feet and eight inches off the gymnasium floor, but he managed to fill several scrapbooks with press clippings from the glory days. He was captain of the team.

"You didn't have to be seven feet tall then to make the basketball team," said Verinis. "Few of our guys were that tall. It was a different game. We did it the hard way."

Verinis also played football and baseball at Hillhouse High.

"I really wasn't that good at football," says Verinis, although he was good enough to be second string halfback at the University.

The family name is Greek.

"My parents came to America shortly after they got married," said Verinis. "All four of their sons were born here. We were a close family. We all spoke Greek at home."

In fact, the elder Verinis didn't hit it off too well when he first came to America. After a short stay, he returned to the old country. But Greece had lost its allure for him and he came a second time and stayed on.

"Dad owned and operated an ice cream and candy store," said Verinis. "It's the only thing he ever did."

The home town in Greece had been Agiou Petro which, translated into English, means St. Peter.

Enough Greeks from St. Peter came to America to form their own St. Peter Society, says Verinis. Which didn't keep him from making it big as an American at Hillhouse. He clinched his claim to being an American by entering the Air Force in July of 1941, as soon as got out of college.

It was shortly before Pearl Harbor.

"A friend of mine at the University had left school after his sophomore year to join the Air Force and become a pilot," said Verinis. "He wrote such exciting letters about his experiences that I decided to go in myself."

America was not yet in the war but the battle was already raging in Europe. Italy and Germany invaded Greece and the Greeks were fighting hard to throw them out. Verinis doesn't deny that this had something to do with his entering the service.

He went to Texas for primary and intermediate training. On his big day he was told to take his Stearman PT-13 for his solo flight. He almost washed out.

50

"I had landed the plane several times," said Verinis, "when the instructor was in the back seat but never when I was in the plane by myself. After about eight hours, you are supposed to solo. So, that day my instructor said, 'OK, Mister. Today you take her up by yourself.'

"So I took the plane up and did several maneuvers. Everything went fine until I tried to land. I failed to level off properly and the plane went into a stall. I was sort of flying it into the ground. The front wheels hit the runway and I bounced hard. I pushed the throttle forward and took off and circled and tried again."

That was when Cadet Verinis almost lost his nerve. He kept circling and circling. Eight times he circled. On the ground, the fire engines were brought out to await a crash.

"I didn't panic," said Verinis. "On the eighth pass I finally got it down properly. But I was close to being washed out. The next day they said they would give me one more chance. The head guy at the school got in the back seat to check me out personally. I did all the flying. He just watched. Everything worked out, but if I had washed out it would have changed my entire life."

Verinis graduated to the hotter planes, the P-39s and the P-40s, and the troubles began again. Only now it was not the pilot's fault. First, the blown tire, then the conked engine and parachuting down into the tree.

Then came the real crash.

"I was flying a P-40 over the field at Charlotte, circling at about 5,000 feet," said Verinis. "I was supposed to practice a night landing so I had to kill time until it got dark.

"My engine quit. I decided I wasn't going to jump this time. I was going to try to make a dead engine landing. With a dead engine you have to keep your air speed up by diving. So I kept diving and circling the field, keeping my air speed up so I wouldn't stall out. I wanted to come in high enough so I wouldn't hit the barracks at the end of the runway, so when I came in for that landing I was too high and I was still going over 100 miles an hour.

"When I got over the runway, the plane just wouldn't settle down but I was too low to make another circle. When I got past the half-way mark on the runway, I was still in the air. I was running out of runway so I just put the stick forward and put the wheels on the runway.

"I tried to apply my brakes, but when I got to the end of the runway, I was still doing about 80 miles an hour. I wheeled back the canopy and applied the brakes. When the plane hit the end of the runway, it flipped over on its back. I put my arm up to keep my face from hitting the gunsight, but in the impact the canopy slammed forward and trapped my arm.

"My head hit the gunsight when we flipped over. I was lying upside down and I had forgotten to turn the ignition off. Gasoline was running all over me, and if it had hit something hot I would have gone up in flames. When the ground crew came running up, I hollered, 'Shut off the damn ignition.' Some guy reached in and shut it off. Then they pried the canopy off and got me out of there. I had to have a bunch of stitches taken in my face and head."

The colonel gave Verinis a week off to go home and recover. It was during that week that he decided he had enough of single-engine fighter planes.

"I had heard about the B-17s and they appealed to me," he said. "They had all those fans up front and you had more people up there with you if something went wrong."

Next stop, McDill Field near Tampa, Florida. B-17 pilots and crews were being trained there. Robert K. Morgan was one of the pilots. Then on to Walla Walla for the final advanced training with the full crew.

"I had qualified as a first pilot but they didn't have enough planes," said Verinis. "So when Bob asked me if I'd like to go with him as co-pilot, I grabbed it. It turned out to be the right move because I'm still here today."

But not without a few more of those hairy experiences. These at the hands of the Germans.

The crew landed in England on the first day of October in 1942 but it would be five more weeks before they would see any action. Whenever the weather was good, they practiced formation flying. Otherwise, from an entry in his diary on October 13, Verinis says they were "Still sitting around." The entry on October 15 says: "Mail reception sure is poor. What is wrong with Uncle Sam?" On October 17 he wrote: "Playing a lot of poker lately."

Six days later, he wished himself a happy birthday. "Had a little party at the American Bar in Cambridge," he wrote in his diary. "Went to the Rex Ballroom where all the charming English girls go."

On October 31, he wrote: "Wing Headquarters today passed on us. We are now ready for combat. It won't be long now."

It wasn't.

52

There were several alerts but no action. He wrote in the diary for November 6: "Off to Cambridge again and the Rex Ballroom. Stayed out until 1 a.m. despite warning that tomorrow might be the real thing. Just had to walk home."

It was the real thing this time.

"I hardly got to bed when they woke us up," Verinis noted. "We're finally off to our first combat. We bomb Brest, in France. A submarine base."

Verinis said the German flak barrage over Brest that day was "terrific." It was a word that would have served him better two days later when he was over St. Nazaire and the Belle came home riddled with shrapnel holes. Some counted 50 holes. Some said it was 82 holes. One of them came through the bottom of the plane right under the co-pilot's seat.

Bob Morgan said Verinis' reaction to it was immediate.

"Verinis went out and scrounged up a steel plate which he put under his seat cushion. He wanted to make sure he didn't get any holes in his rear."

After that, other airmen started using steel plates under them until higher authorities heard about it and put a stop to it. They said that, if everybody started adding their own personal armor to the planes, the weight of it all would cut down on the plane's range, speed and load-carrying capacity.

No more steel plates. The exposure would have to continue.

On November 15, a diary entry says: "Rumor started that we'll be going to Libya to fight down there."

It was true that top commanders, at one point, considered sending the 91st Bomb Group to North Africa where American forces invaded in the fall of 1942. But in the end it was decided that the group was more badly needed in the new daylight bombing program over Europe.

On November 20, he wrote in his diary: "Back from London, tired and broke but happy. Gosh, what a weekend. Our hotel bill looked like the national debt. I'll have to stop having breakfast in bed."

On November 23, he noted: "Sure enough, late getting to bed, so we're up early for a mission. Back to St. Nazaire. Got off the ground and had engine trouble so came back."

That engine balk may have been one of the luckiest things that ever happened to the Memphis Belle for this was the mission when only four of the group's planes managed to get over the target and only two of those managed to get home. One, with several wounded men on board, was riddled so badly it had to be junked. Which may explain Verinis' entry in his diary the following day: "Everyone gloomy as a result of yesterday's tough luck. The group was hard hit but 'C'est la guerre,' I suppose. Sorry to see old P. K. Baxter [a crew member of one of the lost planes] go down. A big, happy boy and his wife is about to become a mother, too. Some of the boys are fighting mad to get back at the Jerries."

For the next several days, the group was grounded because of bad weather and so that they could lick their wounds. On November 26, Verinis wrote: "Doing nothing, sitting around, weather bad. Sleeping an awful lot."

Still, there were certain compensations.

On December 4: "Went to London. Had a gay old time. Went to a new night club, The Bag 'O Nails. Quite a joint."

On December 6, after a raid on Lille, France: "One of the other groups lost two planes. We came through unscathed."

Three days later: "More rumors about going to Africa."

Two days later: "More poker. Lucky today and made a few hundred."

On December 13: "Only 10 more shopping days until Christmas. So what?"

Five days before Christmas, after a raid on Romilly sur Seine and a running fight with swarms of German fighters that lasted nearly two hours, he wrote: "This was really the toughest mission yet. I wouldn't care for many more like it."

On Christmas Eve he noted: "Went to London but got Christmas moody in the evening and came home and spent a quiet X-mas Eve by the fireplace with the boys. Just reminiscing."

December 27: "A Short Stirling four-engined bomber tried to make an emergency landing here. Stalled while turning on approach leg and cracked up and burned. One person got out of the flames. The others gone."

Two days later: "Had our first snow today."

On December 30, he noted: "Up at 5:30, a mission to Lorient submarine pens. Took off with snow falling."

This was the day when Bob Morgan was grounded because of a cold and Verinis took over as first pilot. It would be Verinis' last mission on the Memphis Belle. It was also a day on which the group was hit hard and several were wounded. Verinis wrote on returning: "Joe Yuravicz from West Haven hit in the back of the head by a 20 mm shell. In bad shape."

54

That day had one bright spot, though. "Major Putnam [the squadron commander] complimented me on my formation flying. Said if a string had been tied between my ship and his, it would still be unbroken. The boys in the mess hall cheered."

His mind turned to another happy thought: "Tired but ready for tomorrow night's New Year's Eve party."

But on the eve of the new year, there came a sad note. "Went up on a practice mission and had Spitfires make passes at us for gunnery practice. Two of them collided in mid-air. Only one bailed out and he landed in the water. Rescue boat got there too late. New Year's party here tonight."

Next morning: "Golly, what a headache."

After one of the group's toughest raids on St. Nazaire, two days later: "Biggest losses for us to date. Lost nine bombers. We can't stand trips like that too often. On way home, landed at British field [low on fuel] and stayed overnight. Had eggs for breakfast. The first since we left the States. London, here I come."

On January 11, he wrote: "Boys are getting uneasy. Combat is steadily taking its toll. Everyone thinking in terms of going home for a rest. We have lost about a third of our group to date, with less than half the necessary missions completed. What a dangerous life we live !!!!"

Next day he noted: "I was assigned a new plane. Decided to name it the Connecticut Yankee. Busy getting the kinks out of her."

Verinis took off on January 13 for the first time as the pilot of his own plane.

"I went in with my top turret and tail guns inoperative," he said. "Rather foolish, but I wouldn't turn back on my first mission in my new plane."

Many pilots had turned back with lesser excuses than that.

"I flew the number two spot, on the Colonel's wing. A very good spot. Three bombers lost. None from our Group."

Flying somewhere in the formation outside the Connecticut Yankee's window that day was another plane, the Memphis Belle.

Yet he would always remember his second mission made aboard the Memphis Belle - the low level attack on St. Nazaire, his baptism of fire.

"We went through a fantastic barrage. As co-pilot I had more time to look around. I could see those puffs of black smoke exploding all around us. It was a terrifying experience. That was my toughest raid."

Like Morgan and other pilots, Verinis confessed that he always felt glad when the command sent along a flight of B-24s, the other heavy bomber flown by the Americans at that time. It was commonly believed that the B-24, though bristling with guns, wasn't quite able to defend itself as well as the B-17 because it had more blind spots.

"I was always glad to see a group of B-24s coming along because I knew the Germans would be jumping on them first."

He felt sorry for the crews of the B-24s but he was happy the enemy might be shooting at someone else that day.

"When you saw your own planes going down you tried not to think about it," said Verinis. "You were too busy to think, anyway. And a pilot, or a co-pilot, doesn't shoot the guns. You can't help. It was when you got back and realized that some of your buddies were missing that it would really come home to you."

Did anyone ever finally decide they were not going to make it through the battle, that they were not coming home?

"I never thought I was going to die," said Verinis emphatically. "You feel a strong apprehension, a nervousness, but never fear. You're young and when you're young you don't frighten as easily. You're not afraid as much as when you get older. When you're older, you can't do the things you could do when you were young. Just like taking a fighter plane up to 10,000 feet and then standing it on its nose and coming straight down. You've got to be young and fearless to do that."

Bob Morgan remembered Verinis as being just a bit on the conservative side, as a pilot.

"He wasn't quite as wild as I was," said Morgan. "He wouldn't have done some of the things I did."

Finally, on May 13, following a mission to Meaulte, France, Verinis had his 25 missions completed, four days before most of the crew of the Memphis Belle.

For a short time he was assigned as operations officer for the 324th, a ground job, Then, when the high command decided to send a plane and its crew back to the States for a tour to boost civilian morale they chose the Memphis Belle and needed a co-pilot who had his 25 missions in.

"They picked me because I had started out on the Belle," said Verinis.

After the national tour was completed he was given a choice of duties and elected to attend an engineering school at Yale for flying officers. Yale was in his home town at New Haven, Connecticut.

At Yale he got a call from Bob Morgan.

"He wanted me to go with him to the Pacific," said Verinis. "I told him, 'Bob, I am here at New Haven and I am going to engineering school. Life is pretty serene. There is no war going on here. The answer is, No."

From there he moved on to Mitchell Field in New York where he tested military planes after they were overhauled.

On his testing job at Mitchell, he flew just about every type bomber made, the B-25, the B-26, the B-24 and the B-17. Earlier, he had flown fighter planes.

"The B-17 was the best plane I ever flew," he said. "I enjoyed the B-25. It was a nice handling plane. I didn't like the B-26. Nobody liked it. It had a short wing and a tendency to stall. What they were trying to do was create a faster version of the B-25 and they ended up with a dangerous plane. The B-17 was far more stable and maneuverable than the B-24, which was a sort of sloppy handling plane and the Germans knew it. If they had a choice of attacking a B-17 or a B-24, they always went for the B-24."

Life for Jim Verinis, in the years since the big air battle over Europe, has been mostly serene. He turned down Morgan's invitation to go out to the Pacific on a B-29, but he did team up with him later in the furniture business. When Morgan got out of that, Verinis stayed in and today is a factory representative for several furniture firms.

Married twice, he is now raising a teen-age son by his second marriage, this one to Marie Panagos. "Sort of like starting over again," he said.

His older son Steven and his wife Mary Ann have made Jim the proud grandfather of Alexander and Arielle.

Several years ago, Jim took his family back to Greece for a visit, to see how life had been for his father and mother in that long ago when they turned their backs on St. Peter and set out to start a new life in America.

"It was old and mountainous," recalled Verinis. "Opportunities are not what they are here."

There is a quiet pride in his own long ago, when he flew on the Memphis Belle.

Robert Taylor, noted British painter of military scenes, did a painting of a wartime bomber scene in the sky. It featured the Memphis Belle. It was reprinted in limited edition.

Verinis wanted no print. He wanted the original. So he bought it, and today the huge painting hangs on the wall in his living room, behind the piano. A glint of pride flashes in his eyes when he turns on the soft lighting to show the scene to visitors. He looks at them to see if the majestic form of the soaring Memphis Belle means as much to them as it does to him. To James Verinis it is, somehow, still alive.

Perhaps the only things that might arouse a brighter gleam in his eye is when he can, with a visitor, thumb through the old scrap book of sports page clippings from the days when his team beat Commercial High for the District Basketball Championship.

They called him Angie in those marvelous days. It hadn't been necessary to worry about a parachute then, or about a hunk of enemy shrapnel coming up through the bottom of the plane, seeking his bottom.

Leighton

He Guided Them to the Target

When Charles Leighton chose between a tough chemistry test and doing battle with Adolf Hitler, the dictator won easily.

"With that chemistry exam confronting me, the way to avoid it was to enlist in the Air Force," he said.

He will admit that he volunteered after the Japanese attacked Pearl Harbor in December of 1941, a time when thousands of America's young men would feel the sudden stirrings of patriotism in their blood.

Leighton chose the Air Force because he wanted to become a pilot. However, after being sent to Maxwell Field in Alabama, he found himself involved in the old Army game of "waiting."

"It seems they didn't have enough trainer planes or instructors, so most of us were simply put on 'hold' while waiting to begin flight training," said Leighton. "I got tired of the wait, and when we were told that, if we changed to navigator training, we could start at once, I switched."

Leighton sometimes wonders what might have happened, had he been able to begin his pilot training immediately. For in navigation school he had to fly as a passenger, and found that his stomach had its own ideas about flying.

"Every time I got in an airplane," he said, "I got sick. I found out that a milkshake carton had to be part of my basic equipment. I was afraid that if my instructor knew about it he would wash me out. But it seemed instructors didn't care how sick we got as long as we were able to do our job."

What effect did this air sickness have on his morale?

"I was determined to stick it out," said Leighton. "I just flew with my trusty milkshake carton in front of me.

"I found I was beginning to get sick as soon as I saw the pilot coming, before we ever got off the ground."

When student navigator Leighton graduated to larger planes, such as the B-17, the motion sickness vanished.

"I found I just didn't get sick on the big planes."

During training flights there were three student navigators and one instructor in the back of the AT7 trainer plane. They were given a navigation problem but not allowed to compare notes.

"I usually had the right answer or could make corrections by spotting a familiar landmark," Leighton said.

After three months' training at Mather Field in California, Leighton graduated second in his class as a certified navigator. Now he could wear the coveted gold bars of a second lieutenant.

Leighton's personal journey began in Anderson, Indiana, on May 22, 1919. His memories go back to the age of six when his family moved to East Lansing, Michigan. His father was a tool-and-die maker at the Oldsmobile plant in nearby Lansing.

The Leighton family of five settled at the edge of town, where open fields beckoned a young boy growing up with the spirit of adventure already stirring in his blood. There were rabbits and pheasants in those fields which his father enjoyed hunting, and his sons shared the sport with him.

"I guess I got to be a pretty good shot. As a high school camp counselor I was put in charge of the rifle range."

At East Lansing High School, the young Leighton made quite a mark in athletics. He won letters in track, basketball and football despite the fact that he is of average height and weight - not really the picture book "football hero." He set the record at East Lansing High for the most touchdowns ever scored.

"That record still stands today," he said. "After 50 years. I wasn't very big for a halfback. I only weighed about 145 pounds but I was quick. They called me 'Lightning.'"

His academic scores were something else, he said.

"Really mediocre. There was even some doubt as to whether or not I would go on to college. But then, most graduates were expected to go to college so I enrolled at Michigan University.

"If they asked, I'd say I was going to be an engineer, but I didn't fully realize what an engineer did. I just told people that to get them off my back. My grades were only good when it was something I really liked - as in navigation school."

Leighton remembers a crazy chicken coop "bomb" incident.

"We were on a cross-country training flight from Walla Walla to Dayton, Ohio," he said. "Because of the long distance, we were carrying an auxiliary fuel tank in the bomb bays.

"When we prepared to land in Dayton, the pilot found that the landing gear wouldn't come down. The backup system was a hand crank to get the wheels down. The problem was that the crank was located in the bomb bay and the auxiliary tank was in the way. We had to drop that tank!

"But when the pilot released the tank, it got stuck! The pilot finally ordered the lowest ranking man on board to get on top of the tank and try to kick it out. To keep him from falling out with the tank, we tied a rope around his waist and the rest of us hung onto the other end of the rope.

"The poor guy was scared witless but he jumped up and down on the tank. It still would not budge. Finally, the flight engineer got some tools and managed to turn it loose. When that tank finally fell, it landed on some farmer's chicken coop, smashing it to bits. The next day, the headline in a Dayton newspaper read, "Air Force Bombs Chicken Coop."

Leighton's next scare came when he and the crew of the Belle took off for England, their final journey to the war zone. This time, since he was navigating, it was his fault. They had been flying for several hours when he decided to check their position.

"It was night and we were flying over water," he said. "With no landmarks, I had to use celestial navigation. I got a fix on three stars and when I checked my charts it showed we were flying somewhere over Canada instead of the Atlantic Ocean, halfway to England. God, I was scared!

"I checked and rechecked, with the same results. I didn't know what the hell to do. I was nearly in a panic as I recalled the story of 'Wrong Way Corrigan,' the guy who took off for Canada and landed in England. He also made a mistake in navigation.

"I decided to check my data one more time and I suddenly realized that we had taken off at 11 p.m. and it was now after midnight. I had been using the wrong date in my calculations! The adjusted calculations showed we were exactly where we were supposed to be. But I never told the rest of the crew about that 'minor miscalculation' until we came back from England."

When they arrived in England, they hit their navigation target right on the nose. A perfect piece of navigation.

Before it was over, Leighton was going to find many more problems hindering his navigation skills. For example, the problem with the ammunition boxes.

"They gave us a beautiful compass to work with," he said. "But after we began our bombing missions, we found we had to carry a lot of extra ammumnition for the machine guns. They set metal ammunition boxes right down next to the compass and that created complete chaos. Even a metal belt buckle, too close to the compass, could throw it off. You can imagine what those big metal boxes did to it. They finally came up with a remote reading compass mounted on the wing which we could read inside the plane."

Then the machine guns gave him problems. Unlike the tail and turret gunners, who had been sent to gunnery school, navigators were given no gunnery training but were expected to shoot the guns.

"I had that .50 caliber machine gun up there in the nose," said Leighton, "but I had never fired one. We were even supposed to take it apart and clean it, but we made such a mess of it that on our first mission half the guns on the plane wouldn't shoot. Thank goodness,we didn't have any fighter attacks on that first mission. When the brass found out what was going on, they assigned some armament specialists to take care of our guns for us."

Later, he said, they got in a bit of gunnery practice by flying low over the water and firing at the waves. They watched the little splashes made by the bullets to check their accuracy.

"The first time I fired the gun, it was quite a jolt."

He enjoyed the Belle's first mission, the one to Brest.

"It turned out to be a piece of cake. No flak and no fighters. We just dropped our bombs and went home without a scratch."

Then came the baptism of fire over the submarine pens at St. Nazaire. He didn't have a chance to fire his machine guns.

"It was all flak," he said. "No fighters."

He soon learned that a navigation mistake could cost lives.

It happened twice in raids on those submarine pens at St. Nazaire - on December 30 and again on May 1. They were ordered never to take the direct route home in order to avoid the Brest Peninsula which was loaded with German ack-ack cannon and swarms of fighter planes. The safest route was to head out to sea and fly around the peninsula, then turn north for England.

To aid the planes, the British had a radio transmitter with a homing signal at Land's End, the southernmost tip of England. However, the Germans had learned to duplicate that signal in an effort to lure American planes into landing on enemy territory, the Brest Peninsula.

So, because of the false radio homing signal, an overcast sky which made visual navigation nearly impossible, a strong headwind which cut down your air speed, plus the confusion of a long and hectic air battle, navigators who were leading the groups thought they were letting down for a landing in England. In fact, they were trying to land on the Brest Peninsula, held by the Germans.

Leighton saw them making the wrong turn and told Morgan to continue on their heading, thus averting the same fate for the Belle and those following her.

Leighton quips: "I was the only one who could tell Morgan 'where to go' and get away with it."

The results were tragic for the lead group. Several planes with their crew of ten men each were shot down, and several more were severely damaged.

As Morgan put it, "The ones that got back were an awful looking sight. The leader of that group never led another raid."

Thus it was fate that reached out and tapped Leighton. On January 3, five days after the fiasco, the 91st Bomb Group received orders to hit St. Nazaire again. The Memphis Belle had been promoted to lead ship. The new "up front" navigator was none other than Leighton.

It was one of the toughest raids of them all. Determined, gutsy German fighters flew right through their own flak to get at the B-17s. On this mission, one of the big planes in the group right behind the Belle was hit in the bomb bay, exploding the load of bombs and blowing the plane to bits. No one had a chance to parachute out.

On May 1, in yet another raid on St. Nazaire, it happened again. The 91st Bomb Group was not leading that day. Once again, the weather was terrible. Clouds covered the target and made effective bombing impossible. On the way, the navigators in the lead group made their fateful turn north too soon, heading the two lead groups back into the hell hole of the Brest Peninsula.

The group's navigators and pilots caught the error and turned out to sea in time to escape the worst of the blistering German attack. Even so, the B-17 flying the tail position was shot down. Four planes were lost. Every plane in the formation was damaged.

Leighton survived and did his share of the fighting when the plane was attacked.

Other members of the crew claimed that Leighton shot down a German Ju.88 with his nose gun in one of those tough, running battles in a raid over Wilhelmshaven, Germany. Under the strict rules, requiring outside confirmation, he never got credit for the kill.

He did his share of the shooting. On several raids he did so much shooting that he ran out of ammunition.

"It's a helpless feeling," he said, "sitting up there without any ammunition. The enemy fighters are still coming at you and you can't shoot back."

On Decemeber 20, during a raid over Romilly sur Seine, in the midst of a hot fight with swarms of enemy fighters, Leighton suddenly just "didn't care" any more.

"It was a vicious fight and there were enemy fighters all over the place," he said. "Some came so close that I could see the faces of the German pilots. In the midst of it all I found myself thinking, 'This is a hell of a nice day. What are fighting for?' I looked over at Evans who shared the nose position with me, and he was firing away like crazy. Then I happened to look down and saw that my oxygen hose was disconnected. I was about to pass out! I replugged it and got back in the fight. At that altitude of 25,000 feet, a man can only survive about 20 minutes without his oxygen."

Leighton told of another flight when neither he nor Evans were wearing parachutes. That is, until an ack-ack shell burst just a few feet in front of them, giving the Memphis Belle a huge jolt.

"Neither of us said a word. We just both reached down at the same time and grabbed our parachutes."

Leighton also recalled a day when they were under attack and he noticed some fuzzy stuff floating around in the nose compartment.

"I wondered at the time what it was but I didn't find out until later. A bullet, or a piece of shell, had gone right through the nose of the plane only a few inches from my face. That floating, fuzzy stuff was the insulation that the bullet had knocked loose from the outer shell of the plane."

His closest call, he said, came during a training flight over rural England.

"I had to urinate. There was a funnel and a pipe in the bomb bay for that purpose. I was standing there, relieving myself, when suddenly the bomb bay doors swung open under me. The blast of wind nearly sucked me down and out of the plane. I clung to the framework so tight I must have put fingerprints on the metal beams.

"When I made it back to my nose compartment, Evans was laughing his head off. He had opened the bomb bays as a prank and didn't realize how close he had come to killing me. I was so mad I started punching him. The harder I hit, the more he laughed.

The guy was crazy. He thought it was a great joke. I could have easily been killed.

However, Leighton recalls that when a similar incident happened to Evans he did not find it quite so funny. It was after the Memphis Belle returned to the States and was on the War Bond tour. As they arrived at each city, Bob Morgan liked to put on a bit of a show, including a dive.

"One day, Evans decided he wanted to see the show from the radio operator's station," said Leighton. "At the top and to the rear of the plane. It had an opening in the top to fire the gun. Evans crawled up in there and was standing up half way out of the plane when Morgan put the Belle into a dive. Well, we nearly lost Evans. If Bob Hanson, the radio operator, hadn't been right there to grab his legs, Evans would have gone out."

Leighton admits he was sometimes scared to death.

"A mission flight was an emotional roller coaster. I would come home sometimes and find my pants wet . It is a terrifying experience. It's easier if you stay busy. I often wondered how those co-pilots stood it, doing nothing for hours. I had my navigating to keep me busy and take my mind off the worries of the mission."

One of the toughest jobs was packing the personal property of men who had been shot down. The property was shipped home to the surviving members of the family.

"I only did that two or three times. I always tried to avoid it. You would have to pick out the personal things that you thought the family would want and put them in a parachute bag. Most of us didn't like to deal with death closely.

"One day a plane came back with a dead crew member in the ball turret. I went over and looked in. There was a piece of his skull lying in there. After that, I never looked again."

Then it was over. The national publicity tour ended and the crew was given a 30-day furlough in September of 1944.

"I got married on furlough," said Leighton.

It had been a long wait for him.

"I met Jane when I was in the fifth grade in East Lansing and she was in the fourth grade. In high school and college we dated regularly but not as steadies. When I joined the Air Force, I tried to talk her into getting married. She thought it would be better to wait until I came back."

65

Leighton had taken a bit of kidding about the waiting situation. Bob Morgan said he and Evans had tried to fix up Leighton with a girl friend in England, on their trips to London.

"He never would go for it," said Morgan.

Marriage did not end Leighton's military career. The war was still going. Duty called. At the end of the tour, Leighton was permitted to choose his next assignment. He chose the pilot training he had been cheated out of by the long wait at Maxwell Field.

But that old nemisis returned to haunt him. Even after all that flight time in Europe, through flak and enemy planes, he still got sick when he flew in a small plane.

"I almost washed out because every time I had to put the planes into a spin, I would get sick. Even years later, I would get sick when I took my two daughters on the Ferris wheel."

His older daughter remembers having to leave the amusement park early when her father got sick on the airplane ride!

Leighton stuck it out during training and, this time, got his wings. A pilot at last.

After getting his multi-engine rating, Leighton was happy to be assigned back to the B-17s, this time as an instructor.

In August, the historic atom bomb fell on Hiroshima and Nagasaki. The war was finally over.

"My wife and I debated for a long time whether or not I should stay in the service," he said. "But we had our first child, by then, and we decided we wanted to raise her a civilian."

They returned to East Lansing. He finished college at Michigan State University with a major in education, not chemistry.

"I was a teacher and counselor for 24 years," he said. "I enjoyed working with young people. They kept me young at heart."

Jane also taught but now both are retired. Their two daughters have families of their own.

For their retirement, the Leightons chose to build a nice home near a ski lodge and golf course not far from Bellaire, Michigan. From the top of the mountain you can see Lake Bellaire, Torch Lake and even Lake Michigan, on a clear day. It's a place of singular beauty.

"One of my bridge buddies is an Air Force veteran, too, and occasionally we talk about it," he said. "But not a great deal."

Charles Leighton's voice trails off. He looks out over the tree tops in the direction of Lake Bellaire.

World War II was a long time ago.

Evans

He Hit the Pickle Barrel

The "Kid Wonder," they called him. Because, said his sister Peggy, "You always had to wonder what he would do next.

"Starting with things like, when Vincent Evans was about 11, sneaking off with the family car, leaving his Dad stranded downtown.

"When he got home Mom could barely see the top of his head. We never could figure out how he reached the clutch and brake pedals on that old Whippet," said Peggy Evans.

Then she added: "I guess he lived up to that name for the rest of his life."

Screen scriptwriter for Humphrey Bogart. Friend and confidant of such Hollywood notables as Ronald Reagan in his Hollywood days, Jimmy Stewart, June Allyson. Operator of a nationally famed chain of restaurants. The brash promoter of Anderson's Pea Soup. Flier. Race car driver. Shrimp boat operator. Logging truck fleet operator. Story teller. Romantic wooer of women, including movie actress Jean Ames. Master scrounger of eggs and milk in wartime England.

Then, perhaps we should not forget, the decorated "pickle barrel" bombardier of the Memphis Belle - so nicknamed because , it was said, he could drop a bomb in a pickle barrel on the ground from high altitude. His skill was one of the reasons the Memphis Belle was chosen so often to lead the group on bombing missions.

"This guy was the spark plug of the crew. There never was another guy like him," said Bob Morgan. "Besides, he was one of the best bombardiers in the Eighth Air Force."

Since Evans died in a plane crash in 1980, we had to depend on his sister Peggy and his wartime buddies to fill in the story of Kid Wonder. There were plenty of stories to tell.

It was Morgan who remembered the early days of their combat tour in England and being forced to eat dried eggs and

67

Brussels sprouts. Evans sneaked off the base and got chummy with a nearby farmer's daughter and would come back with fresh eggs and milk.

"Evans became our Egg Officer," said Morgan. Then he added: "She was real cute, too."

They were mostly cute, the girls Evans went for, his fellow crew members recall. There was, for instance, the night club singer named Kaye, whom Evans met in London.

"He was staying with her most of the time," his fellow crew members remember. He would telephone Morgan, or one of his buddies, of an early morning to find out if a "game" was scheduled and if not, he just stayed in London.

There were times when the "game" was on and Evans barely made it back to the base in time to get on the plane.

"One morning he got back so late we were already taxiing out to the takeoff line when he came running and scrambled on the plane," remembers Morgan.

But once he got onto the plane and they were over the target, Evans would hunch over his Norden bombsight and the Germans would lose some real estate down below.

On January 3, 1943, in a mission to bomb the submarine pens at St. Nazaire, Evans won his spurs as a bombardier.

The fact that he had been chosen lead bombardier that day had been due to some good work done by one of his fellow crewmen, navigator Chuck Leighton. Commanders had not failed to notice on previous raids when the formation got into trouble because of poor navigation that Leighton had not fallen into the traps. They made Leighton lead navigator for this trip to St. Nazaire and that automatically made Evans the lead bombardier.

During debriefing he gave a vivid description of the bomb run: "The flak was terrific," he told his interrogator. "I could see flashes of the anti-aircraft fire through my bombsight and an occasional fighter crossing underneath. I could hear the flak slapping the sides of the ship like kicking the door of a Model T Ford.

"Later, we discovered that we had a lot of holes in the plane and one tire was blown to hell. Captain Morgan asked me when the hell I was going to drop the bombs. I told him to take it easy.

"I put my cross hairs where I knew the target to be although I could not make it out at that distance. The second I released the bombs I knew they were going to be good. The bombardier can usually tell. They were squarely on the target."

THE MEMPHIS BELLE

Photographs later showed that Evans' bombs had missed the center of the aiming point by less than ten feet and he was awarded the Air Medal for the feat. It also meant that the Memphis Belle, with a hot shot navigator and a "pickle barrel" bombardier on board, would be leading a lot of raids after that. Incidentally, since the other planes had bombed on his cue, it meant the target really got plastered that day.

Perhaps it is time to remember that Evans' story really began in 1920 at Fort Worth, Texas, where he was born. But the family, Mr. and Mrs. Vinson Evans, moved to Henderson, Texas, a short time later where the boy and his younger sister grew up.

Peggy remembers that Vince played basketball at Henderson High School but is better remembered for his role as cheer leader. That firecracker personality was beginning to sparkle.

And speaking of firecrackers, Peggy says that she was deathly frightened of firecrackers and, in the manner of mischievous boys everywhere, brother Vince quickly discovered this and zeroed in on her fright.

"He'd chase me all over the place with his firecrackers, and I'd sometimes have to hide under the bed to get away from him."

After graduating from high school, Vince attended North Texas Teachers College at Denton, but even while he was still going to school, his firecracker energy had driven him to setting up a business and, while still little more than a boy, he was operating a fleet of logging trucks.

In 1941, with World War II heating up in Europe, with the Japanese attack on Pearl Harbor only a few weeks away, Vince lost interest in the logging business and enrolled in the Air Force.

"He went in with the intention of becoming a pilot," said Peggy. "That was the big thing then but he didn't quite qualify. So he switched to bombardier."

In the meantime this young fireball had also started his career as a lady's man. While still in college he had gotten married the first time. By the time he was in the Air Force, he was divorced.

Which cleared the way for his second marriage to a girl named Dinny, at Walla Walla, Washington, just two days before the 91st Bomb Group completed its final training and was being dispatched overseas. Those two days would be the extent of any real marriage for Evans never came back to Dinny.

There had been at least two young ladies in his life during the tour of combat duty in England and he had planned on going back to England and marrying his Kaye. When the crew and plane

69

came home, one of the stops was in Hollywood and he met Jean Ames. New sparks were flying and it gave him amnesia on Kaye. Poor Kaye.

Poor Dinny, too, for she had spent all that time waiting for her Vince to come back from the war to her, only to find that he had other stars in his eyes.

Peggy agrees it was all true. "My brother was a real skirt chaser," said Peggy.

But perhaps we are getting a bit ahead of our story. In England, at the end of his 25-mission tour, this firebomb character from Texas had a chance to work his charm on the Queen of England.

The Memphis Belle had become a celebrity by this time, the crew reaping their share of the fame. When the King and Queen of England came out to inspect the Bassingbourn air base of the 91st, the Belle and her crew were selected to "receive" the royal couple.

As the queen moved down the line of the crewmen lined up for inspection, she asked each man where he was born. The war correspondents present for the inspection could hardly believe their eyes when the queen came to Vince Evans.

Evans said that he was from Texas. The royal lady surprised everyone by clapping her hands, in rhythm, and singing a couple of lines from "Deep in the Heart of Texas."

Not to be outdone, Evans quipped, "People in England think Texas runs the rest of the United States."

This brought a hearty burst of laughter from the queen.

Evans had accomplished a notable feat during combat duty. Although normally the bombardier doesn't do much shooting with a machine gun, there is a .50 caliber gun mounted through the Plexiglas nose at the bombardier's position and when not busy on the bomb run, he is expected to do his share of defending the plane against enemy fighters. Evans did plenty of this "defending" and it was on that gut-wrenching mission to Romilly sur Seine on December 20, with German fighters swarming in by the dozens, that one of them made the mistake of coming in at the one o'clock position - Evans' position.

Evans got a bead on him, cut loose with a burst of gunfire and the Fw.190 began to smoke, flipped over and went down. This was one time when he had enough witnesses to confirm the kill as an "official" kill. It would be one of the eight fighters credited to the Memphis Belle during its eight months' combat tour.

Evans had his own version of what happens to an airman, psychologically, during a tour of 25 missions. Most of the Belle crewmen say they always clung to the hope and the belief that, somehow, they would be coming back.

In a speech he made at Hartford, Connecticut, on the war bond tour shortly after returning from England, Evans said:

"It's funny but you never quite get over being scared, no matter how many bombing runs you make. During the first five or six raids you're pretty tense. Then you figure, 'What the heck, I'll never come out of this one alive.' You're kinda fatalistic about it, see. Then, when you get to about the 20th raid you begin to realize that maybe you do have a chance, after all, and you tighten up again. Just like a violin string. Boy, those last five missions are tough."

After that little talk at Hartford somebody in the audience asked Evans what he had missed most while stationed in England, a country then struggling to survive, with severe food shortages.

His reply: "What did I miss most? Malted milk. Boy, I dreamed of drinking malted milk so much I would wake up with a pain in my stomach."

In any case, it was not long after that when the next stop on the tour was Hollywood where the crew was scheduled to dub in voice background to the War Department film that had been shot in Europe, including combat scenes. Real ones.

And that fateful meeting with Jean Ames, the glamorous starlet. Until this time, his Dinny, in Walla Walla, had been waiting for him to come home. Evans told a newspaper reporter, "You know how it is. We only knew each other a few days before we got married." And then, after only two days of "married life," he had been gone. To the war.

At first, Dinny swore she would not give him a divorce until he came back to her and tried to make a go of things. In the end, however, she changed her mind and Evans married Jean.

But this, too, was a marriage which had little endurance. Some of Evans' friends say she had a drinking problem.

In any case, it was still wartime. Bob Morgan, a major now, was training on the B-29, the new "super bomber," preparing to go to the Pacific and the bombing of Japan.

"One day I got a phone call from Evans," said Morgan. "He was desperate. He said, 'Bob, can you get me out of the country?'" Quick? I've got to get out of the country.'"

Morgan was able to pull a few strings and get Evans assigned to his B-29 outfit as a bombardier. So Evans went through

71

his second tour of duty in the Pacific. Presumably he didn't meet another Kaye for the B-29 squadrons were now stationed on the Island of Saipan. Not many girls around there.

Which didn't mean he had forgotten about them. Bob Morgan remembered that one day when they had bombed Tokyo, starting huge fires below, Evans suddenly remarked: "I hate to think of what we are doing to those geisha houses down there."

After the war, when Evans returned to Hollywood, people discovered that this ace bombardier also had a talent as a writer.

"He had been writing stories since he was a kid," said his sister, "and he had a great imagination. In college he attracted a lot of attention with his short stories."

According to Peggy, Evans wrote at least one screenplay which was made into a film starring Humphrey Bogart, called "Chained Lightning." He then wrote another called "Loretta," which was scheduled for Bogart until "Bogie" became ill and it was scratched.

It was also during the early years after the war, both before and during the screenplay writing episodes, when Evans, the bundle of energy, became involved in a lot of other things. Such as operating a shrimp boat in Mexico, on which he based another screenplay, managing a restaurant in Los Angeles, and driving race cars at Pomona, California.

But perhaps the most fateful thing that finally happened to him was his marriage to Margery Winkler, a wealthy heiress from Indianapolis. Either Margery was able to tame all those wild impulses in Vince Evans or else he himself decided it was time to settle down. No matter, it was a marriage which lasted and produced two children, Peter and Venetia.

It was during those years of marriage to Margery when Vince's unbounded energy took him into a whole series of business enterprises, and while some might wish to suggest he was able to do so only because of his wife's money, even his critics had to agree that most of such enterprises prospered under his direction. Cattle rancher. Restaurant operator. Promoter of Anderson's Pea Soup, until it was being sold in stores nationwide.

It had all started when, largely on an impulse, he had bought a small, struggling and largely unknown restaurant named Pea Soup Anderson's at Solvang, California, a picturesque little Danish colony near Buellton. Friends said he bought it because he liked the pea soup.

72

But now, he began promoting the restaurant and its pea soup as if he were promoting a Hollywood movie. New chefs were hired, and posted for miles around were huge billboards showing two chefs splitting a pea.

Before it was over, Pea Soup Andersons would do so well it would be claimed that they were serving two million customers per year. Then, not satisfied with one successful eatery, Evans began to expand into other cities - Stockton, Mammoth Lake, Buellton and Santa Nella. All driven by that boundless energy that had earned him that title, "Kid Wonder."

And then it all came to an end on April 20, 1980, when Evans, his wife, their daughter and a pilot, Nancy Meinken, took off from Palo Alto Airport in Evans' private plane, a twin-engine Piper Aztec. Evans had a pilot license but was not qualified on instruments and it was cloudy that day.

Bob Morgan said he checked into the crash with the FAA, and gave this account of what happened:

"He had decided to take up flying again and bought this twin-engined plane. He got his license and was qualified on every-thing except instruments. So when he would go on trips he would take along a pilot from the local flying service. On that day, he was coming home from a trip up the valley and was coming in to the resort where he lived. He was letting down in Santa Barbara, on instruments, when he suddenly broke into the clear and cancelled the instrument flight plan. Then, suddenly, he was back in the clouds. When this happened he obviously became disoriented and crashed into the side of a mountain."

In his description, Morgan referred to the pilot as "he," indicating that Evans may have been piloting the plane. Perhaps the FAA never found out because both Evans and Meinken were gone.

Evans' son Peter was not on the plane that day and thus became the only family survivor.

His sister Peggy remembered a poignant vignette of those last days.

"It was on April 10, when he went to visit our mother, Winnie, who was ill. He told her, 'Mother, I want you to hurry and get well. I want to go to Memphis to see the Memphis Belle. It is a sentimental journey and I want you to go along.'"

Exactly ten days later, Vincent Evans, the ace bombardier, the romantic and the dynamo businessman, was dead.

The journey of "Kid Wonder" had come to an end.

73

Quinlan

Our Lucky Horseshoe

They called him "J. P." and he wore the title comfortably, like an old shoe. It made him feel a part of the crew, a close-knit little "family."

But when several of his buddies tried calling him something like "The Mayor of Yonkers," he bristled a bit.

"I wasn't born in Yonkers and I never lived there," he would insist. "I lived outside of Yonkers, on a farm. My mother was raising chickens. When I was a kid I used to sneak through a hole in the fence on somebody's estate and go hunting. You can't go hunting in Yonkers." He identified his home as Nepera Park, which has long ago been swallowed up in the environs of Yonkers, Greater New York, whatever.

Somebody even tried calling him the Wabash Cannon Ball, and accused him of singing that song on the intercom system of the Memphis Belle, but John P. Quinlan denies that one, too. "It never happened," he insists. He did agree it was one of his favorite songs and his buddies probably heard him singing it.

Still somebody else suggested "Tail End Charley," because he rode the tail, as tail gunner. But Quinlan didn't like that one either.

"That's the name they always used on the tail end plane in the flight formation," he will quickly remind you. It wasn't considered a lucky position because the German fighter pilots liked to pick on Tail End Charley.

It was Bob Morgan, the "Chief," the pilot of the Memphis Belle, who had his own pet title for the stocky little tail gunner.

"He was our Lucky Horseshoe," Morgan told crowds over and over again when the Memphis Belle and her crew came home for her triumphal tour of America's cities.

74

Not only because Quinlan and his twin .50s managed to keep German fighters off the Belle's tail, officially shooting down at least two of them but, said Morgan, "J.P." was a wizard at spotting enemy planes approaching from other directions, spotting flak patterns creeping up on them, calling for evasive action.

"Dive, Chief, dive!"

Morgan is quite certain that if it had not been for his sharp-eyed tail gunner back there, the Belle would never have made it home from several of her tougher missions. It was a comfort to the whole crew, knowing he was back there.

Even though, on at least two occasions, Quinlan had to sit back there in his tail end "office" and watch the plane's tail being shot to shreds around him, being wounded in the leg on one of these occasions, with his guns knocked out. When those enemy fighters attacked in pairs, or in threes, there was a limit to what a guy could do. Especially when they used one of their favorite tricks, of sneaking up on you out of the sun.

Quinlan got so much action, especially in the early months of B-17 missions, because that rear end approach was the favorite method of attack by the Germans at the beginning. Until Quinlan and a bunch of other B-17 tail gunners made that tail end approach so hot they shifted tactics. Like coming in from the front, head on.

Coming in from the front, the closing rate of speed at which the two planes approached each other was terrifying. Each gunner, the German fighter pilot and the B-17 gunner, got only a split-second to fire.

It must be remembered that the Memphis Belle was one of the first of the American heavy bombers thrown into the battle over Europe and Nazi Germany, so there were plenty of attacks from the rear in those early bombing days of 1942 and 1943.

The mere fact that Quinlan was officially credited with shooting down two enemy planes attested to that. Not to speak of the dozens of others he shot at and may have blasted.

"If more than one German fighter was coming at you and you were shooting at them, you didn't have time to look to see if any of them were going down. If you did that, you could get yourself killed. Quick.

"I remember one day it almost happened that way. This plane was coming in at me and I gave him a good long burst. I could see pieces flying off and he started to go down. I was watching him fall, trying to see what really was happening to him. Another plane, right behind him, sneaked up on me out of the sun and almost got me. That taught me a lesson: Never take your eyes off the danger zone to try to see if one of your targets was going down."

Quinlan may not have invented the famous "clock system" fliers used to give a quick location on approaching enemy fighters but he introduced it to the Belle's crew.

The plane's nose, straight ahead, was twelve o'clock. Straight back, the tail was six o'clock with all the other clock positions in between. "Nine o'clock high" meant enemy fighters were approaching high and from the left.

The same system was used to warn the pilot of approaching flak patterns as ground gunners tracked the planes to get their range.

"Flak at seven o'clock and getting closer" gave the pilot a chance to take evasive action.

But then that little tail gunner, Quinlan, sitting astride his gunner's stool, manning his big twin .50s as they chattered and bucked.

"I had to keep telling myself to stay cool. It was easy to get rattled and start shooting wild when you looked out the tail and saw a whole swarm of German fighters coming at you," said Quinlan. "I'd keep telling myself, over and over, 'You've got to stay cool. You've got to stay cool.'

"You didn't have a chance of hitting anything unless you stayed cool and concentrated on one target at a time."

Even today, more than 40 years after it all happened, with only that little board on the wall, containing his medals, to remind him that he was once involved in the great air war over Europe, Quinlan's eyes light up, his hands move in quick gestures as he explains how the German yellow-nosed Me.109s maneuvered in battle.

But before we say more about that, perhaps it is time to go back to that certain chicken farm near Yonkers. Here the gutsy little tail gunner was born on June 13, 1919.

Quinlan remembers that his father worked for the Yonkers sanitation department and the family did not depend completely on Mom's chickens for a living. They helped.

"But Dad died when I was just a kid and things got a bit tougher after that," said Quinlan.

As the son of a staunch Irish Catholic family, he attended , in the beginning, Catholic schools. He went to Sacred Heart Academy in his high school years.

"I guess I didn't conform too well and they didn't like me," he says. "In my third year they more or less let me go. I finished up in public high school."

Quinlan was about 11 years old he began sneaking into a nearby wooded area around an old cemetery, shooting at squirrels.

"My mother decided the BB gun wasn't the proper gun to shoot at squirrels with so she bought me a little Hamilton .22. Then I met up with an older man named Joe, who took me where the hunting was really good."

How did he meet this Joe?

"Well, my sister and I used to deliver his mail to him from the post office. He'd give us a nickel every time. He had a lot of deer heads in his parlor and he'd tell us hunting stories. He said he would take me deer hunting."

When did he kill his first deer?

"Well, there was this woman who told me, when she went to her outhouse a buck deer would scare her and she wanted me to kill it."

Quinlan went to his old friend, Joe, and asked if he could borrow his deer rifle.

"He gave me a .35 caliber Remington and the first time I shot it, it almost kicked me through the door.

"I went and hid in the lady's outhouse and when the deer jumped over the garden wall I shot him, a nice eight-pointer."

When had he enlisted in the Army or Air Corps?

"December 7, 1941." Gee, that was that fateful Sunday when the Japanese struck Pearl Harbor and the war began for America.

"No, actually it was December 8," said Quinlan, correcting himself. "The recruiting offices were not open on Sunday. I had been to church Sunday morning and a man who had been a friend of my father told us about Pearl Harbor."

Why had he enlisted so quickly?

"I just wanted to get into it because we were in it."

One had to be old enough to have been there, that Sunday, to appreciate what happened. The next day, Monday, when the recruiting offices opened, there were long lines of young Americans, waiting, clamoring to enlist. So young John P. Quinlan was one of those, even though his tearful mother was pleading with him not to go. He was her only son and she needed him.

Did he choose the Air Corps?

"I wanted to join any damn thing," he said. "They gave me some tests and decided I fit into the Air Corps. They sent me to St. Louis for basic training. I kept seeing all those crowds of men coming into the Army and I was afraid it would be over, maybe in two or three months, before I could get into it."

After that it was fate that landed him in the crew of the Memphis Belle, part of it stark tragedy, with only a quirk of fate or the kindness of a young pilot that saved his life.

First, it had been an epidemic of meningitis which struck the camp at St. Louis.

"Seems everybody had a cold or flu. Then meningitis. They shipped everybody out of there in a hurry, emptied the camp."

The fast evacuation landed him at McDill Field near Tampa, Florida, where the 91st Bomb Group was being formed. A sunnier climate, less illness. And his first encounter with the four-engine B-17 bombers that were going to play such an important part in his future. For training purposes he was assigned to the crew on a plane piloted by Lieutenant Richard G. Hill.

"Gee, it was almost like getting out of hell and going to heaven," said Quinlan. "All that sunshine, the beautiful, white, sandy beaches. The good food, after that cold, wet winter at St. Louis and all the sickness."

Next episode for the future Eighth Air Force gunner, a six weeks tour at gunnery school, Las Vegas, Nevada. Here he rode in the rear compartment of bucking little trainer planes, firing a machine gun at sleeve targets being towed by other trainer planes.

Had he learned to master the big 50 caliber machine guns they would be using in combat? "I had 'em down pat," he said.

Had his early experience with guns, his hunting, helped with his shooting? "Not much," he said, "but it helped. I knew how to shoot but it was completely different when you were shooting a big machine gun."

Back to McDill, a qualified gunner, and then the 91st was transferred, in June of 1942, to Walla Walla, Washington, for final training. Formation flying, more gunnery practice, bombing practice.

Or a bit of fun like the stunt he pulled on a drill sergeant.

"He kept telling me my hair wasn't cut short enough," remembers Quinlan. "I got it cut but he still wasn't satisfied so I shaved it all off. Then I walked up to him, saluted and jerked my cap off. My head was so shiny it almost blinded him."

Then it happened, that hand-of-fate thing. On July 15, 1942, Lieutenant Hill's crew was assigned to another routine flight but Hill told Quinlan: "I don't need the gunners this trip, only the co-pilot, navigator, bombardier and radio man. You can take the day off."

True, unless it was a gunnery training flight, and it wasn't. There were no German or Japanese enemy planes in Washington to shoot at.

Nobody knew exactly what caused it, or why, but that was the day when the plane piloted by Hill slammed into the side of a mountain and all five men aboard died.

The first thing Quinlan knew about it was when he walked across the grounds at the base that evening and ran into a buddy from another plane. The man's eyes widened in surprise at the sight of Quinlan, as if seeing a ghost. "Gosh, man, you're supposed to be dead," he blurted.

So, Quinlan has at least one thankful memory of a man named Hill.

It was after that, with his original plane gone, when Quinlan was assigned to the crew and plane of another young pilot named Robert K. Morgan.

Even today, after so many years have passed, it is apparent that despite his exhuberant Irish spirit, his zest for life, his pranks, his songs, the family in which he takes so much pride, Sergeant Quinlan is one of those upon whom that war has left its marks, deeply etched into his subconscious.

At times, he is reluctant to talk about it but then, when he starts, it comes tumbling out, his eyes animated by memories, as if it is a relief to get it out to someone who will take time to listen.

We asked him about that wild, hectic air battle over Rouen, France, on March 28, 1943, the day a hunk of shrapnel slammed into his right hip, with enemy bullets shredding the tail around him, knocking his gun out.

"I don't recall that one too well, see," he says. "Something goes vague. Long after the war, after I was married and had children, I had nightmares, bad dreams. Something would bring it back. I would be up in an airplane. I could smell the rubber burning, something you remember from a plane on fire. You wake up at night. You feel cold. Or you hear a noise, maybe a plane flying over your house. I would remember going on a mission, a hell of a lot of ammunition shot. We'd shoot 1,400 rounds easy.

"When we got back, we were losing altitude. We were coming down and actually it was the coast of England, but I thought we were landing in enemy territory. I thought, Gee, we're going to surrender the plane. The pilot said the landing gear was down. I said, 'Hell, we're going to surrender. I want to bail out and get captured because I didn't want to surrender the plane.'

"Then I recognized the landing strip on the ground and we were landing but I didn't remember a damned thing about the mission.

"Well, in a dream I am up there and I am freezing my butt off and we are in trouble. I'm thinking. I'm married and I'm trying to be cool and start putting it all together. Then it finally comes out like a dream and I wake up. Another time I bailed out again. When I woke up, I had jumped right out of bed and landed in the living room."

The dreams went on a long time. Had they finally stopped?

"I don't know. One never knows. I hope so."

There was a pause, then more bits of memory come flashing back.

"It was one hell of a dog fight," he says. "You were half frozen because it was 20 or 30 degrees below zero. Your hands are numb. You are shaking. Scared. We had electrically heated gloves but half the time they didn't work. You would be kneeling down in firing position and the electric suit would burn the back of your legs. The old suits, you couldn't trust them. You had to take off your gloves to get the oxygen mask off. It was freezing up all the time."

Was it possible he didn't remember the missions because the 20 mm shell hit the plane's tail and stunned him?

"No, but it scared hell out of me," he said.

Back on the ground, between missions, the thoughts about the next mission.

"Sure, we were scared," he said. "But most of the guys don't want to be called chicken, so you put on a pretty good face so nobody will know you're scared. Then, when a mission is over, you go to town and drink a few beers and you become one of the knights of the air, a brave man telling everyone who you are.

"Then it came down to those mornings when you were out there with your flying gear on, walking to the plane, and you knew it was going to be a bad one. You had seen that in the briefing session. We knew about the losses we had been taking. Some said it was 100 per cent, counting replacements. It was an awful lot of losses.

"I mean, you knew it would eventually happen to you because a lot of your friends had got it already.

"We all had been together like brothers, all the way from McDill Field. You knew all their stories and all about their girl friends and their mothers and sisters. They were like brothers. Then they would disappear. You move their beds out and replacements come in and you are afraid to be friendly with them because you don't want to get that feeling again about losing them.

"Even then, sometimes you're in the mess hall and you see someone and you say, Gee, that looks like Old Joe and you remember it can't be Old Joe. He's gone.

"If you were one of the old-timers that had lasted through a few missions, you had a little moss on your shell, you had ribbons on your chest. The new ones, the replacements, would figure they would try to get chummy with you. They think you are a man who made it. Maybe you can tell them something that will help them make it. They need somebody to cling to. But you never let them get close.

"The longer you flew the more distant you became.

"You stick around with the other guys who had survived.

"When you knew you were going on a mission you got a little scared. You told yourself you might be able to figure out a way to keep from going. Going over to the plane, I would try to figure a good way out. Maybe I could manage it so that one of the trucks that hauled bombs out to the plane would hit me in the back, just bad enough to put me in the hospital, just bad enough so I wouldn't have to go that day.

"Even after you get on the plane and it starts up, you say to yourself: 'Maybe not all the engines will start and we won't get off the ground. Maybe the plane will slip off the runway and get stuck in the mud.'

"Then you hear the priest up in the tower, blessing you.

"Even after the plane begins climbing, you think: 'Maybe something will happen so we can abort.' But we'd soon gain altitude and be up there and you'd tell youself: 'Well, here we go.'

"Then after you got up there you stop thinking about those things. You lose your fear. Then you want to make sure nothing happens to the plane because of you. You don't want to do something dumb so the plane gets shot down or someone killed. You feel responsible. You want to make sure you do what you're supposed to do and you do it right.

"That was the thing that kept you going.

"One of the worst things was to see one of your other planes get shot up, an engine out, trailing smoke, dropping back and out of the formation. We always wanted to drop back with them and help protect them but our orders were to stay in formation.

"If you dropped back you would lose more planes. You would get your ass shot off.

"Back in the tail, I was the one who got to see most of that. I watched our friends fall back, hit, and the German fighters waiting to pounce on them like a pack of wolves. They always ganged up on a crippled plane. Those guys in the bombers were our friends, and it made you feel bad because you couldn't help them.

"After that, when they come at you, you want to shoot them. You want to kill them because they killed your friends. You got frustrated because you shot at them and you couldn't stop them from coming in. I was shooting and doing everything right. I was leading them right and firing the guns just right. But they just kept coming. Kept coming."

Today it is hard for him to remember what happened on all of his missions. The memories tend to blend together.

Some of Quinlan's memories have a bit of macabre humor, like the day when, for a moment, he thought he had been shot through the head.

To fire his guns, he had to lean forward and place his face against the sighting piece. He had stopped firing, leaned back and it happened.

"A bullet from an enemy plane went right through my little compartment, in one side and out the other," he said. "I felt something wet trickle down my face. When I reached up with my hand, it came away with blood on it. It was crazy but I reached up and touched the other side of my head to see if blood was on that side, too.

"The bullet didn't hit me. A shattered piece of Plexiglas hit me and brought the blood. I wasn't really hurt. But if I had still been leaning forward in shooting position that bullet would have gone straight through my head."

Some memories are of things that happened on the ground, like the time he and another Irish American named McDonald declared war on England.

"McDonald was one of those Irish Republican Army sympathizers," said Quinlan. "He was fun and we buddied around together. One night we were in London and we got drunk. We were out on the street yelling a lot of dirty, four-letter words and we declared war on England and the queen herself. 'Come on out and fight,' we hollered to every Englishman.

"Then I felt a hand on my shoulder. I looked up and it was the biggest Bobby I ever saw. No matter how big he was, I would have taken a swing at him if he had talked tough to me. But the guy was so gentle, just like a father, talking to me gentle and sweet. 'Lads, I believe you have had enough.'

"We went along with him just like a couple of little puppies."

Being Irish makes it tough for him to get all his emotions straight about the day, after the crew completed their 25 missions and were told they were going back to the U.S. for a big tour, when the King and Queen of England came by the air base to tell them goodbye.

"She seemed like a real nice lady," he said. "They shook hands with everybody and wished us luck. But there were some reporters out there and one of them asked how I felt, shaking hands with the Queen. I said my Irish ancestors would turn over in their graves if they saw me shaking hands with the Queen of England. I could see the guy didn't like that answer."

Then they were back in the U.S., visiting war plants around the country, boosting civilian morale.

"People would come up to us, shake hands and tell us what heroes we were," he said. "I didn't like that hero stuff. If they shook hands and told me I was lucky, I could agree to that. Damn right, I was lucky to be on the right plane and the right crew at the right time. It could have been any other plane or any other crew that survived. I never felt like I had done anything great. I figured the country was at war and I wanted to go.

"When I was young I was patriotic as hell. Even now, when they play the Star Spangled Banner at the baseball games I stand up and put my hand on my chest. Red, white and blue American. I'd feel bad about anyone who felt differently. The Memphis Belle was a lucky plane and we were a lucky crew and we were all survivors."

One reason it's hard for Quinlan to remember the details of all his missions is that, after the publicity and bond tour ended he volunteered for another tour of duty, flying tail gunner on a B-29 in the Pacific.

Part of the reason he did it was that Bob Morgan had volunteered to pilot one of the B-29s out there and promised Quinlan he would get him on his crew as tail gunner. Somehow it didn't work out and Quinlan ended up on another plane.

He got back into action and shot down three Japanese planes before he himself, his plane and his crew, were shot down on his fifth mission. At long last the thing he had dreaded in England had happened. He had to bail out.

He landed in Japanese-held territory in Manchuria and was captured by the Japanese. Several days later he escaped and made his way into territory held by Chinese guerrillas.

Before the guerrillas could get him to a protected landing strip where an American plane could rescue him, the guerrilla band had to fight several pitched battles with Japanese soldiers.

"They gave me a rifle and I shot at the Japanese soldiers, too," said Quinlan.

Sometimes during his trek, he was taken to villages where Americans were expected to make patriotic speeches to the villagers.

"I just rattled off a bunch of nonsense, threw in a bunch of swear words and the interpreter would tell the crowd something and everyone would cheer," he said.

One day a B-25 dropped down and landed, took Quinlan on board and flew him back to an American military base.

"The pilot dropped me off at the base and took off again," he said. "The Chinese had given us Chinese guerrilla uniforms to wear and I was just standing there when an Amercian officer walked up and asked me to get him some charcoal. He was surprised when I spoke to him in English and said I was an American airman."

When asked for more details about the shoot-down experience, his times with the guerillas, Quinlan shrugs.

"One sees a lot over there that one doesn't want to remember. I'll tell you one thing, those guerrillas were killers. Some of them were only 15 years old but they had liitle regard for life. I lost a lot of weight. We ate dogs.

"The parachute jump out of the plane over Manchuria didn't help."

He still has a few problems with his nerves.

Back home now, living with his wife and youngest daughter in a tiny village about 200 miles north of Yonkers, or New York, it is enough if he still can get around and go hunting, even if he limps a bit. "This is where I want to be," he said.

There are a few things Quinlan takes pride in. One is that he married his childhood sweetheart, Julie Nicholl and between them they have reared six of their own children and a nephew.

"We went to school together and were going to get married before I went overseas but her father wanted us to wait," he said. "Her mother was dead."

When Quinlan came home, Julie was waiting.

"We had a big church wedding," he said.

An industrial firm in Yonkers, in a burst of patriotism, gave him a job and promised to train him as an engineer.

"Later, they quit waving the flag and let me go," he said. "They had trained me to shoot guns but nobody needed that anymore."

He drove a truck a while, then operated a back-hoe. He worked at various construction jobs.

He is proud of his children.

Jack is an iron worker. Charles is a prison guard. Pat is an attorney. Pete is a psychologist. Matt is in this third year in college in Hawaii. Julie is in her second year at S.U.N.Y. Joe is the nephew whose father died when he was a child. The Quinlans took Joe in and reared him along with the rest. He became a plumber.

Quinlan won't show them to you unless you ask him, but he does have his old war medals mounted on a board on the wall: The Distinguished Flying Cross, the Air Medal with five clusters, the Purple Heart, the China War Memorial Medal, the European Theater Ribbon with four campaign stars, the Pacific Theater Ribbon with four stars and the Victory Medal.

Standing at the board he is stirred to remember once more.

"I was always scared stiff but too proud to admit it," he said. A simple statement but meaningful of his troubled memories.

He doesn't shout of his patriotism but he wants you to know it is there.

He remembers the ceremony at Bassingbourn on April 21, 1943, when the British turned the base over to the Americans.

"The British played their national anthem and hauled down the Union Jack," he said. "Then we played the Star Spangled Banner and raised Old Glory on the flagpole. Shivers ran down my spine.

"I guess I might have had a few tears in my eyes."

John P. Quinlan, the forever patriot.

Winchell

Nor Arrow by Day

"I will say of the Lord, He is my refuge and my fortress; my God; in Him I will trust. Thous shalt not be afraid for the terror by nigbht; nor the arrow that fliety by day. A thousand shall fall at the side, and ten thousand at thy right hand; but it shall not come nigh unto thee".   From the 91st Psalm

It was wartime and the slim young American airman pulled on his flying suit just before going out to climb into the B-17 bomber called the Memphis Belle, which would soon be taking him and his crewmates into the deadly skies of enemy-held territory where bullets and cannon shells would fill the sky around him.

He took a Bible, sat on the edge of his bunk and read for a few moments, silently prayed, perhaps. Then he was ready to go.

"The 91st Psalm was always my favorite. It always gave me comfort and enough courage to go out there and climb into that plane," said Sergeant Clarence E."Bill" Winchell, who flew waist gunner position through 25 missions.

It was only a coincidence, he said, that it was the 91st Psalm and he was a member of the 91st Bomb Group. That Psalm had been his favorite long before he heard of the 91st Bomb Group.

The terror by night - the long, tense hours of lying awake at night unable to sleep, thinking, knowing that a mission was scheduled the next morning, and he would have to go. A bit of fear, perhaps, but not enough to prevent him from keeping his rendez-vous with a target in Germany.

The arrow by day - the enemy bullets that slammed through the aluminum hull of the Belle, searching for human flesh, sounding like hail on a tin roof. Those innocent-looking cotton clouds of anti-aircraft shrapnel, filled with deadly fragments of steel, through which they would have to fly to reach their target.

86

THE MEMPHIS BELLE

Winchell's assignment: Man the big .50 caliber machine gun in the open side window of the plane and make sure that none of Herman Goering's yellow-nosed fighter planes sneaked up on them from his side.

It was cold, bitter cold, sometimes 30 to 40 degrees below zero up there in the sky near 30,000 feet. One had electrically heated gloves and suits but they didn't always work. Sometimes one had to remove the gloves to clear the oxygen mask which would be filled with moist condensation from your breath and freezing up.

You didn't dare take your eyes off the sky for even a second for those Messerschmitts and Focke Wulfs could sometimes sneak up on you in the blink of an eye. Perhaps at the top of every crewman's mind was the resolve never to be the man who would make the mistake that might get the big four-engine plane shot down. To fail to come home.

As Bill himself put it: "A closeness, an *esprit de corps*, develops among a veteran bomb crew. One looks at his crew mates almost as blood brothers. You feel an obligation to defend their backs, as you know they are defending yours, at all cost."

The long journey began at Cambridge, Massachussetts, for Clarence E. Winchell on November 4, 1916, the day he was born. Winchell is not sure why people called him Bill, a name that has stuck with him. It is a bit more obvious why, later, some of his buddies in the Air Force would call him "Winch."

He has few memories of Cambridge, most of his memories beginning after his father, a YMCA secretary, moved with his family to Oak Park, Illinois, for another "Y" assignment.

"I think I was about eight when we moved," he remembers, and then the memories have to do with a lot of swimming, canoeing, camping and all the things a proper YMCA youngster would become involved in. Except, maybe, the bear wasn't on the "Y" schedule.

That little encounter came one day when he was about 12, on a summer camping trip in the Hudson Bay area and he was sent down to the lake to get some water.

"I came around a bend in the trail," he said, "and here was that bear staring me in the face. I don't think he was very aggressive because when he saw me he took off. I took off, too, in the opposite direction."

Winchell also remembers that he became good enough to make the "Y" diving team when he was in high school.

"I wasn't a star. I was just good enough to make the team."

87

One of the big things he does remember was that draft "fish bowl" thing.

It was in 1940 with World War II already raging in Europe, and the threat that America might become involved, when Congress passed a new draft law, requiring the registration of young men for military service.

America had no television in 1940 but Americans by the millions were listening to their radios that day, October 29, 1940, when the numbers of millions of young men were placed in a huge glass "fish bowl" and then drawn out, lottery style, to see who got drafted first.

"My number was the 52nd name drawn out of that bowl," said Winchell. Who wouldn't remember that one, out of all those millions of numbers?

In any case, young Winchell had a decision to make. Those whose numbers had been drawn still had the opportunity to volunteer and choose their branch of service.

"One of my buddies had gone down and enlisted in the famous Black Horse Troop of the 107th Cavalry, Illinois National Guard," said Winchell. "I was in love with horses anyway and I had decided I didn't want to be walking so I went down to enlist, too. The day I went down they closed the books. They said they had all the people they needed.

"So I joined the field artillery. They were still using horses, but a week after I enlisted they took away the horses.

"We were sent to Camp Forrest, Tennessee. Boy, what a mess. We almost had to clear some land so we'd have a place to live. I had a first sergeant I despised. He despised me, which meant that KP and I were synonymous. Cleaning the latrines. All the dirty work. When the Air Force recruiting officer came around, I grabbed the opportunity. I couldn't stand the outfit I was in.

"My captain told me I was up for promotion and if I joined the Air Force, I'd start out as a private again and spend the duration of the war sweeping out hangars. I said I'd take my chances.'

Next stop, Jefferson Barracks near St. Louis, Missouri, in January, living in tents and very cold. Here he had to endure basic training all over again, shivering at night until he managed to make friends with a supply sergeant who slipped him a couple of extra blankets.

Then McDill Field in sunny Florida, where the Air Force trail began for all the men who would, eventually, wind up as the crew of the Memphis Belle.

The first surprise at McDill came when he found that enlisted men were flying, not only officers. The Army and the Air Forces were discovering that if you went to war in big four-engine bombers it took a crew of men to man them, not just a pilot.

But before he would do any flying, this soldier named Winchell had another tough hurdle to pass: his eyesight.

"I was born with an astigmatic left eye and had about 20-50 eyesight. There was no way in the world I could legitimately pass that eye test," he said.

Well, if not legitimate, how about a bit of illegitimate?

"When I got to Europe I was known as the one-eyed gunner," he remembers.

The way he managed it was to get somebody to slip him copies of the eye charts and to memorize them.

"I kept a file of them in my wallet. When I went to take my tests all I had to do was find out which chart they were using, and when they got to the bottom lines I'd just read it off from memory. I had been sitting on my bunk memorizing those charts backwards and forwards. I had a good memory and that is how I maintained my 20-20 status."

Was there a possibility that he would be endangering his fellow crew mates when he tried to shoot with defective eyesight?

"No way. I shoot with my right eye and it's perfect. I was credited with shooting down two enemy planes and some of my buddies, with perfect eyesight, got none."

Shortly after arriving at McDill, Winchell saw a notice on the bulletin board: "Wanted, volunteers for aerial gunnery school." He commited the old military "no-no." He volunteered.

Result: Six weeks at Aerial Gunnery School, Las Vegas, Nevada, and the proud possessor of his gunner's wings. Plus a promotion to corporal. There had been nothing like that in the artillery.

One vivid memory he carried away from Las Vegas, something not so cheery, was a statement made by a drill sergeant: "The average life of an aerial gunner in combat is six minutes." Bill did a bit of worrying about that one but eventually was able to prove the sergeant was wrong.

After returning to McDill, Winchell tried out radio school tu couldn't quite keep the "dahs and dits" apart. But there was something else going on.

"They had enlisted bombardiers then. They put me in a gadget where I had to track a little bug on a screen. I got pretty good at it and soon I was flying regularly as bombardier and ended up with the famed Norden bomb sight as my baby"

Which led to another of those crazy incidents that could happen only in the Army.

"The Norden bombsight was super secret in those days and the bombardier was armed with a .45 caliber pistol, with orders to let no one touch it or look at it. One day, after a training flight to the Houston Air Base, when I knew we would be there overnight, I took the bombsight out of the plane and was carrying it to the base vault to have it locked up when a young lieutenant approached me. He asked me what I had and I said, 'It's the Norden bombsight.'

"He started toward me and said he wanted to see it. I told him to stay away but he kept coming. I drew my pistol and said, 'You take another step and you're dead.'

"He turned white as a sheet. He couldn't believe an enlisted man would do that to an officer. But he never came no closer."

But alsl that Norden bombsight training went for zilch.

A short time later, the 91st Bomb Group went up to Walla Walla for final training before going into combat, and shortly after that the top Air Forces brass decided that bombardiers had to be officers. Winchell was out of a job.

In the meantime they had given him one more training course, learning to service and maintain not only the Norden bombsight but automatic flight controls at the Honeywell Corporation in Minneapolis, Minnesota. Now, with his bombardier's job gone, it appeared he would be put to work as an automatic pilot mechanic.

"A sorry future for a guy determined to fly," said Bill.

It was about this time the brass were changing their minds about something else. Up to this time, the crew of the B-17 four-engine bomber had been considered nine men, with only one man assigned to man the guns on both sides of the waist gunner's position. It was now decided they needed two waist gunners, one on each side. So, if Winchell wanted to be a waist gunner, "You're hired." Back in business.

So the young soldier who had been the 53rd in the nation to be drafted, who tried to get into the horse cavalry, then the field artillery, washed out on radio training, who got cheated out of his bombardier's job, and who had to fudge on his eye tests to get on an airplane, finally made it as a waist gunnery.

Somewhere, sometime, we had to ask the inevitable question about what had been his closest call on the 25 missions he flew over enemy territory.

90

THE MEMPHIS BELLE

Winchell didn't have to search hard for the answer to that one. It had been his 18th mission, as the Memphis Belle, with 21 other B-17s of the 91st, together with formations from other groups, was dispatched to bomb the railway marshalling yards at Rouen, France. It was an important shipping hub for German forces occupying France.

This was a day when almost everything seemed to go wrong and the young airman named Clarence Winchell almost died.

First, the formation of B-17s was supposed to have a British Spitfire fighter escort to protect it from the German fighter planes but the Spitfires missed the rendezvous point and never showed up.

Then a portion of the attack force was ordered to turn around and go home. The 22 planes of the 91st Group never got the turn-around order. They flew on alone.

Then the diversion flight pattern, designed to fool the German fighter pilots, got messed up and instead of flying away from the Germans, they flew right into them.

In the middle of the fight, with German fighters buzzing around them like mad hornets, Sergeant Winchell in his tail position shouted over the intercom, "Fighters coming in at four o'clock. Get 'em. Get 'em."

Four o'clock was the gun position of Winchell's fellow waist gunner, Sergeant S. J. Spagnolo, a substitute gunner on the Belle's crew on this mission.

Winchell turned to look and he saw Spagnalo passed out on the floor. His oxygen mask had frozen and he had passed out for lack of oxygen.

"I had to shove Spagnolo out of the way and fire his gun. I managed to drive them off."

Then his own oxygen mask froze up and he, too, passed out.

Up front, at the controls, pilot Bob Morgan noticed he was getting no response from his waist gunners. He sent Sergeant Bob Hanson, his radio man, back there to investigate.

When Hanson put on his emergency "walk around" oxygen bottle and went to investigate, he found both waist gunners lying on the floor, unconscious. Then he had to get additional oxygen bottles and masks, and go back and try to revive the unconscius men.

"When I came to," Winchell said, "I told Hanson, 'Gee, that was the easiest raid we have been on.' I didn't remember a thing."

This "easy" raid was the one on which the Memphis Belle had a huge portion of the tail shot off and Sergeant Quinlan, in the

91

tail position was hit in the leg by a hunk of hot shrapnel. His guns were knocked out. The plane was saved only by the the fact that several 20 mm shells which slammed through the plane failed to explode as they were supposed to.

What would have happened if Hanson had not come back with his emergency oxygen masks and bottle? "We would have died," Bill said.

But that was not all. On the Memphis Belle's wing, a sister ship piloted by Lieutenant J. a. Coen was shot down, carrying with it Sergeant Jimmie Bechtel, a waist gunner who had been Winchell's roommate.

"Jimmy Bechtel was a comparatively new man to the outfit," said Winchell. "He came to us in January as a member of our first replacement crew. Roomed with me from the start and was, or is, a hell of a swell fellow." Winchell's hope at the time, that Bechtel had made it to the ground and was in a prisoner-of-war camp.

Small consolation came from the fact that, before his guns had been knocked out, Quinlan, from his tail position, had shot down one of the German fighters from a goup of six that had blasted Bechtel's plane.

"One more damn Hun won't fly again," Winchell wrote in his diary that night, "'Beck' partly avenged."

As with other members of the Belle's crew, memories of individual missions seem to blend together in one big blob, but then there are those moments of drama which can never be forgotten.

Like the day over Emden, Germany, on February 4, 1943, when "It was the first time I ever looked right down the barrels of German machine guns and they were firing at me. The bullets went right through our plane, just inches over my left shoulder.

"It was a Focke Wulf fighter. I don't know how he got right into the middle of our formation. He came in at nine o'clock high. his guns blazing. Then he ducked under Lieutenant cliburn's plane on our right wing. His bullets were ripping the side of our plane, coming in right on nine o'clock, my position. I don't know how he managed to miss me.

"I was lucky that day."

The whole crew was lucky all those bullets didn't hit vital parts or men.

It was incidents such as this that earned the Belle a reputation in the 91st Bomb Group as a lucky plane.

Another memory that Winchell was never able to eliminate from his mind has been the acres of flak and the anti-aircraft fire they had to fly through on almost every mission. The Belle was hit several times by pieces of shrapnel but again was lucky never to take a direct hit.

"One day I saw one plane in our formation take a direct hit in the bomb bay before it had dropped its bombs," said Winchell. "The plane simply was blown all to bits. It was a sickening sight. The boys never had a chance.

"I can't forget the flak bursting. When the fighters were coming in at us we at least felt we had a chance to fight back, but when they were throwing that flak at us you felt so helpless. All you could do was just sit there and take it.

"Several times on our first few missions I would ask myself, 'What am I doing here? I could be sitting safe in the bombsight vault with my automatic controls.' But the answer was always the same. I had asked for it and I would never back down. These other guys in the plane were my buddies.

"Even today, after all these years, I haven't been able to forget that flak. When I see a fireworks display now, it makes me nervous and I almost feel as if I am back there again, with all that deadly stuff being thrown at us again. I never watch a fireworks show if I can avoid it."

But then the whole combat thing did finally end for Bill Winchell on May 17, 1943, the last of his quota of 25 missions and the glorious feeling that he was going home.

When the Memphis Belle landed in Washington, D. C., their first stop, that Belle's crew got the most eye-bugging surprise of their lives, an invitation to lunch with the Air Forces, and the Army's real top brass, two four-star generals, General George C. Marshall and General Henry C. "Hap" Arnold.

As an extra bonus, the Belle crew was told that, while the war was not over and they must remain in the service, they could have, within reason, a choice of any future assignment.

"Sir, we would like to become officers," said Winchell and Bob Hanson

As a result, a set of unprecedented orders for two Air Force sergeants to attend officer candidate school at Miami Beach, Florida, "By order of Gen. Henry C. Arnold."

"I got a pair of bars and a wife out of that tour at Miami Beach," said Winchell. It was while at officer candidate school he met a bright-eyed girl named Laura Dickson. After graduating, with his new commission, he was sent to Yuma Air Base, Arizona, and she followed him.

"We were married in the base chapel with Lieutenant Bob Hanson as my best man," said Winchell.

Winchell has few fond memories of the Yuma assignment. They were, he said, supposed to be teaching aerial gunnery and several of the instructors, like Winchell, had been in combat.

"We were too outspoken for them. The people running the school didn't want to listen to anyone who had been in combat."

In any case, he was soon shipped to his next assignment at Aberdeen, Maryland, where his military career almost cracked up in a real disaster. For at the point the Army tried to reclassify him into the Army, rather than the Air Force. Winchell balked.

"I was proud of those wings," Winchell said. "I felt I had earned the right to wear them. I wasn't about to take them off."

There were several other men in the same boat, having seen combat as airmen, but now faced with the threat of reclassification.

At first they tried passive resistance, like turning in blank papers when ordered to take tests. The results of that were threats of court-martial. It was at the bottom of this stand-off when Lieutenant Winchell remembered that Colonel Stanley Wray, who had been commander of the 91st Bomb Group in England, was now in Washington, stationed at the Pentagon.

Wacky as it sounded, Winchell suddenly announced to his fellow sufferers: "I'm going to call the Pentagon and talk to Colonel Wray

"They thought I was crazy but I did it. The Pentagon said Colonel wray was not in. I asked for his home number. At first they refused but I insisted and they finally gave it to me."

With the added advice: "Lieutenant, I wouldn't call him at home if I were you."

Which didn't stop Winchell. "I finally got the colonel on the phone and told him, 'Colonel, I'm about to go over the hill," and then I told him the story.

"For God's said, don't do that," came the reply over the phone. "Give me 24 hours. I'll come down and straighten it out."

True to his word, Colonel Wray arrived at Aberdeen the next day with full military escort. An assembly was called in the base theater.

"After being introduced, Colonel Wray stood up and asked if Lieutenant Winchell was in the audience. I said, 'Yes, sir.' Then he read out an order,a Presidential directive, stating that no airman who had served in combat would be transferred to another branch of service against his wishes."

Winchell kept his silver wings.

After the assembly, Colonel Wray told Winchell his staff had turned the files upside down to find that "no transfer" order. It was a classic example of a top officer going the extra mile to help out a former combat man. Beyond that, Colonel Wray arranged to get Winchell transferred to a B-29 training command where he might have ended up as a crew member of a B-29 in the Pacific as Bob Morgan, Vince Evans and John Quinlan had done. But another of his old bugaboos showed up to haunt him.

"They found out about my bad eye," he said. "I had to take eye tests and this time they threw some eye charts at me that I had never seen before. I flunked. When they asked me how long I had had this condition, I told them I might have damaged it looking into the sun while in combat in Europe. They accepted that."

Bill was at an air base at Pueblo, Colorado, when he was finally mustered out in October of 1945. Before the war he had worked for a chemical company and now, attending school on ois GI Bill of Rights, he got a degree, went back to the Glidden Co. as a research assistant in soyabean chemistry. His daughter, Jacqueline, was born while he was in school.

He travelled extensively as a member of the Glidden sales staff and then , after retirement he dabbled in the travel agency and insurance fields.

Today, with his house in Barrington, Illinois, paid for, Bill and his wife Laura make their own comfortable schedule.

It is easy, in the beautiful hill and lake country 50 miles northwest of Chicago, to forget about that long-ago time in a war, riding through the danger-filled skies over Europe, freezing, squinting into the sun for lurking German fighters, manning his bucking and stuttering gun, facing the flashing gunfire of the enemy's weapons. The ominous black puffs of ack-ack shells. Unable to relax. Wondering if you would make it home.

Unless a nosy book writer shows up to ask questions. Or, perhaps, on a day when a gaudy fireworks display fills the screen of his TV set.

On such days Bill Winchell might indeed remember. A young airman, sitting on his bunk in England, reading the 91st Psalm and somehow deriving from that the comfort, and the courage, to face once more the dangers of the battle-torn skies.

Hanson

Don't Shoot That Tail Off

The military career of Robert "Bob" Hanson, the Memphis Belle radio operator, almost became derailed before it started, with the threat of a court-martial. He did get punished.

"I was only following instructions," says Hanson, laughing.

It all came about because a recruiting sergeant tipped him off about a neat little way to get more pay out of the Army.

This was in a day when a buck private in the Army got $21 a month. The recruiting sergeant tipped him off to a way he could up that to $30. Couldn't blame a guy for wanting a few more bucks.

It all sounds a bit nutty now.

It was in the period before the Japanese attack on Pearl Harbor catapulted America into the war. The war had already started in Europe and the Congress, smelling the possibility of America's involvement, had voted to draft young men into the military service.

"In May of 1941 I knew I would be going off to war so I decided I'd volunteer, enlist, so I could choose the branch of service I wanted," said Hanson in remembering the whole crazy incident now.

"But when I went to the recruiting sergeant and told him I wanted to enlist he said, 'You're crazy. First, let them draft you. Then turn around and re-enlist. That way, you'll get $30 a month.'"

Good advice, decided Hanson. A few months later he was indeed drafted, was sent to Camp Murray, outside Tacoma, Washington. Three days later he followed the sergeant's advice and re-enlisted, choosing the Air Force.

So he was discharged, drawing $2.10 as his pay for his three days of military service, got sent to Jefferson Barracks, Missouri, for basic training.

96

Time to start basic training. All that marching and close order drill stuff. Or was it?

On the first day, a drill sergeant lined them up to begin the whole ritual. He shouted, "Men with previous service, step out."

"I stepped out," said Hanson.

While the other buck privates were out there marching and sweating, Hanson was back in the barracks, loafing, eating, sleeping, having the good life.

The trouble started when, after basic training was over, the men went out on a parade and one of the sergeants shouted to Hanson, "Hey, Hanson, take charge of the squad."

Then the goof-up. After seeing how his new "leader" made it clear he hadn't the slightest idea of how to lead a squad of men, the sergeant blew his cool. And the investigation began.

The brass decided he had used a trick to avoid basic training and threatened him with a court-martial. But when Hanson told his story, they decided maybe a court-martial would be a bit too much.

However, punishment he would have to take. How about kitchen police? It meant the old potato peeling routine, six days a week, week after week. With basic training in between.

But then another twist of fate relieved him of that. On his second day of kitchen police, orders came through transferring him and his group to radio school at Scott Field, Illinois.

"So I never did get my basic training," he said.

Then at Scott Field he almost got into trouble again. This time because the routine was too easy and he became bored.

"I already knew how to type," he said. So when they put the trainees in a classroom with typewriters, taking Morse code messages, it was easy for him. More than easy.

"I could type 30 words a minute and they were sending code at a rate of five or six words a minute. It was so easy I could read a newspaper while taking the code, so I started taking newspapers to class with me and reading them.

"One day the instructor saw what I was doing, but instead of shouting across the room, he began sending me a message through the earphones: 'Hanson, stop reading the newspaper. Hanson, stop reading the newspaper.'

"The funny thing is, I didn't read his message. I was so absorbed in my newspaper. What got my attention was when all the typewriters in the room stopped and everybody was looking at me."

Another blow-up but he escaped with only a chewing-out.

97

THE MEMPHIS BELLE

When he finished radio training and got into the airplanes, it wasn't so easy. "They forgot to put typewriters in the planes and you had to write by hand."

Perhaps it is time to back up to Helena, Montana, where it all began for Robert J. Hanson on May 25, 1920. Three boys and a girl the Hansons had, and just as the youngsters began to grow up, the big economic depression hit the country.

Hanson's father, a construction worker, began chasing all over the country in pursuit of the few construction jobs.

"One year we moved so much we ended up going to seven different schools," he remembers.

"My mother said that was no way to raise a family, so they broke up. I was raised by an uncle, Ford McDaniel, at Garfield, Washingon, a single man who lived with my grandmother."

McDaniel operated a warehouse, storing peas, grain, etc. As soon as young Bob was able, he was put to work in the warehouse, trundling bags of grain, stacked four or five high, on a push dolly.

Along the way the young Hanson decided he wanted a 22 caliber rifle but on his salary at the warehouse he couldn't afford it.

"I went to the bank and borrowed $35 to buy the rifle. I had to pay it back at $5 a month."

Hunting was mostly for ground squirrels which infested the area around Garfield, posing a threat to farmers' crops. So, it was not only fun but an extra bit of income to shoot the pesky things.

"They gave a penny bounty for each ground squirrel tail."

Athletics? The six foot, solidly built youngster was a four-year letterman in football and baseball.

"We won the county championship several times, playing against schools four or five times as big as we were."

Fun or pranks?

"In a town of 500 there really wasn't a lot we could do except walk up and down main street, hollering. One time, as a Halloween prank, we took the wheels off a wagon and hoisted it up on top of the high school building, then put the wheels back on. They never did figure out how we got that thing up there."

Another item in the fun category was to flood the baseball field in the winter, let it freeze and use it for an ice skating rink.

"To keep warm, we set old tires on fire. When we went home we'd be almost black as coal from the sooty smoke."

Hanson said that he stayed with his uncle until he entered the Air Force, but made contact with his father and became friends again, leading to another of those crazy incidents.

THE MEMPHIS BELLE

After completing radio training at Scott Field, Hanson went to McDill Field and met the type plane he would be flying in at war, the B-17. He became a member of the fledgeling 91st Bomb Group and got his first taste of flying. When the group was transferred to Walla Walla, Washington, in June of 1942, he went with it.

What Hanson did not know was that the air base at Walla Walla was not complete, with concrete still being poured on the runways and that his father, the inveterate construction man, was pouring some of that concrete. That led to the wacko incident.

His father somehow got word of the arrival of the group from Florida and even found out which plane his son was on.

Thus, when that certain plane touched down, here came a truck roaring up. Right behind it several Jeeps loaded with MPs who quickly surrounded the pick-up, took its driver into custody and hustled him away.

"It was my Dad but I didn't know it then," said Hanson. "I didn't even get to see him - at least not that day. The war was on and everybody was security-conscious. Unauthorized civilians were not allowed to come barging up to a bomber that way but they never told Dad. He just wanted to see his son."

It was at Walla Walla that he became a regular member of the Memphis Belle's crew and as a radio operator he occupied a little "office" just behind the bomb bay. Here he also had a single machine gun with a limited aiming radius to give a bit of added protection from planes approaching from six o'clock high.

"I was always scared I'd shoot the tail off our own plane," he said. "because that gun was, more or less, aimed in that direction. The gun had a safety pin which stopped the firing when you swung it too close to the tail. I was always afraid that in battle I would get so excited I would swing the gun so hard it would break that pin and I'd fire into our own tail."

Hanson swears the Belle got a couple of bullet holes in her before she ever got into combat or even went overseas. The incident, he said, happened while the crew was at Bangor, Maine, the last staging point before taking off for England. It was here the crews were issued their new planes and were told to fly them for 100 hours, as a break-in and testing period for the new machines.

"One day we were flying over a river and we saw a guy down there in a boat, hauling logs," he said. "Morgan decided to give him a buzz, swooping down low. Lieutenant Evans, the bombardier, hollered at Morgan, 'Hey, can't you get it any lower?' So Morgan circled and this time he flew so low he almost took the guy's hat off. The guy was so scared he pulled a pistol and started shooting at us. When we got back to the base, we found a couple of bullet holes in the skin of the plane. We never did tell anybody what happened. When the ground crew asked about them we said the propellers probably picked up some rocks while taking off."

Morgan says he doesn't remember this incident but at least two other members of the crew said they did, although with slightly different details. One remembers it as a sail boat which almost got blown out of the water by the prop wash. Maybe they were two separate incidents. Bold young airmen did things like that.

No matter, the Belle and her crew finally took off for England and the war. But as in all wars, the men who fought it, including the bomber crews, spent a lot of time in between missions on that old Army game - waiting. It was during these waiting periods when, Hanson claims, he got to see more of England than any other crew member. Thanks to a very strange job of an Englishman Hanson got acquainted with.

It was a time when London was being bombed a lot. To protect their newsprint supply from the bombs, the London newspapers stored their newsprint in empty barns around the country.

"There were days on end when the weather would prevent us from flying and we'd go to Cambridge a lot," Hanson said. "It was only a few miles from Bassingbourn. I met a bartender who had a second job. On certain days he would drive around the country checking on the newsprint and he'd invite me to go along. I was always interested in history, so I liked to see the country."

Hanson readily agrees he was one crew member not credited with shooting down an enemy plane.

"Sometimes I think nobody should have been credited with shooting down planes," he said. "In a battle, when enemy planes were coming in at us, everybody in range would start shooting and sometimes a lot of guys would be shooting at the same plane. If it went down, who could say he shot it down? I shot at a lot of enemy planes, but I don't claim I knocked any of them down."

But things did get hairy up there in the sky.

There was the day he was sitting at his desk in his little radio operator's compartment and had just made an entry in his log. He sat up. *Zip* . A bullet slammed through the desk and his log book.

"I still have that log book with the bullet hole in it. If I had still been leaning over my desk, writing, that bullet probably would have gone right through my head."

But there did come a day when Sergeant Quinlan, back in the tail gunner's position, did get hit.

"I could hear him back there, screaming like a Comanche Indian. So Morgan heard it over the intercom and told me to go back and see what had happened to Quinlan.

"We were flying at 20,000 feet so I had to disconnect my oxygen mask and put on a portable 'walk around' oxygen bottle. I crawled back there and asked him what was wrong and he patted his butt and started screaming again. I got out my knife and started cutting his flying suit. I didn't see any blood. When I finally got down to bare skin we found it was a piece of shrapnel that had gone through his suit and stuck in his thigh. The reason he was screaming was because the shrapnel was still hot and burning him."

There also came a day when some of the control cables on the Belle were cut during a hot air battle, apparently by enemy gunfire, and the plane went into a sudden and sharp dive.

"I was certain we were going down," said Hanson. "and all I could think of was to get out of that plane and jump." [All crew members had parachutes.] "When I got out of my radio compartment and started towards the rear exit door, both waist gunners were flattened out on the floor by the force of gravity. They couldn't get up. The reason I was able to walk was because I had been on my feet when the plane started down - and I was determined to get out."

Before he could jump, Morgan managed to get the Belle under control and pull out of the dive.

Most of the time, after leaving the coast of France, the crews could relax for the rest of the way home but one day, said Hanson, they were almost home, getting ready to land, when a German fighter plane sneaked in on their tail and started shooting at them.

"I think it was one of their long-range Ju.88s," he said. "It scared hell out of us and taught us a lesson. You just couldn't relax until you were on the ground."

One of the first things the American fliers learned when they began their bombing missions was to fly tight formations.

"We had one little red-headed pilot flying one of our wing planes, named C. E. "Red" Cliburn. He was a damned good pilot but he took his close formation flying a bit too seriously. Sometimes we'd look out and he'd be there on our wing, with the tip of his wing almost poking into our waist gunner's windows.

"We finally had to tell him we didn't need his wing lights to read our maps, and to get his wing out of our window."

Had he ever had his moments of panic, when he felt as if he just couldn't face another mission?

"I was just like everybody else. I was scared. Yes, we had guys in our outfit who had problems with their nerves and had to be taken out of the planes. Some guys deliberately exposed themselves to venereal disease so they would be hospitalized. Some guys deliberately overate and drank, to get sick. Sometimes I'd lay there at night, unable to sleep. In the morning when they came to call us, I would already be awake. But there was never any question on my part, it never entered my mind not to go. I was over there to do a job and there was no way I wouldn't go on a mission.

"The worst thing would be the empty bunks. We slept together in our quarters, maybe ten or 15 guys together from several crews. When a guy didn't come back from a mission, they would roll up his mattress on his bed. It would make your stomach do a few turns. You'd ask yourself, 'When is my number coming up?'

"I had to keep telling myself there was no doubt in my mind that I was coming home. If I turned it the other way and said, 'Hey, tomorrow I'm going to get killed,' then a man would really go to pieces. You just had to look at the positive side."

Then Sergeant Hanson did come home to America in 1943 for the great publicity tour, flying from city to city, getting the big welcome. What were his memories of that?

"In some ways it was worse than combat," he said. "They overdid it. Each city tried to outdo the last one. Parties, dances, speeches, day and night. After we had been running all day, somebody would want us to visit the night shift at one of the war plants and we couldn't say no.

"Then we had our schedule to keep up. The next day we would have to fly to another city. We'd be so tired we could hardly stand up. We had to catch up with sleep while flying from one city to the next. Sometimes the pilot would even put the plane on atuomatic pilot and take a rest. I was glad when it was over."

The Air Force brass promised members of the Belle's crew that they could choose their next assignment. Hanson chose officer candidate school and made it, obtaining his second lieutenant's bars.

Since the war was still going on, there had to be another tour of duty. For Hanson it was as a communications officer in a radio-gunnery school at Yuma, Arizona.

"I stayed there until the war was over, but I didn't get along very well with the people running the school," he said. "I kept telling them that their training methods were wrong. They still had that old typewriter system. They didn't teach the men the things they really needed in combat."

Then the war was behind him and he could go back to being a civilian with his wife. Oh, yes, while all that war stuff had been going on, this guy Hanson had acquired a wife. When had all this happened, his first meeting?

It was at Walla Walla, just before he went overseas.

"Several of us guys had gone to a combination beer parlor and restaurant," Hanson recalled. "I remember seeing Irene and several other girls sitting in a booth and there wasn't room for anybody else. But they had the nickelodeon selector in their booth. So we guys would match coins to see who got the privilege of going over to their booth to put in a nickel. I won. That's how we met."

Did he ask her for a date on that first meeting?

"I don't remember. It's possible."

But one thing is for sure: They got acquainted and they got married and after the war, began with the family thing, ending up with three kids.

His job was with a food distributor.

"I did it exactly the way I did it in the Army, started out as a buck private and worked up to lieutenant. In the food business, I started out as a salesman and ended up as a district sales manager."

Today he lives with the lady he met in the nickelodeon booth so many years ago, and is in retirement at Mesa, Arizona. He and Irene now have a new obsession - square dancing.

"I believe this is the square dance capital of the United States," said Hanson. "You can come out here any time of the day or night, and somewhere a square dance will be going on. If you don't like the caller you just go to the next hall and give it a try."

It is only in his memories, the forever kind, that there is the drone of B-17 motors, the oxygen masks, the angry stuttering of those big 50 caliber machine guns, the skies so full of flack you could walk on it, the memory of a young sergeant, lying in his bunk at night, wide awake, thinking, "Are we going today?"

They went, that Memphis Belle crew, and they came home.

Loch

Up There I Could See Them Coming

A bitter wind swept across the Green Bay of Lake Michigan. Ducks were wheeling, trying to find a sheltered cove to land.

A youngster, armed with a battered old shotgun, was trying to maneuver into position for a shot, fighting by paddle to keep control of a 13-foot wooden skiff as the wind whipped at its hull.

Somewhat dangerous, perhaps, for a lone boy not even equipped with a life preserver.

"I tried to stay in shallow water as much as possible in case the skiff got swamped," he would say.

The shotgun, little more than a hunk of junk, the receiver held to the barrel by an old spike. A gap between breech and receiver.

"I bought that old gun for a dollar and two Sunday papers," remembered Harold Loch. "When I fired it, I had to get out my knife and pry out the empty cartridge."

The ammunition? Bought in the summertime at 55 cents a box because it was in the summer when the stores cut their prices.

Why all this risky battle for a few ducks? One reason being that there was a big family to feed, 12 kids plus Mom and Dad. It was the time of the great economic depression. A big, hungry family could eat a lot of ducks. If it was also, to the boy, a bit of adventure calling to the spirit, well - that would be an extra dividend.

The boy? Harold Loch who would one day become flight engineer and top turret gunner on a plane called the Memphis Belle as she fought her way through skies filled with deadly anti-aircraft shells and swarms of enemy fighter planes.

Things could even get worse than that, Loch remembers. For example, a storm hit Green Bay on November 11, 1940, with a bitterly cold wind sweeping across that bay at 55 miles an hour for two days without stopping.

"That wind blew so hard it blew all the water out of the shallow part of the bay and you could walk across it for more than a mile to the light house. They said 32 duck hunters lost their lives in that storm."

Harold was luckier that day. He was out in his dad's old Ford truck, scouting for a place where the ducks were landing. It was so cold - nearly zero - that he had to put a piece of cardboard across the radiator to keep it from freezing, even as he drove. No money for anti-freeze.

"I got out there but, holy cats, the wind was so strong the ducks must have flown past, looking for a quiet cove. The wind chill was unbelievable. I was worried about the truck freezing up and then I would have been stranded. I didn't get any ducks that day."

So young Harold's luck that day, if you could call it that, was in NOT finding where the ducks were landing. His name would not be added to the list of the lost hunters.

But, perhaps, it was experiences such as this that hardened a boy, physically and mentally, giving him the stuff it took to fly 25 danger-filled war missions in a B-17.

For Harold Loch, it was a journey that began in the village of Denmark, Wisconsin, where his father was a tavern keeper until prohibition laws dried up the country during the 1920s. The family moved to Green Bay where the father found a job with a marine construction company. The tough years of the depression were coming.

Harold, born in 1919, one of 12 children, would remember those hard times.

"Sometimes in the summertime I worked for truckers loading and unloading trucks for 10 cents an hour. I sold Sunday papers on the weekends."

Remember? It had been two five cent Sunday papers which, together with that dollar, paid for an old shotgun.

It was around 1935 when things got a bit better for the big Loch family, says Harold. They were paying $20 a month for the house they were living in when Harold stumbled across an opportunity. It was a big house on the southside of town, with 22 acres of land, a small farm that was for rent for $25 a month.

Harold persuaded his father that they could all pitch in and make the extra $5 rent money by raising vegetables and fruit, chickens and things, on the land. There would, for example, be plenty of apples because a third of the land was apple orchard. There was room for milk cows.

His father agreed and the family moved in. They soon began saving money for a tractor. The family began to eat better.

Harold, by this time, had managed to retire that old hunk of junk shotgun and graduated to a $10 double barrel.

"The stock had too much drop on it and it kept shooting low," said Harold. "I finally got an old Model 97 Winchester."

Perhaps all this shooting with a shotgun, learning to lead a duck in a high wind over Green Bay, was part of the reason why, years later, when an Air Force recruit named Harold Loch would face rounds of skeet shooting as part of his gunnery training, he always managed to come out with the top score. And part of the reason why German fighter pilots learned that it was dangerous to expose themselves to .50 caliber machine gun bullets from a certain top turret.

Later, as Loch became a husky teenager, there were better paying jobs, such as the job unloading pulp boats in the harbor at 64 cents an hour. Up to 75 cents an hour on cement and sugar boats. One had to work when the boats came in, around the clock.

"One time I worked 50 hours straight, without sleeping, and I made $50 that week," said Loch. "That was a lot of money. I averaged $30 a week. I always gave Mom and Dad $20 of that."

He was five feet, eight inches tall and weighed 170 pounds, mostly muscle. A guy had to be tough to swing it on the cement boats.

Again, that fateful December, 1941, when the war started for America and the chunky little stevadore became an Air Force recruit. Biloxi, Mississippi, for basic training and then that familiar McDill Field in Florida, where he would meet most of his future crew mates.

In between, a stint at radio training in Kansas City and a course of mechanics for the job of flight engineer.

Loch almost became a war casualty before he would get to the combat zone, he remembers.

"I was up on the wing," he said, "checking the gas tanks one day when John Quinlan crawled into the top turret, just fooling around. It just happened that there was a single live ammunition round left in one of my guns. Quinlan pulled the trigger and the bullet went whizzing right past my head. Just missed me and scared the hell out of me."

Quinlan got chewed out good for that one.

That flight to England, with a stopover in Scotland for refueling.

"There was a cute little Scotch girl helping out with gassing up the plane," he said. "She asked what my name was and when I told her, she was tickled pink to meet an American airman with a Scotch name. It made her day."

Another memory, of the little Scotch children playing around the airfield. They looked a bit hungry and Loch remembered a box of sandwiches on board that the Bell crew had not finished eating.

"I thought the stuff would get stale so I offered the sandwiches to the little kids. They got so excited and began hollering, 'White bread! White bread!' It seemed they had never seen white bread."

Loch would almost regret giving those sandwiches away when they landed in England and were put on British rations, mostly vegetables, Brussels sprouts, cabbage. Even for breakfast.

"And all those cabbage lice. I never saw so many cabbage lice in my life. It was terrible."

It was then, forced by a bit of hunger of their own, that Loch and a couple of his buddies sneaked into the store room and snitched a case of C Rations being kept for emergencies.

"We hid that box up over the door and when nobody was around, we would sneak it down and eat some of it," he remembers. "There was a big investigation. They even called in three or four officers to investigate and we were all questioned but they never did get anything on us."

Then there was the cold, with never enough coal to heat their quarters.

You got the "soldier's curse," if you slept in the British blankets they were supplied with. Quinlan reported being eaten up by the scabies itch he acquired from sleeping in those RAF blankets.

"They were like horse blankets," said Loch. "I decided to sleep in my sheep-lined flight suit, without those blankets. That's what I did. Every night. At least, I never got the scabies itch."

Memories of the pay days, which would set off the flurries of poker games, with most of the pay ending up in the pockets of a few hot shot gamblers.

"I stayed out of those games," said Loch. "I sent most of my money home to help Mom and Dad pay for the tractor."

Then came the bombing missions which were, after all, the reason Loch and his buddies had come this far.

As the day of the first mission approached, the coming of the apprehension, age-old companion of soldiers on the eve of battle.

"The only thing I was worried about was that I might chicken out on that first raid," said Loch. "That scared hell out of me. I was afraid I might freeze up or something. I wasn't afraid for myself but afraid I might goof up and do something that would get us into trouble."

As luck would have it, the first combat mission of the Memphis Belle, to Brest, France, was an easy one. They barely saw a few German fighters, far in the distance. No combat. Little flak. Home safe. Gee, was it going to be that easy?

It wasn't. For the second mission, on November 9, the target was the submarine pens at St. Nazaire. This was the time when somebody in the command structure dreamed up the idea of coming in low to fool the Germans. The command planners forgot that at 9,000 feet, the altitude at which they would be dropping their bombs, German flak was deadly.

"The plane was bouncing around like crazy from the concussion of all those flak shell explosions. I don't know how we got through all that without getting shot down. Now we knew what war was all about."

The education was to continue. There was that big date, January 3, 1943, the day the 91st Bomb Group went back for a third try at the submarine pens at St. Nazaire, the day on which, as several members of the crew remembered, "All hell broke loose." The skies black with flak bursts and then the German fighters.

It was also the day Loch got his first confirmed kill.

"Usually the fighters had been staying away when they had a cloud of flak up there but they must have gotten desperate," said Loch. "I shot at a lot of planes that day. That one was coming right at me, a Focke Wulf 190, the one with the radial engine. I was shooting steady and he went down. I shot up so much ammunition that day I only had a few rounds left when we got back and we started out with 1,000 rounds for each gun."

A man could end up shooting at dozens of planes and maybe get credit for shooting down only one. Or none. A gunner had to have confirmation from other witnesses before getting credit for a kill.

One of the most unnerving experiences Loch can remember was when German fighters came in so close you could see the face of the pilot.

108

One day they were flying through patches of clouds and then, suddenly, there was an enemy pilot popping out of the clouds and staring Loch in the face from no more than 50 yards.

"I could see his face and he was looking right at me," he said. He was almost too startled to shoot but "Guns started going off all around me. I don't know if he was shot down or not."

Another of those days when, on February 4, in a raid over Emden, Germany, the gutsy pilot of a Focke Wulf came blasting right through the formation of B-17s, over The Bad Penny that was flying on the Belle's wing and under the Belle itself. Firing his guns wildly. Although the Belle took a few hits, none were serious.

There were times when, through somebody's crazy errors, American gunners shot at friendly planes with tragic results.

"When friendly planes were in the area, like when they were flying escort, the pilots had strict orders never to come at us head-on," said Loch.

"If a plane came at us, front on, pointing its nose at us, we had permission to shoot .

"One day we were returning from a raid and half a dozen Spitfires were out there, over the channel, buzzing around. Several of them pointed their noses at us and came towards us. From a front-on position, I defy anyone to tell the difference between a German Me.109 and a British Spitfire. We shot a couple of them down. When we got back to the base we expected someone to raise a lot of hell but didn't even get chewed out because it was clear those British pilots had violated the rule never to point their nose at us.

"Later, some pilots from that Spitfire base even came to visit us and they agreed we had every right to fire when a fighter plane came at us, front on. They said, 'Shoot the hell out of them if they do that. They should know better.'"

Then, for Loch too, the 25 missions came to an end. One of the sharpest memories from it all, he said, was the day when the King and Queen of England made their famed visit to Bassingbourn to say goodbye to the crew of the Memphis Belle.

As fate would have it, as the King and Queen went down the line, shaking hands, it was just at the instant when the Queen was shaking hands with Loch that the photographers decided to take a picture. There was that pause, as he stood there, holding the Queen's hand.

"I think I was more scared than I was on a bombing raid," said Loch.

When it was over, Loch, like a lot of other fliers who made it, felt like a very lucky guy. He was even willing to credit some of the slave laborers working in the German war plants, for saving their lives.

Those ack-ack shells which are supposed to explode when they hit a solid object, such as a B-17 up there in the sky. When they do, he remembers, the results are horrible. But, he said, on at least two occasions the Memphis Belle was hit by ack-ack cannon shells which failed to explode.

"One of them lodged in a gas tank," said Loch. "Think what would have happened if it had exploded. Another time, one of those shells hit a solid metal strut in the rear of the plane, near Quinlan's tail gun position, sheared its way more than half way through the strut but failed to explode. If it had gone off, it probably would have killed Quinlan and blown the whole tail end off.

"When I think about those slave laborers working in the German plants, I like to think they were sabotaging some of those shells and that was the reason we lived to come home. Only by the grace of God are we here."

Since the war was still raging after the Belle's crew completed that bond tour, it meant Loch had to take another military assignment.

Perhaps one of the most important pieces of business Loch had to take care of, before the war ended, was to get married. It was in September of 1943, while on a leave home, visiting Mom and Dad and the family, that he met the future Mrs. Harold Loch.

"I borrowed some money from Dad and bought a car," he said.

After the marriage he signed up to train with an air-sea rescue unit to be sent to the Pacific where many American fliers were being shot down over water. The unit flew B-17s which were so familiar to Loch.

"I wanted to see a bit more of the world," he said.

But then another kind of fate intervened, nothing less than a hernia which landed him in the hospital for surgery. By the time he was ready for service again, his air-sea rescue unit was gone. So he took an assignment with a crew that was test flying B-17s that had been damaged and rebuilt, flying from a base in South Dakota.

"One day when we took a plane up for a test, one of the ground crew had failed to connect an actuating arm for the flaps. We took off and and when the pilot turned the controls to go right, the plane turned left. That pilot fought that thing for a while, then he

110

came down over the runway, near stalling speed and then slammed it onto the ground, landing without flaps. If that pilot had not known what to do we would have crashed."

After the war? For several years after the war, together with his father, Loch built houses, a contractor.

"Then I got into local politics. For 28 years I was registrar in the hall of records. I sort of retired but I still build a few houses. I'd be fine if I could just keep my arthritis from acting up. I took my real estate broker's exam and, together with my brother, we are dealing around a bit in real estate."

As we talked, writer and war veteran, in Loch's comfortable house on the outskirts of Green Bay, squirrels were clowning on the back porch, only a few feet away, made bold and tame by the feeding from the Loch family. Behind, the peaceful wooded lot. A good place to live.

Also behind him, in time, that long journey from boyhood, the lad in the skiff on a windy day, in the bay, searching the sky for ducks, fighting the current to make it home. If he was lucky, a few ducks to bring to the family table.

The man of war, gritting his teeth and firing the bucking twin .50's at German fighters boring in for the kill.

Builder of houses, solidly built to withstand the cold winds that could, on occasion, blow the waters out of the bay. An official, keeping trust with the citizens of his town.

But now the time to relax and remember, things as trivial as a battered old shotgun he bought as a boy, for one dollar and two Sunday papers.

"I still had that old shotgun when I went off to war," he said. "When I came back I looked for it but I never could find it. I never found out what happened to it.

"I wish I still had it."

Nastal

He Went Back For More

If Casimer "Cass" Nastal had ever stopped to consider it, he might have decided there were too many ifs in his military career.

If he had not been so anxious to keep up with his older brother Ted, he probably never would have joined the Air Force.

If Ted had not been such short stuff, he would never have been picked for a tail gunner. And if Ted hadn't been picked, then Cass would never have volunteered for the same job.

If a would-be partner had not been killed, Cass might have ended up with a career as a bootlegger in the hills of Virginia.

If centrifugal force had not pinned him down, on that hectic day over Lorient, France, he would have bailed out of his plane and ended his war career as a prisoner of war.

If he had not become fed up with saluting young lieutenants, he would never have volunteered for his second tour of duty in England, becoming the Memphis Belle crewman with the most battle missions.

With all those ifs bouncing around, it had to be somewhat of a hectic career he lived through in the Air Force.

In fact, life had never been a bed of roses after his mother died when he was still a baby. Since his dad had a drinking problem and was not able to take care of four kids, the youngters were sent to St. Vincent de Paul Orphanage, which placed them in foster homes.

"During the time I was growing up, I must have lived in six different foster homes with six different families," Nastal said. Most of the time it was where extra help was always needed. Which meant he and his brothers became young farmhands to pay for their keep. Plus going to school. All this taking place in small towns within 50 or 60 miles of Detroit, where he was born. Howell, Fenton, Clinton.

But life was normal enough that he got a chance to play football in high school at Clinton, Michigan.

"We won a couple of conference championships and when the conference picked an all-star team, I was lucky enough to be picked," he remembers.

As his high school career came to an end, he was staying with a foster mother named Alice Englemeyer who ran a small farm and sold household appliances on the side, placing coin-operated washing machines in apartment buildings.

It was about this time that young Cass discovered he had a talent for fixing things and before it was over, he was making all the repairs on the washing machines.

It was a talent that would serve him well later when the appliances he was servicing were big 50 caliber machine guns in the B-17 bombers.

"I could take those things apart and put them together, blindfolded," he said proudly.

Then it happened - the war which began for America as Japan bombed Pearl Harbor on December 7, 1941.

"I was only 17 but Ted was older than I and knew he was going to be drafted. He decided that if he volunteered, he could get the service he wanted, so he asked for the Air Force.

"I decided that if Ted went, I wanted to go, too. I was too young to enlist on my own so my sister had to sign the papers to get me in. The war started on December 7 and by Christmas Eve we were on our way."

First stop, McDill Field, the famed staging point for the 91st Bomb Group where Cass was assigned to drive a jeep for one of the sergeants and brother Ted was assigned to office work. Then that "short stuff" thing got Ted into trouble.

"One day we were all in the chow line for dinner when a couple of officers came and started picking the short guys in the chow line. They said they needed some short guys to be trained as tail gunners in the B-17s and since Ted was real short he got picked. They sent him off to gunnery school in Nevada.

"After he left, I decided I still wanted to be with Ted, so I volunteered for gunnery training, too. Boy, when I got to Nevada, did he chew me out. 'What the hell did you do that for? You'll be going up there and getting shot at. Don't you have any brains?' He really gave me hell."

In the end, the brothers didn't get to stay together, anyway.

113

"When Ted finished training, they sent him straight into a bomb group and I got sent back to McDill Field," said Nastal.

The biggest thing Nastal remembers about gunnery school was the way he shook with fright when he stood up in the rear cockpit of an AT6 trainer plane to fire a 30 caliber machine gun at a sleeve target being towed by another plane.

"When you stood up in the seat," he said, "all you had to keep you from flying out of the plane was a strap around your waist, hitched to a harness. That first trip scared hell out of me and I couldn't hit a thing. I doubt if I put two bullets in the target."

Later, he said, he got used to it and "I got pretty good at it."

As a qualified gunner he was shipped back to McDill, then to Walla Walla with the 91st. The usual stop at Boise, Idaho, finally Bangor, Maine, the last stop before the flight to the war fronts in England. Bassingbourn, home of the 91st Bomb Group.

"When I got to England, I found out that my brother was already there, on another base," he said. "One day, on a training flight, his pilot flew him down to Bassingbourn so we could have a visit." It was the last time he would see his brother for a long time.

A short time later, Ted's squadron was sent to North Africa to fly bombing missions in the Mediterranean Theater. For a time, there were reports that the 91st would be going to North Africa, too, bringing the brothers together again, but this time the top brass changed their minds and the 91st stayed, making its share of history over France, Germany, Holland and Belgium.

It really isn't part of Nastal's story but Cass likes to feel that it is, an incident of sheer human drama which involved a B-17 named the Thunderbird while on a mission to bomb German-held Tripoli in North Africa. Cass claims a kinship to the story because, "My brother was the tail gunner on that plane."

Nastal pulls out the faded and yellowed clippings of news stories about the incident, written by the late Ernie Pyle, perhaps America's most famous war correspondent of World War II.

The Thunderbird was badly hit just as it dropped its bombs, knocking out two engines, both on the same side, making it almost impossible to keep the crippled plane in the air.

Then, as the pilot and crew struggled to keep the plane going, losing altitude, it was jumped again by German fighter planes which riddled the plane with hundreds of machine gun bullets. Somehow it still hung in the air.

It was long after the other planes on the mission had landed back at their base, and the Thunderbird was still missing. Most men on the base simply assumed that the ten men aboard were dead. And then the miracle. From the control tower, a tiny speck was sighted on the horizon, and the crippled plane could be seen, just a few feet off the ground now, one wing hanging.

With its brakes out, the plane barely reached the runway, slammed down onto it and spun crazily. The ten "dead men" were home. Their plane a shambles and less than 20 gallons of fuel left.

The crew of the shattered plane had shot down six enemy fighters during the hectic ride.

The pilot, drinking a toast that night, had said, simply, "Here's to one damned good airplane."

Cass would be having his own moments of drama. As on that day, January 23 of 1943, only two days after his brother's ordeal, when Cass himself was on a mission to bomb a German airfield at Lorient, France. He was on another plane than the Memphis Belle, that day. It was on the way home when they were jumped by a swarm of German fighters, who began riddling their plane with 20 mm cannon shells.

Fragments of one shell hit the pilot, Lieutenant P. S. Fischer, in the eyes and face, blinding him. The sudden shock and blinding caused Fischer to lose control, sending the big plane into a steep dive.

Nastal, in the tail gunner's cubicle, could feel shells slamming into the plane and when the dive came, he said, "I thought we were goners. All I could think of was that I wanted to get out of that plane.".

He fought to get his parachute buckled and over to the escape hatch. But that was when fate took over, for the violent dive had created such centrifugal force he was unable to move. He was glued to his spot.

Then, suddenly, the miracle. The plane was coming out of that mad dive. The co-pilot had grabbed the controls and was fighting to bring the giant machine under control. But their troubles were far from over, for the German fighters, who always concentrated on a crippled plane, were still slamming bullets and shells into the crippled B-17.

One of the 20 mm cannon shells blasted into the tail, barely missing Nastal but hitting the ammunition box right behind him, which contained his spare ammunition for his machine guns.

"I heard the ammunition exploding. I felt something trickle down my face," he said. "I was sure I was hit and that was blood on my face. When I got my glove off and reached up to feel it, I saw it was gunpowder trickling down my face.'"

Some shells in the ammunition box were blown apart without exploding, spewing unburned gunpowder over his head.

"I was lucky the whole box didn't explode," he said.

The rest of the crew was not so lucky. Aside from the pilot, hit in the face, the navigator was wounded. The engineer had a leg blown off. One of the waist gunners was wounded. One member of the crew was shot in the head and killed. Six of the ten men on board were hit, one was dead.

With all these wounded men aboard, with two engines shot out and the plane smoking, the co-pilot decided not to try to make it back to the home base at Bassingbourn but to land at the closest air strip he could find, landing at the Royal Air Force base at Little Horwood where the wounded were rushed to the hospital. Nastal did not get back to Bassingbourn until two days later.

"After that, they broke up our crew and I was assigned to fly replacement on one crew after another," he said. He finally ended up with the crew of the Memphis Belle.

That didn't end the moments of drama. There was the day when he was hit in the butt by a shrapnel splinter.

"It didn't penetrate very deep. I pulled it out myself and never reported the wound."

On another mission, a German anti-aircraft shell struck the heavy steel strut that held the tail wheel on, just a short distance from his tail gunner's seat.

"The shell cut more than half way through that steel bar but never exploded," said Nastal. Another bit of luck.

While all of this was going on, Nastal was credited with knocking down two enemy fighter planes, Focke Wulf 190s, one on a raid over St. Nazaire on January 3, and another on March 6 on a mission over Lorient.

Then there was that bootlegger business. It was a room mate of his at Bassingbourn, Sergeant Glen Justice, who flew as a crew member on another plane, who cooked that one up.

"He was my best friend," said Nastal. "He kept telling me that when the war was over, we would go back to Virginia and go into the bootleg business. He said he knew all about it and we could make a fortune in a hurry."

That little post-war plan got sidetracked very suddenly, one day, when Sergeant Justice, while on a mission, got hit in the head with a 20 mm shell and was killed instantly.

"That sort of thing made it tough," said Nastal. "When you'd lose a buddy. All at once there was that empty bunk and your friend wasn't coming back."

To compensate for such tragic moments, said Nastal, he and the rest of the men lived things up as fast as they could.

"We'd go to Cambridge, about five or six miles away, go to the pubs, drink a lot of beer and chase girls," he said. "I had pretty good luck with the girls. They liked the Americans because their men were gone to war and we had more money to spend and we spent it.

"There was a lot of gambling going on. We got paid once a month and right after pay day there would be poker games going on, day and night. In a couple of days a few of the guys would end up with all the money and then it stopped."

How was morale among the airmen?

"Generally it was pretty good but there were always a few who couldn't take it. We had several suicides on the field, guys who just shot themselves when they started getting shellshocked."

Like other members of the air crews, Nastal knew that every time his crew took off he would be going along because no man ever wanted to feel that a crew, or a plane, had failed to make it home because he, personally, had failed to do his part.

"On every mission I was scared and would wonder if this would be the time we wouldn't make it back," he said. "I think there was something wrong with a guy who wasn't scared. But once you got up there and got into action, it took your mind off those things."

Unlike other members of the crew who somehow convinced themselves they would be coming home, no matter how rough the odds, Nastal confessed that he had, more or less, resigned himself to the thought that he probably wouldn't make it. Then found it a pleasant surprise when he got home from his 25th mission and found that he had beat the odds after all.

Then, with the rest of the Memphis Belle's crew, he was heading home. That wild publicity and war bond tour, flying from city to city. But even when that tour came to an end, the war far from over, he was given another assignment, teaching gunnery at a gunnery base. It was here that he made the decision to volunteer for another tour of duty on a B-17.

"I guess it was because of the discipline thing," he said. "Over in England, discipline had never been tight. If we did not salute an officer, nobody made a big thing out of it. But here, back

117

at the gunnery base in the United States, somebody was jumping on you every day for failing to salute some Tom, Dick or Harry. I just couldn't take that so I volunteered to go back into combat."

Since he was young and wanted to see the world, he had hoped to be sent to another part of the world but, instead, here he was, heading back for England and another B-17 base, this one at Ipswich.

This time he flew as a ball turret gunner with the 709th Squadron of the 447th Bomb Group on a plane called Miss Minookie. Because conditions and equipment had changed, the tour of duty was stretched from 25 missions to 35. That was why, after Nastal completed his second tour, he had flown 60 missions.

"The second tour was not nearly as tough as the first," he said. "There wasn't nearly as many German fighters around and we had our own fighter escorts on most missions to protect us. Most of our losses were due to anti-aircraft fire from the ground."

The Allied invasion of France came on June 6, 1944.

"By this time, our planes were equipped with radar so they could bomb even on days when the weather was bad, which meant we got in more missions in less time. On D-Day we even flew two missions on one day, bombing ahead of the invasion forces to blast the German positions in France in front of our people."

For all these reasons, that second tour of duty sort of melts together in one memory blob with few memories of incidents or individual missions. He did remember that flying waist gunner was a lot easier now, since the planes now had Plexiglass closures on the side, with the guns shooting through them.

"I don't even remember some of the guys I flew with. I just know it is there on my military record that I completed missions."

Living was much better on that second tour, he remembers, in contrast to the early days on his first tour when they were on British rations and sometimes had to eat beans and Brussels sprouts for breakfast.

"On that second tour, things got to where, if we didn't want to get in the chow lines, we'd just go to the mess kitchen, get a bunch of hamburgers and we'd have a barbecue."

The air war wound down. Nastal came home, looking for a way to make a living. The opportunity to get rich bootlegging in Virginia was gone.

Since he had worked for a short time before the war, repairing washing machines, he now ended up with a washing machine company, demonstrating washers in a sales booth in the Commonwealth Edison Building in Chicago. Somehow, as fate would have it, there was a pretty girl demonstrating vacuum cleaners in another booth just across the aisle.

"There was a place where we would meet for coffee and that's how we met," he said. Love and marriage.

After that, when the washing machine company closed, it was in a grocery store where he worked his way up to manager, later managed a number of stores in the Chicago area. Leaving that, he bought a cookie franchise, first in Chicago and then in Rockford.

It was in 1976 when he had a heart attack. He sold out the franchises. Then a job in a Rockford plant making boxes where, in 1982, he had another heart attack and decided it was time to retire.

He and his wife moved to Apache Junction, Arizona, in 1986 and bought a retirement home. Perhaps one of the deciding factors in choosing Apache Junction was that by this time his two sons, with their grandchildren, had moved to the same area.

"This way," says Nastal,"we get to see their families and the grandchildren."

"It keeps us busy," echoes his wife Doris, who long ago demonstrated vacuum cleaners in Chicago.

It is only a coincidence that another member of the Memphis Belle crew, radio operator Bob Hanson, also lives in retirement in Mesa, Arizona, only 15 miles away. Nastal and Hanson get together sometimes for spaghetti dinner and to exchange memories of the days when the Memphis Belle flew through the flak and fighter-filled skies over enemy territory.

Scott

Curled up in the Belly

Sometimes, perhaps, the stuff of which heroes are made can begin with things like wearing a pair of patched pants to your high school graduation ceremonies.

And wondering what to say to your Mom who is sitting there crying about it. The kind of tears a woman sheds at the help-lessness of being so poor she can't even provide her son with a decent pair of pants for graduation.

Cecil Harmon Scott solved that problem with a trace of ironic humor. "Don't worry, Mom," he said, "I'll have on a cap and gown. Nobody will see the patch."

He had been through a lot of such trying times before finishing high school at Hollidaysburg, Pennsylvania, the kind of soul-tempering things that made a kid tough enough to survive 25 bombing missions as belly turret gunner on a plane called the Memphis Belle.

If Cecil Scott needed a baptism of fire to make a man out of him before finishing high school, that came in one tragic, shattering moment when he and a high school buddy were walking home from school one day, taking a shortcut through some farmer's fields. Those fields were surrounded by barbed wire fences and they would be crawling through those fences.

As they walked, a thunderstorm blew up. The storm, in itself, would not have been so terrifying to a country boy to whom thunderstorms were a part of life. Except that things were going to be different on this day.

They had just come to a point where they would have to climb through another fence. Cecil made it safely and was waiting for his friend to make it when a terrible thing happened. It was a bolt of lightning, sending a massive jolt of electricity through the steel wire on the fence. In a moment, Cecil's friend was suddenly hanging there in the fence, lifeless.

When Cecil saw his buddy hanging there, lifeless on the wire, he could have been forgiven for surrendering to panic and running screaming for home. But wait, perhaps the buddy was not dead. Perhaps he had been warned that if a person were electrocuted you must not touch the jolted person with your bare hands, for fear you might also get a jolt. In any case, Cecil took off his jacket, looped it around his helpless friend and pulled him loose from the fence.

Only then, when he was unable to get any response from the lifeless buddy, did he finally run for help. The police. Then stayed to go with the officers to recover the body.

Meanwhile, at home his parents were worried. What had happened to Cecil? What had he done to keep him away from home?

Only the best he could. It had been fate that lightning struck his friend, not him. The drama of growing up. Hollidaysburg High School, class of 1934.

Part of the perpetual tragedy of those times was what happened to Cecil's dad, Ross Scott. He was a timber and logging operator who got caught in the economic crunch of those terrible depression years that hit the country in the early 1930s.

When he was faced with the choice of using his last few dollars to pay his workers or his creditors, he had simply opted in favor of the workers. Which meant he was out of business. From now on, Ross Scott and his wife Tena would have a tough time keeping food on the table for themselves and seven children. Not even to speak of new trousers for high school graduation.

Which was one of the reasons why Cecil, with his brothers and sisters, would spend the next few years at such chores as picking berries in the woods for food. Trapping animals, including skunks, for their furs. A skunk pelt would bring a few dimes. Making their own maple syrup.

"Mixing maple syrup with clean snow is really declicious," remembers Cecil's sister Mary (now Mrs. Albert Collis of Sebring, Florida) of those times. "We called it 'poor folk's ice cream.'"

Hoeing corn in the summer time. Using wet gunny sacks to fight brush fires. Walking, always walking, to school. They would accept a ride if someone came by, but mostly it was walking.

No electricity in the house. Light came from oil lamps. Mom cooking on a huge kitchen stove heated by firewood. The only water in the house had to be pumped by hand. One of their

121

luxuries, the bear rug in front of the stove the kids could sit on, of a cold morning, to get dressed for school.

If the sisters had dolls to play with, they were the home made kind, stuffed with sawdust. The kind that could spill sawdust when a naughty brother got teasy and played rough with sister's doll.

Their first radio, the headset kind, with Dad using one half of the headset while Cecil and his brother Jack used the other phone by putting their heads together.

Fun? Well, there were times when a guy could hitchhike over to Duncansville and look for a loose board in the wooden wall surrounding the baseball field. Or head for the swimming hole. It was Mom Scott who only learned later that the old swimming hole was an old stone quarry that had become flooded when workers accidentaly struck a gusher spring. Buried under the water was the steam shovel that had struck the water gusher.

"If I had known what kind of swimming hole that was, I'd have been scared to death," she said later when she found out.

There was snow on the ground when it came time to be baptized in the Church of the Brethren, and the kids being baptized, including Cecil, had to walk a quarter of a mile barefoot in the snow to reach the icy waters of the river, for the dunking. Barefoot in the snow because, well, it would have been improper to be baptized with your shoes on.

There had been other little dramas in the process of growing up - like the time Cecil and his brother Jack had been playing in the hay loft over the barn and Jack, after a misstep, plunged down to the barn below, striking a manger, breaking his arm. At the moment it was a bit of tragedy, the kind they don't like to tell Mom about. Hadn't they been warned about playing in the loft?

It could be only the logic of children's minds that came up with a solution, of sorts.

There was pain but the brothers decided not to tell their parents about it. Jack would hide in a wash room until the hurt healed. Cecil would bring him food.

They should have known that one wouldn't work. But Cecil tried, sneaking a plate of food out to his injured brother. Except, as they quickly learned, a broken arm doesn't heal that fast. And the pain, it got worse instead of better. So Mom and Pop had to be told.

But Mom sometimes had a sense of humor in those bad times, and used it one day to teach Cecil something about cheating

122

on his assigned chores. It involved berry picking and a day when the kids had each been given a pail and told to go fill them with berries in the woods. It was his brother, Dale, who remembered this one.

It seems that little Cecil had other things on his mind that day and the pail filled so slowly. So he got the idea of filling the pail half full of leaves and thus would have only half as many berries to pick.

Which explained why, when young Cecil sat down to supper that night and found a nice, juicy blackberry pie in front of him, it wasn't quite what it looked like. When he bit into it, he learned that Mom had her own way of teaching him a lesson. It was filled with a thin layer of berries on top and leaves below. Ugh!

As he grew a bit older, Cecil would be learning other things. Like the summer he got a job working for a farmer, toiled all summer long only to find that the farmer had no intention of paying him. This time it was his Dad who came to the rescue, taking legal action to force the farmer to pay. All of $80 for a summer's work.

Somewhere during this time, as a teenager, Cecil acquired his first car, a battered old Model A Ford that needed a valve grinding. He did that himself. Then he could take his sister Mary to her homecoming football game, and such places, if she paid for the gas and ironed his shirts.

When the Roosevelt administration came up with the idea of the Civilian Conservation Corps to employ the unemployed youth of America at such jobs as tree planting, dam building and other preservation projects, Cecil was one of the first to sign up. He saved enough money to buy Mom 500 baby chicks, to start her in the chicken business. Even if most of the chickens ended up on the family table to feed the hungry family.

Looking back on all that panorama of hard-times living, it is Cecil's sister, Mary, who said it: "I do not think the United States will ever again have people so well trained in the art of survival."

Perhaps she was right. One thing for certain, when America became involved in the war in 1941, and that fateful December became the month when, it seemed, all the young men of America wanted to fight, Cecil Scott would become one of them.

Except that when Cecil showed up at the recruiting office the recruiters told him he wasn't big enough. Too much of a short-stuff guy. Lacking a quarter of an inch of meeting minimum requirements. Not heavy enough, either.

Well, young Cecil had his own way of facing the problem, said sister Mary. He came home and hung on a bar every day, trying to stretch himself a quarter of an inch and gorged on bananas to heft up his weight a bit. Whether he really stretched himself that quarter of an inch or not, when he went back for a second try they took him.

Brother Jack enlisted, too, and opted for the Army Air Forces because it was better than mucking around in the mud with the infantry and, maybe, getting involved in hand-to-hand combat.

Now, suddenly, the Air Force wanted the short-stuff guys. For gunners, for instance, all curled up in one of those ball turrets in a B-17 bomber. And off to war.

It could have been worse. "I once spent seven hours in that ball turret and it wasn't too bad," Scott said later.

In England the other members of the Belle's crew simply called him Scotty, the guy they depended on, to keep the Jerry fighters from hitting the belly of the plane.

"From down there," he said, "I could see everything, and if I saw a fighter coming in too high to get a shot at him, I'd tell the Chief to lift the wing a bit so I could take a shot at the guy."

Sometimes from that belly gun position, Scott would see the German pilots trying the trick of hanging on their propeller, trying to get a shot at the plane from below.

"I think they were trying to hit the bombs in our bomb bay and explode them, blowing us to bits," he said. And it was his job to see they didn't get away with it.

Like most other gunners, Scott shot at a lot of enemy planes, but on the official side he only had one "damaged" to his credit. A gunner had to have confirmation from other sources to get credit for a kill, even if you saw the plane you were shooting at fall apart.

For example, there was that one hellish fight over Romily sur Seine on December 20, 1942, one of the early missions.

"I think about 300 German fighters attacked us in relays," Scott told interviewers later. "That fight lasted at least a couple of hours. They circled us like Indians around a wagon train and were attacking from all directions. I thought I got two of them but I didn't get credit for them."

The Belle's crew shot so much ammunition that day, if the fight had lasted a few minutes longer, they would have been aiming empty guns.

But it was over Lorient, on January 23, 1943, when Scott, along with other members of the crew, got the biggest scare, if you could call it that.

That was the day when a German fighter pilot in a Focke Wulf, armed with a 20 mm cannon, came blasting right straight at the Belle from the front, head on.

As he began firing, Bob Morgan, at the controls, jerked the big plane up at the nose. He was unable to dive because of sister planes right below. So, the shells intended for the nose of the plane got the Belle in the tail, from below. Almost the whole tail surfaces of the Belle were blasted to bits. Then the plane went into a dive. Some of the members of the crew swore they dropped 5,000 feet before Morgan somehow managed to pull the plane out of the dive.

"I didn't think we would be able to pull out, and I was trying to get out of my turret and get my parachute on, but I couldn't move. The force of gravity had me pinned down. Then, finally, I felt the plane coming out of the dive."

The Belle missed two missions after that while she was being repaired.

For Scotty too, as for the other members of the crew, the 25 missions would be over, and they would be going home. After the bond tour, he spent some times as an instructor in an Air Force radio school in South Dakota and was in training as a radar navigator in Virginia when the war ended.

At first he returned to a job he had held before his enlistment with the Tingley Rubber Company at Rahway, Pennsylvania. Then, with the Ford Motor Company at Edison, which he would hold for 30 years. He was living at Iselin. Gone now were the days of wearing patched pants and, in fact, he managed to buy a vacation home at Tuckertown, New Jersey.

It was in 1947 he met and married a bright-eyed young lady named Norma Edwards, who would become the mother of his three children.

Perhaps a wife and mother may be forgiven for saying it, but for Norma this man, whom the Belle crew had called Scotty, "Was the most loving, gentle and patient man. He was the best."

In October of 1978 he retired after 30 years with Ford, and his dream was to take it easy at their shore home at Tuckerton. Less than a year later, on July 6, 1979, the blow came in the form of a massive heart attack, and he was gone.

"He never talked much about those stories from the war," said Norma. "He just felt he had been doing what had to be done, in the line of duty."

By the time it all came to an end for Staff Sergeant Cecil H. Scott, the roar of the engines had faded, the threatening stutter of the machine guns was long silent, the sight of the attacking German fighters fading from memory. But it had indeed happened, and one of the men who did his part, curled up in his ball turret, was the man they had called Scotty.

Dillon

Adele Astaire Bandaged His Wound

Leviticus G. Dillon has a memory, going all the way back to World War II, about meeting Adele Astaire, sister of the world famous dancing star Fred Astaire. Adele was in the Red Cross in England during the war and was manning a first-aid station at Cambridge when she bandaged a leg wound Dillon received while on a combat mission on the Memphis Belle.

Did we say "wound?"

Funny about that. The official record shows that John Quinlan, the tail gunner, was the only member of the Memphis Belle crew who was wounded. He got a Purple Heart for that. "Just a scratch," John insists. He didn't even want to go to the hospital but the other members of the crew made him go.

Oh, yes, we were talking about Levi Dillon, who isn't even listed as one of the original crew members of the Memphis Belle. But he was.

He trained with Bob Morgan, pilot of the Belle, at McDill Field in Florida where the 91st was organized. Flew with Morgan at Walla Walla, where the bomber crews were formed up. Flew with Morgan at Bangor, Maine, the last training stop before England. And then he flew four of the first five combat missions on the Memphis Belle.

After that? Well, he doesn't mind telling the story. He got busted, demoted and transferred to the 306th Bomb Group. There it was only a matter of a few weeks until he had his rank back and finished his 25 missions as flight engineer.

"A bunch of us had been on liberty," he said, "and we were coming back to the base when there was a little fracas at the gate. A lieutenant said some enlisted man grabbed him and ripped his jacket.

"When they brought some of us back down there for identification, the lieutenant pointed at me and said I did it. I hadn't even been close to him, and I found out later who did it, but I never

127

snitched on him. I had my rank back and got along well with the commander at the 306th."

As a matter of fact, Dillon did so well in the Air Force that he stayed in after the war, made a career out of it and didn't retire until 1963 as a senior master sergeant.

About that wound. Dillon remembers it happened on their third raid, over the St. Nazaire submarine pens, where they came under heavy attack by German fighter planes. It was the day the Germans blasted a big hole in the Belle's wing.

"A German machine gun bullet came right through the top turret where I was and hit my right thigh," he said. "It felt like a hot poker and set my flying suit on fire. Lieutenant Verinis came back and beat the fire out. Then he got the first-aid kit, cut my suit open, and put a bandage on the wound to stop the bleeding. It wasn't deep. Just a little flesh wound.

"When we got back and landed, they told me to go to the hos-pital and get it dressed but I saw the liberty bus loading up and I didn't want to miss liberty so I jumped on the bus.

"Later that night, when I was sitting in a bar, drinking beer, somebody looked at my leg and said, 'Hey, man, you're bleeding!'

"I looked and, sure enough, blood was trickling down my leg. So I went to a Red Cross first-aid station there in Cambridge. I found out that the girl who dressed wounds was Adele Astaire, sister of Fred Astaire.

"It wasn't bad and I never reported it," he said. If he had, he would probably have been awarded the Purple Heart, for they were making the awards for almost any kind of wound.

The other event he likes to remember from his days on the Memphis Belle was the one after that second mission, to St. Nazaire, the one that almost turned into disaster. A German bullet, or hunk of shrapnel, cut an oil line on one of the engines, forcing them to come in on three engines and make an emergency landing at an RAF base in southern England.

Dillon remembers that he and Loch, the assistant flight engineer, repaired the oil line but couldn't get the engine to start. Morgan, who had a heavy date back at Bassingbourn, determined to get home somehow. With only Dillon on board, beside himself, Morgan took off on three engines. And then, by windmilling the dead engine, they got it started. Then quickly landed, picked up the remainder of the crew and headed back to base - and the date.

Dillon's story started on July 15, 1919, when he was born in Franklin County, Virginia. His parents moved to Roanoke when he was six. He graduated from William Fleming High School at Roanoke. He enlisted in the Air Force on September 8, 1941, just a month before Pearl Harbor.

Like other members of the crew, Dillon remembers, with an "ugh," that for the first weeks after landing in England they had to live on British rations. It was the period when England was struggling to stay alive against attacks from German bombers by air, and German submarines, by sea, in an all-out effort to strangle the island kingdom.

"I believe we ate Brussels sprouts every day, and mutton," he said. "I got so sick of them I never let my wife cook Brussels sprouts."

On that first raid for the Memphis Belle, on the submarine pens at Brest, on November 7, 1942, "I remember I pulled the pin and tag from the first bomb, arming it, and Morgan wrote on the tag, 'First bomb on Brest, November 7, 1942.' I sent that tag to my sister and I believe she's still got it."

It would be many years later, he remembers, when he made a pilgrimage to the Pentagon and asked to see General Stanley T. Wray who, as a colonel, had been the commander of the 91st Bomb Group in England, the outfit they had called "Wray's Ragged Irregulars." It included the Memphis Belle's squadron.

"He recognized me immediately and pulled out his old rabbit, riding a bomb. We had all signed it in England. This was a cartoon that had been adopted as the squadron's mascot.

When he reaches back in time, into his bag of memories connected with the Memphis Belle, there was the time, en route to England in 1942, when they landed at Gander, Newfoundland, as a stop-over and met Elliot Roosevelt, son of President Franklin Roosevelt.

"He seemed to be a nice guy and his men spoke highly of him. He, too, was on his way to England."

Another memory, from the days at Bangor, a high altitude test flight, to see how high a B-17 would go.

"We got up to 37,500 feet. That's the highest I ever flew on a B-17," he said, "and the highest the Memphis Belle ever flew."

He also clearly remembers a civilian making the first painting of the Petty girl on the nose of the Memphis Belle, shortly before they left Bangor. It was later repainted by Corporal Tony Starcer at Bassingbourn.

129

THE MEMPHIS BELLE

Today, in retirement, Dillon owns and operates a fishing camp and marina at Providence Forge, Virginia, not far from where he was born and raised.

"Come on up and go fishing with me," he says cheerily.

Perhaps, while waiting for the fish to bite, he might come up with another story about the days when the Memphis Belle rode the angry skies over German-held Europe.

Adkins

His Hands Remember

On a frosty morning in Johnson City, Tennessee, Eugene "Gene" Adkins does not have to be reminded of the Memphis Belle. His hands tell him.

It has been so long now he has become used to the fact that the little finger on his right hand is a bit on the shriveled side. His wound from that long-ago bombing mission to Emden, Germany.

"I just took my gloves off for about two minutes to get the cover off my guns," he remembers. "It was such close quarters in there and I couldn't work with my gloves on. Maybe I didn't quite realize it was 50 degrees below zero up there."

The worst part being that it happened at the beginning of the mission and he had to ride it out, a seven-hour mission with frozen hands. It was a mission when they caught hell from the Germans.

"They threw everything they had at us," he recalls.

It meant Adkins had to do his duty, standing by his guns, firing burst after burst at the attacking planes, with his frozen hands.

"In between, when they were not attacking, I crawled into the radio compartment and tried to warm my hands," he said. "It was a bit warmer in there. They were really hurting I would put them between my legs and try to give them a little warmth that way," he remembers.

It was after he landed back in England when he found out how serious it really was. He spent a month in the Oxford Hospital where medics fought to save his hands and succeeded.

Today, it is only that little finger on his right hand, stiff and shriveled, to remind him of that grueling ordeal. That, and the fact that on cold mornings his hands "sort of ache."

131

"Most people don't realize how many casualties we had from frostbite," he said. "We lost more men to frostbite than we did to enemy bullets. The hospitals were full of them."

Many of them lost fingers, toes. Parts of their faces would slough off, Adkins remembers.

He was one of the lucky ones who would recover and go back into service.

"After a long time they let me go back on duty," he said. "I finished my 25 missions on other planes. The Memphis Belle had gone home by then."

But before he finished his 25, that magic figure that allowed an airman to step down from combat duty, something happened, something important. Adkins won his commission as an officer on August 6, 1943, still in England and flying.

"I had qualified as a gunnery instructor at the beginning and now I took all the tests to qualify as a gunnery officer," he said. He flew the last of his 25 missions that month as a second lieutenant.

Strangely enough, it wasn't until his last mission on August 17, a fateful trip to Schweinfurt, Germany, where the B-17 formations took some of the heaviest losses of the war, that Adkins finally got credit for shooting down an enemy plane. He had done plenty of fighting before that, but the requirements were so tough, with witnesses required, to get credit for a kill. It was a Focke Wulf 190, one of those jug-nosed planes so dreaded by American flyers.

"He was coming in at twelve o'clock high all by himself," said Adkins. "I could see his yellow nose. [It was said that Herman Goering's squadron painted the noses of their planes yellow.] I started putting bursts into him at about 1,000 yards. He started smoking. Then he flipped over and went down."

It gave him a feeling of quiet satisfaction, he said.

With his 25 missions behind him, Adkins stayed in England as a gunnery instructor but finally came home in August of 1944, after D-Day.

He came by his interest in a military career quite honestly. His father had been a 30-year career Army man, a veteran of World War I.

"My Dad and I were pretty close," said Adkins. "I guess I decided on a military career while I was still a kid. In the summertime, while I was in high school, I would go to a student cadet training program put on by the 6th Cavalry at Ft. Oglethorpe, Georgia. By December of 1940 I was old enough to enlist and I went in."

THE MEMPHIS BELLE

After basic training, his first assignment was at McDill Field, where the 91st was being organized. He became one of the original cadre from which the group was organized. He had opted for the Air Force.

It was at McDill where he first met a young lieutenant named Robert K. Morgan and flew with him on training flights but did not at that time become a member of Morgan's crew.

At the beginning he flew on a plane that was named Pandora's Box, with Lieutenant Donald W. Garrett as pilot. But, fortunately, he wasn't on the plane when it was shot down on its third mission, in a raid over St. Nazaire on November 23, 1942.

The plane and its crew had been having problems, for it had aborted four missions before it had completed two, and was shot down on its third. It had flown with various pilots.

Originally Leviticus Dillon had been a member of the Memphis Belle's crew as an engineer and top turret gunner but was transferred to another unit after a bit of a dust-up with the Military Police. With his original plane gone, Adkins was a sort of floating crew member at the time and was then assigned to the Memphis Belle.

He flew his first mission on the Belle on December 30, to Lorient, France, and remained on the crew until that day over Emden and his frozen hands.

It had been while a student at Erwin High School in East Tennessee, that Adkins spotted a pretty young girl named Irene Williams and tried to date her.

"She wouldn't give me a date until I was a senior," he said. When he went off to the Army, she decided everything was too uncertain to commit herself.

It was while he was home, on leave after returning from England that the courtship heated up again and a short time later, while he was stationed at Laredo Air Base, Texas, that he persuaded her to come out and become Mrs. Adkins.

"We were married in the chapel on the base," he remembers.

But he was still the Air Force career man, still a gunnery and armament specialist. During his career he trained gunners and gunnery specialists on B-29s, B-36s and B-50s as well as the old B-17s. His service included one tour of duty on Okinawa in the South Pacific in 1953. He retired with the rank of major.

While attending ceremonies in Memphis in 1987, for the dedication of the Memphis Belle Museum, he remembered his first ride on the famed airplane.

"We were at Bangor, Maine," he said. "Just before going overseas pilots were allowed one overnight training flight to their home town. Lieutenant Morgan was flying to Asheville, North Carolina, where his father lived. Johnson City, Tennessee, is only about 50 miles from Asheville so I asked for permission to go along.

"We landed at Asheville and I grabbed a bus for Johnson City."

It had been that frostbite thing that kept him from being a member of the Belle's crew when she was chosen as the first B-17 to be sent back to the United States on a war bond and publicity tour and became the most famed plane of World War II.

Perhaps, at times, as he saw the tumult and sudden fame surrounding the plane and her crew, he had felt a bit left out, that he had, after all, also been a part of the story. He had indeed.

Miller

The Lost Crewman

If anyone qualifies as "the lost crewman of the Memphis Belle," it would have to be E. Scott Miller

Simply because when the Memphis Belle and her crew came home for their triumphant war bond and publicity tour, he was left behind in England. Even though he had flown more combat missions on the Belle than some other members of the crew who did come home to enjoy instant fame as members of the supposedly intact crew.

When he did get home, months later, he dropped out of sight as he returned to civilian life. There was nothing unusual about this for it happened to thousands of military veterans.

Unlike many of his buddies, Miller didn't keep up with his fellow crew members. He didn't make any effort to join the 91st Bomb Group Memorial Association, a kind of get-together group of men who like to remember and, at least once a year, meet for a convention where everyone could drink a few beers with their old buddies, chew the rag about old times at Bassingbourn.

When the other crew members of the Memphis Belle got together in Memphis for a nostalgic look at the old plane, Miller was always missing. In fact, when we began researching the Belle and her crew for this book, and after Miller's name cropped up, none of the crew knew where he was.

It all came about because Miller started his career at Bassingbourn as a mechanic working on automatic pilots, on the ground instead of in the air. By the time he volunteered for combat flight and was assigned to the Belle, the plane and her crew already had ten missions behind them. But Miller became a regular crew-member and flew with the Belle until the end of her combat tour.

THE MEMPHIS BELLE

Which means he had at least 15 missions on the Belle at the end. He did miss one mission because of illness..

When the Belle was selected for that singular mission of going home for the big nationwide tour, one stipulation by the high command was that each member of the crew must have completed his 25 missions. Thus Miller had to be dropped. His place was taken by Staff Sergeant Casimer Nastal who had flown only one mission on the Belle but with that one important difference: he had 25 missions behind him.

Co-pilot James Verinis had also flown only five missions on the Belle, at the beginning, and had then been assigned to another plane to complete his 25 missions.

When Miller's name cropped up, we began looking for him. Since the 91st Bomb Group roster did not have him listed we turned to the Military Personnel Records office in St. Louis. As many Americans know, the mills of bureaucracy grind slowly but when a reply did finally come from St. Louis, it seemed the Army serial number found with Miller's name on an old crew list for the Memphis Belle turned out to be the serial number for another man.

On the weekend of May 17, the big dedication ceremony weekend, we stumbled onto the clue that led to Miller. The 91st Bomb Group Memorial Association had scheduled their annual convention in Memphis on the same weekend so its members could participate in the celebration. At a cocktail party for the Association we met Hilary "Bud" Evers, a vice president of the group.

When Evers learned of the work in progress on the Memphis Belle book, he volunteered: "I've got some records of the Belle's missions. I'll send them to you." The man kept his promise.

Most of the material he sent we already had, but one item, almost overlooked, was a copy of an old news release dated May 17, 1943, telling about the 25th mission for Captain Bob Morgan and five members of his crew. What we almost missed was a listing of the crew members, together with their home towns. It was in a second glance at the release that we spotted that home town for Miller - Albright, West Virginia.

Our heart skipped a beat. Was it possible that the man still lived there after more than 40 years? Most of the Belle's crew had moved, some of them several times. But it was worth a try.

On the phone with the information operator for West Virginia, we asked if she had a number for Emerson S. Miller in Albright. That was how his name appeared in the military records.

"No, but I have a listing for E. Scott Miller," she replied. Please, could I have that number?

When a woman answered the phone, I said, "I'm looking for a man named Emerson S. Miller who served with the 91st Bomb Group at Bassingbourn, England, during World War II."

"That's my husband," came the reply. A moment later we were talking to E. Scott Miller.

"I prefer to use E. Scott Miller," he said. "The Army made us use our first names." After that we had several conversations.

Asked about some of the highlights of his life, he insisted, "I'm just an ordinary guy. I don't remember very many exciting things that happened to me in my lifetime."

You get the same sense of serenity in his replies when you ask about his emotions, his thoughts, his worries in those long-ago times when he flew as a waist gunner on the Memphis Belle.

"I never lost any sleep about the mission coming up the next day," he said. "In fact, I never wore my parachute up there until I had reached something like my 20th mission. Then I began thinking I might make it and started wearing my chute."

Which would suggest that prior to his 20th mission he was somewhat of a fatalist. But, if true, it was not intentional. Just that the former Staff Sergeant Miller is a serene and calm sort of man, today, and wants to keep it that way. Let the chips fall.

Proof that he has put those memories of his war days far behind him may even be suggested by that change in his name, E. Scott Miller, rather than Emerson S. Miller.

If you press him a bit you find that this man does have a few memories. Like that Sunday, May 16, 1943, when he met and shook hands with, the King and Queen of England. It wasn't every day that a West Virginia farm boy got to meet a king and queen.

The Belle and her crew had been on one of their toughest missions the day before. They had been sent to Wilhelmshaven, Germany, but had found it socked in and had bombed Heligoland instead. Switching targets hadn't saved them from a blistering air battle with swarms of German fighter planes which had attacked again and again. Every gunner had been forced to stay on his toes, manning his guns and blasting at the enemy planes every time they came within range.

But the Memphis Belle, on her 23rd mission, had come home safely, living up to her growing reputation as a lucky plane.

It was after the weary crewmen returned to Bassingbourn theat they received the good news. No, nothing about the king and queen. Not yet. But the 91st had sent planes on combat missions three days in a row and now came the announcement that the next day, Sunday, would officially be a "stand down" day, no missions. Beyond that, May 15 had been declared the official first birthday anniversary of the 91st Bomb Group.

Wowee, they could celebrate. It wasn't often that the men were told that there would be no mission the next day. It had always depended on the weather. True, they often stayed on the ground for days, even weeks, when the weather was bad, but it was always understood that if the weather was right,, there would probably be a mission, Sunday or not.

According to Captain S. T. Parker, the official historian of the 91st, the men of the group cranked up a party that night to end all parties, lasting well into the morning of the 16th.

The results of all this, wrote Parker, could be seen the next morning when only 17 men showed up for breakfast at the officers' mess. Virtually the same for the enlisted men's mess.

Which may explain why Staff Sergeant Emerson S. Miller was still sacked out in his bunk when the base public address system began to blare:

"Attention, all crew members of the Memphis Belle. Report immediately to your plane, wearing your class A uniform."

"I would have rather stayed in my bunk at that moment," says Miller, remembering it today. But an order was an order so he got up. At that moment he knew nothing about a king or a queen.

The royal couple had indeed chosen that day to visit the 91st base, perhaps because they had heard about the group's birthday.

"They lined us up in front of the plane and here came the king and queen," Miller remembers.

The Belle and her crew had just been selected for this singular honor, as the 91st historian put it, because they were becoming a bit famous. The plane was being featured in a War Department documentary film and a few days earlier, Captain Morgan, and several crew members had been selected to go to London to make a special broadcast to the people of America.

In any case, here they stood at attention, these ten crewmen of the Belle as the royal cavalcade of limousines rolled up. Dismounting from their limousine, the royal couple nodded as Captain Morgan introduced each member of the crew by name. They went down the line, shaking hands and speaking briefly to each man. The queen doing most of the talking.

What had she said to Sergeant Miller?

THE MEMPHIS BELLE

"You must be proud of your fine plane," is the way Miller remembers it, with Sergeant Miller in agreement, "Yes, Ma'm." They hadn't been briefed on the niceties of "Your Royal Highness."

In any case, after their highnesses had departed, Sergeant Miller could return to his bunk and complete his snooze. If the excitement of the moment hadn't robbed him of his drowsiness.

He doesn't remember clearly his big day on that raid to Antwerp, Belgium, to bomb the German harbor installations, when he was officially credited with shooting down a German Focke Wulf fighter plane.

"I just shot at him and he went down," said Miller. To get a confirmed kill, you had to have several witnesses. "Most of the time you couldn't tell who got a German plane. When you have 25 gunners all shooting at the same plane at the same time and he goes down, how can you say who did it?"

Miller does remember that as the Belle neared the completion of her 25 missions, Captain Morgan tried to help him get his 25 in by scheduling him to fly on other planes on days when the Belle did not fly.

"He was trying to help me get in my 25 at the same time as the rest of the crew but it just didn't work fast enough," said Miller. Which is why, when the Belle went home at the beginning of June for the big tour, a certain young man named Miller had to remain in England.

"I finished my 25 a couple of months later, flying on other planes," said Miller. After that they sent him to Scotland to act as a gunnery instructor at a school for young gunners.

Sergeant Miller could qualify as a gunnery instructor because, after all, he had started his Air Force career as a gunner, with gunnery training, even before being trained as that automatic pilot technician.

The story is that when he enlisted in the Air Force in February of 1942, he was, like other men who flew with the Belle, sent to McDill Field near Tampa, Florida, for his training. From there to Walla Walla, Washington, for that final training before going overseas.

"At Walla Walla I was originally assigned to the crew of Lieutenant Richard G. Hill," said Miller. "Then they decided to send me to the Honeywell Corporation at Minneapolis for training on the automatic pilot controls, to be a maintenance man."

It was on July 15, 1942, while Miller was at Minneapolis that Lieutenant Hill and his crew took off on a routine training flight and crashed into a mountain, killing all on board. Which meant that assignment to the automatic pilot training may have saved his life.

Sergeant John Quinlan, the tail gunner on the Memphis Belle, had been another member of Hill's crew who was told on that fateful day that he could remain on the ground.

E. Scott Miller went overseas as a ground crewman, an automatic pilot mechanic, rather than as a flying crew member.

"I remember I went over on the Queen Mary," he said.

But somehow Miller remembers that he wasn't really cut out to be a technician.

"Those damned things were driving me up the wall," he said. He decided to change his life style.

"I went to the squadron commander and told him I'd like to fly combat. He didn't bat an eye. He seemed happy to hear it."

His assignment - the Memphis Belle.

Again it might have been a bit of fate that arranged all this for it was on a raid over Emden, Germany, on February 4 when Sergeant Gene Adkins, the right waist gunner on the Memphis Belle, received frost bites on his hands, so severe he had to be hospitalized. Which created a vacancy on the Belle's crew.

Since it was about this time that Sergeant Miller decided he'd rather fly than fix gadgets, he flew the next mission on the Belle on February 14, to Hamm, Germany. He could step in and take over as a waist gunner because of his previous gunnery training. Which was probably one of the reasons why, after he completed his tour of missions, he was assigned to the gunnery school in Scotland.

"Our machine guns were fastened to posts and we would shoot at sleeve targets towed past by small planes," he said.

After a few weeks of this, his ears began to hurt because of the constant noise from the big .50 caliber machine guns.

"All we had for protection for our ears was cotton to stuff in your ears," he said. No modern protectors as shooters have today.

So, with his ears hurting, he was finally sent home in November of 1943 and spent the remainder of the war at bases like Miami Beach, Ft. Meyers and McDill once more. As the war ended he was mustered out and returned to Albright, West Virginia.

"I had grown up on a farm there," he said. He couldn't remember how old he was when his Dad first put him in the fields, working with a team of horses.

"From my very first memories I was working. Always working."

After the war, when he was mustered out, he simply returned to the farm and picked up where he had left off. Only now there was something new. There had been this girl named Louise Shaw whom he had known and dated before the war. When he found she was still waiting, he simply popped the question and she became Mrs. Miller. They have two daughters, Mrs. Mary Elizabeth Butler, at Grand Rapids, Michigan, and Mrs. Martha Sue Matherne, at Mobile, Alabama.

Today Miller and his wife live at Kingwood, West Virginia, only a few miles from where it all started on that day in 1918 when he was born.

When he returned home from his military service, he worked for a few years with the West Virginia Alcohol and Beverage Commission, then held a job with the state's Department of Agriculture for 20 years in animal health projects before retiring.

Today? "I'm running a little farm, raising cattle," he said.

Any hobbies or pastimes?

"No, I really don't have any hobbies. Just work. Work is all I've ever done."

As for the famous old airplane, the Memphis Belle, Miller has missed out on all the reunions and activities concerning her.

"I knew when she went home she was going on a tour but that is about all," he said. "One time, shortly after the war, I recall meeting one of the crew members but I don't remember which one. Then I have a friend who once lived in Memphis and he told me the old plane was standing on a pedestal in a park. But I haven't seen her since the last time I flew her in May of 1943."

Which would mean almost 45 years.

When he learned of all that has happened in the meantime, of those years of neglect, the years on the pedestal on Central Avenue, the final and successful campaign to provide the historic old plane with a proper home, it was apparent his interest was perking.

"I'd like to see that old plane again," he said.

Then, after a pause, he said it: "Next time I go to Mobile to see my daughter, I'm going to stop off in Memphis and see the Memphis Belle."

Giambrone

He Kept the Belle Flying

A skinny Italian-American boy named Joe Giambrone never dreamed that when he started showing a talent for fixing things and got a job repairing slot machines at age 17, that such talent would one day land him in England during World War II, as ground chief of a giant four-engine bomber called the Memphis Belle.

"I guess I had a talent for fixing things," he admits.

Never mind that the slot machines were considered illegal in Philadelphia.

"All the clubs had them," said Joe. "Nobody bothered."

Sort of like home-brew beer during prohibition. Everybody had a few bottles down in the cellar.

When beer became legal in 1933, Joe served his time behind the bar in the family restaurant at Norristown, Pennsylvania.

"I was doing my studying in the back room and when somebody wanted bar service, they would holler and I'd come take care of them," he said.

At school he was just one of the seven Giambrone brothers, not to speak of two sisters, the typical, good sized Italian-American family. He remembers that he played basketball and baseball at Norristown High School. "No, I wasn't a star."

It would be in 1940, as the war heated up in Europe and America began building up its armed forces that young Joe decided he wanted in. "I decided to go in before the draft got me," he said of his enlistment.

He started with a National Guard infantry unit at Indiantown Gap, but when the Air Force began expanding and called for volunteers, he decided that sounded better than the infantry. In a few weeks he was at Chanute Field, working his way through aircraft mechanics school.

"I had no trouble with it," said Joe. "It was easy."

The slot machine training was paying off. He became an aircraft mechanic with the 29th Bomb Group, and when the 91st Bomb Group was being formed at McDill Field, he was one of the original cadre as the group came into being. Next stop, Walla Walla, Washington, where the group was going through final flight training.

It was here, Joe remembers, where he became involved in a highly unorthodox and unscheduled bombing incident before he even got overseas. Not to speak of the danger involved. Like, maybe, falling out of a plane.

"Colonel Wray flew to Wright Field in Ohio to pick up one of the new Model F B-17s and I went along as flight engineer," he said. "Because of the long distance they put two auxiliary fuel tanks in the bomb bay. When we took off to leave, the landing gear wouldn't come up.

"There was an emergency hand crank in the bomb bay to crank the wheels up by hand. But we couldn't get to the crank because of the extra fuel tanks. We radioed the tower for instructions and they told us to fly over an open field and drop the tanks.

"Well, we tried that but one of the tanks wouldn't drop. Colonel Wray tried all kinds of maneuvers, trying to shake it loose, but it stayed stuck. That was when somebody told me to get in the bomb bay and kick the tank out."

Giambrone agreed to do it. They tied a safety rope around his waist, just in case he lost his grip on the beams.

"I kicked and kicked but the damned thing just wouldn't turn loose," he said. "We kept circling and circling and we probably didn't realize exactly where we were when the thing finally turned loose and dropped."

The tank landed on top of a farmer's chicken coop, smashing it flat.

Charles Leighton, the navigator, made the flight and remembers the headlines in the Dayton, Ohio, newspaper the next day:

"Air Force Bombs Chicken Coop."

Thank goodness, Joe said, he didn't have to test the safety rope to see if it would hold. His white-knuckled hands managed to keep their grip on the plane.

Joe remembers one joyful dividend from that trip to Dayton. He got to see his brother, Alfonso, who had also enlisted in the Air Force and was stationed at Wright Field.

"Boy, was he surprised to see me," said Joe.

143

Joe soon found out that the life of an aircraft mechanic had its hazards, even on the ground. Or almost on the ground. Like having a ladder blown out from under him by a propeller blast.

"I was up on a ladder, checking the oil pressure sensor on an engine, and I wanted to test it by getting one of the engineers to speed up the engine. He speeded it up so hard he blew the ladder right out from under me and I was left dangling there, hanging onto the plane."

"I gave him a cussing and told him to try again and not speed up the engine so hard. So I got up on the ladder again and he specded it up. And it happened again. He blew the ladder right out from under me again."

Joe was doing his job so well that by the time he got to Fort Dix, the last stop before boarding the Queen Elizabeth for England, he was promoted to the rank of technical sergeant.

When he landed in England, he was sent straight up to Bassingbourn.

If Joe drove his ten-man ground crew hard in England, it was for a cause, to keep the Memphis Belle flying. He was assigned to the Belle as soon as he got to Bassingbourn, new home of the 91st Bomb Group.

"The manuals said changing an engine on a B-17 took 25 hours," he said. "Our crew got so good at it we set a record one day by changing an engine in four hours."

He and his men had to change engines nine times on the Belle during its eight months tour of combat duty, sometimes when checks showed engine compression was low but several times when engines got damaged by enemy gun fire.

It was during good weather when the Belle flew missions on successive days, when they had to work fast, sometimes all night, to make sure she was ready for the next day's flight.

Part of the job was patching bullet or shrapnel holes. "At first we just glued a piece of fabric over the hole but later they came up with the pop rivets and we patched with aluminum," Joe said.

Sometimes, no matter how hard they worked, the Belle had to be grounded. Like the time the plane came home with a huge hole in the right wing and the whole wing had to be replaced.

Or the two times the Belle came home with a good portion of her tail shot off.

"It wasn't so much the work as getting the right parts," he said. "At the beginning, we were so short of parts we had to start cannibalizing the most seriously damaged planes for parts. We called them 'hangar queens.'"

Now that it is so long ago, Joe doesn't mind confessing that he made a few boo-boos. Like the time he put the left wing de-icer boot on the right wing.

"They looked alike to me and I didn't realize they were different," Joe remembers. "We put the darned thing on and the crew took off with it. Then they came back and said the de-icer wasn't working. I got in and took a flight with Captain Morgan and I knew something was wrong. When we got back down I took a good look and realized what I had done. I got the right boot, put it on and everything was fine. But I never did tell the captain what had happened."

Like all the other ground crew who served in England, he remembers how, as the time grew near for the planes to come home, the men would stop playing horseshoes, or pitching pennies, whatever, and start drifting over to the runways. Waiting, listening for the sound of motors. And, when a plane came in sight, trying to read the numbers to "see if it was your plane."

Watching, dreading to see those red flares shooting out of a plane to tell the waiting ambulances that they had wounded men on board, asking for priorities on landing. Or, that a plane was damaged and needed to land fast. Like the day the Belle came home with her tail in shreds and Morgan, the pilot, had his hands full, getting her safely down.

"One of biggest dreads, at the beginning, was a plane coming home with a bullet hole in one of the oil coolers," said Joe. "It meant grounding the plane. You couldn't fly without the oil cooler and we didn't have any replacements."

Sitting on the ground, waiting for his Belle to come home, got Joe Giambrone to wondering what it was like, up there on a combat mission. He wondered if, one day, he might fly a combat mission.

The idea kept gnawing at him until, one day, near the end of the Memphis Belle's tour of duty, he decided to do something about it. He doesn't remember exactly what he said to the pilot, but it probably went something like this: "Look, I've been keeping this plane flying all these months. How about letting me go along one time?"

It was against orders. He knew that. Ground crewmen were forbidden to fly on missions. But maybe he was real good at being persuasive and he got the nod. It was on a mission to

Meaulte, France, to bomb a German airplane factory and repair shop. If they were smashed, it might stop a lot of German fighters from taking to the air to blast the B-17s.

The combat log shows that the mission was a fairly short one, with British Spitfire fighter escort, that anti-aircraft fire was not especially bad on this trip but the German fighters put up a vicious battle. The German pilots knew they had to protect the plane plant down there. They managed to shoot down two B-17s from the 91st Bomb Group that day.

"I was standing up, right behind the co-pilot's scat," said Joe, "and I was beginning to be sorry I had been so brave. It seemed as if every German fighters was aiming right at me. I was so scared my knees were knocking. I had to put my hands between my legs to keep them from knocking."

But at least he could be able to say that he had flown on at least one mission with the boys.

The mission report that day said it had been one of the easier ones. The mechanic from Northtown, Pennsylvania, wasn't so sure.

Then, a few days later, the Memphis Belle completed her 25 missions and went home, leaving a sad crew chief behind. He had hoped, when he first heard that the lucky plane and her crew had been selected to go home for the nationwide war bond and morale tour, that he might get to go along. The answer was, no.

He and his men would have to stay and keep other planes flying. He remembers that one of the other B-17s he kept flying was Pistol Packing Mama. Being promoted to master sergeant helped but, as with a little boy and his first dog, there would never be another plane to take the place of the Memphis Belle.

When asked if he could remember the names of the other men who had served with him on the ground crew for the Memphis Belle, he wrinkled his brow as he tried to remember something so long ago.

"I remember that Robert Walters was my assistant crew chief," he said. "Then there was Charles Blauser and Leonard Sowers. I can't remember all the others."

An English newspaper on June 9, 1943, carried the story of the Belle's departure for home and the publicity tour. The ground crew was listed and it included, in addition to Giambrone, Sergeant Robert G. Walters of Walla Walla, Washington, assistant crew chief; Staff Sergeant Max Armstrong of Albright, West Virginia; Sergeant R. C. Champion of Chicago, Illinois, Sergeant Charles P.

Blauser of York, Pennsylvania, and Corporal Leonard E. Sowers of St. Louis, Missouri.

It was some weeks after the Belle had left when Joe was promoted to squadron inspector which meant he now had all the squadron's ground crews under his responsibility. He stayed until after the war was over.

Back home, mustered out of the service, he found things were going to be a bit tougher, at least at the beginning.

"I had to make a living and got a job with a construction company," he said. "Pick and shovel stuff. It was hard work."

But, just as in the Air Force, he worked his way up. He got married and reared a son, Joseph Gene. His wife Mary Jane was a familiar face at the reunions of the 91st Bomb Group until she died in 1984.

Today, Joe still works as office manager for Henkels and McCoy Construction Company, engineers and builders, at Blue Bell, Pennsylvania, near Philadelphia.

Why doesn't he retire?

"With Mary gone, I wouldn't know what to do with myself," he says. "I'd rather just keep working."

He lives at Glenside, near Norristown where he was born.

Folks said the Memphis Belle was a lucky plane and, perhaps, she was. But there may have been a bit more to it than that. Sergeant Levi Dillon, one of the original crew members, said Joe Giambrone and his crew might have had a lot to do with it.

"Joe was the most dedicated crew chief I ever knew and deserves a lot of credit for this plane's success," said Dillon.

In the spring of 1987 when a new home was finally being dedicated for the Memphis Belle, Colonel Bob Morgan, the Belle's wartime pilot, landed at Memphis International Airport, arriving for the dedication ceremonies. There to meet him as he landed, just as he had met him at Bassingbourn, England, so many times, was Joe Giambrone, dressed in a pair of his old work fatigues that he had worn so many years ago.

The two men grabbed each other and did a bit of an Indian dance.

They had much to remember, the two of them.

The Missions

Author's Note: Three members of the crew of the Memphis Belle kept diaries during their combat tour in England. Clarence Winchell, one of the two waist gunners, meticulously listed each crew member making each mission, noting when someone was ill and a substitute had been assigned. Unfortunately, his diary stops at mission 20. He simply does not remember why he did not continue keeping a diary through the rest of his missions. In fact, his diary was for many years lost, and it was found, after a long search while this book was being written.

Co-pilot James Verinis also kept a diary with entries for each mission, but he flew only five missions on the Belle at the beginning of the tour. He was then assigned as a pilot to another plane. Many of his diary entries do not concern the Memphis Belle.

Navigator Charles Leighton was the third member of the crew to keep a diary, but as time went on, his entries became shorter and shorter. At the end, his entries were only a few cryptic sentences. Here, too, several missions are missing toward the end of his tour of combat. Did he become weary of the thing?

In any case, the following narrative of the 25 missions flown by the Belle and her crew is based on these diaries, on an official narrative of the 91st Bomb Group, and a few debriefing papers found in Air Force archives.

Added to this are the memories of the eight surviving crew members. Unfortunately, it was all so long ago. While the crew has memories of certain events and missions, they all have trouble keeping the 25 missions sorted out in their minds. Perhaps, as some of them suggest, they wanted to forget some of the things they went through.

Two of the ten crew members have died since the war ended and most of their memories died with them. In these cases we have relied on the recollections of relatives and friends.

In the following pages, the main sources of the narrative will be identified as 91st Bomb Group, Winchell Diary, Verinis Diary, Leighton Diary, and Debriefing.

We should further explain that in presenting this combat record, we have been forced by the sheer volume of the material to eliminate many passages. We also have made some changes in punctuation and spelling and, in a few instnces, have inserted connecting words when passages, or parts of them, have been left out.

Other than this we have, so far as possible, used the exact words of the participants as they were written or spoken at the time, when it was all fresh on their minds. This would include Captain S. T. Parker, official historian for the 91st Bomb Group when the Memphis Belle was flying her missions, who wrote it all down, on a day-to-day basis as it was happening. To our knowledge, Captain Parker's history of the 91st Bomb Group has never been published. In those instances where we have added our own interpretation, or amplificiations, we have made this obvious to the reader.

If the author had written this narrative in his own words he, of course, would have attempted to enhance the drama of the events, but the author chose the direct-quote method because even in the short, cryptic passages of the diary, or in the historical record written in stiff "Militarese" there is a certain flavor of authenticity too valuable to lose.

Prelude

They always came for you at night. To awaken you and tell you that you would be going on a mission. Your sleep-fuddled brain would snap awake because of the urgency and danger of what lay immediately ahead. A bit like being awakened by the hangman. No, one didn't want to think about that. Subconsciously, however, you did think about that.

Always with that knowledge in the back of your mind of the buddies who had not come back from previous missions. Less than halfway through your required number of missions, the losses for your group were already past the one-third mark. The odds were constantly growing shorter.

Perhaps you had already been awake when the wake-up sergeant came in. Lying there with your quiet dread, perhaps your hands clasped behind your head, thinking. Unable to sleep because of that nervous uncertainty. Would you be going again today?

Those long, icy journeys through the angry skies where swarms of German fighter planes hovered high, in ambush, waiting. Armed with machine guns, 37 mm aircraft cannons and even the new and deadly air-to-air rockets. The skies filled with so many flak explosions, the black puffs would fill the air, like clouds, even on a clear day. And you had to fly through it.

Perhaps you even caught yourself searching for an excuse not to go. Could you fake an illness? Arrange an injury? There had been that skinny boy from Texas who had shot himself in the foot when he could no longer face the missions. You had heard about one buddy who had deliberately exposed himself to venereal disease so he would be hospitalized. With a macabre sense of humor you told yourself, he at least had a bit of fun making himself unfit for duty.

But no, you would not use an excuse, much as you might like to. Those other nine members of the crew were buddies of yours. They would be going. You would never be able to live with the thought that if they didn't come back, it might have been because you had not been there to do your part. You did what had to be done.

Perhaps, you thought hopefully, there would be another way out. The mission might be scrubbed. It had happened so many times before. You had been rousted out of bed at two or three o'clock in the morning, eaten your breakfast of powdered egg pancakes, marmalade and coffee, had been briefed on your mission, even climbed in your plane and waited on the runway. Sometimes for hours. And then, at the last moment, because a weather front refused to lift, the mission would be scrubbed. Sometimes you weren't even told why. You just didn't go. And you were glad.

The scrubbed missions took their toll, too. It was hard on the nerves. Several of your buddies had said it. Going through one of those scrubs was almost as bad as taking off and going. Then you knew, too, that you had a certain quota of missions to make and each scrubbed mission just set you back that much.

Where would you be going today? The wake-up sergeant never told you. He probably didn't even know. They would tell you later, at the briefing. Would it be one of those hornet's nest targets the Germans defended with utter fanaticism? Because it was one of those targets that would hurt if it were destroyed. Like Romilly sur Seine, that key staging point for German fighter planes. God, that had been a fight. The German fighter pilots had hung on nearly two hours, buzzing like angry hornets, their guns flashing.

THE MEMPHIS BELLE

Gutsy, some of those German pilots, roaring straight at you for a kill, almost kamikaze style, coming in so close your pilot would have to wrench the big bomber into an emergency dive, or into a chandelle, to avoid an almost certain crash. You had seen some of your buddies go down that day.

You had watched for parachutes to come out of one of the doomed planes. Seven, you had counted. At least seven of the ten had made it. Made it for what? To sit in a stinking German POW camp for the rest of the war. For the three who did not get out, well, for them the war was over.

Then, there had been that time over St. Nazaire when one of the B-17s in your group, still carrying its load of bombs, had been hit in the bomb bay. The big ship had simply disintegrated in a horrible ball of fire. No parachutes that day.

It had started with the first mission, the one to Brest, France, on November 7, 1942.

You were a pioneer then, among the first crews of the big bombers that tried to prove that daylight bombing was possible and could help end the war.

The British, who had been at war since 1939, said it could not be done. Losses were too high in daylight raids. The stubborn Yanks replied that they would prove that it could be done. Our new B-17, bristling with guns and called the Flying Fortress, will be able to hold its own against the German fighters. As for the flak, they said, we'll fly so high our planes will be out of range of the German anti-aircraft guns on the ground.

But from the beginning of time, in wars, every new weapon has met with a new counter weapon. The Germans constantly developed new weapons and tactics for their fighters. On the ground, they constantly improved their ack-ack guns until they were reaching 35,000 feet and more.

So the Yanks did their daylight bombing but they paid a heavy price, in lives and planes. You were a part of that.

As time went by, it sometimes seemed as if your memories of the individual missions merged into a dreamlike thing. As if there were some sort of defense mechanism in your brain, trying to wipe out what was unpleasant.

Until, in the morning, you heard those footsteps on the stairs. The voice through the door. "Time to get up. Breakfast at 3:30. Briefing at 4."

Then, suddenly, it was all real again.

You were going on another mission.

The Missions - First Half

October 31, 1942

91st Bomb Group: "The combat crews tended to become restive as the training program continued week after week. Most of them felt, with good reason, that the almost endless succession of ground school classes, practice missions and study had carried them as far as it was possible to go until they had undergone actual combat experience. By the end of October this feeling had spread to many members of the ground echelon as well. Their patience was gradually becoming a bit worn."

November 1, 1942

91st Bomb Group: "Several officers of the Eighth Bomber Command visited the station and made a detailed evaluation of the progress of the group. They made their report to the commanding general. They stated in no uncertain terms that the 91st Bomb Group was ready for combat."

November 2, 1942

91st Bomb Group: "The announcement of the long-looked-for day arrived as a secret teletype message: the first field order addressed to the 91st Bomb Group. This unheralded event occurred during the late afternoon of Nov. 2. Everything about the airdrome was suddenly shrouded in a mysterious secrecy. At 1535 hours the post was closed. No one was told why, but all gates were unceremoniously shut tight. Automobiles and trucks attempting to get into or out of the station caused a traffic jam which by 1800 hours had attained serious proportions. Men returning from pass were unable to regain admission to their own airdrome without a long delay. At the same time, all telephonic communications was cut off except for urgent official messages which were routed through the intelligence office. While all this secrecy was being enforced, the public address system, which could be heard in at least two neighboring settlements without difficulty, was blasting forth requests and orders at a tremendous rate. As one civilian caustically observed the following day, 'Only an operational mission could have caused so much excitement.'

"The target originally selected was the submarine base at Brest. Only 14 of the group's aircraft were required for the mission. Preparations for this target were completed at about 0200 hours on Nov. 3. Just as the ground crews were about to relax and get some sleep, Wing Headquarters sent a supplementary order changing both the target and the bomb load. The group was directed to attack a diversionary point on the Cherbourg peninsula. Considerable haste was needed to make the necessary changes. Somehow the corrections were made and the new target was prepared. Just before 0700 hours, when these preparations had been completed, Wing Headquarters changed its mind once more. This time the group was ordered to attack the German airdrome at Abbeville. This assignment required a still different bomb load and entirely new briefing information. No questions were asked; the weary ground crews proceeded to meet the requirements of the last order with extraordinary energy, even though most of them had been working all night.

"These changes produced much more confusion than had been occasioned by the original order. Breakfast for the combat crews was served at 0700 hours and the briefing had been scheduled for 0800 hours. But because of the last change in targets, practically nothing was ready when they began to assemble in the briefing room at the appointed hour. After waiting about an hour, the first of the briefing notes for the latest target had been completed and the first operational briefing began. The briefing was completed at about 1000 hours. At the appointed time they arrived at their dispersal areas only to find that the bomb loading had not been completed. There they first learned of the work and changes and confusion that had been going on all night. In several instances the combat crews helped to load the last of their bombs. A few comments were passed.

153

"They taxied their aircraft into position at the end of the runway at 1100 hours. Word was then radioed to them that the mission had been postponed by one hour. They sat and waited. Finally, about 1230 hours, a half hour before the delayed takeoff time, they were advised that the mission had been cancelled.

"When the combat crews learned all of the story they credited the whole series of incidents to higher headquarters and did what they could to forget it. Colonel Wray assisted in this process by granting an extra 24-hour pass to everyone who had been scheduled to make the flight. Needless to say, most of them did not spend this time on the airdrome."

Who says war is not confusing?

November 6, 1942

91st Bomb Group: "On Nov. 6, the group received its second field order, which sent the first of its aircraft over Europe on their first operational mission."

Brest - November 7, 1942

Author's Note: The time was 10:15 and the damp, misty air hanging over the runways of the Bassingbourn airdrome was vibrating with the thunder of Wright-Cyclone engines. B-17 bombers of the 324th and 322nd Squadrons of the 91st Bomb Group of the Eighth Air Force were preparing to take off for the group's first attack against German-held Europe.

Against the light, misting rain the windshield wipers on the waiting planes swished back and forth to provide a clear view for the anxious eyes of the waiting pilots as they peered eagerly at the control tower. In that tower, peering out just as anxiously, were General Carl Spaatz, commander of the Eighth Air Force, and General Ira C. Eaker, commander of the Eighth Bomber Command.

At 1022 hours the pilots saw a man walk out onto the balcony of the tower, one arm high in the air, holding a Very signal pistol. The pistol fired. A signal rocket flared into the air and First Lieutenant Duane L. Jones gunned the engines of B-17 No. 503, Pandora's Box. He would be the first to take off on that historic first combat mission.

THE MEMPHIS BELLE

Flying as co-pilot of Jones' plane was Colonel Stanley T. Wray, commander of the 91st, who insisted on leading his men into their first battle.

The second plane to take off would be none other than the Memphis Belle, piloted by Lieutenant Robert K. Morgan, destined to become one of the most famed warplanes of World War II. If surviving operation logs are correct, the Belle and her crew made their share of history that day as the first plane of the 91st actually to take off and carry out her missions. For the logs show that Jones' plane aborted, due to trouble with the plane's guns. They apparently froze up at high altitude and the plane was forced to turn back before reaching the target. At least one published account of this raid shows that Jones and his plane completed the mission and led the squadron over the target. However, both the missions logs and the engineering logs show that the plane aborted and did not complete the mission.

Now for the official version of that first mission:

91st Bomb Group: "Breakfast was ordered for the combat crews at 0500 hours. Briefing, which began an hour later, was carried through without delay or unusual incident. No important changes were made in the original order. The target to be attacked was the submarine base at Brest and the 91st was one of three heavy bombardment groups to fly on this mission. Colonel Wray gave the combat crews an excellent pep talk. Everyone was in high spirits. There had been no delays such as had attended the fiasco four days before. At 0945 hours, the 14 aircraft began to take their positions at the end of the runway. The takeoff was scheduled for 1015 hours. The pilots began to warm up their engines. Finally, at the signal from the control tower, the first aircraft began to roar down the runway on the first operational mission of the 91st Group against Nazi-occupied Europe. At 1034 hours the last of the 14 aircraft became airborne."

Winchell Diary: "Ninety-first bomb group starts her trip along the glory road, her first combat mission. Were to have started on the author's birthday Nov. 4 but mission postponed. Took off in the morning on ship 124485 - the Memphis Belle.

"Everybody was tense and very anxious to get going. No opposition until we reached the French coast and target. Flak was moderately heavy but there were no enemy fighters to speak of. The ship, the squadron and the group came through with no casualties to personnel. During the run over the target everyone was keyed up, nervous and excited, naturally, our first taste of combat."

Verinis Diary: "Hardly got to bed when they got us up. We're finally off on our first combat mission. We bomb Brest, in France, a submarine base. Started off with 14 ships but six dropped out half way across because of gun trouble.

Made a turn after crossing the coast of France and ran into terrific anti-aircraft fire at our level, 20,000 feet. Three ships hit but none seriously damaged. Ours rocked a couple of times but came through without a scratch. Saw one Focke Wulf 190 go down in flames - shot down by the tail gunner of another ship. Most fighters sat in the distance, not daring to attack. Much damage to target but not completely destroyed. Home to base, tired but mighty happy. All ships returned. Used 500-pound bombs."

Leighton Diary: "The ack-ack that was meant for us burst mostly below and behind, so I didn't see too much of it. The plane bounced a few times, but all in all, the trip over the target was not too bad. A few fighters jumped on us on the way back and our group got three of them. I only saw one enemy aircraft and I couldn't get a shot at it. Came back to base happy and excited, feeling like we had won the war. The Memphis Belle did not have a scratch on it."

Debriefing: Lieutenant Bob Morgan: "Our first raid was to Brest. It was very successful, even though the weather was not the best. We encountered a bit of flak. Brest at that time was one of the hottest flak areas. We were at 20,000 feet, flying a formation we thought up ourselves - a pretty loose formation. There were some enemy fighters in the sky, but the groups just saw them. They made one or two feeble attacks at the end of the last group. We all came home with the idea that this was a snap."

91st Bomb Group: "The first combat mission of the 91st Group can hardly be judged an outstanding success. Six of the 14 aircraft that took off left the formation and returned early because some of their guns froze up after they had reached altitude."

Author's Note: The freeze-up of guns on many planes in the bitter cold of high altitude caused many of those planes to return to their bases before reaching their target. In the early day, gunners had instructions not to have a cartridge in the chamber, for safety sake. The guns would not fire until a cartridge had been jacked into the chamber by hand, operating the gun's bolt. But when the oil in the gun's action "froze" at high altitude, the gunner could not move the bolt. Later, gunners were instructed to have a cartridge in the chamber before reaching high altitude, and the firing of that shell would activate the automatic actions of the guns. Beyond that, in most cases, gunners were told to fire a short burst to test their guns before reaching the target area.

91st Bomb Group: The remaining eight flew behind the larger formation of the 306th. Group and was followed by the 301st Group. A small formation of Focke Wulf 190s attacked the formation of the 91st for a few minutes on the way to the target area. Sergeants W. G. Griddy and Thomas Hansbury were credited with destroying one German aircraft each. Moderate to intense anti-aircraft fire was encountered over the target and at one point along the French coast. Five of the eight aircraft returned to the base without serious difficulty. The beginning had been made and although it was not a perfect performance it was not too bad for the first attack"

November 8, 1942

The Eighth Air Force attacked German transportation targets at Lille, France, and the 91st Bomb Group was ordered to make a diversionary attack on a German air base at Abbeville, the two simultaneous attacks designed to confuse the German gunners and fighter groups. The 91st sent 12 planes, four from the Belle's 324th Squadron, with one of the four aborting. The Memphis Belle was not assigned to this mission.

St. Nazaire - November 9, 1942

"A raid none of my crew will forget." - Pilot Morgan

"I'll never have another run like that one." - Navigator Leighton

"The kind of raid Hollywood dreams up." - Co-pilot Verinis

"We were convinced that war can be hell." - Gunner Winchell

91st Bomb Group: "All four squadrons had to be called upon to furnish planes because so many of the aircraft had suffered damage the two previous days. The mission was against the German submarine base at St. Nazaire. The 91st was one of five groups to participate. Three groups were ordered to make the attack without fighter support at altitudes ranging from 7,500 feet to 10,000 feet, while the remaining two groups would move in to the attack immediately afterwards at 20,000 feet to 21,000 feet. The three groups attacking from the lower altitudes were ordered to fly at approximately 500 feet until they reached a point off the French coast which would barely enable them to gain their bombing altitude before reaching their target. The object was fairly obvious. The two high-flying groups would attract the attention of the German radio detection stations and lead the Germans to believe that these two groups constituted the entire attacking force. Meanwhile, the three low-flying groups would be able to reach the target without serious fighter opposition. As they would be making their bombing run at low altitude, it was expected they would be able to bomb with excellent results. The plan did not allow sufficient credit for the action of the German ground defenses.

"The 14 aircraft of the 91st Group took off between 0945 and 0955 hours. Everything went according to plan until the formation began its bombing run. Apparently the German fighters were outwitted completely. Even the German ground forces seemed fooled for a while.

"Unfortunately, the German gunners did not remain in a state of indecision very long and just before our aircraft released their bomb loads, they opened up with every conceivable type of anti-aircraft weapon."

Verinis Diary: "Holes were appearing in the plane all around us and one directly beneath me. Many narrow escapes on our ship but none wounded. Other ships not so fortunate. Some fatalities and many wounded. All ships returned completely riddled but still flying. One of the groups following us to the target lost three planes. Target completely destroyed by terrific bombing. Altitude good for effective bombing but well near suicide for us. Landed at Exeter because of fuel shortage."

Winchell Diary: "It seemed as if every flak gun in Germany was there to meet us. Don't know how one ship survived, let alone the whole group. Our ship came out of it with 40 holes and we were fortunate compared to some. When it was all over we were convinced that war can be hell."

Leighton Diary: "Sighted the coast of France about one o'clock and we were right on course, headed for the docks at St. Nazaire, not a cloud in the sky. Started our bombing run and the flak started bursting. It seemed like every shell was going off in our bomb bay. One barrage was following us down the run. I could see every burst getting closer and moving in at two o'clock. Vince Evans did a swell job and laid our five 1,000-pounders right in there. Evasive action didn't seem to stop the flak. We were soon out of there and headed for home, over the water. Landed at Exeter about 5:30, completely tired and plenty shaky."

Morgan Debriefing: "We came down to France outside the water area down low. We were almost on the deck. We came straight into St. Nazaire and then began to climb to 8,500 feet. The main idea was to surprise the Germans. It did surprise the pursuits, which never got up, but it didn't surprise the flak guns. Our ship got 62 holes and we got off better than anyone else. We went back to St. Nazaire four times, but a mission at such low altitude has never been run again. We learned a lot."

91st Bomb Group: "This mission did not produce all the results which had been anticipated by some of the officers who planned it. The Flying Fortress had been designed to fly at altitudes safely above all but the heaviest anti-aircraft guns.
"On this particular mission an attempt had been made to out-maneuver the German radio detection system and German fighter aircraft, but this was accomplished only by neglecting the margin of safety in altitude. The Fortress had been exposed to murderous fire from the ground. The 91st suffered less than either of the other two groups, one of which lost three planes. Every aircraft in the formation sustained some battle damage."

November 10, 1942

Author's Note: We remember that the group had landed at Exeter, an RAF base, because the planes were low on fuel after the long run. One of the Memphis Belle's engines was running rough and after landing it was discovered that flak had hit the oil line. But even after repairing the oil line the engine refused to start for the flight home to Bassingbourn. We remember how the pilot, Bob Morgan, with only flight engineer Levi Dillon aboard, managed to take off with three engines and then started the balky engine by windmilling the propeller in flight. Verinis, the co-pilot, remembered a bit more.

Verinis Diary: "Finally got the engine re-started after five hours but in near darkness and fog, combined with nightfall to make visibility near impossible. Our good luck held up and we found the field just before what would have been too late. Landed and thanked the Lord for guiding us home. That flight turned out to be the most exciting of all, a close call."

Leighton Diary: "Just barely made it back as we could hardly see the ground."

November 14, 1942

91st Bomb Group: Bad weather and the necessity to repair battle damage to planes ruled out any missions for several days after that November 9 raid to St. Nazaire. On November 14, a mission was scheduled for La Pallice where the Germans were building new submarine pens. However, the bomber formations found La Pallice covered with clouds and went back to hit St. Nazaire, a secondary target, with good results. The Memphis Belle was not assigned to this raid.

St. Nazaire - November 17, 1942

Morgan Debriefing: "This was the day on which the Memphis Belle received her first real 'spanking.'"

91st Bomb Group: "The assigned target was St. Nazaire. Twenty aircraft were ordered to attack several buildings which were described as storage sheds for torpedoes, ammunition and spare parts. The first aircraft took off at 0915 hours. Six of the aircraft returned to base because of mechanical failures. The remaining 14 attacked the target at 1245 hours and dropped 140 of the 500-pound bombs from approximately 18,000 feet. German defenses were very active. Anti-aircraft fire was moderate to intense and at times very accurate. Between 90 and 100 Focke Wulf 190s came up to attack the formation but, fortunately, most of their fire was directed against the formations of other groups. Only six were damaged and only two members of the group were wounded. Considering the intensity of the German defenses, the results of the bombing were pretty good and many of the bombs were seen to explode in the target area, some of which were very close to the aiming point. During the course of the encounters with the German fighters, the gunners of the 91st claimed five enemy aircraft destroyed, two probably destroyed and eight damaged."

Leighton Diary: "We were the number-two ship in the last flight. No action over the coast of France but on the bomb run Evans lost his gyroscope so he targeted on the No. 3 ship. [This meant Leighton watched No. 3 and released his bombs the moment he saw the other plane drop theirs.]

"Not much flak over the target. Dropped ten 500-pound bombs at 20,000 feet. Ran into Fw.190s on the way home. The fight lasted about 20 minutes, but we maintained a good tight formation which was too tough for Germans to crack. Quinlan and McNally, each got one. I took a few shots at one but he was about 1,000 yards away. The Memphis Belle got a big hole in the left wing and a .30 caliber bullet in the number three prop. Spitfires met us at the coast after the fight was over and escorted us home. Went to London the next day on a 48-hour pass. Gordy and I saw the sights. Big Ben, Parliament, Westminster Abbey, etc. Had a swell time."

Verinis Diary: "Just as I expected, I didn't get to bed until 1:30 a.m. so naturally they got me up at 5:30 for another raid to St. Nazaire. This time we were after the oil storage tanks and ammunition dump. Peaceful trip going in. Bombed from 20,000 feet so flak didn't bother us much. Hit target and set it afire. Then came the storm. Focke Wulf 190s and 110s all over the place. Attacked us for 20 minutes. We could see them peeling off and coming at us. Our gunners got two of them but we were riddled with holes, lost a propeller and got a hole shot in our wing. Dillon got hit, a grazing blow in the leg - just a scratch.

"Finally sighted the English coast and here came the Spitfires to protect us from the target home. A bit late. Off to London tomorrow for a couple of days of rest."

Winchell Diary: "Back to St. Nazaire again on mission number three, by a different route this time. Nothing doing in the way of opposition until we neared the target. Were picked up by quite a few enemy fighters, Fw.190s, just before the target. Intense flak again over the target, 'Flak City.' 'Bombs away,' then chased by fighters all the way to the Channel. Quinlan got a Focke Wulf, as did McNally who flew the ball turret. Six enemy planes down for the day, no losses on our side. Ship okay, crew okay. Crew members same as first two trips except Sergeant H. M. McNally flew in Scotty's place. Scotty sick with a cold.

Author's Note: Crew members with colds were not allowed to fly, since, at high altitudes, it was necessary to breathe oxygen, which was difficult to do with a stuffy nose. McNally was a regular crew member on the plane "Jack the Ripper" which was not assigned to this mission.

"We are becoming somewhat accustomed to combat missions. The flak scared hell out of us but the brush with the fighters was rather fun. When you fly through flak you just sit tight and hope. Fighters you can fight back at."

November 18, 1942

Author's Note: The 91st Bomb Group took part in a mission on November 18 to La Pallic. The mission was plagued by bad weather. Bombing results weren't satisfactory. Five out of 17 bombers from the group that took off, aborted. When they returned to England, the weather was so bad two of them collided in the air as they attempted to land. It was a miracle that neither pilot lost control of his plane and both landed safely with only minor damage. The Belle was not assigned to this mission.

November 22, 1942

Author's Note: The 91st Bomb Group took part in an attempt to bomb the German submarine base at Lorient, France, with St. Nazaire and Brest as secondary targets. Seventeen planes from the group took off but after flying to France found all three targets socked in by clouds. They were forced to return without dropping any bombs. The Belle was not assigned to this mission.

November 23, 1942

Author's Note: This was a day that could be described only in terms like "drama," "tragedy" and "disaster." A day on which the Memphis Belle may have been lucky by being unlucky, saved from disaster by engine trouble which forced the pilot to turn the Belle around and head for home before reaching the target.

The target was St. Nazaire, once more, that vital submarine base the Germans were defending with such fanatic effort. Due to battle damage from previous raids the 91st was able to put only ten planes in the air. Five of these aborted and a sixth apparently was lost over the English Channel, leaving four lonely planes out there.

Their loneliness became stark tragedy when they failed to rendezvous with other groups and found themselves heading for the target utterly alone. Major Harold C. Smelser, squadron commander, apparently made the decision to go on when he obviously would have been justified in turning back. It was well-known what kind of punishment Germans could dish out to small groups flying alone. The German pilots this day must have licked their lips in glee when they saw the pitiful, tiny formation bravely boring on for the bombing attack.

Smelser might have thought, or hoped, that the other groups would show up before they reached the target. In any case, he paid with his life and the lives of his crew for making that "into the valley" decision. One of those crew members was none other than Lieutenant Duane Jones, the pilot who had been the first to take off for the 91st on November 7, that first raid. Smelser's plane was last seen, smoking and struggling along on two engines. Two more of the four planes barely managed to cross the English coast before crash landing, heavily damaged and with wounded and dead crew members on board. Only a single plane, that of an indomitable little redhead, Lieutenant C. E. Cliburn, made it home to Bassingbourn.

The 91st, licking its wounds and hampered by bad weather, would fly no more missions until December 6. Major Claude E. Putnam was assigned to replace Smelser as squadron commander.

THE MEMPHIS BELLE

As the writer of the 91st Bomb Group's official narrative history put it, "November 24 was probably the gloomiest day the 91st had spent since its arrival in England. The loss of three of its aircraft and more than 25 of its personnel produced an extremely heavy reaction among all personnel. This was not just a question of morale as much as it was the fact that practically everyone in the airdrome had lost a personal friend."

Lille - December 6, 1942

91st Bomb Group: "Target, the locomotive factory and steel mill at Lille, France. Three aircraft aborted. The remaining 18 proceeded to the target area and bombed at 1215 hours. Opposition from German ground defense rather intense and many of their shells burst too close for comfort. Several formations of German fighters attacked the Fortresses but, fortunately for the 91st, most of their attacks were directed at the other two groups. Confirmed five enemy planes shot down. Nine aircraft received battle damage. The results of the bombing were not too good. Out of approximately 150 bombs dropped, only six were identified as bursting on the aiming point. Short and to the right of the target. A meeting was held after the mission to determine the cause of the relatively poor showing but no decision was reached."

Leighton Diary: "Jumped by enemy fighters shortly after entering France and since they were coming in at eleven o'clock. I was able to get a crack at a few of them. A large number of Spitfires met us over the target and were a big help. I saw a B-17 go down in flames. Only one guy got out. No holes in the Memphis Belle."

Winchell Diary: "Our first crack at an inland target. Lille. Went in over Calais and came out over the immortal Dunkirk. Quite a few enemy fighters and flak over the coast and at the target, of course. How I hate that stuff. All in all, it wasn't as bad as St. Nazaire. Oddly enough, the fighters weren't nearly as persistent or tough. Maybe I'm getting used to it, if that's possible."

Verinis Diary: "Went in at 20,000 feet with 500-pound bombs. Fighters from the coast to the target. Scored some hits on the target. One of the other groups lost two ships. We came out unscathed."

THE MEMPHIS BELLE

December 12, 1942

91st Bomb Group: "The primary target was a large German plane assembly park at Romilly sur Seine, near Paris. Fifteen planes from the 91st were assigned to the mission, but when they found the target covered with clouds they turned to the secondary target at Rouen. Here only a few holes were found in the clouds, giving a few planes a chance to drop their bombs but most of the planes brought their bombs home." [The Memphis Belle was not on this mission.]

Romilly sur Seine - December 20, 1942

91st Bomb Group: "Target, Romilly sur Seine. Some of the combat crews were a little uneasy when they learned of our objective, not only because it meant flying over enemy territory for two-and-a-half hours, but also because they had been briefed for this target several times already and had, so far, been unable to reach it. The mission was uneventful until the formation had passed Paris. From then on the aircraft of the 91st were intermittently engaged by formations of German fighters that proved to be the longest and stiffest air encounter the combat crews had yet experienced. Twenty-five of the German aircraft were claimed as destroyed by combat crews of the 91st but, in turn, two of the group's aircraft were shot down. Several of the crew members were seen to bail out. While all the remaining aircraft returned safely to England, every one of them sustained some battle damage. Major Bruce Barton's aircraft was so badly damaged he got no further than Fletching, just inside the coast. With his ailerons gone and an eight-foot hole in his vertical fin, he crash-landed in a meadow. The only additional casualties were two sheep and one rabbit. His plane was so badly damaged it was broken up for salvage.
"The results of the mission were generally good and certainly better than the average of previous missions. Many of the bombs took effect in the hangar and dispersal area. The loss of two aircraft and their crews was quite a blow to the 401st Squadron, but some satisfaction was derived from the fact that the mission had been a success."

THE MEMPHIS BELLE

Leighton Diary: "On the way to Romilly we flew over Rouen where we were attacked by about 25 German fighters. They were all coming at the nose so I got in a lot of shots. Bob said I got one, but I was firing so fast I didn't have time to notice. We continued southwest, just missing Paris. I could see the Eiffel Tower very clearly. After bombing the target we headed northwest, back to Paris, over Beauvais and then back to the coast. We were under constant attack for about two hours. I never thought I would get that many shots and I shot over 700 rounds. I saw two B-17s go down in front of us. One went straight down in a dive, with its tail shot off and we saw only one guy get out of that one. The other one went down in a glide and we saw seven guys get out of that one but they opened their chutes too quickly and we could see the Germans machine-gunning them as they floated down. When they open fire at you head-on, it looks as if their whole plane is exploding. I was surprised that I wasn't in the least frightened, but I sure felt helpless when I was out of ammunition once and when my gun jammed once. I don't mind the fighters at all but the flak scares the dickens out of me. The fighters like that nose attack, which is O.K. with me. No holes in the Memphis Belle."

Cecil Scott, ball turret gunner, in a 1943 interview: "On the Romilly sur Seine raid about 300 fighters attacked us in relays. They circled us like Indians. They started attacking from all directions at once. I thought I got two but I didn't get credit for them. Practically all our ammunition was gone when we got back. But as many times as they shot at us, we didn't get a single bullet hole in the plane that trip."

Verinis Diary: "We were supposed to have a fighter escort on this mission, but I didn't see it until we were practically home. We were attacked by Fw.190s from the time we hit France 'til we got out, an hour and five minutes later. The sky was full of them, more than I have ever seen before. Our group shot down 19 Fw's, our ship got two. [The official list showed one plane destroyed by the Memphis Belle that day, Vince Evans getting credit for it.]

Winchell Diary: "The briefing said this one was going to be tough. It was tough, plenty tough. One long, nerve-wracking 'dog fight' all the way in and all the way out. Saw two Forts go down. A sickening sight. As we flew further and further I thought the bomb bay doors would never open. Finally, 'Bombs away,' and we turned to fight our way out. Finally, the English Channel with practically no ammunition left. Not much flak but more fighters than I ever want to see in one day."

Bob Morgan, from a 1943 debriefing: "First one squadron hit us and then another, and another. We were shot at on the way to the target, over the target and then on the way out. By the time it was over, some of the Germans had attacked us, landed and refueled, picked up some ammunition and were up attacking us again. For one hour and fifty-eight minutes they followed us. I never saw so many attacks in my life.

"We learned one lesson that day, to keep our eyes open. This was one mission when the Germans sneaked up on us without our seeing them. Two German fighters came in at two o'clock high and I still don't know where they came from. The first tip-off I had was when our top turret gunner began firing his guns. We were caught asleep that time and if they had been able to shoot straight we would have been shot down. We hit the hangars and the depot. We wrecked 100 German fighter planes on the ground and we hit a German officers mess at lunch time. We heard later that we also blew up their cellar full of cognac."

91st Bomb Group: "By the middle of December, all the personnel of the group realized they were pawns in a great experiment being tried by the Army Air Forces. Daylight bombing had long since been given up by both the German Air Force and the Royal Air Force. With new methods, the Eighth Air Force was attempting to do that which had been accepted as a failure by both our allies and their enemies. The members of the group even referred to themselves as 'guinea pigs.' But on this occasion they had fought the Luftwaffe for more than an hour and, in addition to bombing their target successfully, they had given more than they had been compelled to take. Maybe these men were guinea pigs but they were doing what others had failed to do."

Author's Note: It was also about the middle of December when the 91st Bomb Group, along with other groups, realized they had a bit of pie on their collective faces. All the elaborate security measures that had been in effect on mission days, with the gates closed, the traffic jams, the blaring public address system shouting orders that could be heard even in the English villages surrounding the base, were actually proving to be a tip-off that a mission was being prepared rather than a security measure. It would have had to be a very stupid spy stationed anywhere near the base who would have failed to know what was going on. The men of the crews, and even intelligence officers, were suddenly seeing evidence that the Germans were not surprised by the raids but seemed to have been, somehow, tipped off that the Americans were coming. As a result, the intelligence people suddenly switched orders. On mission days the gates remained open, traffic continued to flow and the loudspeaker messages were carefully monitored to keep them from disclosing information abut the missions. Even the departure of the planes would not, necessarily, be a tip-off since the group often flew practice missions on days when they flew no bombing raids. Christmas came. The 91st flew no raids from December 20 to December 30, mostly because of bad weather. The group did fly big practice missions on December 23 and 24 over England. On Christmas Eve, Colonel Wray, group commander, said all officers and men would have Christmas Day off, except those needed to man vital stations. With tongue in cheek, the 91st historian wrote: "Many of the men had already begun their celebration and, needless to say, not a few were barely able to appreciate the fine Christmas dinner."

Lorient - December 30, 1942

Author's Note: Another navigational error, more tragedy. That pesky Brest peninsula sticking out there to make pilots believe they were seeing their friendly old England when they were actually seeing the coast of France bristling with German anti-aircraft guns.

91st Bomb Group, Summary: Target, the submarine pens at Lorient. The weather, good. Only two aircraft aborted. "Shortly after reaching enemy-occupied territory, formations of German fighters began to attack. Over the target they withdrew and the formations came under an intense anti-aircraft barrage. As soon as the formations were beyond the range of the anti-aircraft guns, the fighters returned to the attack. A large percentage of the bombs fell in the target area, and several of the bombs exploded on, or very close to, the submarine pens. However, the reinforced concrete pens were so strong that even the 2,000-pound bombs which made direct hits failed to destroy them. [It was said that the Germans were building the roofs and walls of the pens up to eight feet thick.] Many subsidiary buildings located around the pens were destroyed."

Leighton Diary: "Bob was sick but Jim did a swell job. The wind blew us off course and some of the navigators had their heading off, so when we got back up north they thought the northwest corner of France was the southwest tip of England. They started to let down right over Brest. Their flak and fighters got two more B-17s. No one got out. Just off the coast I saw another B-17 go down in flames. The bastards were sending out radio signals just like at Land's End. Nevertheless, some of the navigators caught hell for the mistake."

Verinis Diary: "Nobody shot down over the target but as we went out to sea we had a 100 mph head wind. Everyone thought we were back over England and got careless. Bill Bloodgood got over some flak batteries and was shot down in flames. It took us five hours to come back home compared to only two going out."

Author's Note: The 401st Squadron had been in the lead that day, and it was this squadron's navigators who fouled up, due to that head wind. Major Myers, flying the lead plane, may not have been responsible for the error but it cost him his life. He did realize the error in time to order the formation to veer sharply away from the ack-ack batteries and head for the real England, but not before his ship had been heavily damaged and he was fatally wounded. His warning did save the trailing formations, including the 324th, with the Memphis Belle.

Aside from Bloodgood's plane being shot down, said the 91st narrative, almost every plane in the formation was damaged, two so heavily they barely made it to Exeter, the closest British landing base. Major Myers died a few minutes after his plane landed.

The results of this tragic error led to a change in plans for future missions. Instead of flying with flight plans only to the target, and then getting home as best they could, from now on all navigators would be given complete flight plans to the target AND RETURN. Beyond that, all navigators were warned that they must continue plotting their courses on their own instead of simply following the lead planes. Said the 91st narrative, "The loss of Major Myers was a severe blow to the morale of the 401st Squadron which had already taken the heaviest losses in the group." Myers was the third squadron leader, out of four in the group, to be lost.

THE MEMPHIS BELLE

January 1, 1943

91st Bomb Group: "To many officers and men of the 91st Group, the New Year began almost as a nightmare. The party held in the officer's club the night before had been too much for many of the officers. The mess hall appeared almost deserted at breakfast."

St. Nazaire - January 3, 1943

"I could hear flak slapping the side of the ship like kicking the door of a Model T Ford."

Bombardier Evans Debriefing

Author's Note: The Memphis Belle not only led the Group but the entire bomber formation, promoted to this responsible job because Charles Leighton, the Belle's navigator, had not fallen into the Brest trap on the previous raid and because Vince Evans, the Belle's bombardier, had been doing some of that "pickle barrel" bombing. Morgan and his crew repaid the trust by turning in one of the best jobs of bombing ever for the group. Evans would be awarded an Air Medal for the accuracy of his bombing.

91st Bomb Group: "The first mission of the year was against the torpedo sheds and submarine pens at St. Nazaire. Sixteen aircraft took off, with three aborting. The remaining 13 dropped their bombs, scoring several hits on the aiming point. This was the best job of bombing done by the 91st until this time and was certainly better on this day than that of any other group in the formation. Two crew members from the 91st were killed, ten wounded. Lieutenant Anderson's plane, from the 323rd Squadron, failed to return and is believed to have been shot down near the target.

Evans Debriefing: "Our target was a building we were after that day. It was a small target but, we were told, it was very important and we were glad to lead the Eighth Bomb Command. As we turned to make a run on the target, which I knew by its relation to other buildings, we ran into a strong head wind which we had not anticipated. That caused the plane to go wide on the initial aiming point and also caused our ground speed to drop to 85 or 90 miles an hour. So we were sitting up there like clay pigeons. I told Captain Morgan and Major Putnam, who was riding along as wing commander, that it was going to be a long run. They said to settle down on it. We were anxious to get it right. We had a two and a half minute run. The usual one is 55 seconds. We were really sweating it out the last few seconds of that run. The flak was terrific. I could see the flashes of the anti-aircraft fire through my bomb sights and an occasional fighter crossing underneath. We had a lot of holes in the ship and one tire was blown to hell. Captain Morgan asked me when the hell I was going to drop the bombs and I told him to take it easy.

"I put my cross hairs where I knew the target to be, although I couldn't make it out at that distance. The second I released the bombs I knew they were going to be good. The bombardier can usually tell. They were squarely on the target. [Photographs showed later that Evans' bombs missed the center of the target by less than ten feet.]

Leighton Diary: "Big raid on St. Nazaire today., with super-duper navigator Leighton leading the whole group. Good weather made the trip down a snap. As we turned towards the target we were a little left off course so we rolled over a bit. Turned over target just in time but we still got flak. A strong head wind made our ground speed about 96 mph. Flak started to burst just before we went into the bomb run and towards the end it was pretty hot. Those bastards down there are pretty good shots. The group over to the left of us was getting the hell knocked out of them. As we turned back over the water the fighters jumped us right away. We sure had a fight on our hands. Most of them came in on the nose, but Major Putnam [Apparently Putnam was flying the plane at this point.] did such a swell job of evasion so we came through without a scratch. We landed at St. Eval in southwest England with a flat tire, stayed overnight and came back home the next day, bringing with us Lt. Fischer. Fischer's plane was sure a mess. A direct hit by a 20 mm shell had blown it apart. Made me sick to see it. Lieutenant Burke, Fisher's navigator, was hit, too. So that just leaves Carr, Kurt, Leisure and myself out of the eight navigators who started with the 324th."

Verinis Diary: "Off today to our old friend, St. Nazaire. Ran into heavy flak over the target. One B-17 hit in bomb bay and exploded. Fighters then jumped us in fierce attacks. The toughest

bunch of fighter pilots we've met to date. They crippled Ed
Gaitley's ship and swarmed in for the kill. Good old Ed outsmarted
them and went out to sea. Biggest losses for us to date. We lost
nine bombers. We can't stand trips like that too often. Our ship
was shot at plenty but we managed to dodge most of their shots.
Only a few holes. Many wounded on other ships."

Winchell Diary: "As we approached the target, all hell broke
loose. Heavy flak and fighters at the same time. First time the
fighters have come in right through their own flak at us. Bored in
close, too. Saw a direct hit by flak in a bomb bay of a B-17 in the
group behind us. The ship was blown to bits, a horrible sight.
Over the target now and caught in the apex of a solid cone of flak,
but the fighters are still boring through it. Captain Gaitley's ship
falling behind with its number two engine on fire. Fischer's ship,
the Jersey Bounce, dropping down to cover. [If this was true,
Fischer apparently paid for his Good Samaritan deed by getting
himself shot up. Pilots had orders not to drop out of formation to
help a crippled buddy but some did it anyway.] To date, for flak
alone, the worst was St. Nazaire, at 10,000 feet, on November 9.
For fighters alone, the worst was Romilly on December 20. For
flak and fighters combined, the worst was St. Nazaire today.
Sergeant Cornwell flew with us today as nose gunner as Lieutenant
Evans was lead bombardier."

January 4, 1943

91st Bomb Group: "Coca Cola was offered for sale today
for the first time. This Coca Cola, concocted in London, is not quite
up to the standards we have been accustomed to. However, it is
universally hoped that the English will learn how to manufacture this
product to our satisfaction. All those desiring to purchase Coca
Cola had to bring their own canteen cups or other containers.
Bottles were too scarce to be allowed out of the PX."

Lille -January - 13, 1943

Author's note: Perhaps the best lesson the crew members
learned on this day, after a raid on the Fives-Lille Locomotive
Works at Lille, France, is that if you are superstitious and believe in
jinxes, keep your dad-gum mouth shut.

THE MEMPHIS BELLE

At the briefing that morning the men of the 91st discovered that 13 ships from the 91st would be flying on this 13th day of the month. Only Lieutenant Felton of the 322nd Squadron mentioned it. His plane was the only one severely damaged that day, with three of his crew being wounded.

Leighton Diary: "Easy raid on Lille   I was lead navigator again and Colonel Wray went with us. Everything went pretty much as scheduled, except our bombing run was longer than usual. Evans did OK. Two B-17s went down in front of us and it looked to me like a Focke Wulf 190 crashed into it. Four guys got out. This makes my eighth raid and still O.K. None of our crew had been hurt yet, either. We are about the only crew still on the field and still intact. [This was not quite true since Sergeant Dillon, flight engineer, had been transferred to another squadron after the fourth raid and Lieutenant Verinis, co-pilot, had been given his own plane and was flying it for the first time on this raid.]

Winchell Diary: "Memphis Belle is the flagship again today. Lille should be fairly easy but you can't be too sure. Passed over Calais on the way in. Light, inaccurate flak at St. Omer. Rather light flak over the target, surprising but gratifying. 'Bombs away,' and here come the 'Focke-Wolves.' The rat race didn't last long and here we are over Dunkirk, on the way home. The Belle came home with many a hole this trip but crew okay."

Verinis Diary: "I flew in the No. 2 spot on the colonel's wing. A very good one, too. Flak was light and the fighters busied themselves with the other groups. They didn't care to attack our tight little formation. However, Lieutenant Felton, flying on the tail end, was hit badly. He had three wounded on board."

Author's Note: Verinis began flying his own plane on this mission but we will continue using excerpts from his diary when he flew on the same missions as the Belle, and where his remarks may be pertinent.

91st Bomb Group: "This mission was more to the liking of the combat crews as the briefing was relatively late and the aircraft did not take off until 1235 hours. Lieutenant Felton's aircraft was the only one to suffer any material damage on the mission. Three members of his crew were wounded. However, other groups participating in the raid lost three aircraft. Enemy fighters which came up to oppose the formation concentrated most of their fire on the other group. In this respect, the 91st was extremely lucky. [The 91st was known for its very tight formations, giving the gunners overlapping fire power. It was believed this was one reason fighter pilots sometimes shied away from the 91st and attacked groups flying in looser formations.]

January 16, 1943

91st Bomb Group: "The station soccer team played a very exciting game with the 70th Battalion Welsh Regiment. The local boys did fairly well during the first part of the game, but in the latter part they appeared to be rather seriously outclassed. The final score was five to one in favor of the Welshmen."

January 17, 1943

91st Bomb Group: "Authority has just been received by Colonel Wray to grant seven days leave to all personnel who have completed three or more months in the European Theater of Operations. However, Colonel Wray decided against this. The 91st is very short on personnel and, as a result, seven-day leaves cannot be given to members of the air echelon. In view of these facts, Colonel Wray stated that he could not justify himself in granting seven-day leaves for ground personnel, inasmuch as similar privileges could not be accorded to the flying personnel." [The shortage was due to the high number of killed and wounded, plus the lack of replacements.]

January 18, 1943

91st Bomb Group: "After the show [presented by a Royal Air Force troupe in the base movie theater with 900 members of the 91st attending] an air raid alert was sounded. Several German aircraft could be heard flying over our airdrome, apparently on their way to London. After a few minutes you could see the flash of anti-aircraft guns and occasional dull flashes of bombs exploding to the south. It was a beautiful moonless night. The progress of the entire raid on London could be witnessed from the vicinity of the officers mess."

THE MEMPHIS BELLE

January 21, 1943

91st Bomb Group: "The number of aircraft available for service in the group has been seriously reduced because of the lack of spare parts and tools. Seven of the group's aircraft are out of service because of damage to the outer wing sections. Replacements have arrived. However, the group has not been able to procure a reamer needed to prepare the holes to receive the pins that hold the wings to the main plane body. These reamers have been on order for more than four months, but not a one is available in the United Kingdom. Major Stogner, our group engineering officer, has now placed an order with a firm in Sheffield, to have one made to order. It is anticipated that the reamer will arrive in a week or 10 days."

Author's Note: Between January 13 and 23, the 91st Bomb Group flew no missions. The group was alerted for missions at least four times, but each time the takeoff was cancelled because of bad weather, or for other reasons. On each of these alerts, while waiting for the word that they could either go or stand down, the crew had nothing to do but, as the 91st narrative said, "to stand around getting nervous and fidgety." This is why men dreaded the cancelled missions almost as much as the real ones.

Lorient - January 23, 1943

Author's Note: On this day the crew of the Memphis Belle would experience sheer drama and the ship itself would suffer its worst damage to date. Only six planes would be flying in the 91st formation - a formula for disaster. It came.

91st Bomb Group: "Target, the German submarine base at Lorient. The 91st was able to dispatch only 13 aircraft. This mission was one of the worst. The weather was bad and three of the planes became separated from the rest and returned to the base. Of the remaining 10, two had mechanical difficulties and returned. At least two more of the planes became separated from the group and attached themselves to the rear of another formation."

Morgan Debriefing: "One of the other groups was over the target first. Through the flak the fighters were beginning to attack us because we were the smallest of the four groups. They concentrated on us. For about 22 minutes they gave us hell. Most of the attacks were coming from the front. One Focke Wulf 190, attacking straight in from twelve o'clock, was heading right into us. One of us would have to move. The usual procedure would be to dive. I couldn't do that because another group was right below us, so I pulled her straight up. The shells that were intended for our nose got our tail. I didn't know what had happened until Sergeant Quinlan started giving it to me, play by play.

"'Chief, the tail is hit, the whole back end is shot off. Chief, it's blazing! The whole tail is leaving the plane.'!

"There was silence then. I asked for a report. Nothing happened. Finally, I heard Quinlan's voice again. 'Chief, it's still on fire! There goes another piece!'

"Another silence for a minute and then Quinlan said, 'Chief, the fire has gone out.'

"I don't need to tell you that was the sweetest music I had ever heard.

"I climbed up to look back to see what had happened. It looked like we had no tail at all. I got back into the cockpit and flew for two hours back to the base. It was tough flying and tougher than that to set her down. The elevators were damaged so badly that the controls jammed.

"But we somehow managed to get down safely.

"That was a close call."

Leighton Diary: "We were the lead ship for our group again today. Everything was O.K. until we reached the target. Then the fighters and flak began to hit us. The group ahead of us turned off the target so we turned off, also. Then the fighters really came at us and we just about got our tail shot off. Fischer got shot up bad. He had one dead man on board and two wounded. We had to have a whole new tail put on the plane, also a new nose."

Author's Note: Leighton explained later about the nose:
"We had the extra gunner along that day because we were the lead plane and the extra gunner was to take Evans' place as a gunner while Evans was busy with the bomb sight. But after the bombing run Evans was firing one of the nose guns and Sergeant Markle [the extra gunner] was manning the other one. I was sitting there with nothing to do but when all those fighters began coming in at us, I remembered we carried an extra .30 caliber machine gun on

board. They had a rubber plug in a round hole right in the center of the Plexiglas nose. You were supposed to push that rubber plug out and then you could just stick that little gun out through the hole and shoot. But that plug was frozen in and I couldn't get it out. I guess I was excited. I was trying to knock it out and I hit it so hard I knocked a big hole in the Plexiglas. After that, we almost froze from the cold wind coming in through the hole."

Winchell Diary: "Not much doing until we passed over the 'Hun' airdrome just north of Lorient, but after that, wow, the usual hell in large quantities. The Belle was hit by 20 mm fire from a German fighter. The fin and rudder in tatters. Quinlan was fortunate, only dazed for a few minutes. Upon landing, we of the crew were O.K. but the tail of the ship was hanging in shreds."

Verinis Diary: "Easy going in but what a fight coming out. We had only six ships so they picked on us, coming in with head-on attacks so close we had to get out of their way to avoid collisions. I had some bullet holes, one right between me and the co-pilot. Phil Fisher's plane badly hit. Many wounded on board. Phil got glass splinters in both eyes from a burst of a 20 mm cannon shell which shattered the cockpit glass. It seems he might lose sight in one eye. Seven ships lost, all by the 303rd Group. One of the roughest raids to date. When will it stop?"

January 24-February 3

91st Bomb Group: "Lieutenant Fischer was unable to bring his plane back to base and was compelled to make a crash landing at the RAF airdrome at Little Horwood. The mission was not really a credit to the group."

Author's Note: The Memphis Belle crew flew no missions from January 23 to February 4. The 91st Bomb Group took part in a mission to Wilhelmshaven, Germany, on January 27.

January 25, 1943

91st Bomb Group: "The group was alerted for an attack on Ghent. The planes took off, but before they had reached an altitude of 5,000 feet, the mission was cancelled and the aircraft recalled. The effect upon morale was to further deepen the depression.

"The mail situation continues to be badly snarled. A vast majority of the officers and men report that they have not received letters and packages which they know have been addressed to them. Colonel Wray addressed a letter to First Base Post Office requesting a re-check."

Author's Note: The explanation for the bad mail service was that in November of 1942, when American forces invaded North Africa, several of the Air Force units in England were sent to North Africa to support the invasion. The 91st Bomb Group had been scheduled to be sent to North Africa, too, and the Army Post Office was instructed to send all 91st mail to the North Africa Post Office. Then, when the orders were changed, with the 91st remaining in England, mail continued to be sent to North Africa. It was months before the snafu was corrected. Months later, when the lost mail was finally found and redirected to England, the packages from home were badly battered from the back-and-forth handling and any edibles, such as cakes and cookies, were stale or smashed.

January 26, 1943

91st Bomb Group: "Members of the Intelligence Section have just completed arrangements with the commanding officer at the Duxford airdrome for an inspection of captured German aircraft on display there. There are approximately eight German aircraft, several of the latest models, several in flyable condition. The combat crews are anxious to go over and examine them. Weather permitting, the commanding officer at Duxford has promised to give each group of officers and men a demonstration of the flying characteristics of these planes."

January 27, 1943

Author's Note: Up to this date, all bombing missions by the Eighth Air Force had been on German-held bases and installations in France or other occupied territory. But, on January 27, bomber groups were alerted for their first raid on Germany itself. The target Bremen, with secondary targets at Wilhelmshaven and Emden. The

Memphis Belle was not assigned to this mission. She was still under repair.

91st Bomb Group: "Everyone who attended the briefing realized that, sooner or later, they would have to attack Germany proper, as that was the real stronghold of the enemy. Clouds obscured the primary target, so all the B-17 formation turned off to attack the secondary target at Wilhelmshaven. Here they found more cloud cover and this, together with a smoke screen, made aiming difficult. Some of the bombs landed in the vicinity of the docks and it is believed they did considerable damage. However, some of the bombs landed in the water and probably did no more than kill some German fish. There was some confusion as the formation left the target. As the leading group was unable to drop its bombs at Wilhelmshaven, the air commander led the entire formation of four groups back across Emden so they could bomb the target there. This produced some ill feeling on the part of a few combat crews. Fourteen planes dropped their bombs on the target at Wilhelmshaven and the remaining two dropped their bombs on the target at Emden."

"Many of the pilots reported that the German pilots did not appear to be as experienced as the ones they had been encountering over France, and many of them did not press home their attacks.

"When the combat crews returned to Bassingbourn, they were met by a host of newspaper correspondents. [Obviously because this was the first raid on Germany proper.]. Many newsmen were rather considerate but others became so eager for anything that would make a good story that it became literally necessary to corral them and keep them away from the interrogation tables."

January 29, 1943

91st Bomb Group: "Today a meeting was held at which all unit commanders, medical officers, first sergeants and medical enlisted men were in attendance. Among other problems discussed was the need for more cleanliness in the kitchens, barracks area and latrines. Matters of personal hygiene were also discussed."

January 30, 1943

91st Bomb Group: "The sky was dull gray with fast flying low clouds. There was a good deal of rain and the wind velocity was higher than it has ever been since we arrived in the British Isles. The aircraft which were parked in unprotected areas had to be tied down but, even so, some of them suffered damage. The wind and rain also inflicted damage on buildings and other installations. Under such conditions it was impossible to attempt anything."

Emden - February 4, 1943

Author's Note: At 8:30 a.m. Captain Bob Morgan cranked his engines for the takeoff. Today there was a special air of tension and excitement among the members of his crew, just as there had been on their very first mission back on November 7 They were taking off on their first combat mission into Germany itself.

Prior to this day, they had bombed only German-held targets in France, but everyone had known that, sooner or later, they would have to hit the German homeland. Everyone also knew that the Germans would fight that much harder to protect their homeland. It would be a rough trip.

The weather over the Bassingbourn airdrome, for once, was bright and sunny. They wondered how the weather would be over Hamm, Germany, that harbor city which was their primary target. If it was socked in, their orders were to go to Osnabruck, with the last alternative at Emden.

Morgan and his crew were flying a plane called the Jersey Bounce. Their own Memphis Belle was still being repaired after that terrible beating it had taken on January 23. But they would be leading the formation again and they had a special guest on board, none other than Colonel Wray, commander of the 91st Group, who once again would be leading his men into battle. He would be riding in the co-pilot's seat. A commander needed to experience battle to know what his men were facing. Furthermore, a trip to Germany was something special.

The 91st had actually gone to Germany once before, on January 27, but the crew of the Belle had missed that one because their plane was grounded.

They would be crossing Holland before reaching Germany and long before they reached the Dutch coast they could see that the continent was covered with clouds. But they flew on, hoping they might find a hole, or a break in the clouds, over their target. They didn't. No chance. Osnabruck was the same. They headed towards Emden.

THE MEMPHIS BELLE

91st Bomb Group: "Even here the cloud cover varied between 8/10 and 9/10. [Cloud cover was rated between 0/10 (clear) and 10/10 (completely covered, visibility zero).] But there were sufficient breaks in the clouds to enable the bombardiers to drop their bombs with a reasonable degree of accuracy. Strike photos indicated the bombs of the 91st Group fell within 2,000 feet of the center of the harbor and probably did considerable damage. However, these photographs also indicated that a good many bombs might just as well have been brought back. Two of our aircraft failed to return. More than half the aircraft which returned received heavy damage. This was a most unsatisfactory mission and the combat crews labelled it their 'Cook's Tour.'"

Leighton Diary: "Our first raid on Germany today and I [as navigator] led the pack of 60 Fortresses. We started out for Hamm but all of Germany was overcast. We finally found a hole and dumped our bombs on Emden. Flak and lots of fighters made the day eventful. Smoke pots had the target covered with smoke. No one hurt in the 324th Squadron but the 91st Group lost two planes."

Winchell Diary: "As consolation for missing the big one [the first attack on German soil] we were the first crew to cross the German border today, lead ship for the Eighth Air Force. Mission was briefed for another target but the weather changed our minds. Passed over a new country today, Holland, across the Zuider Zee. Colonel Wray gave orders to bomb the nearest target of any size [after the sock-in at Hamm] and Emden got it. Apparently the Huns don't like the idea of our bombing their home country for they threw Fw.190s, Me.109s, Me.110s, Me.210s and Ju.88s at us, from the looks of things, every plane they could get off the ground. One Focke Wulf came directly at my waist window through the formation, over Cliburn's ship and under ours. Thought my number was up for sure. I could see 20 mm and 30 caliber shells passing over my head and on top of this he almost rammed us. Landed at the base with a few holes in the ship. The crew, except Adkins, all okay. Gene froze his hands rather badly and will be grounded for some time. Hope the Belle is ready to go next trip."

Author's Note: In an interview a few weeks later, Winchell gave another version of that fight: "The fighters were after us. I never saw such crazy flying as they were doing. One Focke Wulf

181

came in at nine o'clock and seemed to be concentrating on me personally. I was looking down the barrel of a 20 mm cannon. He went over our left wing ship and under us. I don't know yet how he managed to slip through. I was petrified."

Verinis Diary: "Fought a fierce fight for about an hour and fifteen minutes. We didn't shoot down many [German fighters] because most of our guns were froze up because of the 45 degree below zero temperature. Rather rough trip."

February 5-13, 1943

Author's Note: Although the Memphis Belle had been patched up and was ready for a return to combat, she flew no missions from February 4 to 14. The group was alerted and briefed for four missions during this period, three on three consecutive days, but all missions were scrubbed due to bad weather.

February 8, 1943

91st Bomb Group: "The 91st Group received some much needed replacement personnel. Eight officers and men were assigned to the 324th Squadron. Two additional combat crews, consisting of seven lieutenants and 10 sergeants were assigned to the 401st Squadron. Many more replacements are needed. Not one of the squadrons of the 91st Group is able to muster sufficient combat personnel [for] our table of organization."

February 9, 1943

91st Bomb Group: "Today has almost set a record for excitement and frustration. [A mission was scheduled, then scrubbed.] Just as life was returning to normal, Group Headquarters received word that a new mission had been scheduled against a very special target. A German steamship fitted out as a commerce raider had gone aground off the coast of Belgium, near Dunkirk. The group was ordered to prepare all available aircraft for immediate takeoff. Everyone wanted to go on this exciting mission. [Just as briefing was about to begin, the mission was postponed and a bit later cancelled.] Disappointment was very keen.

"In the evening three officers who had been shot down over enemy territory talked to the combat crews. They had evaded capture and had made their way, with the help of the French underground, into Spain, from where they had been returned to the United Kingdom via Gibraltar. The stories they told excited the greatest admiration for them and their ability to endure hardship. The information they imparted was very valuable to combat crews in the event the same fate should overtake them.

"There have been some instances of petty thievery on the station and several men have reported the loss of their wallets and other valuable personal belongings. Several members of the Criminal Investigation Detachment have arrived to investigate. All personnel have been advised to keep a record of the serial numbers of any notes in their possession."

February 12, 1943

91st Bomb Group: "The mail situation has improved during the past week. Four to six sacks of mail have been arriving every day. It has just been learned that most of the mail for the 91st Group has been going to Africa because someone in the Army Post Office had failed to correct the routing slips after the War Department decided not to send the 91st Group to Africa.

"Just before 1100 hours, Lieutenant Riley, pilot of 41-24431 met with bad luck. He was taxiing along the perimeter track when a strong cross wind lifted one side of the aircraft. It rose several feet in the air and came down with a tremendous thud. The aircraft was completely demolished. Lieutenant Riley is thought to have been taxiing at an excessive speed in view of the general weather conditions"

February 13, 1943

91st Bomb Group: The findings of a Special Court-Martial were finally published today. Technical Sergeant Edward Corrigan [was acquitted]. It seems that someone from the 323rd Squadron had imbibed too freely at one of the village pubs on November 23, and in the midst of his exuberant reactions had taken a Thompson sub-machine gun and fired out the window, just to see what it sounded like. Sergeant Corrigan managed to establish his alibi. The real culprit remains a profound mystery."

THE MEMPHIS BELLE

Hamm - February 14, 1943

91st Bomb Group: "The weather promised to behave for a change. Twenty took off [to hit the railroad marshalling yards at Hamm, Germany]. Two returned because of mechanical failure.

"As the formation flew over the North Sea, cloud layers began to build up in front of them. By the time the coast had been reached the cloud cover was 10/10. After the leading group had proceeded about 30 miles beyond the Dutch coast, the entire mission was recalled."

Winchell Diary: "Took off this morning in the good old Memphis Belle. Staff Sergeant E. S. Miller, my new buddy at the waist guns. Crossing the channel, we picked up 10/10 overcast. We picked up a fighter or two and a few bursts of flak but way out of range. No use to bomb in this sort of weather so we all came back home with our bombs. Got credit for a mission although it seems almost a joke to call it that. More like a 'cross country' back in the States."

St. Nazaire - February 16, 1943

Winchell Diary: "Nothing phony about this one as the heading will show the oft-bombed St. Nazaire again. Over the target, Goering's fighters met us and they are every bit as tough as ever. Who said they were pulling their ace squadrons to Russia?

"Flak was heavy, intense and accurate but didn't seem as bad as previous trips. Can it be that I am getting used to this hell hole? Battled it out with swarms of fighters all the way back across France. Some Forts knocked down a few but our own ship had no claims. Got two bad hits, one in the right wing and another put our number two engine out. Got it feathered and came home on the remaining three. Number three engine leaked oil badly but we made it home. Crew all okay but the old girl will be laid up for a while."

Leighton Diary: "Weather was 10/10 when we hit the French coast but cleared over the target. Fighters hit us after we dropped our bombs. The fight lasted for about 45 minutes and was pretty rough. We had a good spot between two groups and good evasive action helped us complete our 12th raid with only a hole in the wing. I didn't get any real good shots, only short mini-bursts as attacks were too much head-on. Six B-17s were lost."

91st Bomb Group: "Eighteen aircraft from the 91st took off at 0830 hours. Five returned because of mechanical failure, but the remaining 13 flew on and dropped twelve 1,000-pound bombs with more devastating effect than on any previous mission. At least six bombs from the 91st formation fell within 50 feet of the pinpoint target. It was a lucky day for the 91st inasmuch as each of the other groups lost two aircraft. Lieutenant Brill of the 324th Squadron was the only aircraft from the group to receive heavy damage. Staff Sergeant Middleton, who was killed, was the group's only serious casualty."

February 17, 1943

91st Bomb Group: "An average of four to seven packages of mail has arrived daily now for more than a week. However, the group has not yet received any of the mail which should have arrived during the first six weeks of the year and there is some speculation as to whether all of this mail will ever be delivered."

February 19, 1943

91st Bomb Group: "Two Red Cross hostesses have been assigned to the station to take charge of the canteen and recreational facilities. Everyone seems to be well impressed by their sincerity and industry."

February 20, 1943

91st Bomb Group: "The past two days have been very warm and conducive to a widespread epidemic of spring fever. Even those who appeared for the ground school classes had difficulty remaining awake, even while the instructor dismissed them."

February 22, 1943

91st Bomb Group: "This morning, Headquarter's 1st Bombardment Wing issued an order that liberty runs may not travel more than 11 miles from their station. On the face of it, this new order automatically cancels all hope of continuing the liberty busses which have been running to Cambridge every night. However, the officers of the group put their heads together and discovered by actual measurement that the distance from the nearest corner of Bassingbourn airdrome to the end of the bus line in Cambridge was just under the prescribed distance. As nothing was said in the order about stopping the busses on the edge of town, or even in the middle of a wood, if necessary, Colonel Wray has decided to continue the liberty runs to that point. Under this new arrangement, the liberty busses stop at the southern edge of Cambridge. This new order has produced a situation that would be downright amusing if it were not so serious.

"Most of the town's available taxicabs have already learned of the new program and are waiting for the arrival of the liberty busses. The people of Cambridge are rather sorely upset and feel their wishes in the matter have been given no consideration at all.

"It appears that some of the enlisted men have been selling cigarettes and other Post Exchange supplies to their English civilian friends while on pass. A new regulation prohibits all enlisted men from carrying more than two packages of cigarettes on their persons when departing on their usual 24-hour weekly pass."

February 23, 1943

91st Bomb Group: "Close order drill and calisthenics were re-introduced today. All enlisted men of the ground echelons are to be given a minimum of one hour close-order drill one day a week. On other days, when the pressure of operations permits, additional close-order drill, organized sports and physical training will be a part of the training program. The combat crew members, both officers and enlisted men, are excused from close-order drill but, in lieu thereof, must report at least one day each week for calisthenics and on a second day for organized sports. These measures are considered necessary to maintain physical standards and to improve on military bearing and appearances."

February 24, 1943

91st Bomb Group: "It has become necessary to publish a memorandum enforcing more strictly the discipline [regarding] the parking of heavy aircraft on the grassed areas. Bassingbourn airdrome has been built on low, marshy ground and much of the grassed area is drained by an intricate system of tiling. Heavy aircraft have done considerable damage to this tiling system. In the future, no heavy aircraft or vehicles will drive on the grassed areas except in extreme emergencies."

Wilhelmshaven - February 26, 1943

"Well, here it is, number thirteen for our crew ..."

Winchell

91st Bomb Group: "Last night the 91st Group was alerted to attack the harbor facilities at Bremen, with the secondary target at Wilhelmshaven. Twenty took off. This was one of those missions when nothing happened as it should.

"The wing formation was late arriving at [the rendezvous point] and there was some difficulty when the various group formations attempted to find their proper places. On the way across the North Sea, the lead navigator neglected to check wind velocity with the result that the entire formation flew several miles south of the briefed course and encountered a good deal of anti-aircraft fire over the Frisian Islands. As the formation approached Bremen, they could see the target was completely covered by clouds. They then turned to Wilhelmshaven, which was partly covered and further obscured by a heavy smoke screen. The results of the bombing were not too good. Many of the bombs fell in the water, doing little, if any, damage. The 91st Group had the dubious honor of placing at least one bomb pattern closer to the aiming point than any other pattern dropped.. This landed in one portion of the harbor area and did accomplish some real good. The 91st formation reported the second instance of air-to-air bombing carried out by an Me.109G, equipped with six external bomb racks, which dropped its bombs from a position approximately 3,000 feet above the formation." [The narrative mentioned no hits by this unique attempt at destroying B-17s. It was reported that two planes from the 401st Squadron failed to return, but no one was able to give specific information as to how or where they were lost.]

"Nineteen members of the combat crews suffered frostbite with varying degrees of intensity. The group could ill afford to lose this many men from among the combat personnel when

187

replacements are so hard to get. The total losses to the group were 41 men, which was equivalent to four full combat crews."

Winchell Diary: "Well, here it is, number thirteen for our crew and the target is a tough one. Heavy overcast over the primary target, so we turned off and headed for Wilhelmshaven, constantly accompanied by and attacked by German fighters. Still not many anxious moments for our particular group. They seemed to be concentrating on the B-24 outfit below and to our left. Approaching the target now and have been forced up to 28,000 feet. Damn cold. 'Bombs away," and we swung out to sea."

Author's Note: The crew of the Belle was flying in the Jersey Bounce again since the Belle was still laid up for repairs.

Leighton Diary: "Raid wasn't too rough. Clouds over target so bombing not so good. Got a few shots at Me.109s and Ju.88s."

Brest - February 27, 1943

Author's Note: In one of the few instances of flying missions on two consecutive days, the 91st Group sent planes to bomb Brest on February 27, following the raid on Wilhelmshaven on the 26th. The Memphis Belle was still undergoing repairs so did not make this raid. The available documents indicate that the majority of the Memphis Belle's crew did not make the February 27 mission. However, Captain Morgan did fly another plane, the Jersey Bounce, with another crew. According to Charles Leighton's diary, he also was assigned as navigator with another crew and flew that day. Winchell made no entry in his diary that day and said in an interview that he and the remainder of the crew did not go. This was Captain Morgan's 13th mission.

91st Bomb Group: "Eighteen aircraft of the 91st took off at approximately 1045 hours. Again the navigation was not too good and the wing formation made landfall over the French coast approximately 50 miles too far to the southeast. It became necessary to abandon the original 'initial point' and make the bombing run from a point on which the crews had not been briefed. Consequently, the results of the bombing were not too good. Again, the 91st Group made a good showing, placing several patterns of bombs within

1,000 yards of the aiming point. Only a few did any substantial damage to military installations. Several patterns fell in residential areas of the city and probably did a great deal of damage. The interrogation reports indicate that the bombardiers were not sure when the bombing run began and as a result did the best they could after they had selected tentative initial points while making their approach. No aircraft of the 91st Group suffered serious damage."

February 28, 1943

91st Bomb Group: "The mail situation is rapidly being restored to normal. Mail has been arriving at the rate of approximately four to eight bags per day. This afternoon a whole truckload of mail arrived. This is only a small fraction of the mail which has been sent erroneously to North Africa but [its] arrival raised the hopes that, sooner or later, the rest of the mail would find us."

Author's Note: The 91st Bomb Group narrative also discussed the fact that the large number of mission alerts in February, during which the crews were briefed and sometimes even boarded their planes, with missions then scrubbed at the last moment, had hurt morale. The narrative said morale was helped by the fact that on the four missions actually flown in February, the 91st made the best showing of all the groups. Improved weather also had helped.

March 1, 1943

91st Bomb Group: "A mission was scheduled but, fortunately for the combat crews, it was scrubbed before the time to arouse them from their slumbers. This makes a total of 50 missions that have been prepared. Out of this number only 21 have so far been completed.

"The station provost marshal made a check of identification tags and Adjutant General's Office identification cards. Two per cent of the enlisted men and 16 per cent of the officers had neither the tags nor AGO cards. Nine per cent of the enlisted men and 38 per cent of the officers did not have their tags. All personnel who do not have tags or AGO cards will be confined to the station until they have been obtained.

"Limitations on liberty runs [to 11 miles from the base] are working a hardship on the personnel of this base. Men patronizing

189

the liberty runs [bus service] to Cambridge are compelled to walk three and a half to four miles to get into and out of the city."

March 2, 1943

Author's Note: The 91st Group received an alert to bomb the marshalling yards at Rennes, France. All preparations were completed and the planes were actually taxiing for the takeoff when the order came to scrub the mission. No reason was given for this.

91st Bomb Group: "The station Special Services officer announced there would be a special music night every Tuesday. This would be an informal jam session held in the snack bar. Several members of the group had agreed to sing and it was hoped to turn these weekly affairs into singing contests. The first of these events took place this evening and the singing of Bill Moskovitz evoked hearty applause."

March 4, 1943

Author's Note: The Memphis Belle was assigned to fly this mission but aborted because of mechanical problems, possibly as a result of the damage on its last raid. Since the Belle did not fly this mission, we would normally skip it, but because it turned out to be one of the most successful and most costly raid to the Group to date,we will present a brief summary.

The target was the railroad marshalling yards at Hamm, Germany. If the target were reached, it would mark the deepest penetration into Germany by the Eighth Air Force. Twenty planes from the Group took off at 0730 hours. Four, including the Memphis Belle, turned back. The 91st was scheduled to be the lead group, with Major Phil Fishburn as air commander. Over the Channel, with some clouds creating problems, the two groups assigned to follow the 91st, the 303rd and the 305th, turned off to bomb a secondary target at Rotterdam.

Major Fishburn, with his single flight of 16 planes, continued toward the target. As the 91st Bomb Group narrative tells it, "However, realizing that he had received specific orders to bomb Hamm, he made the decision to follow through." Due to the small size of the formation, enemy fighters had a field day, shooting down four of the B-17s. As one returning pilot put it, "It was like trying to fight off a swarm of hornets."

Persisting in their bomb run, through all that hail of enemy fire, the small formation did what was described as a classic job of bombing. "Almost every bomb hit," said the group's narrative history, scoring direct hits on vital buildings and installations in the target area. It was judged the best job of bombing ever done by the 91st and was even cited in reports to Washington as one of the best bombing jobs on record. Photographs taken three days later showed that the Germans still had been unable to restore rail traffic.

The small formation was attacked by at least 60 German fighters before and during the bomb run, with some 75 more entering the battle on the way home, with the German fighters attacking fanatically. Said one B-17 pilot of the German pilots, "They were either crazy or inspired." Many of the planes which made it home were severely damaged.

Lieutenant Verinis, who flew the Connecticut Yankee on this mission, wrote in his dairy, "The worst raid that any USAAF bombers ever had took place today. Our group continued to Hamm, just 16 planes. We had a running fight for one hour and forty-five minutes. It was hell. I thought none of us would make it. I was fortunate. We had no crew members hurt and only a few holes in the plane."

Author's Note: Suddenly the crew of the Memphis Belle had their half-way mark behind them in this dangerous game of 25 missions. At the beginning there had been a spirit of anticipation, of an adventure in which they would be "winning the war."

That second mission, to St. Nazaire on November 9, 1942, had rudely snatched away any thought that carrying bombs into German-held territory could be a lark.

But they had some of their toughest raids behind them. They had seen many of their buddies shot down. Their plane, on several missions, had taken an awful beating. But then, with that half-way mark behind them, perhaps the thought that began to sneak into the uppermost spot of their minds was, "Will we make it?"

Missions - Second Half

Lorient - March 6, 1943

Author's note: It was time for one of Captain Bob Morgan's crazy stunts again. He barely pulled it off. Yes, it was on a combat mission. The Memphis Belle was back in service.

91st Bomb Group: "The target was the submarine base at Lorient. The aiming point was the power station and transformer installations on which the base depended for light and power. The secondary point was the railroad bridge near the transformer station. The 91st was able to muster only 14 planes for this mission."

Author's Note: On this raid the Air Force's planners once more ordered the same tactics which had been so disastrous on the group's second raid, on November 9, 1942, to St. Nazaire. The planes were ordered to remain over the water for the entire trip, in and out, which meant they would have to fly all the way around the Brest peninsula. They were also ordered to fly at low altitude until just a few minutes before reaching the target and then quickly climb to bombing altitude. The main difference this time was that, instead of trying to bomb from some 8,000 feet, as on that November 9 raid, they would climb to a safer altitude, above 20,000 feet.

To appreciate what all this means, one has to look at a map. There one can see the Brest peninsula sticking out of the west coast of France like a huge thumb, with both St. Nazaire and Lorient located on the south side. The shortest route, of course, would be to fly across the peninsula, but that would expose the planes to the murderous fire of whole nests of German anti-aircraft batteries. Thus, those orders to stay over the water, going all the way around.

It was hoped once more that the low approach would allow the bombers to near the target without being detected, leaving the German defenses relatively disorganized. And this time it did work better than it had the first time.

192

THE MEMPHIS BELLE

91st Bomb Group: "Visibility at Lorient was excellent. Anti-aircraft fire was moderate but relatively accurate. A flak ship anchored in the harbor was extremely active but seemed to be directing its fire at the group ahead of the 91st. Several flak guns just outside Lorient seemed to be directing their fire at the group behind the 91st. So the 91st was lucky. Bombs were seen bursting on the transformer station and on, or near, the power house."

Author's Note: Now for Morgan's crazy stunt, as revealed by that official log/history of the 91st Bomb Group:

"The return trip over the water did not bring the formation back to Bassingbourn. The trip was too long to permit such plans. Only one of the 13 aircraft of the 91st to attack the target succeeded in accomplishing this feat and this pilot landed with just enough gas to fill a cigarette lighter. The reason for this rather foolhardy feat was the fact that one of the 91st famous parties had been scheduled for the evening and he did not intend to miss it. The remainder of the 91st formation landed at Davidstowe where they spent the night."

Author's Note: The official narrative did not identify the "foolhardy" pilot but the answer is in Leighton's diary entry for that date: "We came back with only about five minute's gas left but we were the only crew to make the party."

How did Morgan manage it? The clue to that may be found in Winchell's diary, as he wrote at the end of his entry for that day, "Crew okay, one bad motor on the Belle, otherwise she wasn't scratched."

Was it possible that Morgan had deliberately shut off one of the motors and feathered the prop to save gas and make it possible to fly non-stop back to Bassingbourn that night?

It was well known among B-17 pilots that you could fly one of these planes very well on three engines, especially after the bombs had been dropped, lightening the load. Even on two engines, just barely, if you threw out all excess baggage. There had been that other stunt Morgan pulled when he had a heavy date back at Bassingbourn and he took off on three engines to make it.

Well, if Morgan did indeed do that, it had to be done with the consent of his commanding officer, Squadron Commander Major Eddie Aycock, who just happened to be riding in the Belle's co-pilot seat that day.

Can we imagine a conversation in the cockpit, after the bombs had been dropped and they headed for home, that might have gone something like this:

Morgan: "Hey, Major, it looks like we'll be missing that party tonight."

Aycock: "Yeah, sure does. And I had a nice date all lined up."

Morgan: "Me, too." The motors drone on a few minutes. "Hey, Major, reckon we could make it back to Bassingbourn?"

Aycock: ; "I don't know. It's a heck of a long haul. We're supposed to land at Davidstowe."

Morgan: "I know. I was just thinking. If we stopped one of the engines and feathered the prop, it would save some gas. Want to give it a try? We could tell the crew the engine picked up some flak damage."

Aycock: "I dunno. Maybe."

Morgan: "Mind if we try it?"

Perhaps Aycock only shrugged his shoulders and Morgan took that for an O.K. His fingers reached for the switches on the No. 2 engine.

End of conjecture.

Incidentally, when they did make it to Bassingbourn and landed, Morgan's flight log showed the Memphis Belle had been in the air nine hours and thrity minutes - a long haul, indeed.

Was it worth it? For the answer to that, we tune in once more to that 91st Bomb Group's history/log:

"The party in the evening did not measure up to those standards which had been established by previous parties. The obvious reason was the fact that many of the officers were compelled to spend the night at Davidstowe. A good many of the officers had invited young ladies from Cambridge, London and other towns to the party. Most of the young ladies appeared [on] schedule, only to find that their escorts were spending the night at another station.

"Another reason the party did not measure up came from the fact that the commanding general of the 1st Bombardment Wing, Brigadier General H. S. Hansell, attended as a special guest of Colonel Wray. [It had been reported] that the general took a dim view of the parties which had been held at Bassingbourn in the past and his attitude was generally known. When he insisted on staying long after midnight, many of the officers disappeared. However, the lunatic fringe made merry, according to the usual formula, and those who managed to outsweat the general reported having a very good time."

March 8, 1943

Author's Note: The 91st Bomb Group participated in an attack on Rennes, France. The flight log of the 324th Squadron shows that the Memphis Belle was assigned to this mission with Captain E. D. Gaitley as pilot and Colonel Wray as co-pilot. However, the log shows, the Belle aborted that day becaue of mechanical defects. Results of the bombing were described as very good, with heavy damage to the railway marshalling yards. It is not known why Morgan was not shown as pilot of the Belle and he does not remember.

91st Bomb Group: "While the group's formation was on the Rennes mission, Special Services Section conducted a series of bicycle races. There were between 50 and 60 entries. The races varied from one and three quarters miles to seven miles. The most amazing race was the [seven mile event] in which the contestants wore full field equipment. It was a sight to behold, watching these would-be champion peddlers coming down the home stretch with full packs, carbines and gas masks."

March 10, 1943

91st Bomb Group: "The group was alerted to attack the harbor and dock facilities at Emden, Germany. The combat crews reached their aircraft. However, just before [take off] the mission was postponed and then scrubbed. Just as the combat crews were returning to their squadron rooms, word was received that 1st Wing Headquarters had ordered a practice mission.

"The combat crews were not the least receptive to the idea. Captain Baird of the 323rd Squadron expressed the sentiment of many crew members when he said, "If these people haven't learned to fly a mission by this time, it is a bit late to start practicing now."

March 11, 1943

91st Bomb Group: "The 91st Group today received 14 lieutenants, a flight officer and 10 sergeants as replacements. They were distributed among the four bombardment squadrons."[It was noted that the distribution was not made on the basis of the losses by each squadron but according to which squadrons had the most flyable airplanes on hand.]

Rouen - March 12, 1943

Author's Note: They called it "the perfect mission," the raid on the railroad marshalling yards at Rouen, France, on March 12. The weather was good. They flew a diversionary flight pattern before approaching the target to fool the German defense and for once it worked. But most gratifying to the bomber crews was the fact that also, for once, they had British Spitfire fighter cover to keep the German fighters away from them on their bomb run. Both the British and the American fighter commands were beginning to equip their fighters with auxiliary fuel tanks so the fighters could protect the bombers all the way to the target.

To cap it all off, the bombardiers, able to make their run in peace, plastered the target. Aerial photos made during and after the raid showed the target was virtually wiped off the map. Since the 91st Bomb Group had led the formation of four groups, it was a feather in its cap.

Making it even more perfect for the 91st was the fact that they put into the air every single one of the 18 planes of the group still flyable, and not a single one aborted. A textbook raid.

Said the 91st Group narrative, "Only two German fighters were able to break through the friendly escort but their attacks resulted in practically no damage.

The only casualty for the group was one gunner who suffered a frostbite.

Winchell Diary: "Squadrons of Spitfires in any direction one cared to look. A beautiful sight. The target was wiped out."

Verinis Diary: "Raid [aboard Connecticut Yankee] definitely in the 'children's department.' It's about time we got an easy one."

Abbeville - March 13, 1943

196

Author's Note: If everything went right on the March 12 raid, everything seemed to go wrong in a raid the following day on the railroad marshalling yards at Amiens, with the secondary target at Abbeville. It seemed that the Eighth Air Force was suddenly concentrating on the railroad centers in France to disrupt the transportation system.

The first snafu came as the four groups attempted to gather for the trip to the target. Said the 91st Bomb Group narrative, "One group, the 306th, insisted on flying at the altitude and in the position assigned to the 91st and it was only with difficulty that the 91st was finally able to reach its assigned place."

Then, said the narrative, the formation went into another diversionary flight pattern. As on the day before, somebody goofed and failed to keep the formation on the designated pattern. The result was a failure to make a scheduled contact with a Spitfire escort at the proper point and the formation had to fly, at first, without fighter support.

The next result of navigation errors resulted in crossing the French coast at Dieppe, instead of Cayeux, forcing the formation to approach the target on a different heading than the one for which the bombardiers had been briefed.

To cap it all off, said the narrative, as the formation approached the target area, the 306th Group was still trying to fly at the altitude and position assigned to the 91st. Said the narrative, "Rather than contest the position with the 306th, the 91st made a left turn northwest to Abbeville where they bombed the air-drome which had been assigned as the secondary target."

At Abbeville a cloud cover gave problems, although at least some of the planes managed to drop their bombs on the target. "The results of the bombing were not very good," said the narrative.

The only bright spot remaining was that the Spitfire fighter cover finally caught up with the group. Otherwise, the group might have run into heavy opposition from German fighters, taking advantage of a small group of planes flying alone.

Winchell Diary: "Poor navigation led to a wild scramble over our primary target. Our own group inched back to Abbeville to bomb the airdrome dispersal area. Saw no enemy fighters. Spit support was beautiful."

Leighton Diary: "Messed up good today. Started out for Amiens but a new navigator got screwed up and took us almost to

Rouen, then up to Amiens but couldn't make a run because of the 306th, so we turned west to bomb Abbeville. Big waste of effort."

Morgan Debriefing: "We had a raid on Abbeville airdrome which was not scheduled. We were going to Amiens. The lead group was supposed to turn northeast of Dieppe but instead went over Dieppe. I figured we had missed it so we turned back and found Amiens. But there was only one little hole [in the clouds] which was closing fast. [The lead crew] made so many zig-zags trying to find the target, because they couldn't find a checkpoint. So we had to quit our run because we were afraid of dropping some of the bombs on the planes [below us]..

"We had fighter protection up in the vapor trail. We could see them occasionally and knew they were up there. We knew the fighters were about to run out of gas and would go home any minute. And there were a lot of enemy fighters in the area. We had to make a decision. While [trying to make a decision] we made a left turn and saw the Abbeville airdrome. We made a bombing run and hit a great deal of it.

"We found out later that we were lucky because we had just got to the French coast when 120 German fighters were screened [intercepted by British fighters] just behind us. If we had made another run we would have had every one of those planes on top of us.

"When we checked the next morning, we found almost everyone had bombed a different target. We were the only ones that hit Abbeville. We learned the lesson about not going back on a target again unless everyone goes."

Morgan later talked to new combat crews about the lessons learned in Europe and cited the March 13 raid as the way NOT to go about bombing targets.

March 14, 1943

Author's Note: As the weather gradually warmed for spring, Bassingbourn was plagued by heavy morning ground fogs, so heavy that it was impossible for planes to take off even when the weather reports showed clear weather over target areas. This was caused partly by the fact that Bassingbourn air base had been built on low-lying ground which normally would have been a swamp, except for a tile underground drainage system. These fogs usually lifted later in the day. In any case, it was during this period when a number of missions were planned but scrubbed, due to this fog problem. One solution was to schedule missions for later in the day but this would work only on targets relatively closer by. It ruled out strikes at targets in Germany.

March 17, 1943

Author's Note: A mission to hit Rouen was ordered for this day and 18 planes of the 91st took off. About three hours later, too soon to have completed their mission, they appeared over the airfield and landed. It was then learned that they had been recalled by a radio message from wing headquarters. The reason was that the fog had not lifted from the airfields of fighters scheduled to protect the bombers. The commanders recalled the mission rather than expose the bombers to German fighters without that fighter escort.

The 91st narrative said the combat crews already had reached 22,000 feet when recalled and would have preferred going ahead with the mission without the fighter escort.

91st Bomb Group: "Last night, Staff Sergeant H. A. Carter, a combat member of the 324th Squadron was killed when he was knocked down by a hit-and-run driver between Royston and Baldock.

"The 91st had a near-serious accident this afternoon. While Technical Sergeant J. A. Peterson, a ball turret gunner, was removing the guns from his ball turret, he accidentally hit the trigger bar. The trigger bar was jammed, resulting in a 'runaway gun.' The whole village of Bassingbourn was sprayed with 50 caliber machine gun bullets. The consequences might have been serious but no one was injured. A few tiles were knocked off several roofs in the village. Peterson was absolved of the blame when it was determined that a defect in the gun caused the barrage."

March 18, 1943

Author's Note: Planes of the 91st participated in a raid on the submarine pens at Vegesack, Germany, on this day but the Memphis Belle did not go. Planes of the formation came under heavy attack by German fighters, including Me.110s equipped with a new free-mounted 20 mm cannon in the nose. It was believed to be the first time guns of this size in fighter planes could be aimed by any method other than aiming the nose of the plane. American airmen said the cannon might have been more effective if the German pilots had the nerve to come in close enough to use it properly. Despite the fighter attacks and heavy anti-aircraft fire, the bomber formations were credited with carrying out one of the most effective bombing missions to date. Said the 91st historian in the narrative, "Bombs of the group dropped squarely on the target. Strike photos showed that not a single bomb dropped by the 91st was wasted. Within six days the 91st and the other three groups participating, received messages of commendation from Prime Minister Winston Churchill."

The narrative also said several drivers had to be reminded to observe the base's speed limit of 20 mph.

March 19, 1943

91st Bomb Group: "An itinerant USO show visited the base this evening [and] was attended by approximately 1,000 officers and men. [It] was a much better show than many that have visited in recent weeks."

March 20, 1943

91st Bomb Group: "Preparations for the mission [to Emden] had just been completed at 0400 [when] it was scrubbed. All the work done by the ground crews had to be undone. The kitchen crews were probably more annoyed than any other section. They had all but completed a fine breakfast for the combat crews and they were put to extreme exertions to preserve the meal when they finally learned the mission was [scrubbed]."

March 21, 1943

91st Bomb Group: "News has just reached Eighth Air Force Headquarters that the pocket battleship Admiral Scheer and the cruiser Admiral Hipper were in the naval base at Wilhelmshaven, and the commanding general was very anxious to attack both ships.

THE MEMPHIS BELLE

The Group was alerted to make a special attack. [Preparations were completed but then the mission was scrubbed.]

Wilhelmshaven - March 22, 1943

Author's Note: Today the attack on the big warships was finally made and the 91st was assigned the job of leading the formation of four groups to Wilhelmshaven. The group's narrative history said the 91st put 21 planes in the air, indicating the group had received at least three replacement planes. This would still leave the group far short of the 35 planes needed for a full group roster.

91st Bomber Group: "The 91st took the lead, made two 'S turns' to allow the other formations to close, then set course for the target. The cloud cover had dwindled to less than 2/10. The bombardiers had no difficulty identifying the target. Not all the bombers of the 91st Group reached the aiming point. Some bombs were released too late to hit the Admiral Scheer but were not wasted. Many fell in the industrial area that surrounded the harbor. Strike photos showed at least one bomb from the 91st exploded just off the port bow of the battleship and undoubtedly inflicted rather severe damage. German opposition was stiff and the 91st, as the lead group, sustained more than its share. The more experienced crew members said the evasive action taken by Captain Oscar O'Neill, the air commander, was the chief reason no more damage was done."

Author's Note: The narrative said 50 German fighters swarmed in as soon as the bomber formations crossed the German border, attempting to break up the tight formation. At the target they backed off to allow flak to take over but, after the target, fought bitterly all the way to the coast.

"Most of the attack was made from the front. Many times the German pilots came in pairs, or in formations of three to six.. Nine of the group's aircraft suffered battle damage. Captain Cliburn had two engines shot out. Major Wallick had one engine shot out and before he reached Bassingbourn the propeller dropped off. Captain H.C. McClellan's plane was shot down in the North Sea just off the German coast. The interrogation following the raid revealed that the Germans were experimenting with new tactics. At least four Ju.88s were employed to drop aerial bombs. Maintaining a tight formation paid handsome dividends and was undoubtedly responsible for the [safe] return of at least two or three of our aircraft."

Leighton Diary: "Got in a lot of shooting but only scared the fighter pilots. Lost Captain McClellan. He was flying on our wing, a swell fellow."

Winchell Diary: "An Me.110 slipped in on us just before we got to the target and almost shot us down. Only a violent dive and evasive action threw him off. Lieutenant Cliburn on our other wing hit badly in No. 1 engine. His engine on fire now and he is losing altitude.

"The group dropped down to 10,000 feet [to help Cliburn]. Half way home we were jumped by five Me.110s and two Ju.88's. They slipped in on the Belle and we had to go into a steep dive to get away. They came so close I could see the 20 mm shells bursting right over Loch's head in the top turret. Cliburn still with us but flying just off the water. Fire is out but engine still smoking badly. Two Me's spotted him and dove in for the kill. The group's guns caught one of them in a cross fire and he went spinning into the sea. Serves the bastard right. The other one was driven off. Cliburn limped home on two engines."

Author's Note: Captain Charles Cliburn,was a close friend of several members of the Belle's crew. The protective action of the 91st Group saved his life that day. Although Cliburn barely made it home on several occasions, flying badly crippled planes, he survived and flew his 25th mission on May 14. He flew most of his missions in a plane called the Bad Penny.

Verinis' Diary: "My electric system went out [during mission aboard his Connecticut Yankee] and four of my crew were at 43 degrees below zero for an hour and a half without heat. All of them frostbitten but they stayed at their posts. I have recommended them for a decoration. Three bombers lost, one from our squadron, Captain McClellan, a wonderful guy. His wife just had a little girl."

Author's Note: The 91st did not fly another mission until March 28. They were alerted several times but each mission was scrubbed because of bad weather.

March 23, 1943

91st Bomb Group: "During the late afternoon Sergeant Joseph A. Totusek was repairing an oxygen leak in the nose of aircraft 545. He decided to light a cigarette while the oxygen was draining out. The oxygen ignited and in a moment the nose of the plane was a mass of flames. [Two other ground crew men were in the plane helping Totusek.] All three received first degree burns and had to be evacuated to the station hospital at Didington. The plane was so badly damaged it had to be salvaged. It had previously completed 18 missions without an abort and was considered one of the best planes on the station. The three men [had to]remain in the hospital for many weeks.

"This evening an air raid alert was sounded. A few minutes later, several German aircraft could be heard flying over a corner of the airdrome. Some members of the group suggested that possibly the Luftwaffe wanted to retaliate for the damage we had done at Wilhelmshaven the day before. [Apparently] these German bombers were on their way to London.

March 24, 1943

91st Bomb Group: "An inter-unit softball league has been formed on the station and nine teams are now competing for the base championship. In addition, a regular baseball team has been organized to represent the 91st. Several veteran sandlot baseball players are stationed at Bassingbourn and it is anticipated that our club will make a good showing."

March 25, 1943

91st Bomb Group: "This morning the ground school training program was resumed. A new emphasis was placed on ditching procedures [getting out of a plane downed at sea]. The loss of Captain McClellan's aircraft in the North Sea [with the entire crew listed as missing in action] has brought home to all crew members the necessity for more knowledge in this phase of their training.

THE MEMPHIS BELLE

"The station library has grown to 1,800 volumes. The books are loaned under the supervision of the American Red Cross. Miss Ritchener, who is in charge, estimates that 300 books are loaned each day.

March 26, 1943

91st Bomb Group: "Arrangements have been made to enable members of the group to purchase money orders [to send] home their surplus funds. It was considered advisable to encourage individuals to send their money back to their families rather than spend it foolishly in England for commodities they do not need.

"During the past several months the pantry in Officer Mess No. 1 has been left open as a convenience for those personnel who must work at night. However, certain officers and men have persisted in abusing this privilege. Some property has been destroyed and a good deal of food wasted. As a consequence, an order was published today placing all kitchens and pantries out of bounds to all unauthorized personnel."

March 27, 1943

91st Bomb Group: "All personnel were advised to improve their personal appearance and to adopt a more soldierly standard of behavior. [It was] directed that all officers and enlisted men observe the salute ritual with the greatest possible precision and propriety."

Rouen - March 28, 1943

Author's Note: It was another fateful day for the Memphis Belle. For the second time, her tail was badly smashed by enemy cannon fire, the tail guns were knocked out and tail gunner John Quinlan was wounded. Beyond that, right in the middle of a desperate gun battle with German fighters, two of the crew members passed out for lack of oxygen and would have died if Captain Morgan had not noticed something wrong and sent Sergeant Bob Hanson back with emergency oxygen bottles to revive them."

91st Bomb Group Narrative Summary: The group was alerted to fly the same mission that had been scheduled yesterday, to hit the railroad center at Rouen, France. Twenty-two planes were

204

sent up but four aborted. This time the diversionary flight pattern failed to fool the Germans and they actually sent fighters to attack the flight formation while the diversion pattern was being flown, damaging two planes and forcing them to return to base before the formation could approach the target. Then, some 150 Spitfires had been scheduled to fly cover for the bombers, but the bomb crews said they saw few British fighters. Apparently, something had gone wrong here, too. As the formation neared the target, they found it covered by clouds but they had a bit of luck when a hole appeared right over the target, allowing them to drop their bombs."

Flak was relatively light this trip but the gutsy German fighter pilots swarmed in for the kill, from beginning to end. Some attacked from the front but some were trying a new tactic from the rear. "The enemy aircraft would slip down on the tail, fire one quick burst, slip under the formation and then stand on their tails to take one parting shot at the Fortresses from below." It was such an attack that got the Memphis Belle. Just before the French coast a vicious attack managed to bring down one of the group's planes, piloted by Lieutenant J. A. Coen, one of the recent replacements. Just before going down, Coen was seen to circle back towards the French coast so his men could parachute down onto land instead of water. Five men were seen to jump.

Still a further snafu came when, just as the formations were about to begin their bombing run, a radio signal from Eighth Air Force Headquarters was received, recalling the mission. It was Major Phil Fishburn, the air commander, who decided to go ahead with the bombing anyway. It was reported that despite the problems the bombs of the 91st plastered the target.

Winchell Diary: "This was the first time we were jumped by 'Jerry' fighters as we paralleled the French coast. Two B-17s were shot down, a rough-and-tumble fight all the way back to England. We were 'tail-end Charlies' today and the enemy fighters were after us with a vengeance. Six Focke Wulfs bore down on us just after we released our bombs. The second one shot down Lieutenant Coen's ship, flying on our right wing. My roommate, Jimmy Bechtel, was a waist gunner aboard her. Quinlan poured a long burst into this same second fighter and the devil dropped off, smoking, and then blew up. One more damn Hun who won't fly again. 'Beck' partly avenged. The third Jerry peppered us with 20 mm shells and one of them exploded right at the end of Quinlan's guns, riddled the tail and knocked our tail guns out. [Quinlan was struck in the right leg.] Jimmy Bechtel was a comparatively new man to the outfit, came to us in January as a member of our first replacement crew. He roomed with me from the start and was, or IS, a hell of a swell fellow.

"I said IS because I'm sure he is alive, a prisoner of war. Lieutenant Coen went down but under control and I saw the boys bail out. Good luck, Beck. See you back in the States when it's over. The next Nazi bastard I get is for you, fella.

"Jim was on his first flight since returning to duty after being shot down in the North Sea and fished out, on the raid to Hamm on March 4, perhaps the roughest raid our squadron ever pulled. He only made four raids altogether. Went down at sea on the third and now shot down again on his fourth."

Harold Loch, the top turret gunner, in an interview: "I'll never forget our March raid on Rouen. We flew over the French coast, feinted, and flew back across the Channel. We knew the Jerries would get wise some time and they did. They jumped us over the channel, 30 or 40 of them. They attacked from every position. Then, just after we dropped our bombs, more fighters came out of nowhere. Our tail got hit. Six of them jumped us, circled around our tail from seven o'clock to five o'clock.. Shells were bursting everywhere. Finally the foremost fighter began to smoke. He turned away and the rest followed him.

"We hear they get an Iron Cross every time they shoot down a B-17. They are a pretty determined bunch.

"The upper turret is a good position. You can see almost any plane that is in a position to damage you. And from there you can let [the other gunners] know when a plane is coming in from which direction so that they can take a crack at him. We had good teamwork on our plane. I think that is the reason we were able to complete 25 missions without a casualty."

Verinis Diary: "A close call for men [in the Connecticut Yankee]. Hits on No. 1, 2, and 4 engines, but not serious. Most dangerous mission to date."

91st Bomb Group: "While the combat crews were in their attack on Rouen, one of those strictly serious comedies of life took place on the airdrome. It was not intended as a comedy at all but, rather, an exercise to prove that we could defend ourselves and our airdrome."

THE MEMPHIS BELLE

Author's Note: Hitler had planned an invasion of England after conquering France in 1940. Although that plan had, more or less, been shelved, the British with their American allies had continued to maintain a semi-alert against a surprise attack, commando raids or possible parachute saboteurs.

91st Bomb Group Continued: "It was a sham battle which turned out to be a sham from start to finish. Every Sunday the English Home Guard holds its weekly [drill]. Our commanding officer had arranged [for the Home Guard] to attempt to capture Bassingbourn airdrome. The home of the 91st would be defended by a detachment of a Royal Air Force Regiment stationed here, augmented by various detachments of the 91st. It would be impossible to record all the often amusing incidents that took place during the exercise. A few cannot be overlooked. About an hour after the 'attack' began, a whole truckload of the 'enemy' entered the main gate without a challenge from the guard. A glider landed on the field and, unchallenged, its crew walked over and 'captured' the control tower. Our forces recaptured the place and having concluded that the 'war' was over, they advanced as stragglers up the road [and] walked into an ambush. All 200 of them were either 'killed' or 'captured.' The most serious loss came when all four of the main hangars were 'destroyed' during an attack by fifth columnists.
"One serious accident did mar the otherwise humorous side of the activities. While repelling a counter-attack Sergeant Ambrosio Martinez had a faulty hand grenade explode very close. He received serious wounds on the face, right hand and right leg. [Three other men] were also wounded as a result of this accident. The exercise proved beyond any question of doubt that a small but well organized force could capture Bassingbourn without too much difficulty.
"A special directive has been received from 1st Wing Headquarters today. It stated that enlisted men in the area have been wearing non-regulation items of uniform, dark coats and trousers, officers' short coats, officers' service caps, non-regulation garrison caps, trench coats, officers' shoes, etc. Those who went to the other extreme were appearing in public in such unauthorized articles of clothing as sweaters, field jackets and other paraphernalia of a generally disreputable nature.
"The directive ordered that, in the future, all enlisted men would be properly dressed before leaving the station."

THE MEMPHIS BELLE

Rotterdam - March 31, 1943

Author's Note: It was another day full of gremlins, according to the 91st Bomb Group narrative. First, an air raid alert came over the alarm system just as the briefing began for a raid on the shipyards at Rotterdam, Holland. False alarm, somebody's idea of a joke. The jokester was never caught.

Next, clouds over England made it impossible for planes of the formation to assemble until they climbed to 7,000 feet, burning up lots of gas before the flights were ready to head for the target.

Next gremlin, the order to fly a double diversion pattern over the English Channel before heading for the target. The American bomber formations had been flying these diversions in an effort to confuse the German fighter commands, make them wonder where the Yanks were going. But the Germans had finally gotten wise and had begun to attack while the Flying Fortresses were in the diversion pattern, usually triangles.

So, this time, the order was to fly a double diversion. This led to the biggest snafu of the day for, as the formations began flying their triangles, they could look out towards Rotterdam, their target, and see it was clear. By the time they completed their double triangles the target area was completely covered by dense clouds.

Crew men said they could have bombed the target if they had flown straight in, without the diversions. Now, with the harbor socked in, the 91st had to lug its load of bombs back home.

Luck was a bit better for the groups following the 91st. They found a few holes in the clouds and plastered the target. The pesky clouds also turned out to be lucky for Captain Edward Gaitley of the 91st. He got an engine shot out and was forced to drop behind his formation. As the German fighters closed in for a kill, he was able to duck into a cloud and escape. He made it home with his crippled plane.

Lieutenant Verinis added a tragic footnote:

Verinis Diary: "As the planes struggled through the clouds, in their efforts to form up for the flight patterns at the beginning of the mission, two Forts collided and one exploded. Only four men were able to bail out."

Author's Note: Winchell noted that the 91st had so much trouble finding its way home through the dense clouds that they had to request an emergency homing beacon to get back to the airfield. These radio beacon signals were used only in emergencies for fear the Germans would "home in" on them, too.

In fact, the group was so badly lost it committed a no-no, coming in over the Thames Estuary, a forbidden zone. British ack-ack gunners had instructions to shoot at any planes which invaded this area, no matter who. Apparently, however, the ground gunners got word in time that the intruders were a bunch of lost Yanks and they held up their fire. Mark it down as one last gremlin that plagued the day.

Incidentally, the Memphis Belle and her crew flew as the lead ship. Once more Captain H. W. Aycock flew it as pilot.

One final word from the writer of the 91st Bomb Group historical narrative. He noted that 130 men of the group had been promoted during the month and 32 demoted. Of this last group, said the narrative, "several got into difficulties because they went too far from Bassingbourn without an adequate knowledge of the deficiencies of the British transportation system." In plain language, they got lost.

April 2, 1942

Author's Note: Nobody liked it when orders came to start night flying training for pilots, co-pilots and navigators, the 91st Bomb Group historian wrote in the narrative. They preferred daylight attack and did not want to join the Royal Air Force in night missions

On another matter, the narrative noted, "One of our co-pilots, apparently suffering the effects of a party, decided to take a ride in the cab of one of the shunting locomotives [at King's Cross Station in London]. Without warning he scrambled into the cab just as the engineer opened the throttle. Those who were with him began to wonder what the outcome would be when, to their amazement, [the co-pilot] appeared riding in the cab of another locomotive at the head of a through passenger train at another platform."

April 3, 1943

91st Bomb Group: "During the day, seven [replacement] combat crews reported to the group, 26 officers and 40 men. Three of these crews were assigned to the 324th Squadron.

"A spot inspection of the fire equipment on the station indicates that some personnel are making unauthorized use of the fire buckets. A warning has been issued that fire equipment must be reserved for fire use only."

April 4, 1943

Author's Note: The 91st Bomb Group historian wrote in the narrative that the group was ordered to join an attack against the Renault automobile plant near Paris. The plant had been converted to build tanks for the German army. The Memphis Belle took off on the mission but aborted because of mechanical troubles. Weather conditions over the target were perfect and the mission classified as a 'success.' Little opposition was reported, going in. Coming out, the formation was attacked by up to 75 German fighters. A good many continued their attacks until they were within 100 feet of the formation. Enemy pilots appeared not to have had too much experience but everyone agreed they had plenty of nerve

Two planes of the 91st suffered heavy damage but got home safely. The group was credited with shooting down 11 German fighters, and four probables. Other groups in the U.S. formation lost four planes.

Antwerp - April 5, 1943

Winchell Diary: "It seemed like there were millions of enemy fighters over the target [when the group hit the aircraft engine repair shop at Antwerp, Belgium].

Author's Note: The Eighth Air Force formations were hit hard this day, with German fighter planes boring in almost as soon as the Fortresses cleared the enemy-held coast, continuing all the way over the target and on the way home until a flight of some 40 British Spitfires finally met the battered planes shooing the Germans away. The 91st Group and the crew of the Memphis Belle were lucky this day, even though the crew was flying on a different plane, the Bad Penny. The Belle was still being repaired for mechanical problems.

91st Bomb Group: "Most of the attacks were made from the front and against the lead group [which lost four B-17s on the mission]. The German pilots attacked the lead group in waves of from four to 10, broke away after their initial attack to attack the third or fourth group either from above or below. After attacking the lead group, most of the German fighter pilots flew over or under the 91st to make further attacks on the groups behind."

Winchell Diary: "They seemed to peel off at us in squadrons at a time. Got one for Beck [his roommate shot down March 28 on the Rouen raid] shortly after we left the target. Caught a Focke Wulf in my sight and poured about 50 rounds into him. Saw him stall, the left wing buckle and fall off. He went down in a tight spin. No one to help me confirm, however, so I don't expect [them] to give it to me. One of the roughest 10 minutes of my life."

[The 91st Group shot down six enemy planes.]

Author's Note: He did get credit for the kill. Winchell also noted that Vince Evans, the bombardier, now promoted to Captain, had been appointed lead bombardier for the group. Navigator Charles Leighton, who had won a reputation as an unflappable navigator, also had been promoted to captain. This was the 20th mission for Winchell and other members of the crew but it was the last entry in his diary. He did not remember why he did not make entries for his last five missions. Lieutenant J. H. Miller, a co-pilot, flew with the Belle's crew for the first time on this mission.

Verinis Diary: "I'm almost through fighting. What a day that will be."

April 6, 1943

91st Bomb Group: "The weather was cold and windy today. No alerts. Staff Sergeant Harold Litke (wounded in previous day's raid) was awarded the Purple Heart in a special pre-sentation at 2nd Evacuation Hospital."

April 6-15, 1943

Author's Note: Neither the Memphis Belle nor her squadron flew any mission during this time.

April 7, 1943

Author's Note: An order was published demanding that all life preservers that had been snitched from the various planes, be returned at once.

91st Bomb Group: "Life preservers taken from the aircraft were being improperly used as pillows or rest cushions. An order requiring certain items of uniform to be worn at all times created rumors that the base was about to be visited by high dignitaries, possibly the theater supreme commander. Or, possibly, the King and Queen of England, with oddsmakers betting on the King and Queen."

April 8, 1943

Author's Note: In view of standing orders that prohibited the sending of photographs from England to the United States, several officers from Bassingbourn who went to London on pass and there saw, in a movie theater, newsreel pictures of the raid on Hamm, Germany, on March 4, came back a bit upset. They asked why they were not allowed to send pictures home but theater managers could show newsreels in which men and planes could be recognized. Sympathetic to the men's complaint, Colonel Wray sent a note of protest to Wing Headquarters but got slapped down. None of your business to question orders, Colonel Wray was told. No pictures could be sent home.

April 9, 1943.

91st Bomb Group Narrative Summary: Technical Sergeant Leroy Wolfington was wounded by shotgun fire this afternoon on the skeet range. He was a recent replacement. He said he thought he heard an order to cease fire and had stepped out into the line of fire to pick up his jacket. He was wounded in the arms and face.

April 11, 1943

91st Bomb Group: "There have been a number of thefts of bikes in recent weeks and having them registered [with the Provost

Marshall's office] will give investigation officers a better chance to identify the bikes and return them to their owners.

"Anyone caught throwing cigarette butts or trash on the grounds, or floors of buildings, will be subject to disciplinary action without benefit of clergy or appeal."

April 14, 1943

Author's Note: The group was alerted to take part in a mission back to Antwerp but, at the last moment, it was scrubbed due to bad weather over the continent.

Lieutenant Colonel F. S. Kamykowski and Sergeant Campbell were recognized for inventing a device to change a B-17 tire, cutting the time from the usual 14 hours down to only one-and-a-half hours. The gadget was made from scrap metal found around the base. The two inventors demonstrated it for the command officers and were recommended for a commendation.

Lorient - April 16, 1943

Author's Note: This was a day when the commanding officers snafued their own mission to the submarine pens at Lorient. The orders read that, during the rendezvous maneuver at the beginning of the mission, the planes were to climb to 23,000 feet at an indicated air speed of 170 mph. As it turned out, such a rate of climb was too much for B-17 engines and superchargers.

The group had put 21 planes into the air but eight of them had to turn back because of problems with the superchargers and engines. Other planes from other groups were having the same problem, and so many planes were turning back, said the 91st Bomb Group narrative, that "group formations and single aircraft were strung out all along the route from the English coast to France. Luckily, the German Air Force did not realize this in time to order attacks while the planes were strung out in an unfavorable position to defend themselves." Jim Verinis flying his Connecticut Yankee, was forced to turn back.

The reason for the call for high speed had been to try to get the planes at altitude and over the targets before enemy fighters had a chance to assemble.

But many of the planes that did make it to the target and dropped their bombs, burned up so much fuel at the higher speed that they were forced to land at emergency bases on the way home.

Although a ground haze prevented some of the bombardiers from getting a good aim, strike photos showed that some of the bombs hit the target and others came very close.

Verinis Diary: "We just got over the French coast when two of my superchargers went out. One came completely out and went through the wing. I turned around and headed for home like a bat out of hell. With my nose down I was doing 450 per. One fighter gave chase but gave up after a while. One of my tires was flattened by the runaway supercharger. I made a landing with my right tire flat but no further damage to the plane."

Author's Note: Charles Leighton wrote in his diary that the Memphis Belle also had to turn back but gave no details, except to say they had crossed the French coast and were in enemy territory before they turned back, so they got credit for a mission. That was the last attempt to beat the German fighter pilots to a target.

91st Bomb Group: "Headquarters 101st Provisional Heavy Bombardment Wing has established itself on the second floor of the main administration building in Bassingbourn. Brigadier General F. A. Armstrong has been designated commanding general of the echelon. With more men and planes pouring into England, the Eighth Air Force was expanding."

Breman - April 17, 1943

Author's Note: All the men had wanted to go on this one. It would be something special. There was that big plant at Bremen, making the famed Focke Wulf 190s, considered to be the best, the fastest and toughest of the German fighter planes. Hitting it would be like hitting back at a tormenter, getting a bit of revenge for all those times these planes had come snarling in at you, spitting bullets and cannon shells. They had killed a lot of your buddies.

But it would be tough, too. It was always tough when you went after one of Germany's prime targets. These they defended like cornered rats. Swarming like hornets, they could come, the

Fw.190s, the Me.109, the 111s and the Ju.88s with their twin engines.

The Germans also had their best anti-aircraft crews and guns around targets like this. So many anti-aircaft shells bursting that Bob Morgan said it was like flying into a thundercloud filled with steel.

It had all started that morning, this mission to Bremen, Navigator Charles Leighton would remember. . You lay in bed and heard those footsteps on the stairs, the wake-up officer coming to today was a mission day.

"Breakfast at 5, briefing at 5:30," said the voice through the door.

Breakfast of flapjacks, made with powdered eggs, and toast, jam and coffee. Somehow, nobody ate much on mission days. Too much tension.

Leighton had always made a game out of second-guessing the target. They never told you when they woke you up. Would it be St. Nazaire again? No, they had been there several times and there wasn't much left to bomb. Rotterdam, perhaps? The big shipping center for the Germans.

At the briefing, Colonel Wray, station commander, wasted no time. Aiming a pointer at the chalk board he said, "Gentlemen, the target for today is the Focke Wulf factory at Bremen."

A bit of a gasp ran through the briefing room. Most of the targets they had hit so far had been in France. This would be the first trip so deep into Germany.

The flight plan called for the group to assemble at 3,000 feet over the field and then head for the city of March where they would join the other groups going on the raid.

Flying low, they would fly parallel to the German coast for half an hour, forcing the Germans to guess where they were going. Then make an abrupt right turn straight into Germany.

Crossing the German coast they would be climbing to their bombing altitude of 26,000 feet. Up there, they were harder for the flak guns to hit and the German fighters had to scramble a lot higher.

What would be waiting for them? Major John McNaboe, an intelligence officer from New York, told them, "There are 200 flak guns within 100 miles of the target. You will encounter 275 fighters." No picnic.

The communications officer gave them their code name for the day. As lead ship of the third group, the Memphis Belle would

THE MEMPHIS BELLE

carry the code name, "Stinky Three." Hopefully, they wouldn't have to use it. Orders were to maintain radio silence except in case of emergency. The Germans were too good at using the radio beams for location purposes.

After the briefing, everybody headed back to quarters to climb into their flying togs. Which meant putting on their good luck pieces. Bob Hanson, the radio man, had a rabbit's foot. A real one that a British hunter had taken off a real rabbit. John Quinlan, the tail gunner, had his horseshoe. Somebody had a pair of lucky socks, knitted by a girl friend back home. Part of the fetish was never to wash them but always to wear them on missions. Bob Morgan carried a ribbon.

It was Morgan, known to his crew as "Chief," who gave them a last-minute boost as they climbed into the plane.

"Okay, gang," he said, "give 'em hell."

As they started the engines and warmed them, you could look out of the windows and see the ground crew standing there, headed by the big crew chief, Jim Giambrone. Anxious. Sweating it out almost like air crew members. Were the engines right? The guns? The bombs? The bomb releases? Lives hung on the answers to those questions.

On time, at 0815 hours, Morgan gunned the engines and the Belle struggled to get off the ground, weighed down by a full load of fuel and five 1,000-pound bombs. She made it up and then, in the manner of airplanes to look clumsy on the ground but graceful in the air, the Memphis Belle swept upward to her "wild blue yonder."

Out over the North Sea, where stray bullets could do no harm, the order was given to test fire all the guns. Sometimes, in the bitter cold of high altitude the oil in the guns would freeze, locking the guns. You always made sure there was a shell in the chamber and the gun cocked. Firing that first shell would jar a cold-jammed gun into action.

There came the jarring stutter as the big .50s at the various parts of the plane jolted into life.

"Ball turret guns okay."

"Top turret guns okay."

"Something wrong back here," reported a nervous Quinlan. "Pete's stuck."

He named his twin guns Pete and Repeat. With two kills to his credit, if anyone could free a jammed gun, Quinlan could.

A blast of gunfire came from the tail end.

"Okay, Chief," Quinlan reported. "I've got 'em working."

216

THE MEMPHIS BELLE

It was when the first flak began filling the sky with those ominous puffs of black smoke that Vince Evans, bombardier, came up with one of his quips.

"You know, " said Evans, "I'm beginning to get the idea that the Germans don't like us."

It was the Chief, now, who put the squelch on chatter. "All right men," said Morgan, "quit the chatter and man your stations. Keep those eyes open for fighters."

Time now for serious business.

Morgan remembered some of that serious business later:

"We went out at less than 5,000 feet to stay off the German radar screens until we were ready to turn in. We began our turn and began to climb so that, by the time we crossed the German coast, we had our altitude. We had learned as long ago as our second mission never to fly into flak territory at low altitude.

"At first it looked as if Bremen was covered with clouds, but Wilhelmshaven was open I thought we might have to bomb Wilhelmshaven as a secondary target. But then I looked over to the left and saw a black cloud sitting there. It was flak. I figured that must be Bremen and, sure enough, when I took a good look, I could see Bremen.

"The flight plan had called for a course that would let us duck around as many flak guns as possible.

"We went in from the southwest to the northeast. I could see German fighters getting off the ground and I've never seen so many at one time. But I had to forget about the fighters because we were going into our bombing run. We were the high group that day. The flak was pretty bad, bursting all around us. The boys in the low group really caught hell."

The formation lost sixteen B-17s that day.

Navigator Charles Leighton said, "Our group lost six ships, all out of the 401st Squadron. So it almost wiped them out.

"Some of those Yellow Nose pilots were damned good. The hottest in the outfit was supposed to be No. 14. None of us knew his name but we had been seeing him in action. He was a fancy Dan who would dive in at a B-17 at 500 mph, his guns blazing and he wouldn't pull out until he was so close you could almost count his whiskers. Even when he was attacking, you could see him stunting all over the sky to attract attention. We were itching to lay our hands on him."

The German pilots were not fooled, said Leighton. Instead of coming straight at the B-17 formations, they scrambled for altitude in a position to head off the bomber flights aiming at Bremen.

Then there was the bombing run to be made. Leighton, navigating, spotted the River Weser, a long and heavy line on the landscape. It was one of the navigation points at the target.

"There it is, Vince," he called to the bombardier. "See it?"

Now it was all up to Vince Evans, a bombardier considered one of the best and the first bombardier to be awarded the Air Medal for his sensational "pickle barrel" bombing on earlier missions.

Evans would also remember that day later.

"The guys gave me a lot of kidding about being the highest-paid man on the crew because my work only took a minute or two but it was a terrific minute, I can tell you."

Evans had to man a gun, too, except when he was on a bomb run. Fighters were swarming in.

"I had to tear my hands off the gun and get over to the bomb sight," said Evans.

Suddenly the fighters were gone. The old German strategy of trying to hit the bombers while on the bombing run with flak instead of fighters, because on the run the big planes had to fly straight and level, making them better targets for flak than fighters. During the run, the bombardier also flies the plane with remote controls.

"We were just 45 seconds off the aiming point," said Evans. "I worked like crazy to make the course corrections. The anti-aircraft guns were giving us hell. In the last five seconds, I got the aiming point square in the bomb sight and pulled the release lever. It was what everybody was waiting for.

"The moment I yelled, 'Bombs way,' Bob Morgan pulled the Memphis Belle into a sudden and steep climb. The sudden release of the heavy bombs helped the big plane leap upward to get out of the range of the flak."

Sergeant Quinlan in the tail was acting as observer for the pilot.

"He reported that the group was intact and in position," said Evans.

There was a close call just as the plane left the target.

"At the very moment we left it a Yellow Nose came hurtling in from my side. He got a line on us with his tracer bullets and then cut loose with his 20 mm cannon. Somehow he missed us but he came so close to us that we almost crashed before we peeled off.

THE MEMPHIS BELLE

"I got his number. It was No. 14 again."

Evans was firing now and swore his bullets were smashing into No. 14 but he was never given official credit for kill.

It was also right after leaving the target that another Focke Wulf got on the Belle's tail. Quinlan was trying to get a bead on it but Morgan was whipping the big plane around like crazy, now, trying to make it as hard to hit as possible. In the tight formation that the 91st was always famous for, gunners from several planes were shooting at the same FW that Quinlan was. The plane faltered, hit.

"The Nazi pilot jumped out," said Quinlan. "I saw his parachute open."

Meanwhile, Morgan was whipping the plane around so wildly, said Quinlan, "I felt like a flagpole sitter in a high wind."

Verinis wrote in his diary, "Easily the greatest show I have ever seen, flak from 200 guns and 150 fighters. Black puffs for miles around. The fighters fought us for more than an hour. Our group lost six bombers, a total of 16 for the Bomber Command, largest number to date. The previous high was seven. What a trip. Captain Oscar O'Neill went down, a great guy. I don't care to go after that target again."

But then, somehow, it was over. As soon as he could, Morgan streaked for home, dropping to 10,000 feet over the North Sea to give the crew members a chance to get out of their oxygen masks. The nerve-wracking tension was over. The signal came from the control tower to land. A sound for joy.

At least it had not been in vain. It was a mission when so many bombs hit home, the intelligence people estimated that at least half the plant, maker of the hated Fw.190, was destroyed.

But once again the men of the 91st were in a state of mixed emotions. Happy for the destruction of the plant but in mourning for the crews of the six B-17s that had been lost.

The historian for the 91st Bomb Group wrote: "Practically every aircraft in the formation received some serious battle damage. Several patterns of bombs from the 91st were seen to explode among the buildings of the FW factory."

One last poignant note to the mission. A party had been scheduled at the Officers Club that night and many of the men had invited guests, girl friends from the English villages.

"Many of these arrived," said the 91st historian, "to find that their escorts were missing from the day's mission."

April 21, 1943

Author's Note: The 91st Bomb Group was alerted to bomb the submarine pens at Brest, but the mission was scrubbed due to weather. Despite this, it was a big day for Bassingbourn. It was the day the British flag would be hauled down and the American Stars and Stripes would be raised over the administration building. When the 91st had arrived at Bassingbourn in October of 1942, the base had been under the jurisdiction of the Royal Air Force and administrative personnel of the RAF had remained to run the field, the canteens, the entertainment, and so on. As manpower became available, the 91st had gradually taken over from the RAF and, on April 21, the takeover was completed.

91st Bomb Group: "Approximately 200 officers and men represented the RAF while the formation representing the 91st Group numbered well over 1,000. The RAF provided a band and, after short speeches by Squadron Leader J. S. Ellard and Colonel Wray, the Royal Air Force flag was taken down and the flag of the United States raised. A formal inspection and parade in review concluded the ceremony."

April 22, 1943

91st Bomb Group: "The commanding officer received orders to engage in a low-level practice mission. Approximately 25 planes were dispatched to fly at zero altitude for a period of approximately six hours. The combat crews reported they had a great deal of fun. It seems the low-flying aircraft played havoc with flocks of sheep, herds of cattle and even the barnyard fowls. One pilot reported that the driver of a tractor stopped abruptly and sought shelter under his machine when he saw a Flying Fortresses formation coming towards him at approximately 50 feet over his head."

There were rumors that it meant low-level night missions with the RAF could be planned. Nobody liked the idea.

April 23, 1943

91st Bomb Group: "During the past six weeks, an agricultural project has been launched under the direction of Captain G. M. Marshall. He hopes to furnish enough fresh vegetables and produce to supplement the rations of the entire station. To date, ten acres have bee prepared for seeding and planting began yesterday. It is anticipated that 25 acres will be under cultivation. Captain Marshall is attempting to purchase a small tractor to assist in this work. The captain has a good deal of experience in [farming] and, with the assistance of several enlisted men, there is no reason why he cannot realize his present ambition."

April 24, 1943

91st Bomb Group: "During the past few days, several pilots from other organizations have arrived at Bassingbourn to take a special course in the technique of standard beam landing approaches. Some have flown in Africa and other theaters of operations. By and large, they are a lot of individualists and some of them have been giving our ground officers a bit of trouble."

April 25, 1943

Author's Note: The group is flying low-level training flights, but the crews still do not approve of Flying Fortresses performing at such low altitude.

April 26, 1943

91st Bomb Group: "Prior to the arrival of our visitors [members of the newly formed 94th Group] Kneesworth Hall was occupied by some eight or ten of the more sedate and subdued officers of the 91st Group. The influx of approximately 60 flying officers turned the sanctified precincts of Kneesworth Hall and gardens into a sort of pandemonium.
"Some of the more common offenses: loud and boisterous talking, spilling drinks on the tables and floors, littering the lounge with books, papers and cigarette stubs, throwing darts into the walls and ceilings, emptying contents of fire extinguishers on floors, walls and ceilings, failing to clean lavatories and bathtubs after use, burning holes in the furniture and floors. [A new set of house conduct rules was announced.] It is anticipated that this order will bring an improvement in the behavior of the officers at Kneesworth Hall during the remainder of their stay."

221

THE MEMPHIS BELLE

April 27, 1943

Author's Note: The 91st Group was alerted to bomb the Ford Motor Comapny plant at Antwerp, Belgium. The plant was reported to be making 400 trucks per month for the German army. The mission was cancelled due to bad weather.

91st Bomb Group: "Headquarters is becoming concerned about the practice of officers fraternizing with enlisted personnel of the WAAF, particularly in towns and other public places. Colonel Wray has threatened dire consequences upon any officer caught violating this order."

April 28, 1943

91st Bomb Group: The farm and garden project continues to make progress. Approximately five acres have been planted. However, it becomes necessary to publish an order warning all personnel not to walk on the cultivated ground. The commanding officer stated that he would take disciplinary action against all offenders, regardless of rank or position."

April 29, 1943

Author's Note: The 91st Group was alerted to bomb an airframe factory at Meaulte, France, but the mission was cancelled due to bad weather.

91st Bomb Group: "This afternoon approximately one truckload of mail arrived at Bassingbourn. A large portion of it seems to be the last of the mail misdirected to Africa last winter."

St. Nazaire - May 1, 1943

It was a day when the gremlins were at work again. The Memphis Belle had to dump her bombs in the water.

The target was the one they had bombed so many times before, the submarine base at St. Nazaire. It seemed the bomber formation was doomed to repeat a mistake they had made before, flying low over the Brest peninsula, thinking it was England. And once more the mistake would be costly.

THE MEMPHIS BELLE

The lead group, for some reason, headed for France ten minutes too early, leaving for the trailing groups the chore of trying to catch up.

The 91st was one of the groups trying to catch up. Running their engines wide open, trying to catch up, some of the pilots found this was burning their engines up, and five of the 20 planes had to turn back.

Then the weather gremlins took over and covered the target with heavy clouds. Leaders of the group attempted to drop their bombs blind and succeeded in dumping them in the water, wide of the target.

Following planes were supposed to drop when the leader did.

"The formation leader," said Bob Morgan, "made the mistake and salvoed his bombs in the water and everybody else did the same thing."

At least the crew of the Memphis Belle did not have on their conscience the tragedy that resulted from the bombs dropped by other groups. Some of their bombs fell wide and created considerable destruction in the village of St. Nazaire, which was still inhabited by French citizens. It had always been a touchy situation when the Americans bombed targets in occupied France, for, if their bombs missed the intended military targets and hit populated civilian areas, it alienated the French. Some French workers were employed by the Germans on and around their military installations and there was always the chance of killing some of them. Otherwise, the Americans tried their best not to hit civilian areas.

Along came another gremlin. The lead group pilots returning to England mistook the Brest peninsula of France for the tip of England and dropped down into the waiting sights of German anti-aircraft gunners.

91st Bomb Group: "The lead group seems to have gotten off course and turned north before they should. Three or four of their aircraft were lost here. The leader of the 91st Group saw the error in time to make a sharp left turn."

But the turn had been so sharp, with clouds limiting visibility, that some planes got separated. One of the planes of the 91st, flown by Lieutenant James Baird, came out of the melee all alone, something the Germans always looked for. Sure enough, here came the enemy fighters to pounce on the lone plane. Lieutenant Baird ducked down to the ocean, flying low over the water with his guns blazing. His plane was badly damaged and four of his crew were wounded but he made it after his gunners shot down three enemy planes. He landed at an emergency RAF field from where the wounded members of the crew travelled by train to Bassingbourn.

Eight of the planes of the 91st got lost so badly on the way home they landed at RAF bases scattered all over the southern half of England. The last of the gremlins? Not quite. One waited until the next day to strike.

May 2, 1943

Author's Note: Two officers of the 91st, Lieutenant Joseph Reynolds and one of his best friends, Lieutenant Leathers, were going through the personal effects of Lieutenant Rand, shot down the day before, preparing to ship the material back home to Rand's family. Among the effects was an automatic pistol. Somehow, while Lieutenant Leathers handled the gun it began to fire. Six of the bullets struck Reynolds who died before he could reach a hospital.

91st Bomb Group: "The Bassingbourn baseball team travelled to Alconbury to play the team from that station. Weather conditions were bad. However, not bad enough to postpone the game. Bassingbourn was defeated by a score of 18-6."

May 3, 1943

91st Bomb Group: "Approximately 500 officers and men attended a performance of 'Swing Time,' one of the better travelling USO shows. The show was well received and the participants were royally entertained at the senior officers mess after the [show].

Author's Note: Members of ground crews and non-combat personnel began asking if they would be rotated back home as their combat crews finished 25 missions and were returned to the United States. The 91st Bomb Group historian said in the narrative, "Those who do not come under the [combat] category continue to wish and think and hope. However, nothing specific has been received which is applicable to ground crews." Concerning another matter of importance, the narrative recorded a new order stating, "Only authorized drivers will be permitted to operate motor vehicles in the future. Members of the combat crews are not permitted to ride motorcycles at any time."

Antwerp - May 4, 1943

The 91st Bomb Group flew the mission that had been scheduled for the day before, then cancelled, the Ford Motor Company plant at Antwerp, making trucks for the German army.

The Memphis Belle did not go on this mission although her pilot, Captain Bob Morgan, flew as pilot of The Great Speckled Bird with the regular Belle crew.

The weather was perfect, wrote the 91st historian in his narrative account, and the bombing was nearly perfect. Enemy opposition was light. No planes of the 91st were shot down and only two were slightly damaged.

The only snafu of the day, said the narrative, came because the combat crews were not told that American P-47 and British Spitfire fighters would be flying escort. Some of the gunners of the B-17s mistakenly thought the friendly planes were enemy and fired some shots at them. Said the narrative, "It is sincerely hoped that none of our friendly escort received damage at the hands of our own gunners."

91st Bomb Group: "Many enlisted men have been using their blue passes [for evening only] to leave the station prior to 1730 hours. All commanders have been notified today that no enlisted man would be permitted to leave the station prior to 1730 hours unless he has more authority than the blue pass."

May 5-13

The Memphis Belle and her squadron flew no missions during this time.

May 5, 1943

The group was alerted to bomb the Meaulte aircraft factory today but the mission was scrubbed due to bad weather.

Three officers and four enlisted men left Bassingbourn for a leave of seven days at a special rest home for combat crew members. Such rest homes were for combat crew members who were showing signs of nervous tension from combat.

The two top softball teams from Bassingbourn played an exhibition game to which British civilians were invited. According to the 91st Bomb Group historian's narrative, the British spectators soon learned to cheer when the Americans did. The Bulldogs beat the Bears by a score of 7-5.

May 6, 1943

Author's Note: Bad weather again kept the planes on the ground. More than 1,100 men attended two showings of an orientation film called "The Nazis Strike." The softball season is in full swing with eight Bassingbourn teams swinging away.

May 7, 1943

Author's Note: Bad weather kept the planes on the ground again but the Memphis Belle was "in the movies."

91st Bomb Group: "During the past several days, Captain William "Ace" Clothier has been busily engaged in taking colored motion pictures at Bassingbourn. Captain Clothier has had extensive experience [with] some of the best known Hollywood studios. He hopes his efforts will result in a relatively long motion picture similar to the Royal Air Force Command's 'Target for Tonight.' The chief difference being that this will present the Eighth Air Force Bomber Command in their daylight bombing program. The whole effort is being built around the aircraft Memphis Belle and its crew, commanded by Captain Robert K. Morgan. Approximately 5,000 feet of the film have been shot, to date. He has already gone on six operational missions. He plans on going on two or three more missions in order to complete the picture."

May 8, 1943

Author's Note: The 94th Bomb Group, which had been housed and trained at Bassingbourn while it was being formed, began moving to its own base at Earls Colne. Undoubtedly, the men of the 91st, who had been forced to share their quarters with the 94th visitors, were glad to see them go. Sir Stafford Cripps, [prominent British diplomat, serving as Minister of Aircraft Production],visited Bassingbourn today with his official party.

91st Bomb Group: "They were preceded by a horde of newspaper reporters. Judging from their activities, a small fraction of their number could have accomplished their purpose. Sir Stafford and party arrived in several limousines, accompanied by rather ferocious-looking police detectives. They rode through the airdrome, hangars, dispersal areas and a few other buildings without bothering to dismount from their automobiles. All personnel of the station had received special instructions on how to dress and behave. Everyone was all primed for the occasion.
"During recent missions, personnel for the control tower have sometimes been hindered because numerous unauthorized personnel have gone to the control tower to observe the takeoff or landing of the planes. In the future, unauthorized officers will not be admitted to the control tower at any time unless they have written permission from the station commander."

May 9, 1942

91st Bomb Group: "During the recent spell of inclement weather, several instances of personnel using electrically heated flying clothing for other than actual combat or high altitude training flights have been brought to the attention of the station commander. An order [was issued] stating that electrically heated flying clothing will be used for high altitude flights [only]. Violations of these instructions will be dealt with severely."

May 10, 1943

91st Bomb Group: "Personnel at Bassingbourn have been able to draw hospitality rations to take when they visit British civilian friends. Unfortunately, a suspicion has arisen that a few officers and men have been abusing this privilege. In the future, no one will be permitted to draw hospitality rations unless they can present a written invitation indicating a request that they visit."

91st Bomb Group: "Captain Robert K. Morgan, Lieutenant Charles Leighton, Sergeants Bob Hanson and John Quinlan departed from Bassingbourn for London. It is anticipated that they will participate in one of the regular monthly broadcasts to the United States. Several of the personal friends of those officers accompanied them on this mission to furnish the necessary moral support."

May 12, 1943

91st Bomb Group: "It has been more than a week now since the group has participated in an operational mission. This has brought about a gradual loosening of morale. It has tended to produce a restlessness on the part of many of the combat crews and a feeling that they are not making the proper contribution to the war effort. Many have completed 15 or more missions and are really anxious to complete their assigned 25 missions and go back to the States. It is believed that an operational mission in the near future is really necessary to prevent a further deterioration in morale."

Meaulte - May 13, 1943

Author's Note: Lieutenant C. L. Anderson and another crew flew the Memphis Belle on a mission to bomb the aircraft repair depot at Meaulte, France. The 91st narrative writer gave no clue to the reason, but it is possible that Captain Morgan and the three Belle's regular crew members who had accompanied him to London had not yet returned, so the Belle's regular crew stood down. The 91st put 25 planes in the air and 13 squadrons of British Spitfires were to fly escort. The group flew the lower formation and lost two planes but strike photos showed nearly all bombs hit the target.

91st Bomb Group: "There is some difference of opinion concerning the quality of this fighter escort. All combat crews report having seen the Spitfires engage in dogfights with some of the enemy aircraft. However, they did not appear to be as eager as our own P-47s have been. On the mission of May 4, several P-47 pilots had followed the German fighters right on through the bomber formations in order to break up their intended attacks. It appears that the Spitfires did provide good cover for the high squadrons but did not exert themselves very strenuously towards breaking up the attacks made on the low squadrons."

Kiel - May 14, 1943

For the second consecutive day, the Memphis Belle flew off to the wars without her regular crew. This time it was Lieutenant J. H. Miller who took command, with a crew of his own. Captain Morgan and his men may still have been in London.

The target today was the shipbuilding installations at Kiel, Germany. This time the 91st put 27 planes in the air, the largest number ever. Which meant the group finally had begun to get replacements. Only one of the 27 aborted.

The Germans put up at least 125 fighter planes to stop the mission but, as the 91st narrative writer reported, they gave most of their attention to several flights of B-24s taking part in the mission. The 91st lost no planes although a number were damaged. Results of the mission were classified as excellent.

Heligoland - May 15, 1943

"We bombed Heligoland," reported the crew of the Memphis Belle and other crews of the 91st Bomb Group after they returned from the May 15 mission.

The trouble being that nobody would believe them.

This is one of the strangest stories of the entire career of the Belle and her crew. Yes, Bob Morgan and his regular crew were back and flew the Belle on this one. But, what a crazy story!

The primary target had been the submarine and ship building facilities at Wilhelmshaven. But when the formation of which the Belle was a part, approached the target area, they could see that the entire northern part of Germany was completely covered by dense clouds.

What to do? Bremen, their secondary target, was also "socked in."

They had flown over the island of Heligoland on the way in to the German coast and the weather had been clear there. The island contained important naval installations and submarine pens.

The crews had not been briefed for an attack on Heligoland, but now, with no target visible in their assigned area, and rather than carry their bombs back home, the flight commander simply decided to hit Heligoland. They did - and plastered it.

As the 91st narrative writer put it, the bombardiers had no maps or briefing information to guide them. So they simply set their release mechanisms to drop a bomb every 100 feet and "walked their bombs across what appeared to be the most important parts of the island's installations. Practically every bomb from the 91st Group was seen to break on the military installations on the island. Strike photographs indicated that hardly a bomb was wasted."

Bravo. But now for the complications, described by the Group narrative:

"The 24 aircraft of the 91st Group returned to Bassingbourn in mid-afternoon. The interrogation went along in a routine manner during the first few minutes. But as soon as the intelligence officers began to ask the combat crews what they had bombed, everyone, including the commanding officer, began to get excited. This state of tension continued to increase until someone suggested that the target had been the German naval base at Heligoland. This information was phoned to Headquarters, First Bombardment Wing, who received the report with a great deal of skepticism. During the next six hours, the situation was genuinely intense. However, a comparison of the strike photographs with the casual photograph that one of the intelligence officers located in a magazine convinced all and sundry at Bassingbourn that the target had been this important naval installation.

Headquarters still refused to accept our verdict. Consequently, as soon as our photographs had been processed by the Photographic Section, the duty intelligence officer, Captain Parker, took all the reports, the photographs and the other information to headquarters and was able to convince the officers that Heligoland had been the target. For some strange reason, no mention of our attack on this target was made in the newspapers, radio broadcasts, or other channels of public information during the days that followed. Many formed their own conclusion as to why this omission was made. In view of the excellence of our bombing and the extensive damage which obviously had been inflicted upon the island, it was rather strange that our Public Relations Office neglected this, one of its golden opportunities."

Author's Note: Opposition to the attack was stiff, with some 100 German fighters boring in, but once more the 91st was lucky, with the fighters concentrating mostly on other groups. The 91st lost no planes but was credited with shooting down eight German fighters.

To compound the confusion even further, the historian for the 91st Bomb Group, as part of his entry for May 15, wrote, "The Memphis Belle, piloted by Captain Robert K. Morgan, completed its

25th mission today. Although this crew does not have the record of completing its 25 missions without a turnback, it is one of the first crews to complete 25 mission for the 91st Group intact. [The crew, of course, was *not* intact.] It is rumored that the Memphis Belle, with her highly publicized crew, will shortly depart for the United States where it will tour the entire country in supporting the forthcoming bond drive. Preparations have been made to take extensive moving pictures of this aircraft and its crew, although the purpose of this project has not yet passed beyond the rumor stage.

"This day, May 15, is recognized as the official birthday of the 91st Group. The party of all parties was in full progress in the senior officers mess when the announcement was given. Three generals and nine full colonels from other stations were present to assist in the celebrations.

"Approximately 300 civilian guests had accepted invitations for the buffet supper and dance which formed the major entertainment for the celebration. Shortly after the announcement which outlined the day's success, further announcement was made to the effect that in recognition of the excellent work done by the First Bombardment Wing during the past three days, everyone would have holiday on the 16th. This seemed to release any inhibitions which may have been in evidence prior to this time. One may best judge the success of the party by recalling that only 17 officers appeared for breakfast the next morning."

Author's Note: In the official missions log for the 324th Squadron the target for May 15, 1943, is shown as Wilhelmshaven. However, several group and squadron mission analysis sheets clearly show the target bombed was not Wilhelmshaven but the island of Heligoland.

May 16, 1943

It was Sunday and a holiday. No war today. The 91st had been on three missions in three days. The ground crews had to work on the planes of the 94th Group, still their guests. "The men were literally worn out," Captain Parker said. They deserved a rest.

The birthday party for the 91st had lasted nearly all night. Most of the men skipped breakfast and were "sacking out."

There was something special afoot, however. The King and Queen of England were coming to visit.

Some of the men would have to be roused to greet them. Like the crew of the Memphis Belle. William Wyler, they said, was responsible for that.

Wyler had been making that War Department documentary, centered around the Belle, and when he heard that the Royal couple was coming to visit the base, he immediately arranged for them to make a special visit to his favorite plane, the Memphis Belle.

That explains why Sergeant Miller, asleep in his bunk and sleeping off the effects of the big party, was aroused by a blaring loudspeaker that called out his crew to put on their Sunday best and report to their plane.

Captain Parker, in his diary-log, described the visit this way:

"The King and Queen of England, accompanied by a rather large retinue, visited Bassingbourn shortly before lunch today. Rumors of the impending visit had been going the rounds for the past two weeks. They arrived in six large, comfortable-looking limousines at approximately 1115 hours, were met at the gate by Colonel Wray and his staff, received a salute from a guard of honor and proceeded to give Bassingbourn one of the most cursory goings-over that this old and well-established airdrome has ever had. Generals Baker, Longfellow and Hansell and several unidentified United States Army Air Force officers were also present. The King and Queen drove around the taxi strip through the hangars and into one of the dispersal areas. The King and Queen met Captain Morgan and the crew of the rapidly-becoming famous Memphis Belle.

"Captain Morgan did a good job of meeting the King and Queen and showing his aircraft. At the conclusion of this ceremony they returned to the main administration building where the formal farewells were said. As soon as they had concluded their tour and received another salute from the guard of honor, the entire party returned to their limousines and proceeded in the general direction of Brampton Grange."

Lorient - May 17, 1943

The biggest day of all - the day on which Captain Bob Morgan and several members of his crew would complete their 25th mission. That magic day, that glorious day when they could stop flying into those angry skies full of flak and angry fighters.

THE MEMPHIS BELLE

It was the day in which Sergeant Winchell, the indomitable waist gunner from Oak Park, Illinois, would write his own blazing finale to his mission tour by blasting one more German fighter from the sky.

Other crew members, such as tail gunner Quinlan and navigator Leighton, had already finished their quota of missions by flying missions on other planes.

It was the day on which the pilot, Bob Morgan, would be able to come back and buzz the hell out of the field without being punished for it. It was, as one of the men put it, "like dying 25 times and then waking up in heaven."

It was a day on which, after they had landed at Bassingbourn, they would kneel down and kiss the earth. Morgan himself would be hoisted on the shoulders of his men so he could kiss that perky Memphis Belle painted on the side of his plane. A day which none would forget.

For the plane herself, it would be her 24th mission. She still owed one to the books. But she would get that, too, two days later, with another pilot and crew. Then they would all go home, to fame on a nationwide tour where they would be hailed, in newspapers and on the radio, as heroes. Real wartime heroes.

On this final day, the target would be Lorient once more. They had been there three times before, with some of their toughest battles fought over that target. This time it would not be quite so bad and it would be one of the times when the bombs would plaster the target. It would be a proper farewell.

Replacement planes and crews had been coming and the 91st was able to put 24 planes in the air, one of the largest numbers ever. The weather was perfect. In fact, visibility was so good the bomber crews were able to spot their target from a distance of 40 miles. And for once there was little anti-aircraft fire or enemy fighter opposition during the bombing run.

With all these things going for them, perhaps the smashing bombing success was not exactly a miracle. According to the 91st official history, one bomb from the group's salvo was seen to land smack in the center of the aiming point and others smashed storage and repair sheds surrounding the submarine pens. Several bombs smashed squarely into the roofs of the pens themselves.

The Germans tried to fight back, sending some 40 or 50 fighter planes into the air. One of these roared in on the Memphis Belle. It was Winchell, in his waist gunner position, who got the Fw.190 in his sights and cut loose with a long burst from his .50

caliber. The enemy machine blew apart and went down. This was one time when Winchell had enough witnesses to make it official.

Fortunately, most of the enemy fighters concentrated on other groups in the bomber formation, letting the 91st go home virtually unscathed. The Germans tried some of their air-to-air bombing once more but, except for one near miss, that didn't do any damage either. The 91st was home free - and the Memphis Belle with it.

For Bob Morgan, it was a time to celebrate. It was, more or less, understood that when a pilot completed his 25th mission he would mark the occasion by buzzing the field. For the man with a tradition of buzzing lawn parties and such, it would have to be a super buzz job. And everyone said he did it.

There had been reports that he knocked the flagpole off the administration building but he says it isn't so.

"I did 'cut the grass,'" he admits.

The war, or that part of it, was over for Morgan and his crew. They would now be going home. They didn't know it yet, but they would be taking the proud but battle-scarred Memphis Belle with them.

May 18, 1943

Today Colonel Stanley Wray, the man who had taken a group he called "Wray's Ragged Irregulars" and turned them into one of the best bombardment groups in the European Theater, was relieved of command, effective May 22. It was a promotion for he would be taking command of a wing, the 103rd Provisional Heavy Bombardment Combat Wing. Colonel William M. Reid would take his place as commander of the 91st.

Kiel - May 19, 1943

Today the Memphis Belle, the battered plane that had carried Bob Morgan and his crew through flak and fighters so many times, and had taken her share of a beating on several occasions while dishing out more than her share of war, flew her last combat mission.

This time, since most of her crew had completed their 25 missions, it would be Lieutenant C. L. Anderson, who had flown her on another mission, at the controls with his own crew.

THE MEMPHIS BELLE

It would be one of the tough ones, an attack on the shipbuilding center at Kiel, Germany.

This time the Germans tried everything to stop the American bomber formation. First they tried more of that air-to-air bombing, dropping what were called "relatively heavy bombs." Fortunately, the bombs missed. It wasn't the best way to knock down a B-17. The second wave of fighters, Ju.88s, were armed with some of the heaviest cannon yet to show up on airplanes - 40 and 50 mm guns. With these weapons, the Germans stayed out of range of the .50 caliber machine guns on the B-17s and fired. Again, their gunnery was not of the best.

The third attack wave came in the form of conventional fighters blasting in at the nose. Said the 91st narrative, "This aerial engagement was one of the most prolonged and vicious which the aircraft of the group have had to contend with. Enemy aircraft were attacking some element of the wing's formation for an hour and ten minutes."

The 91st gunners were credited with four kills. One B-17 was lost. Other groups were hit harder.

There was one snafu on this mission. The group flying just ahead and a bit higher than the 91st was carrying small cluster bombs for a change, and some of these bombs apparently were defective, going off as soon as they were dropped instead of waiting to hit the ground.

And here was the 91st, flying right into this mess, sending the pilots into a frenzy of maneuvers to dodge these "friendly" bombs. At least three of the 91st Bomb Group's B-17s were damaged by these blasts. The worst part being that, in dodging the cluster bombs, the bombardiers of the 91st were unable to draw a bead on the target. The result, the bombing of the 91st that day was less than satisfactory. Other groups did a better job.

As for the Memphis Belle, her luck was still holding.

She had come home to Bassingbourn after her mission for the 25th time. Her tour of combat duty was at an end.

People around Bassingbourn had been saying she was a lucky plane.

She was, indeed.

The National Tour

It was August 11, 1943, when a huge four-engine bomber swept in over Asheville, North Carolina. It was flying low, barely skimming the tops of the buildings. The roar of its engines rattled the windows below.

For some people, it must have brought a moment of horror when they saw the big plane fly straight at two tall buildings, the City Hall and the Courthouse. There was a gap between the buildings but not nearly enough to accomodate the 103-foot wingspan of the big plane.

Just a second before the plane would crash, it flipped up on its side and blasted between the two buildings, one wing pointing straight up and the other straight down.

It was an incredible feat of skill. Perhaps it was foolhardy and dangerous. Some who watched thought the pilot should be court-martialed. The commander of the U. S. Weather Station on the top floor of the Courthouse actually tried to get the pilot punished for the stunt.

But, for the time being, the pilot seemed to lead a charmed life, immune from punishment. After all, he had just completed a tour of 25 combat missions over Europe and survived everything the Germans could throw at him.

On a triumphal tour of the nation, he had been given permission by General H. H. Arnold, commander of the U.S. Air Forces, to fly his plane as low as he pleased. This would allow the pilot to buzz the airfields of the cities he visited. It is almost certain that the general never dreamed the pilot would also buzz city roof tops and slip the big bomber between tall downtown buildings.

The plane: the Memphis Belle. The pilot: Robert K. Morgan, already a national celebrity and enjoying the role.

It took a bit of that "go to hell" spirit to fly warplanes into the skies Europe filled with daring German pilots. America, in the biggest war in its history, needed a few daring pilots of its own. America should be glad if it had pilots who sometimes gave vent to a crazy "can do" spirit and flew the gaps between tall office buildings.

Morgan and the other nine men of his crew had been on that tour for nearly two months. In city after city, Morgan flipped the big plane around as if it were a sporty single-engine fighter plane.

The crowds were thrilled.

Morgan may have put on his best show in Memphis, Tennessee, which had been the second stop on the tour. He had a special reason to pull out all the stops. Waiting on the ground was the girl he loved, the girl he was engaged to marry. A cocky young man always wants to strut in front of his girl. A high ranking military officer who saw the Memphis show muttered something about a "court-martial for that pilot."

Now the inspiration for the Asheville caper was simply that it was a homecoming for Morgan. He had been born and reared here and gone to school here. These were his home town folks who watched his plane hurtling past. He would give them a show they would never forget.

Actually, when the Air Forces top brass had first come up with the idea of sending home bomber and crew after completing 25 missions, the purpose was primarily to send the plane and crew to air bases where new crews were being trained. There they would give the trainees a chance to benefit from their combat experience.

In his order to the commander of the Eighth Bomber Command, Major General Ira C. Eaker wrote on June 1, 1943: "The Theater Commander has approved my recommendation that one especially selected crew which has completed its operational tour, be allowed to return to the United States, flying its airplane which also has completed 25 operational missions. You are charged with the responsibility of selecting this plane and crew. You must make it clear to your operational personnel that this is in no sense a precedent. It is done because of the beneficial effect it is believed it will have on the Operation Training Units system at home, particularly in the Second Air Force.

"It may be that as a result of our continued operations in the coming summer we may allow one especially selected crew from each wing to go back with their aircraft. That has not been definitely determined and will not be until the effect of sending this first crew back has been analyzed.

"As soon as you have selected the crew and plane in question, advise me showing the particular reasons for its selection with good historical and biographical sketches, including the performance of the crew in combat, so this can be sent back to the United States. In this way we can make sure that the crew will be properly used for morale and training purposes on arrival in the United States."

Taking a careful look at that order indicates the primary purpose was to expose the plane and crew to military men in training but public relations officers and the newspapers would make much more out of it.

Why were the Memphis Belle and its crew chosen?

The number of planes that had completed 25 missions was small. That narrowed the choices. Also, everyone knew that a War Department film was being made that centered around the Memphis Belle and her crew. The Belle got more publicity when the King and Queen of England visited its bomb group at Bassingbourn, and the plane and its crew were inspected by the royal couple. Captain Morgan and members of the crew also had participated in radio broadcasts from London back to the United States. The plane and crew had a good combat record.

Captain S. T. Parker, the official historian for the 91st Bomb Group, had made several entries about the Memphis Belle and her crew in his daily diary and log, noting "the rapidly becoming famous Memphis Belle."

Furthermore, word had gotten out about the romance between the plane's pilot and a pretty "belle" back in Memphis. It was a natural for the news media.

Even the name of the plane was poetic and easy to romanticize. Other planes had completed 25 missions, planes with names such as Hell's Angels and Delta Rebel, but those names might be objectionable to some.

Considering all of this, it seems inevitable that the Memphis Belle be chosen for the grand national tour.

General Eaker should have known what would happen with the arrival on home shores of the crew of "heroes" and their plane with such a romantic name.

When word got out that the plane was going to land at National Airport instead of a heavily guarded military base, the news media and the public took over.

General Arnold and the Secretary of War, Robert Patterson, were to meet them, with mobs of reporters and patriotic Americans.

It was a photo opportunity that the media could not pass up. Pictures from the National Airport were flashed across the nation and printed in hundreds of newspapers. The message with them was that the famous plane would be flying to major cities across the nation. America, here they come!

Before starting the big tour, the men of the Belle were special guests at the Pentagon at a luncheon hosted by General Arnold and a whole string of top brass.

"We weren't used to anything like that," said John Quinlan, the tail gunner from Yonkers. "There I was, an enlisted man sitting down to eat next to a general. I was so nervous I shook like a leaf."

That wasn't all. General Arnold told them they could each have their choice for their next assignment. It was like being handed an Alladin's lamp to rub.

Bob Morgan decided he wanted to fly one of the new and bigger B-29s. Bob Hanson and Clarence Winchell said they would like to be officers. Charles Leighton said he had been cheated out of going to pilot training school and that he'd still rather be a pilot than the navigator he was.

They all got their wish.

Only it would have to wait until their tour was over.

Memphis was their first stop after leaving the Pentagon.

One Memphis newspaper headline screamed: "Proud City Awaits Plane." A banner across the top of The Press-Scimitar, crowed, "MEMPHIS BELLE IS HERE!" Columns and articles were sprinkled liberally throughout. One cartoon showed a proud Uncle Sam welcoming the heroes with a bouquet of War Bonds. There were countless reports on the radio stations.

There was a long string of speeches, parties, receptions and an army of photographers popping flash bulbs. The crew visited the Fisher Body Plant where hundreds of "Rosie the Riveter" girls were busy making wings for B-25s.

The Commercial Appeal, the city's morning newspaper, which missed out on covering the earlier landing of the Memphis Belle on June 19 because of the time of day, made up for it the next day with Belle stories scattered throughout the paper. One big headline read, "WAR SCARRED MEMPHIS BELLE KEEPS DATE WITH CUPID."

The plane and crew stayed in Memphis three days. The War Department put the crew up at top hotels. The hoopla never stopped. It was heady, intoxicating stuff.

It took the ten young men a while to accustom themselves to their roles as conquering heroes.

Margaret Polk accompanied Morgan and the crew on their tour of the city. The young beauty was the central figure at all the parties and receptions. Hostesses vied with each other to nab the true Memphis Belle for their parties.

The next stop was Nashville, Tennessee. More headlines and parties. More receptions and galas. Then on to Hartford, Connecticut, where workers at the Hamilton Standard plant made those huge propellers which drove the Memphis Belle and her sister bombers through the air. Morgan and the crew were presented at a mass rally of factory workers.

They went on to a rally of workers at the Chance-Vought aircraft plant at Bridgeport, Connecticut. Then on to more of the same in Boston, Pittsburgh, Detroit, Akron and Cleveland. More headlines and flash bulbs, banquets, rallies, parties and bouquets.

Each city tried to outdo the last one.

Cleveland was the home of the Addressograph-Multigraph Company, where Morgan had worked before entering the Air Force. The firm scheduled a gala banquet and rally of all company workers.

Secretly, without Morgan's knowledge, arrangements were made to fly Margaret Polk to Cleveland. She was to walk on stage during the rally and into the arms of her lover.

It was another photo opportunity. It produced the Picture of the Tour. It was the perfect shot. It made newspapers from coast to coast. Life Magazine featured it.

It was then and there that Morgan wanted to defy War Department edicts and get married. Margaret hesitated. Marriage must wait, she pleaded, for a more appropriate time and setting.

The tour swept on to Dayton, Las Vegas, Los Angeles.

In Los Angeles, the Belle's crew members were guests of Douglas Aircraft plant which was turning out B-17s under a contract to Boeing. They were welcomed by Governor Earl Warren.

Then on to San Antonio, Oklahoma City, Wichita.

Wichita was the home of another Boeing plant that was turning out the super bomber B-29 which was destined to carry the war to Japan and drop the first atom bomb ever on an enemy.

Morgan was invited to visit the plant and inspect the Air Force's newest baby and to sit in the pilot's seat.

"There I sat," recalled Morgan, "surrounded by all that new, sophisticated instrumentation, in that powerful, huge plane. I just knew this plane had to be for me."

Then Morgan claimed the one magic wish, granted him by General Arnold in Washington.

"I told them I would like to have a B-29 squadron," Bob said. This explains why this young North Carolina pilot, promoted to major, became the man who led the first formation of B-29s to bomb Tokyo. Morgan entered another page of history.

They continued on to Cheyenne and Denver. In a Denver hotel room, Bob Morgan held the fateful telephone conversation with Margaret Polk in Memphis which would lead to the break-up of their storybook romance. This was at the end of July.

The tour had originally been scheduled to run for one month only. But Air Force public relations officers were a bit drunk, perhaps, on the fabulous success of the Memphis Belle's 26th mission. All those headlines and wildly cheering crowds, the banquets and the hoopla, had gone far beyond their wildest publicity dreams.

"Let's extend it another two weeks," the public relations men said. Then they asked for yet another two weeks' extension. The rapidly tiring crew agreed.

Panama City, Mobile and Orlando, here we come.

It was after the Belle had landed at Orlando that a heart-warming little drama took place that put more cheer into the tour.

The Belle was at the airport when a young airman in a private's uniform asked for permission to board the plane. There was something about the way the young man asked that led the authorities to give their permission.

The young soldier clambered aboard the plane as if he were quite familiar with it, then made his way to the pilot's compartment and the bomb bay.

"I found it!" he shouted a moment later.

He had found his own private identification mark. Before he was drafted into the military, Ralph Thielen of Seattle, Washington, was employed as a riveter at the home plant of the Boeing Company. He had helped build the Memphis Belle and he had left a cryptic little mark of identification on the plane. This was, for him, a reunion.

The Air Force public relations men who directed the tour were happy to include Asheville, North Carolina, home of the Belle's pilot, Major Morgan. Asheville accepted the challenge and planned a reception Morgan could never forget. He responded to his home folks by giving them a demonstration of flying skill such as they had never seen before and might never see again.

Morgan, still operating under the permission granted by General Arnold to fly as low as he wished, put on a show over the city, buzzing the field and doing aerial acrobatics that the B-17 manual never mentioned. It was a dazzling display. To climax it, he slipped the Flying Fortress, tilted up dangerously on one wingtip, between those two big downtown office buildings.

His caper in Chicago was a little different.

"We were there several days," said Morgan. "They had assigned a couple of Red Cross girls to drive us around. When we left we were going to Los Angeles and Hollywood, and these girls wanted to go out there with us. So when we left, we just told them to hop on board. It was strictly forbidden to carry civilians on a military plane, especially girls, without permission."

It might have turned out fine if there hadn't been engine trouble.

"One of the engines went out," said Morgan. "We had to land at Ogden, Utah, to fix it . The Air Force officers on the field welcomed us with open arms until they saw the two girls climb out of the plane. I could see they didn't like it. But after we got our engine fixed, we took off without any more problems."

What Morgan didn't know was that the commanding officer at Ogden had filed a report on the unauthorized personnel aboard.

"It finally caught up with me while I was out in the Pacific, about one year later," he said.

"My base commanding officer called me in and said he had a letter that came through channels, dated the previous year. It had to do with my flying civilians in a military plane from Chicago to Hollywood. He said they wanted him to take some action. I explained what had happened and he let the matter drop."

The old immunity magic still worked, all the way out in the Pacific.

The trip from Chicago to Hollywood, via Ogden, was the Belle crew's second trip to Hollywood. It lasted a week during which they were feted, wined, dined and partied in high West Coast style. The crew went to the film studio in Culver City to dub their voices on the Memphis Belle film that was being put together there.

There was no sound track on the 16 mm film that was shot in England for the movie. Sound was being added now. The film makers wanted the voices of the real crew speaking as they would have in combat.

The tour began to peter out after the crew left Los Angeles the second time.

San Antonio, Texas, and Camden, South Carolina, were the next stops.

Camden was the air base where Morgan had begun his pilot training.

At times the crew of the Memphis Belle were getting a little weary of all the parties, the banquets and meetings, the plant rallies and the speeches, the wine, women and song.

Some of the crew said that they were almost too tired from the previous night's parties to get out of bed and stumble to the plane to fly to the next city.

Sometimes they would set the plane on automatic pilot.

Everybody would, well, sort of relax.

The most alert member of the crew might be asked to stay awake and watch the plane, waking either the pilot or co-pilot if they were needed.

"Finally I got fed up with it all," said Morgan. "I don't remember where we were at the time, but I called the crew together and told them I was fed up. I asked them how they felt. They all agreed with me that it had been a bit too much of a good thing. We were all ready to quit.

"So we flew to Washington and I told the Air Forces brass we wanted to quit. We had had enough. They wanted to extend the tour another time but we said no. They said we had not been to New York, yet. We would have to make one more stop.

"So I said, 'O.K. New York will be our finale.' We flew up to New York and landed at Mitchell Field. They put us up at the Waldorf Astoria for three days. We had another round of parties. The Bulova Watch Company gave us Bulova watches. Our names were all engraved on the back.

"That was the end of the tour."

One thing was certain. By the time the tour ended, there was hardly a man, woman or child in America who had not heard about the Memphis Belle and her crew of heroes although the crew hated it when people called them heroes.

At the beginning of the tour in June, somebody had said that her tour of the nation was the Memphis Belle's 26th mission.

The men, too, had now completed their 26th mission, the longest one of them all.

In some ways, it had been their toughest.

Stuka

A Female on Board

Stuka - such a fearsome name for a gentle little girl puppy.

It had been the name the Germans gave to their dreaded dive bomber, the Junkers 87. Their Stuka was a plane that struck terror into the hearts of Polish citizens when the war opened in September of 1939. Sometimes, it was said, German pilots attached air whistles to the bellies of their Stukas to make them even more scary as they screamed earthward to release their bombs.

When Germany attacked France and, later, Russia, the plane lived up to its reputation. It was a synonym for terror in the skies.

Stuka is a contraction of the word Sturzkampf-flugzeug, which translates into English as something like "diving battle plane." To the Americans, it simply meant "dive bomber."

In the spring of 1943, Jim Verinis, the Memphis Belle co-pilot, gave that name of Stuka to a frisky little Scottish terrier girl puppy whose best idea for creating terror was to chew up her master's socks on the floor of his barracks bedroom at Bassingbourn.

Stuka, to millions, could mean a dreaded dive bomber. At Bassingbourn it also meant a perky little black dog known as the 11th crew member of the Memphis Belle.

There were rumors that became newspaper stories that Stuka actually went on one of the bombing missions with the Memphis Belle, enclosed in a little box that had its own oxygen supply.

Verinis says it isn't so.

"I don't know where that one got started," he said. "Some-body made it up. Stuka never flew with us unless we were staying below 10,000 feet and we never flew a mission that low."

244

THE MEMPHIS BELLE

The Stuka story began sometime around February or March of 1943. Verinis said he and Leighton, the Belle's navigator, made one of their escapes to London for a little relaxation.

"We were just walking down the street," he said, "when we passed a pet shop. I saw this little puppy in the window."

The frisky little terrier appealed to him so mightily that he went straight in and bought her.

"I don't remember the exact price, but I believe it turned out to be something like $50 in American money."

With the puppy under his arm, he returned to the base.

Stuka, naturally, began doing all the naughty little things that puppies do before they are trained.

Somehow, both master and puppy survived each other. When the Belle returned to the United States, Stuka came along.

"I believe that was her first plane ride," said Verinis. "When the engines started and the plane began to move, she got nervous and ran back and forth. She didn't bark or yelp, though."

Later, the little dog settled down and enjoyed the rest of the flight across the Atlantic Ocean.

So it was, as the Belle began barnstorming around the country, at each landing in a new city, there would be Jim Verinis, sticking his head out of a plane window, Stuka cuddled under his arm.

Stuka's tail would be wagging up a storm.

The little dog didn't seem to mind all the stunt flying Morgan did as he arrived over each new city on the tour.

"After she got used to flying," said Verinis, "Stuka seemed to enjoy all the wild stuff.

"She was a big hit with the crowds. People went wild over her. She seemed to be enjoying all the attention. When the cities put on parades for us, she would ride in it as if she were a queen."

Newspaper photographers and newsreel cameramen had a field day, taking pictures of the flying dog.

A man could start a conversation with a pretty girl by telling her about the little black terrier that flew with them.

"They would always be surprised to see her waiting for me at the door of my hotel room," said Verinis. "They would say to me, 'Gee, you really do have a dog, don't you?'"

Word got out that Stuka liked whiskey. Some people would slip her a saucer full.

"She'd lap it up," said Verinis. "She'd stagger around a little, act silly and go off somewhere and lay down to sleep."

Then Stuka had her own "short snorter."

Those were dollar bills which overseas GIs would collect autographs on. When one got filled up, they'd start on a new one. Some soldiers had big collections of them.

"Stuka's short snorter had signatures on it such as Clark Gable, Burgess Meredith and William Wyler, the director who made the Belle movie," said Verinis.

One time, Verinis said, he left Stuka with his buddy, Leighton, when he went into London on a date. He got homesick for the pooch as soon as he got to London and turned around and came back to the barracks.

After the tour was over in America, and Verinis had finished his duty with the Air Force, he went back to being a civilian and Stuka came along. Her days as queen of the parade were over.

Verinis got married, settled down, and a son was born.

"Stuka didn't know what to make of a baby," said Verinis. "She never really became attached to him. It almost seemed as if she resented having to share our affections with the baby. But Stuka behaved herself. Her good breeding and manners prevented her from taking her resentment out on the baby. "

Stuka ended her days as a watchdog, house pet and some-what less than ardent companion for a boy named Steven Verinis.

If gifted with memory, she must have gloried in her younger days as queen of the parade.

It would be nice to say that Stuka finally just died peacefully of old age. It didn't quite happen that way.

"She was about eight or nine years old when she got sick," Verinis said. "The vet said she had eaten a chicken bone. The bone punctured her intestine and she died."

It was the end of the glory road for a little flying Scottie named Stuka.

Romance

I Love You So Much

"I love you so awfully, awfully much. You are so wonderful. Lovingly yours. Margaret."
From a wartime letter written by Margaret Polk in Memphis to Bob Morgan in England.

"My heart cries out to you from this distance. Forever I adore you and only you. Your Bob."
From a wartime letter written by Bob Morgan in England to Margaret Polk in Memphis.

Yes, it had its glorious moments in the sun, that romance between Margaret Polk and Bob Morgan, pilot of the Memphis Belle, before it sputtered and became a failed thing.

Perhaps it would not have been fair to have asked her then, in 1943, when the hurt was raw and alive, but now, from a distance of some 45 years, had she truly been in love with Bob?

Her reply: "I believe I was more in love with love."

The fact that Margaret Polk has repeated this statement to friends several times would indicate that she is now comfortable with such a thought. Or at least that she has come to terms with it, in seeking to rationalize what happened to her in 1942 and 1943 when she was suddenly hurled into the vortex of a storm, an experience bigger than she was able to control.

Perhaps it was asking too much of a girl of 19, reared in a genteel and protected environment, to cope with what happened. At

247

times she was not even allowed to make her own decisions about her own personal love affair.

As for Bob Morgan, the other half of the romance, it has sometimes been suggested that it was his somewhat casual approach to his romances which was at least partly to blame.

He was something of a lady killer, folks said, and he knew it, sometimes taking advantage of it, with this factor creating part of their problem. But it wouldn't be fair to Bob to suggest that his wartime romance with Margaret was just another casual encounter.

There is plenty of evidence to indicate that this was one time when he may have truly been in love and wanted desperately to marry Margaret. He was deeply wounded when it did not work out.

Bob has said it himself that he, too, was caught in a hurricane, too, being hurled around by forces he could not control. Beyond that, Morgan has proved, through two rather substantial marriages since then, by his pride in his children, that he was capable of more than casual relationships.

It all began on that fateful day in June of 1942, in the midst of wartime, when her mother suggested that Margaret take a trip to Walla Walla, Washington, with her sister, so Elizabeth wouldn't have to make that long car trip alone.

Perhaps we should really start at the beginning, on that day in 1922, when a baby girl was born into the family of Mr. and Mrs. Oscar Boyle Polk of Memphis and named Margaret. Her father, a lawyer, lumberman, planter in the old southern tradition.

A girl growing up and somehow managing to become some- what of a tomboy, despite her attendance at girls' private schools.

"My daddy didn't believe in coeducation," said Margaret.

Her first schooling, grades one through five, were at Miss Emma Cook's School, operated by two elderly ladies who never assigned home work because "they didn't believe in grading work done by the parents."

After that, grades six through twelve, were at the very proper Miss Hutchison's School for Girls. The tomboy thing could develop mostly in the summertime because that was when little Margaret was taken to the family's country place at Hickory Valley, Tennessee, and, more or less, allowed to do as she pleased.

A great deal of the time what she pleased to do was play with the black children of families working on the place.

"Sure, I had a lot of fun with them," she said. "It didn't make any difference to me that they were black."

Fun, because she didn't have to do it, were things like picking strawberries that ended up on the most delicious pies made by the black cooks in the big farm kitchen, separate from the big house. That big house, a huge white structure put together with wooden pegs. Heated in the winter only by fireplaces.

More fun at things like riding the ponies and going skinny dipping in the big cow pond. For pranks, things like taking the porch furniture and hoisting it up in trees.

Did her family feel any of the effects of the great economic depression of the 1930s?

"I remember Dad had to drop his membership in the University Club and we couldn't go swimming over there any more," she said.

After high school?

"My Daddy told me if I stayed home and went to school in Memphis for two years, then I could go anywhere I wanted to," she said. "So I went to Southwestern [now Rhodes College] for two years."

Then a year at the University of Wisconsin, lured there by a girlfriend. But, disappointed, back to Southwestern for her fourth year.

It was somewhere about this time that the Walla Walla trip beckoned.

All because her older sister Elizabeth had married a young doctor named Edward McCarthy. "They just called him Mack."

It was wartime when the young men of America had to serve in the military forces, doctor or not. In fact, the Army Air Force and Navy were grabbing up every young doctor they could get their hands on.

As fate would have it, young Doctor McCarthy was assigned as physician to a Air Force unit being formed at McDill Field in Florida that would come to be known as the 91st Heavy Bombardment Group.

Then, that fateful June when the 91st got orders to move to Walla Walla for final flight training before being shipped overseas for combat.

The air echelons of the 91st flew in their planes, but the ground personnel would go by train - five train loads - and since young GIs sometimes get sick on long train rides, it meant that a young doctor, but not his wife, would travel by train. The wife, Elizabeth Polk McCarthy, would drive the family Ford from McDill to Walla Walla, with a stopover in Memphis to say hello to Mom, Dad and sister Margaret.

It was when sister Elizabeth complained about the loneliness of a long trip by car, that Mom suggested, "Margaret, why don't you go along with your sister so she won't have to travel alone?"

The fate thing was churning now, for Margaret, a slim, winsome and pretty maid of 19, said, yes. It was an age when romance beckons.

In fact, during a stopover at Yellowstone National Park, she met a handsome young park ranger and, for the moment at least, the sparks of a budding romance were flashing.

But then, on to Walla Walla and her rendezvous with fate - that meeting with a young second lieutenant named Robert K. Morgan.

Neither Margaret nor Bob have a clear remembrance of their first meeting. It must not have been one of those South Pacific type things, with sparks flying "across a crowded room," signalling love at first sight.

"I just remember that Mack and Elizabeth lived in a house off the base and sometimes somebody would be bringing Mack home in a car. I believe Bob did the driving on several occasions and Mack invited him in for a drink. I guess Mack introduced me to him. There was nothing special about it at the time."

In fact, if anything did set the sparks to flying, awakening a romance, it had to be a certain argument with her sister and brother-in-law.

"I had made a date with another young man for July 31," she said. "Then Bob invited me to his birthday party which happened to be on the same day. I wanted to go to Bob's birthday party and wanted to break my date, but my sister and Mack wouldn't let me. They said it wasn't done. We had a pretty hot argument about it."

The argument thing got Margaret's dander up and became the factor which, more or less, threw her into Bob Morgan's arms.

"I started dating him and we got pretty close," said Margaret.

In the manner of exuberant youth, things became somewhat exciting after that. For Bob Morgan was smitten now, in love and determined not to let Margaret forget it. And what could be more exciting than using a huge, four-engine bomber in which to go through the rites of courtship?

They were flying every day now, their final training before going overseas to battle, with formation flying, beginning early in the morning, the major routine. Perhaps Bob would take off a few minutes before the others and then, before getting into flight formation, take a quick buzz over the house where Margaret was asleep.

"Here Bob would come," she said, "around four or five o'clock. He came so low and it was so loud you would have thought he was flying right through my window. The whole house shook. It was so exciting."

There was the suggestion that Morgan might be disturbing the whole neighborhood but he was in love and didn't care.

"She was a pretty southern belle," said Bob. "Way up there in Washington and I liked southern belles. I liked her better than the other girls I had met in Walla Walla."

The summer grew late. It soon was time for Margaret to head back to Memphis. She was enrolled for the fall term at Southwestern. It was time to go back to school.

Margaret stopped at Yellowstone National Park on the way back to Memphis. She renewed her friendship with the young park ranger. His picture went in her scrapbook. Tall and handsome, curly hair, almost another Bob Morgan.

"Bob and I had not really made any commitment," she said.

The sight of the young park ranger warmed her heart to the point that she was having a hard time deciding which one she liked better, the pilot or the park ranger.

The difference was that Bob had that big four-engine plane at his command and he was not about to let Margaret forget him.

There was a letter from Bob waiting for her when she got home. The language was unmistakable.

My dearest Polky,

I miss you, 'little one.' I miss you more than you'll ever know or understand. And if you miss me this much you will come to me. I know I would be on my way to you if I were a civilian once again.

I know now that I have never loved before. I have never felt towards anyone as I do to you. If we can't have OUR LIFE before the war is over, I know I shall come to you afterwards.

I flew all yesterday afternoon. I flew for you and went to bed early. I was up at 4 a.m. this morning and flew the dawn patrol again.

Never worry, God will keep me safe until we are together again.

Must go, now. Write soon, 'little one.'

I send you all the love in my heart.

Forever yours,

Bob

For his first letter to a girl named Margaret, Bob Morgan was doing all right. It would take a stone-hearted young maiden not to respond to something like that.

There followed a storm of telephone calls and telegrams.

"Almost every morning," she said, "while I was getting ready for school , the phone would ring. If he didn't call me in the morning it would be in the afternoon."

Always the words, "I love you."

On August 14, after flying to Ogden, Utah, Bob sent a telegram.

Darling. Be here until Saturday. Busy 24 hours a day. Tired but happy when I know I am doing this for you. Miss you awfully. It must be soon that we meet again. All my love always. Bob.

The next meeting did come soon. Towards the end of August, the 91st Heavy Bombardment Group was declared ready for combat. The orders were to fly to Gowan Field near Boise, Idaho, and turn in their old B-17s used for training purposes. There they would pick up new B-17s which would fly them overseas.

But at Boise only six of the new planes had arrived from the plant instead of the 35 or 36 the Group needed to equip its four squadrons. Two of the new ones went to Bob's squadron, the 324th. One of those was taken by Colonel Stanley Wray, commander of the 91st.

Their orders were to fly to Dow Field in Bangor, Maine, where they would get the remainder of their new planes. Morgan managed to get a ride with Colonel Wray who planned to stop overnight in Jackson, Mississippi, and he sent this telegram to Margaret:

Jackson, Mississippi, Army Air Base tonight. Will call. Love. Bob.

"I jumped in the car and took off for Jackson," said Margaret. "It was midnight before I got there."

She was in his arms, listening as he told her for the millionth time, "I love you, 'little one.'"

There was a green card with a string on it to hang on the doorknob outside. It said, "Do not disturb." It went into her scrapbook later. On the back of the card Margaret wrote, "Room 931, Hotel Heidelberg, Jackson, Mississippi, August 31, 1942."

Then another telegram suddenly:

Plans to come south are good but keep fingers crossed. Love. Bob.

Morgan had finally been issued his new B-17F. It was getting its last fitting out, with the latest in war equipment. It was being given a final test. Part of the test was 100 hours of flying that would tell about fuel consumption and so on. Each crew was given one flight to the destination of their choice, often the hometown of the pilot. Any crewman living near that destination could come along.

Morgan's official destination was Asheville, to visit his father, David, but he sent another telegram came to Margaret:

See you Saturday.

Sergeant Levi Dillon was Morgan's flight engineer. He said Morgan, after landing at Asheville, sent a message to Dow Field saying the plane had brake trouble. There would be a layover of three days while they were repaired.

Dillon went home to Roanoke, Virginia, during those three days. Sergeant Eugene Adkins wangled his way on the trip and caught a bus for Johnson City, Tennessee, to see his folks.

Morgan used those three days for something else. He sent another telegram from North Carolina:

Land airport [Memphis] about 10 your time Saturday.

On September 12, 1942, a United States plane bearing the number 42-24485 landed in Memphis for the first time. This was the first landing of the bomber in Memphis. At that time, the plane had not been named. A young lieutenant had to get special permission to allow a Miss Margaret Polk to enter the Air Force part of the Airport so he could proudly show her his plane.

One more night to remember.

Margaret's memento, in her scrapbook, would be the dance stub ticket from Hotel Peabody, Number 782. On the back of it she wrote, "Us. September 12, 1942." On the same page in the scrapbook she placed an orchid corsage.

This time the young lieutenant brought her a Love Knot ring. The commitment was coming closer.

It was perhaps a week later when a bright-eyed young lady of 19 signed for a registered package dated September 21, 1942. She opened it carefully.

Inside was a diamond ring. Her engagement ring.

There was another of Bob's notes:

To the dearest person in the world - you. With this ring your are mine for as long as you love me. God make that forever. I'll return to make you a happy person.

Yours.

Bob.

It was on September 27, unable to cage all his exuberance, that Bob Morgan sent another telegram:

Congratulations on our engagement. I am the luckiest person in the world I ever found you.

Morgan

Not satisfied with that, he also mailed Margaret a letter:

My dearest Darling,

This is our day. I can't write you very much, but at least you know I am thinking about you all the time. Our job is a big one and you and I will do it together, always. I hope the ring and the picture arrived safely. The Memphis Belle [The name was on now.] will ride the sky safely, always. You can be sure. To you I send all my love. Forever yours.

Bob

Then he was gone. Off to the war.

A few days later, there came in the mail one of those little official messages from the War Department. It was on Form No. 206. It said:

I have arrived safely at new destination. Address me as shown below. First Lieutenant Robert K. Morgan, 324th Squadron, 91st Bomb Group, A.P.O. 3043, New York, N. Y.

There was no room for a love message on this one.

Then, dated October 5, 1942, his first letter came from England:

My dearest darling,

I sit here so many miles from you and write you my first letter from England. It is quite hard to write, darling, for there is so much on my heart, and it is so hard to put it on paper. You must always have faith that I'll be back one of these days. You and I have a wonderful life ahead of us and I am sure we will both dream of it much in the near future. Our life was meant to be and it will be, my love. I shall cable you as often as possible to give you assurance of my well-being. I read your old letters, over and over. They are such a great help, as is our record, 'Just as though you were here.' I play it over and over, my darling. The Memphis Belle will always stick by us and it will make our future secure.

Your Bob

There were more letters and cables during the next eight months.

"After every mission Bob would send me a cable that he was safe," said Margaret.

"They didn't always arrive promptly, of course, due to wartime security and censorship. They were not always dispatched on the day he wrote them Nor could he say that he had been on a mission."

It was after that first mission to Brest on November 7, 1942, that he cabled:

Safe and happy. Missing you with all my heart. Chin high, darling fiancee. I adore you. Your Bob.

Nobody in Memphis was aware in the beginning that there was a plane called the Memphis Belle or that there was a romance between Margaret Polk and Lieutenant Robert K. Morgan.

That was about to change.

After the Memphis Belle's fourth raid, on Lille, France, on December 6, 1942, a war correspondent in England named Dixie Tighe of International News Service (INS) wrote a story about the raid. It was published in the Commercial Appeal newspaper in Memphis.

The story told how the fliers had referred to the raid as their "answer to Sunday, December 7," the anniversary of the Japanese attack on Pearl Harbor.

"Every man and every plane returned safely to base," the dispatch said.

The story gave the description of the raid, reporting that three men were wounded. It then listed a number of the planes by name,the Delta Rebel, Jack the Ripper, the Bad Penny and so on.

In the very last paragraph of the story, it said, "Lieutenant Robert K. Morgan of Asheville, North Carolina, was at the controls of the Memphis Belle, named to honor his fiancee, Margaret Polk of Memphis."

That was all it said. But that was enough. A sharp-eyed news editor named Null Adams, of Memphis' afternoon newspaper, The Press-Scimitar, spotted the paragraph. He called a young cub reporter named Menno Duerksen to his desk.

"Duerksen, if you can find this young lady named Margaret Polk, we'll have a good story," he said.

He was right.

There were a number of Polks in the Memphis telephone book. After a few calls we hit the right one. Margaret was not at home. She was at school but her mother, Mrs. Oscar Boyle Polk, not only confirmed the romance but agreed to give pictures of Miss Polk to the newspaper, along with a picture of Lieutenant Morgan.

For the first time, on December 7, 1942, the secret was out. It was a front page story with pictures of a B-17 and of the real belle of Memphis. The last paragraph of the story said, "The couple plans to marry as soon as Lieutenant Morgan can come home."

From that day on, the story of Bob Morgan and Margaret Polk belonged to the world. Everything the Memphis Belle and her crew did were in the limelight. That fact did nothing, for the time being, to quench the romance.

The letters and and cables flew back and forth across the Atlantic, warm and passionate, full of the explosive emotions of young people in love.

On December 15, 1942, for Margaret's birthday came:

Happy Birthday. My dearest Darling Angel.

You are no longer my little girl. You have grown up darling and now you are my 'Little Lady.'

How does it feel to be out of your teens, my darling? I hope now that you are older that you'll take your fiance in hand and make me behave. I have been the bad boy again. I worked again the whole week and didn't take a pass to London. Therefore I am a very tired man and since I have a big game (code for a raid but the censor apparently missed it) I shall mind the ship. Now spank.

The boys on the Memphis Belle have always called me the "Chief" and now the whole flight is doing it. [The Memphis Belle had been the lead ship on several of the recent missions.] I act as if I don't like it , but you know it helps my ego and I love it.

I am dying to get the socks, darling. I know they will fit. [Margaret had knitted a pair of socks for him.]

Darling, I adore my "Little Lady" even more than my "Little Girl," if that is possible. Good night, Angel. I shall dream of you forever.

Your Bob

On December 21, the day after the raid on Romilly sur Seine, one of the toughest of the Belle's missions, came this letter:

My dearest, darling,

I guess you have been reading all day about our latest "Game." It was one we shall never forget and I am sure the Huns won't either. I am sure their respect for the 'Fortress' is improving.

You have a just right to be proud, dearest. Your plane wasn't even hit all day and we were attacked more than any of the rest for the Memphis Belle was taking her place in the lead. So once again I return with all my crew and not one injury. That makes me a very proud man to be flying your plane for US.

257

Darling, there is no use denying that I was scared, for I was scared to death. It was a real nightmare. But I guess I have learned now that you are flying with me each time and that God does ride with me and guide me home to safety and to you. He will always do that, my angel.

When I landed after the raid I was so tired I could hardly hold my head up. I took a small drink and came to your arms and slept like a baby, just yours.

I have at last received the rank I always wanted. I am now Captain Morgan. I am really happy about that. I got my letter from the War Department last night. I have been waiting to get to town so I can send you a cable.

Now you will be able to wear the other earrings. [He had given her a pair of earrings made from small captains bars and she had been waiting to wear them.] It will be so much better to marry a captain.

Angel, I am going to bed again as I am so tired, so I shall say goodnight to the dearest person in all the world, you, who I adore now and forever.

Your Bob

The Memphis Belle was making more headlines. On January 13, a story from International News Service said: "Memphis Belle Beats Jinx."

It was the 13th day of the month and the Memphis Belle was designated Number 13 in the mission, said the story, but the Belle came home, breaking the jinx of the 13th.

On February 4, after a raid on Emden, Captain Morgan and his co-pilot, Colonel S. T. Wray, commander of the 91st Bomb Group, reported a new trick by the Germans. They were trying to drop bombs on the Fortresses from above. The bombs that day had missed.

The stories never failed to mention that the Memphis Belle was named in honor of the girl from Memphis, Margaret Polk. Romance was now stealing the spotlight.

After most missions, Morgan managed to send a cable that said he was safe, pledging his eternal love.

The letters began to be fewer.

On March 24, Morgan wrote that Major H. W. Aycock, squadron commander, was in the hospital suffering frostbite from an earlier raid, and that Morgan was the acting operations officer.

It keeps me on the ball. I am really doing my share. We have lost Brill, Henderson and McClellan [other pilots] this month and that has made me very tired and upset, too. About the end of next month I shall step down from combat duty. The Major wants me to take over "operations" and quit flying for a while. [This did not happen.]

Darling, I wish I could tell you I'll be home in a month, or two months, or something but I can't. We are the test tubes [The early B-17s were testing the feasibility of high altitude bombing.] and when we have taken all we can take we will be sent home. Til then I have no news.

Please, darling, no matter what, remember I LOVE YOU and no one else. You are my life and without you I know I should suddenly die somehow.

Your Bob Forever

Somehow, the tour that was assigned to Bob Morgan did come to an end. On May 15, 1943, Morgan returned from his 24th mission, one of the Memphis Belle's toughest, with only one mission to go before completing his tour. He wrote Margaret:

The Belle finished her 24th today and after one more she will be retired from Captain Robert K. Morgan's hands and given to some other person to carry on with. I am going to have the name painted off, though, for I feel that she has done her part, and when I begin again somewhere else, I will have Belle the Second. You have done your share (known over here as sweating it out) and I know now that I would never have been able to finish my tour of duty over here if it had not been for the fact that you were behind me at all times. We have done a good job, darling, and I hope that our life job turns out as well as this one has. I realize now that you did the right thing in making me wait till we saw how things were going to turn out. Now you must realize that the young kid full of hell and stuff isn't the one who is coming back. The war has done many things to me, but I am sure one of them is to make a better man out of me.

To you I send all the love in the world to the sweetest person that God ever gave the light of day to.

Forever, I am yours.
Bob

259

Morgan's tour ended two days later.

Margaret had given him a little white bow the last time she had seen him, on September 12, 1942. He had attached it to his officer's insignia and had worn it on every mission.

Just before his last mission, on May 17, 1943, another bow, a blue one this time, arrived. He wrote her:

My Dearest Darling,

I am writing to you before I taxi the Belle out to takeoff position. You see, this is number 25. The whole tour will be finished. A big load off my shoulders, and yours, too.

There isn't a lot to say but, Margaret, you were riding beside me at all times and, darling , I'll finish this later when I have buzzed the hell out of the field. That is what I have longed to do, my sweetheart. I have both your ribbons on this morning and, darling, may God be with us both.

Well, sweetheart, this is it and so take this kiss and hug and keep me flying, darling angel."

There was to be one more message from England. It was a cable message:

Safe. Tour of duty completed. Fingers crossed. Adore you. Bob.

Morgan did not need to have the name painted off of his plane. He was coming to Memphis and would be flying the Belle. Margaret did not know that yet.

On May 21 she told The Press-Scimitar, "Robert cabled me that he was coming to Memphis as fast as he can get here. I don't know how he is coming, but I do know we are going to get married as soon as he gets here."

In her last letter to Bob in England she had written:

Bob, my dearest, dearest, angel,

I love you, darling. I really have a one-track mind, for you are all that runs through my thoughts. You are so wonderful. I just wish I could see you tomorrow. I have wished that for almost nine months now, but soon, real soon, my wishes will come true and I will be divinely happy.

Their throbbing young hearts would have to wait another long month.

It would be June 9 before it was officially announced that Morgan and the crew of the Memphis Belle were coming home.

Margaret and Bob no longer belonged to themselves alone. Now, in a sense, they had become public property. When the Memphis Belle swooped down on the runway at National Airport in Washington on June 16, 1943, the newspapers blared the news of their arrival.

Pictures and stories flooded the newspapers of the nation.

In the midst of all the hullaballoo, the hectic meetings and the news conferences, Bob Morgan managed to make a few telephone calls to Memphis. He sent a telegram:

Memphis Belle will arrive tomorrow. Don't forget there are nine other men. You are going to have one heck of a busy time. Am so tired I hope there will be some rest. Won't leave until Tuesday morning. Adore you. Bob.

And then it was Saturday, June 19, the roar of motors and the big bird with the lilting name Memphis Belle and the leggy Petty Girl painted on the side of her nose, swooped down onto the runway at Memphis Municipal Airport. A tall, slim young Air Force captain loped across the tarmac to grab the girl in his arms.

Bob Morgan was home.

The first inkling of what was about to happen, came a few days later with the announcement that the wedding would be postponed until after the national tour was completed. The tour would take one or two months.

Young love must wait.

It seems the public relations people at the War Department realized what a tremendous publicity coup they had on their hands. They decided it would hold public interest longer if the wedding were postponed until after the tour. The image of a romantic couple was better than a married pair, they said. There was no time for a honeymoon. The publicists couldn't see transporting a bride around on the tour.

"It was war time," said Margaret. "If the War Department asked you to do something, you did it."

THE MEMPHIS BELLE

The tour continued, from one city to another. Each city tried to outdo the preceding one in entertaining Morgan and his men. There were girls everywhere, most of them anxious to entertain the celebrated heroes.

There is a touch of sadness in his voice as he remembers it. "Too much wine, women and song," said Morgan.

Deprived of the presence of his beloved Margaret at a time when he needed her, with pretty young girls being pushed at him from all sides, perhaps it was inevitable. The first little glitch in the romance came when the crew made its stop at Cleveland, Ohio, home of Bob's peacetime employer, the Addressograph-Multigraph Corporation. The company, bursting with pride at what their former service engineer had become, staged a giant rally of the company's workers and a gala banquet at Hotel Cleveland.

Secretly, with no word to Morgan, the company arranged to fly Margaret to Cleveland to make a surprise appearance at the rally. As the Cleveland News put it, "Captain Robert K. Morgan's jaw dropped to his bootstraps when his 'Memphis Belle,' willowy Margaret Polk, came smiling but wet-eyed to his side before the cheering throng."

He swept her into his arms and, since photographers were present, it made a picture that flashed from coast to coast to the nation's newspapers. Even Life Magazine published the picture.

Perhaps part of the reason why Bob Morgan's jaw dropped was that, somehow, the presence of another young lady became known to Margaret. Was the strange young lady a date provided for Bob?

With Margaret on the scene and in his arms, Bob was willing, even eager, to forget the other girl. In fact he wanted to get married. Immediately. That day. To hell with the War Department.

Margaret demurred. She said she didn't have the proper clothes. She had no wedding dress. Someone arranged for a Cleveland store to open up, at night, to supply her needs. Margaret remembers that she was now the one to refuse. It seemed too sudden. Too rushed. Did not every girl dream of a proper wedding? And, perhaps the image of the other girl bothered her.

Then on August 1, 1943, Morgan and the Memphis Belle arrived in Denver on the tour. With it came the final break.

Margaret did not go to Denver. The break came during a phone call when she became aware that Bob was not alone in his hotel room. A female voice was heard in the background. Bitter and hurt, she told Bob it was over.

Now it was the turn of the War Department to be outraged. "You can't do this to us," officials screamed. Here they had the Memphis Belle on a nationwide publicity tour, all centered around that beautiful romance with a willowy girl in Memphis, and suddenly they were told it was all over. What would they tell the public now? What about their storybook ending to a storybook romance?

It was a time of war and Americans hungered for romance, for love stories. They needed it to take their minds off the tragedy and the violence in the world. It had been so beautiful. Now it was all over?

A bit of pressure was applied and Margaret agreed to allow the love story to continue. She would keep her mouth shut about the broken romance. After all, wasn't it a part of her war effort to play a role?

The conspiracy of silence did not work well. Margaret may have told friends what happened. Maybe they guessed it. Somewhere it leaked out. A few days later the newspapers had it.

The romance was over.

Bob Morgan had his special side of the story to tell. When the break came, he fought desperately to keep alive his thing with Margaret. He made phone calls, sent telegrams and wrote letters.

"They took you away from me," he told Margaret.

He blamed the War Department and the tour business. He wanted to come home to his beloved and get married immediately. He had dreamed about it through all those terrible months of combat flight in England when he was addressing the letters and telegrams to his "Dearest Darling." But the War Department had ordered him and his crew to make a big tour. They were soldiers. They were subject to orders.

Bob's wedding to Margaret would now have to wait until after the tour. If the military allowed Bob to stop the tour now and marry, they would have to make similar concessions to other crew members.

At least half the crew had girls waiting for them to come home.

Vince Evans, the bombardier, for example, had married just two days before leaving Walla Walla. His bride was waiting, but he would soon meet another girl on the tour and divorce his Dinny.

Girls continued to fling themselves into the arms of the heroes as they continued their triumphant tour of the nation. Only stone-hearted men could have resisted. They were hot-blooded young men, home from a bitter war and hungry for love.

263

THE MEMPHIS BELLE

Maybe it was anger or resentment at the thing fate had done to him that flung Bob Morgan into the arms of another girl so quickly. He met a girl named Patricia Anne Huckins when the crew arrived in San Antonio on the national tour. On August 11, the newspaper announced his engagement to the lady.

When the newspapers asked him about his engagement to his "Memphis Belle" he suggested they had never been engaged.

His engagement to Miss Patricia Anne Huckins lasted only a few days.

The romance with Margaret refused to die. Bob tried to get it back on the rails. Once, on a trip through Memphis, he tried to contact her. She was not home or chose to have that message given to him.

He poured his heart out in a letter on October 27, while training on a B-29 with the 395th Bomb Squadron at Pratt, Kansas:

The public took a tired young man away from you. I loved you and never have ceased. Yes, I was blinded by the actions I had to face because I wanted to come home to you. You know the only way I could come home was to be the pilot of a famous bomber. I wanted to come home for one reason, you. We kept our love going, through hell and high water.

God gave us life and happiness. I gave you all that. I came home. I am made a hero when all I want is you. I warned you in Memphis that this tour was not to my liking. The public damn near killed me and got me to the point where I wanted to tell all of them where to go. You had told me that at any cost I had a job to do even here in the States. I did it and a damned good job. I made an awful error by blowing up but I couldn't help it, darling. I needed you and your pride kept you from coming to me.

I need you now forever. I need you now more than at any time over Germany. You belong to me and God gave me the strength to come back to you. Why don't you admit that our love was the love of the year and always will be.

This is our last chance, darling, as I can't take it any more. I can't even fly a B-17 without looking up for your picture. I can't even look at my dog tags without looking for your ribbons.

You belong to me.

They were the words of a man in love even if, under the pressure of public adulation, he had not been able to remain completely faithful. In the rest of his letter he said his colonel had

264

promised him 15 days off if he could persuade Margaret to come back. They would be quietly married, he promised, and the public would learn nothing about it until weeks later.

In her reply, the next day after receiving Bob's plea, Margaret was trying hard to be cool:

Here I sit in the midst of downy cushions. Do I hear you ask why? As usual, I have just returned from the farm. The horse went one way and I went down and hit rock bottom. Won't I ever learn? O.K. laugh. It's worth it.

I received your letter yesterday. Some parts of it beat the hell out of me. So I must make the next move. Well, here goes. I am asking you to come here so we can have a little talk. There are a few rough spots. If the Colonel will give you 15 days after you "talk me into it," surely he will give you a few days to "talk me into it." Perhaps one of the main difficulties is the fact that we have never been with each other except for a few hours. I think we should have another speaking session, or a good facsimile.

Bob, do you agree with that old axiom now? You really don't realize the value of something until you lose it. If it was of any value in the first place, it should be worth working for. The days of "Pennies from Heaven" are past.

You say you can't go on like this, Bob, if we don't marry I will still be on your mind. I am linked to the most important thing in your life. If we can't talk things over and recover our old feelings, you will always wonder what it would have been like being married to me. Oh, do you want my opinion? O.K. I will save it for future reference. Just as you say, Chief.

Something to tuck you in bed tonight. Have you ever tried to reflect yourself into my place? What would you have done, or would you do now, under existing circumstances? I do hope I will see you soon.

Sweet dreams
Margaret

P.S. People here are bursting with curiosity as to what we are doing.

Somehow, it didn't work. On November 17, still at Pratt Air Base, Bob wrote what should have been his farewell to the girl he had loved so much:

THE MEMPHIS BELLE

*Yes, I guess I do understand how you felt when you got that
letter from me while I was in Denver, but I will never feel that you
could have loved me as you said and let us go our ways without
doing anything about it. If I could feel that you ever truly loved me,
I'd try to win it back. We have been apart now for a long time and
the wound is nearly gone and I feel we would open it once again if
we tried to start over again.*

*I hope we will always be friends and that any time I am in
Memphis, I will give you a call. I hope you will do the same when
you are near wherever I am. I hope I have as much luck this next
trip [his next tour of duty] as I did last time. I guess I'm the only
member of the 8th Air Force who is crazy enough to go back to
combat, but I am fighting for something still.*

As ever. B.

And then he was gone, back to the wars. This time he
would be flying a different kind of airplane and would lead the first
B-29 raid over Tokyo. Destiny, somehow, was keeping this man
Morgan in the headlines.

But, before leaving for the Pacific he made a trip back home
to Asheville, North Carolina. There on December 29, 1943, he
married Dorothy Grace Johnson. He had met her on one of those
earlier trips home, after his furlough at the end of the grand national
tour. Now it was in her honor that he named his new plane, a B-29,
the Dauntless Dollie. It would be Dorothy who would give Bob his
children.

The Dauntless Dollie, at least the plane, would not be as
lucky as had been the Memphis Belle. On July 8, 1944, the Air
Force announced that she had crashed off the Island of Kwajalein in
the South Pacific, while taking off for a trip back to the United
States with another crew, killing ten of the 13 men aboard.

The marriage to Dorothy ended, for all practical purposes,
the storybook romance of the Memphis Belle.

Except there would be one time, during the years that
followed, when it almost came back to life once more. They wrote
each other. They met again and the old flame was alive again.
Margaret likes to remember it, that flaring of the old flame, as proof
that their love had not been just another casual weekend affair. It
proved, for her, that there was something durable and undying
about it, after all.

"I would have married him at this time if circumstances had permitted it," she said. But those circumstances had their way of interfering and it couldn't happen.

Even Margaret agrees that, after that last little flaring of what had once been a marvelous thing, it was indeed ended.

"I knew it was over for good," she said.

For one thing, Margaret had a new battle on her hands.

She had always enjoyed a drink. It had helped make things spark when she had been together with Bob. Later, even as early as her airline stewardess days, she found that her drinking had become a problem. She lost the stewardess job.

"I'm glad that marijuana and cocaine were not around then or I probably would have gotten into them, too," she said.

The hell lasted nearly 16 years and only ended in 1963 when she collapsed in a coma which lasted five days.

After coming out of the coma in a hospital, her health was shattered. She had to spend months in a hospital in Dallas, Texas, slowly recovering her health and the will to live.

It left her, she says, with a slight brain impairment and an equilibrium problem. "I had to have railings put in my house to hold onto, at times," she said.

She does not mind if Memphis Belle fans know about her long journey into hell and back.

"It might help someone to stay away from what I went through," she said.

Had it been the bitterness and disappointment of her failed romance which helped catapult her into her battle with alcohol?

"I believe that our romance was something that simply was not meant to be," she said quietly. "You see, Bob and I never had a chance to be together for any length of time. My mother adored Bob. They were great friends. But mother said several times that, in her opinion, Bob would be a wonderful lover but a hell of a poor husband.

"I believe if Bob and I had married, we would have torn each other to pieces."

She pauses to think of it again.

"I believe I was more in love with love than with a man," she said. "I believe God had a hand in it all along."

It had been in its best moments a thing of such splendored beauty. It had seemed to be a love affair made in heaven.

Bob Morgan is as hesitant in discussing it now. He, too, has come to terms with what life, in the end, has brought him.

His marriage to Dorothy finally broke up, but he is married again and, he says, this one is successful.

"I have a fantastic marriage now," he says.

He prefers not to reflect on what might have been.

Postscript

They call her "Polky" today. It is a term of casual endearment from the best of her oldtime friends from school days.

Bob Morgan called her "Polky" when their romance was young and blooming. It survives, shorn of its romantic shading but with a special meaning for those who love her in a different way.

Not that she has a lot of friends. Some might say she almost leads a monastic life in her modest home in midtown Memphis.

There are those other friends. The family of raccoons, for example, that comes sliding down a certain pole in her backyard every evening to claim those generous offerings of bread, dog food and sweet marshmallows.

For those marshmallows even the mature raccoons willingly surrender a certain measure of their dignity, sitting in the shadows, smacking and chewing in shameless joy.

"Some of them, especially the younger ones, will take the food out of my hand," she says with gentle satisfaction.

The chipmunk friends are a bit more wary by nature. They must be watched from indoors as they arrive like nervous thieves to snatch the food Margaret has left for them, also.

A rabbit used to come every day, hopping down the driveway, in search of the tasty morsels she offered him. One day he did not come back.

"Maybe a dog got him," said Margaret with a touch of resignation in her voice, as if it was something that you had to expect.

Birds feed freely in her back yard. They know where lives the generous heart.

Margaret must act with a measure of firmness to enforce an uneasy truce between her dog Shelly, a Shetland collie, whose genes stir her to make warlike gestures towards all those hungry visitors.

There have always been dogs in her life, especially in the later years. A favorite was Columbo, the German shepherd who failed miserably at obedience school because he refused to leave her side as is required by some exercises.

Her friendship for all little creatures has filled a large part of her life since the time in 1963 when she crawled painfully out of the private hell she had been living with for so many years.

She has worked for years with the Humane Society, on the edge of things because she cannot abide close relationships with the real action of the society.

"I can't go in where the cages are, looking at them and knowing," she says, her voice trailing off.

She spent five or six years working with Alcoholics Anonymous, helping other victims struggle out of their own hells. But there came a time to give it up.

"I wasn't thinking like an alcoholic anymore," she said. "This is something you need if you work with these people."

The specter of alcohol never leaves her, she says. Alcohol has claimed many members of her family as victims including her father, her brother, her sister and her sister's husband.

It claimed her husband.

Margaret Polk had married in 1950 but the marriage had lasted only five years.

"It was never really a marriage," she said. "I was in the midst of the drinking problem and he had the problem, too. It couldn't have worked."

When it ended, she legally resumed her maiden name.

She spends some of her time working with the Women's Exchange, a place where good clothing is made available at bargain prices.

"I sell and wait on tables in their tea room" she said.

She has been there to help whenever Memphis Belle fans have tried to raise money to restore the old plane and build a permanent home for it. She always lends her presence and her support as the real Memphis Belle.

Has she turned to religion, perhaps? Tom, her brother, is a retired Episcopal minister.

"I am not one for organized religion," she says gently. "I have my own religion. I believe in God and believe He had a hand in all the things that happened to me but it is something I keep to myself."

Doctors tell her to slow down. They have told her she has a damaged heart valve and will have to have surgery. She must reduce the swimming she has always loved, in her own backyard pool.

She accepts it all in serenity.

A visitor said recently as he left her, "Well, I'll go and leave you in peace."

She had a most simple reply.

"I am at peace. I'm always at peace."

The Search For the Legend

This might be called the mystery of the Memphis Belle Legend.

It is the legend created by the War Department and its spokesmen in 1943 when the Memphis Belle and her crew completed their 25 mission tour of combat duty and were chosen to fly back to the United States for a nationwide publicity tour.

The legend was spread throughout the U.S. by countless newspaper stories, magazine articles and books. It has been kept alive all these years.

It is a neat little package, that legend. Simply put, it says that the Memphis Belle was the first B-17 Flying Fortress to complete 25 combat missions over German-held Europe, that it did so with its original crew of ten men, that the crew of the Memphis Belle shot down eight enemy planes, that only one member of its crew was wounded. Finally, May 17, 1943, was the date always given for the Belle's 25th mission.

Even today, as this legend reveals cracks and flaws, one who attempts to unravel the mystery is faced with a tangled thicket of conflicting records, official and otherwise, claims and counter claims, and the fading memories of the men involved about the things that happened to them more than 40 long years ago.

Perhaps Exhibit A in the creation of the legend is a little booklet of 36 pages published by the War Department in 1943, as the Belle and her crew were on that triumphant tour. Entitled, "Twenty Five Missions," it has a foreword by General W. H. Arnold, commander of the Air Forces, and there can be little doubt about the official status of this booklet.

It is true that the booklet does not flatly state that the Memphis Belle was the first B-17 to complete 25 missions, but there is little doubt that War Department spokesmen were responsible for that legendary story.

271

THE MEMPHIS BELLE

Colonel Bob Morgan says: "There was never any doubt in my mind, even for a minute, as to whether the Memphis Belle was the first to complete 25 missions. That is what General Arnold wrote and what General Eaker told us. We had no reason to doubt it. It is the official record."

The booklet does state that the Belle was the first plane to complete 25 missions *and be sent home.*

It is easy to miss the importance of the last part of that statement.

The booklet also states that it was "the same crew to a man that was organized ten months ago in Maine."

Colonel Morgan has never made any attempt to argue that this is true. But he does insist that neither he nor any member of the crew that flew back from England with him did anything to promote such a claim.

"To my knowledge, we were never asked about it."

As to the eight enemy planes destroyed, as symbolized by the eight swastikas painted on the sides of the plane, Colonel Morgan is willing to argue with documents showing up now that indicate that claim is too high.

"When we returned from missions and claims for 'kills' were made," he said, "we were never allowed to paint the swastikas on the plane until the claim was verified and we had official permission to do so. There is no way you can take that record away from the men."

As to the number of the Belle's crewmen wounded in combat, it does little to change the over-all story, but research for the Memphis Belle story brought up information indicating the number should be three, possibly four. Colonel Morgan insists that there was only one official wound, with a Purple Heart medal awarded, and this seems to be true.

When this writer began the background research for this book he believed the story told in the War Department booklet, "Twenty Five Missions." He had written about it in several newspaper articles. After he began digging into old Air Forces records and encountered conflicting data, he began to wonder.

We spent months writing letters, making phone calls, interviewing the surviving crewmen, checking and re-checking everything we could get our hands on. True, we did not always find what we wanted. Some documents we wanted had either been destroyed or could not be found. What we did find was impressive.

For example, we have two copies, obtained from two separate sources, of the operational flight log of the 324th Squadron, compiled during the time when the Memphis Belles was on her combat tour. We have records from the engineering staff of the 324th Squadron, showing which planes went on missions and on which days. We have a copy, running into hundreds of pages, of the narrative diary-log of the 91st Heavy Bombardment Group, as written daily in 1942 and 1943 by Captain S. T. Parker, the group's official historian. The Memphis Belle was one of the original nine B-17s assigned to the 324th Squadron, one of the four squadrons of the 91st Bomb Group. We had the diaries kept by three members of the Belle's crew during the combat period, James Verinis, Charles Leighton and Clarence Winchell.

There are many other documents.

First, let's examine the claim that the Memphis Belle was the first B-17 to complete 25 combat missions. Several books about Air Forces history during World War II, published since the war, have repeated the claim that the Belle was first. Others have said no.

One document found is a letter written by Major R. H. Hodges of Pelham, New York, a retired B-17 pilot of World War II. The letter was published in the Aerospace Historian, a magazine devoted to aviation history, in its Winter 1986-87 issue. It said, in part: "It is incongruous to read again that the 91st Bomb Group's Memphis Belle was the first to complete 25 operational missions in the European Theater of Operations. This myth-error is evident on pages 295-296 of James Parton's newly published biography of General Ira C. Eaker, Air Forces Spoken Here. It also keeps showing up in magazine articles but was shot down many years ago. The false claim, e.g., was demolished by Roger Freeman in his 1970 book, The Mighty Eighth."

Freeman's book is considered one of the most authoritative histories of the Eighth Air Force. On page 47 he writes, "May 14th, 1943, was a milestone for the Eighth. For the first time, over 200 heavies were dispatched. Another notable occurrence was the completion of 25 missions by the Molesworth Fortress Hell's Angels. Not once did it have to turn back due to mechanical failure and only one bullet hole and a few flak patches bore witness to its hours in hostile skies."

On page 74 he writes of the 303rd Bomb Group's Flying Fortresses: "One, Hell's Angels, had been the first B-17 of the Eighth to reach 25 missions."

After finding these passages in Freeman's book, we wrote to the author in England, asking him for his sources of information about Hell's Angels.

He replied, "My information as used in The Mighty Eighth, was based on squadron and group reports and PR handouts. All contemporary records of the Eighth Air Force stated that Hell's Angels, of the 303rd, was the first B-17 to complete 25 missions. It can be said with some certainty about the Memphis Belle that it was the first Eighth Air Force B-17 to complete 25 missions and be returned to the U.S."

He added, "Few, if any, crews flew all their assigned 25 missions in one particular aircraft."

After receiving Freeman's letter, we contacted Parton, author of the Eaker biography, and Irl E. Baldwin, Colonel, USAF Ret., who had been the pilot of Hell's Angels.

Parton, who had been an aide to General Eaker in England during World War II, wrote to say that since his book had been published, he had discovered from several sources that he had been in error in the book about the Memphis Belle being the first B-17 to complete 25 missions and that he would correct this in a subsequent edition of the book.

Baldwin said in his letter that he, as the pilot, had completed his 25th mission on May 14. He also said, in later letters that at least part of his crew finished their 25th mission on the same day. However, he said his diary showed that the plane itself had not completed its 25th mission until May 17, the same day on which, as the available data show Captain Morgan and five members of his crew completed their 25th mission.

Certified copies of the logs of both Baldwin and his plane, Hell's Angels, confirm what he said. These records were compiled by James Rodriguez, Master Sergeant, USAF Ret., who had been a crew member of Hell's Angels.

The record of the 324th Squadron should be illuminating.

Its operational flight log shows that Colonel Morgan, then a captain, completed his 25th mission on May 17, but the Memphis Belle did not complete its 25th mission until May 19. The Belle had been grounded several times for repairs to battle damage and on several of those occasions, the Belle's regular crew had been assigned to fly combat missions on other planes. Therefore, in order to bring the plane's mission numbers up to the crew's, the Belle was sent out on combat missions with other pilots and crews.

THE MEMPHIS BELLE

At least two of these missions, the log shows, were flown before May 17 and one, May 19, was flown after.

The log shows that B-17F No. 485 was sent on a combat mission to Kiel, Germany on May 19 and that this was the plane's 25th mission. The pilot that day was Lieutenant C. L. Anderson. The co-pilot was Lieutenant D. F. Gladhart. The only member of the Belle's regular crew on the plane that day was Staff Sergeant Emerson S. Miller who flew as tail gunner. Miller had previously flown as a waist gunner.

Documents obtained to verify the record of the May 19 mission include a second copy of the 324th Squadron Operations Log, from a second source, a copy of the engineering records of the squadron and a copy, from the U.S. National Archives (Military Division), Washington, D.C., of the Interrogation Form for the crew of the Memphis Belle on May 19, 1943, showing that they did indeed fly the plane to Kiel on that date. All of the above documents confirm the May 19 mission. Three of the documents show it to be the 25th mission for the Belle.

Colonel Morgan, however, does not agree with these records. He believes the flight logs are in error.

"I flew the Memphis Belle myself on May 19," he said.

He said it was a noncombat flight to shoot additional movie footage for the War Department documentary film being made by William Wyler, featuring the Memphis Belle. Wyler was aboard that day, said Morgan, and the plane did not enter a combat zone.

Morgan provides copies of his own pilot operations log for this period which show that he flew a B-17F on May 19, for two hours and fifty minutes. This log does not show that the plane was the Memphis Belle.

"My records do," he said.

Two hours and 50 minutes would not be long enough for a combat mission since they usually took at least five hours, sometimes as many as eight or nine.

Consulting the 91st Bomb Group's official narrative log-history, compiled at the time by Captain S. T. Parker, only confuses the issue further. In an entry dated May 15, 1943, Parker wrote, "The Memphis Belle, piloted by Captain Robert K. Morgan, completed its 25th mission today. Although this crew does not have the record to complete 25 missions without a turnback, it is one of the first crews to complete 25 missions for the 91st intact."

Two days later, on May 17, Lieutenant Carlton Brechler, a public relations officer for the 91st Bomb Group, corrected the May

15 narrative log entry by writing a news release which stated that Captain Morgan and five members of his crew completed their 25th mission on that day.

An International News Service dispatch from England, dated May 17, 1943, also stated that Captain Morgan and five members of his crew completed their 25th mission on that day. The INS newsman may have obtained his information from Brechler's release. A news clipping of the INS dispatch is preserved in one of the scrapbooks belonging to Margaret Polk, then Morgan's fiancee.

If you can stand a bit more confusion, another official document, found in the records of the 324th Squadron, is a sheet showing percentages of missions begun and completed by each plane of the squadron. This list, compiled after June of 1943, shows the Memphis Belle started on 28 missions and aborted, or turned back, on four. Subtract four from 28 and you have 24.

Still more confusion comes from the operational flight log for the 324th. It shows that the Memphis Belle aborted on only three missions, on Nov. 23, 1942, March 8, and April 4, 1943. The only possible explanation for the four aborts on the abort sheet might come from the fact that Captain Morgan and the Belle's crew started a mission on March 4, 1943, flying on a plane called Jersey Bounce, but aborted due to mechanical problems. It is possible that a squadron clerk entered that abort for the Memphis Belle.

Is it possible that the Memphis Belle flew only 24 missions, rather than 25? This is highly unlikely, since General Eaker, when he wrote the order that a plane be selected to be sent to the United States on a morale-building and training tour, specifically stated that such a plane be selected and that each member of the crew must have completed 25 missions.

Research into this question leads into recurring references to still another plane in the 91st Group with a high number of missions, the Delta Rebel II of the 323rd Squadron with Captain George Birdsong of Clarksdale, Mississippi, as pilot. Birdsong, who also retired as a colonel, now lives at Pleasanton, California.

Roger Freeman said his records showed the Delta Rebel II had completed its 25 missions on May 17.

Birdsong said his own personal diary showed that the Delta Rebel, as a plane, had completed its 25th mission on May 15. He agreed that neither he nor the crew had flown all of their 25 missions on the Delta Rebel II.

Through Birdsong's assistance, and through Dan Bauer of Monroe, Wisconsin, a copy was obtained of the personal log-diary of Bob Abb, bombardier on the Delta Rebel II. Abb's log shows that the Delta Rebel II completed its 25th mission on May 1, not May 14.

Although this record is not official, it is possible, for this was the 91st Group's 36th mission, which would have meant that the Rebel had flown 25 out of 36 missions. Abb's description of the May 1 mission agrees with other descriptions of that mission.

Checking the missions record of other planes of the 324th brought another surprise. The log shows two other planes of that squadron completed their 25th mission on May 17 and 19.

One of these, the Jersey Bounce, according to the log, completed her 25th mission on May 17. Then, on May 21, while on her 26th mission, this plane was shot down. Her pilot on that day was Lieutenant P. S. Fischer who had flown as Captain Morgan's co-pilot on at least one occasion. The Belle crew had flown this plane several times when the Belle had been laid up for repairs.

The other plane was none other than James Verinis' Connecticut Yankee, which, the logs show, completed her 25th mission on May 19, the same day shown for the Belle's 25th mission. The surprising factor here being that the Yankee had been a replacement plane which did not complete its first combat mission until January 13, 1943, Verinis' first in this plane. The Yankee had previously aborted two missions with another pilot.

Which meant that the Connecticut Yankee had to do some fast and furious catching up.

Verinis had said that there was a stretch when he had to fly almost every day.

The missions record of the Jersey Bounce and the Connecticut Yankee are confirmed by engineering records of the 324th Squadron.

Which raises the question: If three planes from a single squadron completed their 25 missions on or about the same time, what would one find in a check of other squadrons and groups?

All of which leaves a lot of unanswered questions about which plane was first. However, the weight of the evidence seems to lean in the direction of Hell's Angels.

Concerning the matter of the Memphis Belle's "intact" crew.

A copy of the original flight order, sending the 324th Squadron overseas from Bangor, Maine, in September of 1942, includes the list of crew members of each plane.

The list shows Robert K. Morgan, pilot; James A. Verinis, co-pilot; Charles B. Leighton, navigator; Vincent B. Evans, bombardier; Leviticus G. Dillon, flight engineer and gunner; Harold P. Loch, assistant flight engineer and gunner; Robert J. Hanson, radio operator and gunner; Cecil C. Scott, assistant radio operator and gunner; and John P. Quinlan, tail gunner. The order lists as being on board a Lieutenant John K. Rickles, a Group S-2 officer. Morgan and the other crew members remember that he flew over only as a passenger and never flew on the Belle in England.

When the Memphis Belle returned from England in June of 1943 for the national tour, Dillon's name was missing and two others had been added, Clarence E. Winchell and Casimer A. Nastal, both listed as waist gunners. So, it immediately becomes apparent that the crew that came back was not the same as the one that went over, no matter what the War Department booklet said.

We have already explained Dillon's disappearance from the crew. After flying four missions on the Belle, he had a bit of a controversy with the Military Police and was transferred.

As for Winchell, originally trained as a bombardier, he said he was shipped to England on the Queen Mary, together with other ground personnel. He was assigned to the Belle's crew before it began flying combat missions and flew all of his 25 missions on either the Belle or with the Belle's crew on other planes.

Some crew members of the Belle were reluctant to talk about some parts of the crew's record when research first began on the Belle book. This was most apparent with Nastal.

"I don't want to talk about it," he said flatly.

After insistant questions and a promise to be fair, Nastal finally explained his reluctance. He had flown only a few missions on the Belle, "maybe two or three" toward the end of the Belle's tour of duty.

He explained why he was chosen to go home with the Belle crew.

"I was sitting there with my 25 missions completed," he said. "One of the Belle's crew didn't have enough missions and, since I had flown a few missions on the Belle, they simply told me to pack my gear and go with them. I didn't have any choice in the matter. It was an order."

He added, "I've been uncomfortable about it all these years, that story that I was a member of the original crew."

He seemed relieved to be able to talk about it at long last.

Sure, he had flown his 25 combat missions but they had been mostly on other planes. In fact, that original order taking the 324th Squadron to England listed Nastal as a tail gunner on a plane

278

called Pandora's Box, with Lieutenant Donald W. Garrett as pilot. Pandora's Box was shot down after seven missions but luckily, Nastal was not on her that day.

Amazingly, Nastal had not only completed his 25 missions before the crew of the Belle had, but later on volunteered for a second tour of duty as a B-17 gunner and flew 35 missions on that second tour of duty. The normal tour of duty increased from 25 to 35 as the number of bombers increased and the missions were protected by more and more fighter escorts. He had flown 60 combat missions at the end of the war.

The records show only two missions for Nastal on the Belle, with crews other than the Belle's regular crew. He flew most of his missions as tail gunner, rather than waist gunner, as he was listed for the Memphis Belle.

Nastal was credited with shooting down two enemy planes during his first tour of duty, one on January 3, 1943, in a raid on St. Nazaire, and the other on March 6, in a raid on Lorient, France. The first was while flying as tail gunner on the Jersey Bounce. The second was on Jim Verinis' plane, the Connecticut Yankee. Neither kill is credited to the Memphis Belle or her crew.

Thus, Nastal flew more combat missions than any member of the Belle's crew. It is a record any man could be proud of, for very few gunners volunteered for a second tour of duty. The only possible question about his record is that he was listed, not by Nastal but by the War Department, as a member of the original crew of the Memphis Belle.

Bill Winchell did not go over on the Belle, but it can be said truthfully that he was an original member because he flew combat with the Belle from the very beginning.

However, there was the matter of his diary, which he kept during his combat days. Dr. Harry Friedman of the Memphis Belle Memorial Board had a copy of Winchell's diary, a typewritten transcript of the original. It had lots of blank spaces, some filled in by pen. The person making the transcript apparently had trouble reading Winchell's handwriting in the diary so he left blank spaces.

Winchell's diary listed the names of the crew members on each mission, showing when substitutions had been made, as well as the names of the other planes they flew when the Belle was grounded for repairs to battle damage.

Winchell said his original diary had been misplaced and he couldn't find it. He was urged to make new searches for the diary but each time he reported the diary still could not be found.

One night he called this writer and said, "My wife, Laura, and I have been doing some soul searching about this diary thing. I found the original diary. I'm making a clear copy of it and sending it to you. It's all very clear."

He sent along a typed copy of the original plus a photo machine copy of the original handwritten note book in which he had kept his combat diary.

Then the picture began to clear up.

The diary told how, when Dillon was transferred off the Belle's crew, his place was taken by a Sergeant Eugene Adkins. After flying some six missions on the Belle, Adkins suffered frostbite to both hands and had to be hospitalized. Adkins' place on the Belle crew was taken by Sergeant Emerson S. Miller who remained with the crew until the plane was sent home. He was the one who did not have his 25 missions behind him. Nastal took his place.

The problem with Winchell's diary was that it stopped at mission 20. He said someone probably had reminded him that combat crews were forbidden from keeping combat diaries.

Many men did keep diaries, despite the order forbidding it. Two of the Belle's crew, James Verinis and Charles Leighton, kept diaries although they did not list crew members on each mission or the names of the substitute planes they flew.

Verinis' diary changes in value when he stopped flying the Belle. Leighton's became sketchy towards the end, petering out before the 25 missions were complete.

The talkative tail gunner, John Quinlan, pointed to the tape recorder during an interview on the Belle and said, "Turn that thing off and I'll tell you about it."

With the tape recorder off, Quinlan said that during his tour, on those days when the Belle did not fly but other planes did, he had been assigned as a tail gunner on some other plane.

"That is why," he said, "I had my 25 missions in before the rest of the crew and they [the commanders] would not let me fly with the Belle on her last couple of missions."

After all those years, the "intact crew" thing still remained in his mind and he wanted to be a good soldier and protect that image. He felt reassured when he was told that such things happened to just about every combat crew in England and that the other crew shifts were widely known.

THE MEMPHIS BELLE

Charles Leighton said that he had flown an extra mission on another plane and had to sit out the last mission of the Belle as it flew its 25th.

The co-pilot's seat in the Belle changed hands more than any other position on the plane. At least ten different pilots flew co-pilot on the Belle during her time in England.

Neither Bob Morgan nor any member of the crew made any bones about that. Although, according to the "Twenty Five Missions" booklet, Verinis rode as co-pilot for all 25 missions.

The story here was, simply, that Verinis had qualified as a first pilot before going overseas. There was no plane available for him when the 91st Bomb Group moved to England, so he had to take the co-pilot's seat of the Memphis Belle.

He flew five of the first six missions with the Memphis Belle, once as first pilot because Morgan was ill, and then was given his own B-17, which he named the Connecticut Yakee in honor of his home state. He flew his own plane for the remainder of his missions and completed 25 before the other members of the Belle's crew. He was chosen as a member of the crew to go home on the national tour because he had started out on the Belle and he had his 25 missions.

On several flights of the Memphis Belle, according to flight logs, Colonel Stanley T. Wray, commander of the 91st Bomb Group, rode in the co-pilot's seat on the Belle. He was a qualified pilot and went on missions, riding in various planes, to get a first hand look at bombing results and combat conditions.

Sometimes squadron commanders would fill the co-pilot's seat, men such as Major C. E. Putnam, Major Haley Aycock and Lieutenant Colonel B. R. Lawrence.

Other pilots who sat in the Belle's co-pilot's seat were Lieutenant C. W. Freschauf, Lieutenant J. S. Jackson, Lieutenant J. M. Smith, Lieutenant J. H. Miller and Lieutenant D. F. Gladhart.

The Belle flew with 11 men on her crew several times. This happened when the Belle was designated as the lead ship for a mission, making Vince Evans the lead bombardier. A bombardier usually had a machine gun to man, as well as the bomb sight to operate. When he had to act as the lead bombardier, that job was considered so important that an extra crewman was assigned to handle the bombardier's machine gun so he could devote his full time to his bomb sight. One of the men who flew as the 11th man was a Staff Sergeant Markle, first name not known.

281

THE MEMPHIS BELLE

On the March 28 raid to Rouen, France, on a day when Sergeant Miller had a cold and was grounded, his place on the Belle was taken by a Staff Sergeant Spagnolo. It almost became his last flight. During the battle, Spagnolo's oxygen mask became unplugged from the oxygen source and he lost consciousness. When Winchell went to his rescue, Winchell also passed out. Bob Hanson, the radio man, went back with portable oxygen masks to revive both of them. They both would have been dead in minutes if Hanson had not come when he did.

Cecil Scott missed a raid on November 18, 1942, because of a cold and was replaced on the Belle by a Sergeant McNally. Scott apparently had to fly a make-up mission before reaching 25 but, since he died of a heart attack since coming home, that cannot be verified by the sergeant himself.

On the last mission of the Belle's crew on May 17, the navigator who took Leighton's place was Lieutenant Raymond Y. Kurtz of Bellerose, New York. The gunner who took Quinlan's place was Sergeant Robert W. Cole of Beverly, Massachussetts.

According to Winchell and other members of the crew then, the men who flew all their missions on the Belle or with the majority of the Belle's crew were Winchell, Bob Hanson, Vince Evans and Harold Loch. Since Scott is shown as making the May 17 mission, he apparently had done his make-up mission prior to that.

In reviewing all these facts about the crew it becomes apparent that it is impossible to reconcile the real record with the War Department's document.

If the crew members of the Memphis Belle played any part in this, their role was confined to the matter of an unwritten and unspoken agreement to cooperate with what the War Department had said in "Twenty Five Missions" and to remain silent.

They have all agreed that now, with so much time elapsed, there is no use to continue the silence. Most said they felt better with the true story now being told.

There are still a couple of little items on the record which raise questions. There are eight swastikas painted on the side of the Memphis Belle, indicating the number of enemy planes shot down by crew members of the plane. However, two of the official records acquired during research, indicate that the number of enemy planes shot down by the 324th Squadron is only four for the Memphis Belle. One news dispatch sent from Bassingbourn in June of 1943 speaks of six. Why the discrepancy? Was it really four or six or eight?

THE MEMPHIS BELLE

As Colonel Morgan and other crew members emphatically state, whenever the planes came back from a combat mission with claims of enemy planes shot down, each claim was carefully examined by the intelligence officers. No crew was permitted to add a swastika until given official permission to do so.

There is only one possible explanation. In the narrative history-diary kept by Captain S. T. Parker at Bassingbourn, there is a mention in one of the entries that the Air Force command had become aware of the fact that the number of shoot-downs being recorded was too high. As a result, the command decided to revise the figures downward, reducing the number of enemy planes claimed as destroyed.

There would, of course, remain the question as to what to do about those claims already allowed, with swastikas already painted on the planes. We have no official documents to prove this, but our guess would be that the commanders decided not to demand that the extra swastikas be removed from the planes.

We must once more point to the War Department's booklet, "Twenty Five Missions." It says of the crew of the Memphis Belle, "They shot down eight enemy fighters, probably got five others and damaged at least a dozen."

We certainly are not going to suggest that any of those eight swastikas on the Memphis Belle be removed.

One little matter that might be looked at is the fact that only one official wound is claimed for the crew. That was a slight upper leg wound for tail gunner John P. Quinlan on March 28, 1943, on a raid to Rouen, France. He was, upon landing, sent to the base hospital, kept one day and awarded the Purple Heart, the official combat wound medal.

There may have been three more injuries suffered in combat by members of the Belle's crew.

Leviticus Dillon, who flew four of the Belle's first five missions, said he was struck in the leg by a hunk of shrapnel, causing a bleeding wound, on the third raid, which was on St. Nazaire.

Dillon said he reported it at the time, on the plane's intercom system, and that Lieutenant Verinis, the co-pilot, came back to look at it and apply first aid. Verinis' diary confirms this.

Dillon was ordered to report to the base hospital when the plane landed, but he didn't go.

"When we got back to the base," he said, "it wasn't hurting or bleeding and I saw the liberty bus was about to take off. I decided I had rather go on liberty than go to the hospital, so I jumped on the bus and took off."

Later that night, while at a bar in town, someone told him his leg was bleeding. He said he went to a first aid station were he got a fresh bandage for the wound from Adele Astaire, the sister of Fred Astaire. He said he never reported it as a wound and never was given a Purple Heart.

Then there is the matter of Gene Adkins' frostbitten hands. Bob Morgan says that frostbites were never officially considered to be war wounds. However, since Adkins suffered the frostbite while in combat and then spent a month in the hospital, almost losing both hands, it might be said that he suffered far more than did Dillon or Quinlan and that his frostbite should be considered a war wound.

Another such incident involves Nastal, who said he was struck in the butt by a piece of shrapnel.

Nastal said it was not serious and he applied his own first aid and never reported it or went to the hospital. He is not even certain if it took place on the Memphis Belle or on some other plane. However, since Nastal is listed in theTwenty Five Missions booklet as an original member of the crew, how should this be viewed?

One of the most baffling mysteries connected with the Memphis Belle remains unsolved. Why did the War Department documentary film about the Memphis Belle insist on centering that film around a mythical bombing of Wilhelmshaven on May 15, when the official record clearly indicates that the 91st Bomb Group on that day bombed naval installations on the island of Heligoland?

Why did that film, shown in private to President Roosevelt, then later to millions of Americans in theaters throughout the nation, call it the 25th and final mission for the Memphis Belle and her crew? Official records of the 91st Bomb Group show that the May 15 mission was the 24th for the crew and the 23rd for their plane.

True, the primary target for the 91st Bomb Group and other groups on May 15 was Wilhelmshaven. However, the record shows that the bomber formations found Wilhelmshaven completely covered by what the Air Force meteorologists called 10/10 clouds, meaning visibility zero. After this finding, the record shows, the bomber formations turned back and bombed Heligoland with excellent results.

If there was some reason for the deception, that reason must have existed from the very beginning for Captain S. T. Parker, the 91st Bomb Group historian. In his daily log he asked the question,

Why had the base public relations officers put out no news release as they usually did after a successful bombing raid? Only silence.

On other occasions when bomber formations found their targets socked in they turned to secondary targets that were less covered by clouds. There had never been an attempt to keep such diversions secret, especially when they were successful. It had simply been the fortunes of war.

Obviously, William Wyler, the award-winning Hollywood film director who had put the film together for the War Department, knew something about the Wilhelmshaven-Heligoland deception, as did General (then a colonel) Stanley T. Wray, commander of the 91st Bomb Group. Both men are dead now and, presumably, left no record about it.

No one surviving, who had any connection with the film, has been able to cast any light on this question. There is William Clothier, now 85 years of age, Joseph Josephson, George Siegel and Mrs. Wyler, the director's widow.

"Obviously the answer died with Willy Wyler," said Clothier, who shot much of the footage used in the film. "When we finished shooting the film, Wyler packed it up and left for the U.S. with it. He put it together in Hollywood. I stayed in England and had no idea why it was done that way."

He said he had never discussed the matter with Wyler.

One possible explanation is that it was done knowingly. They had planned to make the film that way. Wilhelmshaven had better name recognition. It was a well-known target. When the clouds spoiled their plans, they decided to go ahead with it anyway.

From an altitude of 25,000 feet, most targets look alike, except to experts. The 91st Bomb Group bombed Wilhelmshaven on two previous occasions, the last on March 22. Wyler and his crew were shooting film on that date and they might well have used some footage from the March 22 raid for their May 15 film.

The film makers used extensive charts that showed the routes taken to the target, the feints and deceptions made by the bombers prior to the bombing, in an effort to confuse the German defenders. Is it possible that Wyler, steeped in the Hollywood tradition of making fictional films, could not resist the opportunity to insert a bit of fiction in a film meant to be a documentary? If so, he did it with the best intentions and with the approval of the War Department. The film, after all, was intended to boost war morale and promote the recruitment of airmen, who were then badly needed

285

for the war effort. A filmed raid on Wilhelmshaven could simply be more effective for that purpose

As for saying in the film script that this was the 25th and final mission for the Memphis Belle and her crew, again it was much more effective that way. When the Belle's crew did make their final mission, two days later, it would be a bit anti-climactic. The May 17 target was Lorient, France, but everybody knew that Germany was the real enemy. So a mission into Germany, with the target Wilhelmshaven, was more dramatic.

There may be a bit more deception in the film. The narrator speaks about as many as 1,000 allied planes being in the air that day, a number that was possible six months or a year later. Freeman, in his book The Mighty Eighth, says it was May 14, one day before the Wilhelmshaven-Heligoland raid, when the Eighth, for the first time, was able to put 200 heavy bombers in the air.

Of course, the narrator of the film was counting fighter planes, both American and British, plus a number of B-26s, but the record is clear that it would have been impossible to send out 1,000 planes on May 15. This exaggeration, no doubt, was done deliberately to impress the German enemy, if no one else.

Bob Morgan said: "Don't pay too much attention to the charts and numbers in that film."

To sum it up, even knowing of the discrepancies, Wyler's film remains one of the most impressive and dramatic documentaries ever made.

Even if the Belle was not *the* first B-17 to complete 25 missions, and we have shown that respectable sources are in disagreement regarding this matter, it was certainly one of the first. Why was it selected as the one plane and crew to represent the Eighth Air Force on that national publicity and morale tour? Why was Hell's Angels or some other plane not chosen for the honor? A number of other planes had completed their 25 missions by June 1, the day General Eaker wrote his order directing that a plane be selected for such a mission back home.

Most believe that it was largely because of vigorous and active lobbying by William Wyler, who had been making the documentary, largely centered around the Memphis Belle. He wanted the Belle chosen for the national tour. Also, the Belle and her crew had received a great deal of publicity by virtue of the visit of the King and Queen of England. Wyler was said to have had a hand in that visit. Then Captain Morgan and several members of his crew had been selected for a special radio broadcast to the U.S.

THE MEMPHIS BELLE

In addition, there was the "intact crew" matter. As Roger Freeman and others have pointed out, very few, if any, planes completed their 25 missions with a single, intact crew. Nor did the Memphis Belle. But after General Eaker's order on June 1, the search for the right plane began. It may well have been that the crew of the Memphis Belle came closest to being an intact crew. Except for one waist gunner position and the co-pilot, most of the crew had indeed flown most of their missions together, including the pilot. Again, most of those missions had been on the Memphis Belle.

There also remains the question of why that Twenty Five Missions booklet was written as it was, over the signature of General Arnold.

One answer could be that in compiling the booklet in the United States, the War Department writers did not consult the Eighth Air Force records in England or else those writers knew but decided that the "intact crew" version made a much better story. As for the Belle being first to complete 25 missions, it could have been easy for War Department writers to read that statement, "First B-17 to complete 25 missions and be sent home," then, either inadvertently or otherwise, to drop the "*and be sent home*" part. When it had been done, it was easy to repeat, as it was repeated, until it had acquired a certain appearance of truth.

Whatever the facts may be, the Memphis Belle and her crew have a proud record. Each of the men, and the plane, flew their required combat missions. Each man looked danger and death in the eye and felt its cold breath. They saw their friends and buddies die. Each fought his own battle of the will to remain faithful to the trust that had been placed in his hands, not to let his fellow crew members down in the presence of the enemy.

If, for certain reasons, they were chosen to star in a War Department documentary film which was shown to the nation and brought them a measure of fame, to take part in a nationwide tour which reaped for them even more fame, it was not as if they had asked for or demanded such fame. If they had been made, unwittingly, symbols of all the men who were fighting and dying in the warplanes of the Eighth Air Force, it was not without good and fitting reasons that this had been done.

The story of the Memphis Belle is still a great story that deserves to be told.

A great plane and a great crew!

The Belle Becomes a Movie Star

When Franklin D. Roosevelt took a look at the movie he said: "Every American should see this."

The film was the color documentary sponsored by the War Department and titled "The Memphis Belle." Its director, William Wyler, one of Hollywood's top directors, had just made the double Oscar winning film, "Mrs. Miniver," before donning an Air Force uniform.

The Belle film was, said film critics from coast to coast, one of the most realistic wartime documentaries ever made.

The President almost was not given a chance to see it.

After the film was completed, Wyler took it to Washington to show it to General H. H. Arnold, commander of the Air Forces.

Arnold liked it so well he set up a screening at the White House. It was assumed that the President would be present, but when Wyler arrived with his film in the screening room in the basement, he found the room filled mostly with Navy brass.

An admiral told him, "Roll the film."

It rolled. When it was over, the Navy told Wyler that he did not need to come back.

It just so happened that one man present there that day, not a member of the Navy, was Judge Sam I. Rosenmann, one of the president's top advisors, who sensed Wyler's disappointment that the President had not been present. He was also well aware of the intense rivalry between the Navy and the Air Force.

"You want the President to see it?" Rosenmann asked Wyler as the director was leaving.

The next day, Wyler got a call from the White House. He was asked to bring the film back. This time, all of the top White House officials were there - except those Navy men. This time they wheeled the crippled President into the screening room.

288

After the film had rolled to an end, before a hushed audience, the President made his suggestion that every American should see it.

If not all Americans, certainly millions did see it. The film was distributed without profit by Paramount Pictures. It was shown in major theaters from coast to coast. It became one of the factors which made the Memphis Belle and her crew perhaps the most famous war plane and crew of that global war.

"The Memphis Belle" ranked with such war documentaries as John Ford's "Battle of Midway" which, incidentally, was a Navy film. Perhaps the Navy men were fearful that Wyler's film might take away a bit of their glory in the Midway film.

William H. "Ace" Clothier, who played a major role in making the Belle movie with Wyler, nearly got roped into making the Midway movie for the Navy.

"When director John Ford went into the Navy, he tried to talk me into going in with him as a cameraman," said Clothier, who once shot most of John Wayne's films and now lives in retirement at Studio City, California.

"My wife talked me out of that. She didn't think I would like it on board the Navy ships."

So, when Clothier went into the service with the rank of captain, he was assigned to a motion picture unit with three other men and sent to England in 1942 to do combat and flying film footage of war planes in action.

Willy Wyler was commander of the small unit.

Clothier remembers that shooting battle pictures was something that had been done in England to produce footage for the famed wartime documentary featuring the Royal Air Force, called "Target For Tonight." The British film provided the impetus to do the Memphis Belle picture. It had been an instant and smashing success in England, a desperate country then fighting for survival and much in need of a boost to morale. The film was shipped to the United Staes and widely shown here.

"It was felt that something like that should be done for the United States Air Force," said Clothier.

There was no mystery about why William Wyler chose Bassingbourn as the place to shoot the film.

Wyler told an interviewer, "I picked the base because of its nice, comfortable quarters."

Beyond that, Clothier said, it was only 50 miles from London. When Colonel Wray was approached, he just welcomed the film makers aboard. The film would be made at Bassingbourn.

Wyler, in the interview, gave Colonel Wray the credit for selecting the Belle as the heroine of the film.

Clothier remembers it another way.

"When we first started going on missions and shooting film, we had chosen a plane named Invasion II, piloted by Lieutenant Oscar O'Neill," said Clothier, indicating that the Memphis Belle was not even involved at first.

Then, wartime fate stepped in and changed the picture.

"Invasion II got shot down on one of her missions," said Clothier. "We had shot thousands of feet of film around that plane and suddenly the plane was gone."

Several days after that, Clothier and Wyler decided to look for a new plane to feature.

"We got in a Jeep and started driving around the base," Clothier said, "going from one plane to another, looking them over. All at once, there was that perky Petty bathing suit girl staring us in the face and that romantic name, Memphis Belle. Willy pointed his finger at the name said, 'That's it.'"

In the meantime, another tragedy struck the film group.

"There was this man, Lieutenant Harold Tannenbaum," said Clothier, "who had originally come over as a soundman, but the ship carrying his equipment and our 35 mm cameras was sunk. That is why we ended up shooting the film with small hand-held 16 mm cameras. When Tannenbaum lost his sound equipment, he switched to cameraman."

Then came the day when Tannenbaum was chosen to go on a mission with a B-24 group. Clothier said the Air Force wanted some footage shot around B-24s to keep the B-24 flyers from feeling slighted.

Men who served in the Air Force at the time remember that the B-24s' were sort of considered the ugly ducklings of the Air Force, more vulnerable to being shot down by the Germans.

Bob Morgan said the same: "We were always glad to see a B-24 outfit included in our bombing missions. We knew the German fighters would concentrate on them and leave us alone."

War correspondents shunned the B-24s.

Tannenbaum went along on a B-24 to get some film footage and that day his plane was shot down.

"He was a good cameraman and we hated to lose him," said Clothier.

Wyler himself one day almost became a war casualty.

"We were on a high flight," said Clothier, "and Willy knocked his oxygen hose loose. Somebody just happened to look and they saw him lying unconscious on the floor. We got him hooked up again to his oxygen, real quick, and he came to. If we hadn't noticed him he would have been a goner."

People who have seen Wyler's documentary remember those dramatic shots of the Memphis Belle's landing wheels leaving the runway and touching down on the return landing.

Talli Wyler, Willy's widow, told how he got those shots.

The Flying Fortress had a belly turret which protruded from the plane. It was strictly forbidden for anyone to be in the belly turret while landing or taking off. There was always the chance of a landing gear collapse, or a failure, that would simply wipe out anyone riding inside the belly turret.

Mrs. Wyler said Willy had told her he ignored the rule in order to get some dramatic film footage.

"He stayed in the turret while taking off to get the shot."

Clothier made such shots, too, he said, but he fastened a camera inside the belly and operated it by remote control.

"I wasn't about to get down in the turret during a landing or a takeoff," he said.

Wyler was so eager to get a good shot for his camera, said Bill Winchell, that he sometimes butted in on the gunners.

"One day, we were under attack and I was trying to man my gun out the side waist window to fire at a German fighter plane that was coming in. But there was Wyler, trying to stick his camera out my window and get a shot of the attacking plane. I had to push him out of the way."

Shooting a machine gun was more important than shooting a camera, at that moment, said Winchell.

Wyler had to be checked out on a machine gun's operation before he was allowed to fly on combat missions. But crew members don't remember him ever doing any real shooting.

"He was too busy taking pictures with his camera," one crewman said, adding that Wyler often stuck his camera so far out of the plane they were afraid he was going to fall out.

Wyler, in a taped interview, said he missed some of his best camera shots because of gunners getting in his way.

"I would see a good shot, like a B-17 exploding, but by the time I could get lined up on it, the thing would be gone. I was always in somebody's way.

"Sometimes I would crawl up to the front, to the bombardier's position, and get some good shots. But I couldn't go up there during a bomb run. They were busy up there."

Wyler remembered that he got a few good shots through the open bomb bay doors while the plane was over the target. Even here he had to be careful not to be sucked out of the plane.

Frank Donofrio, who led the long campaign to save the Memphis Belle, adds a bit to the film story from his own memories of a visit to Wyler's home before the veteran film director's death.

"One wall of his home was literally covered with all the awards he had won during his lifetime. There, in the center of all those awards, in a place of honor, was his Air Medal that he won for flying five combat missions.

"Willy told me that he valued that Air Medal above all the awards he had ever won because, he said, 'When I won that, they were shooting at me - with real guns and real bullets.'

"He also told me that he was the one who arranged for the King and Queen of England to review the Memphis Belle and her crew. He said he had heard that the King and Queen would be visiting Bassingbourn so he got busy and made sure they would make a specific visit to the Belle and her crew."

Donofrio remembers Wyler telling about being forced to use two cameras while on those missions because it was so cold at high altitudes that his little 16 mm cameras would freeze up.

"Wyler said he would use one camera until it froze up and then would slip it inside his fur lined flight jacket to thaw it out while he used the one he had been keeping warm in his jacket," said Donofrio. "He had to switch cameras every few minutes and missed some good shots because his camera froze up."

Wyler remembered that at first he flew only a few of the so-called "safe missions" over targets in France but wanted to go on one of the tougher missions over Germany.

He talked to Colonel Wray about this and the commander promised to call him the next time one of the tough missions came up. When that call came in, it was for the raid which Wyler would feature in the Memphis Belle film.

The announced target for that May 15 was Wilhelmshaven.

Daniel A. McGovern of Northridge, California, one of the men in the film group working on the Memphis Belle picture, said the original title for the movie was "Twenty Five Missions over Germany." He said the name was changed to "The Memphis Belle" simply because it had such a romantic and clean-sounding name. He said other planes high up on the list that they considered were planes such as Hell's Angels, Snafu, Tiger Lady and so on.

"Hell's Angels is a sort of a naughty name," he said. "Snafu would be a no-no. The picture of a Tiger Lady was a bit on the obscene side. But on the Memphis Belle, both the name and the picture were perfect. "

He said he never flew or did any camera work on the film but processed the film and was an equipment man for the team.

The film crew had shot about 10,000 feet of film by the time the Memphis Belle took off from England on June 10, 1943, to go back to the United States.

Four days later Major General Ira C. Eaker, commander of the Eighth Air Force, ordered Major William Wyler to return to the U. S. with the film, there to assemble it into a finished product.

Said Eaker's order, "The Theater Commander has authorized me to return Major William Wyler, Photographic Section, Eighth Air Force, to the United States on temporary duty to complete a project in which I am very much interested because of its potential value to this Air Force and to the Army Air Forces.

"Major Wyler is bringing with him approximately 10,000 feet of Kodachrome 16 mm film, most of which he shot personally, depicting our combat missions and activities on the ground. The crew of the Memphis Belle has been used as a central theme."

The order requested facilities and funds in the U.S. to complete the processing. It further stated that the film footage had been accumulated, rather than released piecemeal, because a complete documentary "should provide the public with a documentary film of powerful impact."

Joseph Josephson of New York, a film technician who worked on the film in England, said Wyler almost ruined the footage.

"Wyler was used to working with professional grade 35 mm film but we had to use 16 mm non-professional grade film. You had to make a negative. Apparently Willy didn't know that. He started screening the original film after developing. He almost ruined it . He ended up with a lot of scratches. It would have made the film unusable.

"Willy came to me and asked what he could do. I remembered a young film processor in New York who had developed a

293

technique for saving scratched film. Very few people knew anything about this at that time. But I told Willy to take the scratched film to my friend and the guy saved the film. Otherwise, it would have been ruined."

Josephson, who worked on such films as "The Blue and the Gray" and "Vietnam, the Forgotten War," confirmed that Wyler had crawled into the belly turret of the Memphis Belle to make that famed takeoff scene.

"He shouldn't have done it," he said, "but he did."

In April of 1944, the Public Relations Office of First Motion Picture Unit, Army Air Forces, finally issued a news release announcing the completion of the film.

The release said, "All aerial combat film was exposed during air battles over enemy territory by an Army Air Forces Combat Camera Unit under the direction of Lieutenant Colonel William Wyler, assisted by Major William Clothier, former RKO cameraman, now overseas as commanding officer of an AAF Combat Camera Unit, and Lieutenant Harold Tannenbaum, former RKO sound man."

The release noted that Tannenbaum had lost his life on one of the missions. It said the film cutting had been done by Staff Sergeant Eric L. Harrison, with the narration by Lester Koenig, Eugene Kern and Corporal John Beal. The voices heard in combat had been dubbed in by crew members of the Belle, brought to Culver City, California, for that purpose during one of their stops on their tour. The original footage had been shot without sound.

One spokesman at the time said that 20 versions of the film had been put together before Wyler had been satisfied.

The War Department and the Air Forces, aptly enough, chose Memphis for the premiere showing of the film on April 5, 1944. After all, the Memphis Belle was the star of the show.

Colonel Stanley Wray came to Memphis for the premiere as did Major William E. Clancey, commander of the 324th Squadron. Wyler came, together with a line-up of veteran bomber pilots.

There was a band and Walter P. Chandler, mayor of the City of Memphis, officiated at the opening ceremonies. Other government leaders were present.

The real stars of the show, Major Bob Morgan, the pilot of the plane, and Margaret Polk, for whom the plane had been named, were missing from the list.

Memphians did not have to be told why they were not there. The beautiful romance which had sparked the Memphis Belle story was over, the engagement broken. It just wouldn't be appropriate to try to put them back into the picture.

Morgan, at the time, was training in the big B-29 at Pratt Air Force Base in Kansas. He could have easily been brought back to Memphis but he wasn't.

A short time later, when the film was first shown at the Barron Theater in Pratt, Kansas, Morgan appeared at the opening and made a short talk.

Elizabeth Ballenger, reviewing the film for the Memphis Press-Scimitar the next day, wrote, "It's about as far removed from the movietown pictures of American fighting men and planes as Peter Pan. Without any stars, without any Hollywood, it is one of the most beautiful and thrilling films that has hit the Memphis movie screens.

"We have REALLY been on a bombing raid now. Nobody should miss it."

Then the film belonged to the nation.

Even Time Magazine wrote in a glowing review: "The Belle's mission takes its crew among prodigious scenes that have seldom been so well recorded. Even the take off into the mild sunlight, has grandeur. As the swift ground shrivels into easy, floating legibility, cinema addicts feel that sudden magical suction in the midriff which the actual experience brings. Climax of this effect: a magnificent close-up of the landing gear as it retracts, flattening like the feet of a bird in flight.

"It is one of the few genuinely exciting U.S. documentaries. Memphis Belle is a remarkable film."

Liberty Magazine, a leading magazine of the time, said it even more dramatically. Ending its review, the magazine said, "Your heartbeat is tuned to the roar of motors, the skull shattering vibration of guns. Home at last, you watch the broken bombers limping in, heavy with wounded men. There is nothing faked about this superb Technicolor document; its making took thirteen combat flights and a man's life. If you don't come away dizzy from the indescribable impact of air war, we're sorry for you!"

The Chicago Daily Tribune said, "Here is one of the most thrilling and beautiful real life air movies ever made.

"Up 25,000 feet the flyers were, as they swept over the Nazi base. You note the close formations, which are the squadron's greatest protection; you see the streaming, swirling vapor trails, the nasty black shell smoke. You hear the controlled voices of flyers. Commands given and answered. You are in a strange, terrible, beautiful world, like something out of your dreams. Here is a movie not to be reviewed but to be SEEN."

The newspapers of America picked up the refrain. The film became a smash hit. The Memphis Belle, a four-engine B-17, had become a star.

There is a poignant, heart-warming little footnote to the story of the Memphis Belle film, told by William Clothier, the man who had played such a big part in the making of the film.

As he had said, the filming first centered around a plane called Invasion II, whose pilot was Oscar O'Neill. Then, after Invasion II was shot down, the film makers had been forced to find another plane around which to build their story. They had chosen the Memphis Belle.

"It was more than 20 years after the war and I had, more or less, forgotten about the Invasion II incident," said Clothier. "I was working with John Wayne as his exclusive camera man."

Clothier said he had a contract with Wayne as the exclusive camera man on all of Wayne's films.

"We were working on one of his films, on location in Arizona," said Clothier. "Jennifer O'Neill was playing the female role. One day we were riding out to location in a chauffeur-driven limousine. I was up front with the driver. Jennifer was in the back seat.

"I happened to look out the window and saw an old B-17 flying in the sky. I pointed and said, 'Gee, there's an old B-17.' When I said that, Jennifer suddenly became excited and shouted, 'Where? Where? I want to see it!'

"I pointed it out to her and I noticed she watched it as long as it was in sight. Then I asked her why she had become so excited at my mention of a B-17.

"She said, 'My father flew a B-17 during World War II.'

"I asked what her father's name was. When she said, 'Oscar O'Neill,' I nearly jumped out of my pants.

"Then she told me the rest of the story.

When O'Neill's plane was shot down he got out of the plane and parachuted to safety. He was taken prisoner by the Germans.

"But it seemed that he had been in love with a British girl and after the war, when he was freed and repatriated, he went back to England to marry the girl.

"'They were my parents,' Miss O'Neill said."

Petty Girl

Daring Young Girl on the Flying Machine

Millions of Americans from coast to coast, especially those of the World War II generation, have heard that name - The Memphis Belle.

Who was she?

An airplane? A Memphis girl named Margaret Polk? A movie actress named Joan Blondell? Jenny Blake, a Mississippi gambling queen of the 1870s? A Lady for a Night? An Esquire Petty girl from 1941? A bathing beauty painted on the side of a B-17? Something about a movie that had been banned in Memphis for fear it would embarrass Boss Ed Crump?

The truth is that if you guessed any of the above you would be at least partly right. Which means, of course, that we have some explaining to do.

Many of us of the World War II generation remember that it was in 1943, in the midst of the greatest war ever fought, at a time when American bombers were bearing the brunt of the battle against Hitler's Fortress Europe, when the War Department decided to bring one of those bombers home from the war, with her crew, for a nationwide morale building tour. To let America see one of the big machines that had been in actual combat and her crew. They chose the Memphis Belle.

Most of the newspapers, in that day before television, in explaining that name, simply said the plane's pilot, Bob Morgan, had named the plane in honor of Margaret Polk, his Memphis sweetheart. And that was it.

Okay, good enough. But where did the name come from? It was when we tried to find the answer when we found more story than we had dreamed possible.

297

First we asked Bob Morgan. His answer: "I liked Southern belles. Margaret was a Southern belle so I just called it the Memphis Belle."

The search would have ended there if James Verinis, who had been the Belle's co-pilot and Morgan's buddy, had not remembered a little more.

"It was up at Bangor, Maine, in September of 1942, just before we flew overseas, when Bob and I went to a movie. I don't remember its title. I only remember Joan Blondell starred in it. In the movie there was also a Mississippi River gambling boat and I remember that either Miss Blondell or the boat was called the Memphis Belle.

"We were walking back to our quarters, after the show, and Bob suddenly said, 'Gee, that would be a good name for our plane, the Memphis Belle.'"

Oh, the plane had been named in honor of Miss Polk, all right. Never any question about that but still ...

We went to the Memphis Public Library to do a bit of research on movies made around 1941 or 1942, starring Joan Blondell, one of Hollywood's hot hunks of sassy feminine property in those days.

The library had movie reviews from the New York Times, in bound volumes by the year. And there it was, a movie called "A Lady for a Night," with a Memphis setting and starring Joan Blondell as a Mississippi River boat gambling queen and entertainer. Gee! We were getting close to pay dirt.

The only problem, the Times review said not a word about the Memphis Belle.

A hint of despair crept in until the lady behind the desk at the library piped up, "You know, I think I saw that movie, years ago."

Her next remark was what set our hopes to soaring again.

"You know, I wonder if that movie is listed in the VCR tape catalogs? Let me take a look."

And yup, there it was. We resisted a temptation to kiss the lady. We had to resist all over again when she said: "I'll order it for you and let you know when it comes in."

Perhaps a couple of months went by and we had nearly forgotten about Joan Blondell and her movie when, one day, came a postcard in the mail.

From the Memphis Public Library: "Lady for a Night" has arrived. We are holding it for you."

298

Maybe we broke some sort of speed record getting to the library. Grabbing the tape and heading home to our VCR.

We were ready to dance all night when, barely five minutes into the film, it happened. The Memphis Belle was on stage.

Oops, maybe we should start at the beginning.

As the Republic Pictures film began to roll, the city of Memphis was preparing to celebrate Mardi Gras. They probably hadn't invented the Cotton Carnival in the 1870s. People parading in the streets in costume. Big billboards blaring that the Mardi Gras Queen, whose identity was a big secret, "Will be unmasked tonight." Big gala. All the city's gentry would be there.

Gala - the queen descended the stairway, masked. The governor of Tennessee rips off the mask. A shudder of horror ran through the audience.

"Why it's Jenny Blake of the *Memphis Belle*, the Jezebel who runs a gambling house," gasps one of the town's leading ladies. Bong! We had our Memphis Belle.

The reason for their indignation? Jenny had been born on the wrong side of the tracks, in a swamp shanty, was now kicking up her heels in some bawdy shows on a Mississippi River gambling boat called the Memphis Belle and wasn't fit to be seen in proper society, much less as queen of the carnival.

Then it is revealed that Jenny got elected queen because her boyfriend, who is a behind-the-scenes political boss, to whom all the prominent gentry of the city owe money or political favors, more or less put the screws to the gentry to force them to vote for Jenny.

It is then, faced with the walk-out of the town ladies that the mayor of Memphis turns to Jenny's boyfriend, played in the movie by John Wayne, and says it, "I told you society would not put up with your making a queen out of your Memphis Belle."

Bingo! The Memphis Belle a second time. The boat and the girl.

Before we tell you more about the film, and we won't tell you much, perhaps we had better warn you, as the New York Times did, "to check your wits outside." "For," said the Times reviewer, "this costly concoction whipped up in 'Old Southern' costumes by a company of well-known actors out of a badly dog-eared script, is as muzzy and stereotyped a picture as you're likely to encounter in these times."

Now, for the remainder of the film, as briefly as possible, Jenny vows revenge on the society dames who turned their backs on her and does so by paying off a large hunk of gambling debts for one of the town's down-and-out members of Memphis' top society who is drinking himself to death. In return for the rake's promise to marry her and thereby force her into that elite circle of society which she covets.

Poor John Wayne is still so much in love with Jenny that he helps out, even though it means throwing her in the arms of another man.

So, Jenny Blake does indeed become a "Lady for a Night," at a gala party with John Wayne pulling some strings to force the town's gentry to attend. In the end, Jenny is accused of murdering her hard-drinking husband but she is cleared and walks off into the sunset on the arms of poor, long-suffering John Wayne.

Oh, there has to be a little kicker: We left it for last. In the film, John Wayne's name is Jack Morgan. Any wonder that a young man named Bob Morgan, pilot of a B-17 Flying Fortress, should have been smitten by the film?

That should be all of this story but it isn't. The Boss Ed Crump part.

After having learned about the film, seeing it with its Memphis setting, the next question in our mind was, in view of the Memphis setting to the film it certainly must have gotten some kind of special reception in Memphis. No?

It didn't. In fact, Memphians didn't even get to see the film. A crazy story.

We dutifuly trekked back to the Public Library and began poring through the microfilms of the Memphis newspapers for 1942, searching for news stories about the film. Or, at least some movie reviews. Or ads.

We searched and searched and searched. Nothing. No news stories. No reviews. Not even an ad to show that the film had been shown anywhere in Memphis.

Gee, what happened? We had to know.

We finally found it.

In the Memphis Commercial Appeal for January 14, 1942, a story written by Harry Martin, then the movie reviewer for the paper. It seemed, said Martin, that "Lady for a Night" had suddenly been transformed into something that could best be described as a huge white elephant.

Republic Pictures, said Martin, had been planning big things for the film in Memphis. A gala premiere in Memphis, with John Wayne and Joan Blondell to arrive for personal appearances.

Then sudden silence.

He had learned, said Martin, that the owners of the top Memphis movie palaces had viewed the film in private and had become disturbed about the way it portrayed a political boss, pulling strings behind the scenes, in control of the city.

For you see, in 1942, Memphis indeed had such a boss. None other than the genial, white-haired Ed Crump who, it was said, did control the politics of the city.

The movie house owners feared that the movie would be a public insult to Boss Crump. Thus the sudden and complete silence. The people of Memphis would not be allowed to see the film.

Without having a gala premiere, the hoopla, eventually the film would be booked in other cities in the United States. In Bangor, Maine, for example, where Bob Morgan and Jim Verinis saw it in September of 1942. And from it grabbed the name for a plane called the Memphis Belle.

"Yes," said Morgan when we told him what we had found. "I remember it now."

In fact, with his memory jolted, Morgan remembered that he originally wanted to name the plane Little One. It had been his favorite pet name, up to this time, for Margaret Polk.

But Bob remembers now, as do several of the crew members, that after seeing the film, he had changed his mind. Memphis Belle suddenly sounded better.

Next chore, to tell Margaret Polk about it. We hesitated a few days. Wondering how she would take it. Would she feel a bit upstaged by a movie actress named Joan Blondell? By Jenny Blake? By the "Lady of the Night?"

We should not have been worried. Margaret has always had a great sense of humor. It was a trill of laughter we heard through the telephone.

"Gee, that's great," she said. She wanted to see the film. Wanted to get a copy of it.

But still not the end of the story. That perky bathing suit girl on the nose of the Memphis Belle. Where did she come from?

That part wasn't much of a mystery. Bob Morgan remembered it well.

"I was a reader of Esquire magazine," he said. "I always admired those Petty girl paintings they ran every month."

Artist George Petty was well-known for his paintings of sexy girls.

301

"I wrote to the magazine and told them what I wanted," said Morgan. "They sent me the picture, and we had it painted on the nose of the plane, next to that name, The Memphis Belle."

Simple as that. Except for one thing. Who was the artist who painted it on the plane and when did it happen? Was it painted on at Bangor, before the flight to England, or later, in England?

The crew members were not sure. The consensus seems to be that it was first painted on by a civilian worker at Dow Field at Bangor, just before the departure. Perhaps this civilian was not the best of artists and the art job may not have been the best.

In England, they found a talented young artist in the uniform of a corporal assigned to the 91st Bomb Group, 441st Lab Depot, named Anthony "Tony" Starcer, who was busily painting names and artwork on B-17s all over the base. Starcer, who did the artwork on more than 150 planes, was drafted to touch up or repaint the girl on the nose of the Memphis Belle. Perhaps all the planes, after the rigors of high altitude flying and battle damage, had to have their artwork touched up from time to time.

The story got around, during the Belle's tour of duty in England, that the German fighter pilots had spotted the sassy girl painted on the nose of the plane called the Memphis Belle and vowed to shoot her down.

It was said that, in an English language propaganda broadcast, by radio, the Germans had broadcast such a threat. A German radio announcer reportedly said: "If the Memphis Belle comes back to Germany, she will never go home again."

But we have noted elsewhere in this book, the Memphis Belle was a lucky plane and while the German fighter pilots gave it a mighty try, they never got the Belle. Several of them paid with their lives for their attempt.

The daring young girl kept flying.

Again, this should be the end of the story except that we wanted to pin down the Esquire issue in which the Petty girl first appeared. If possible, to look at it. Get a copy. We assumed, since the plane was named in September of 1942, it would have to be 1942.

Back to the library. Yes, they had file copies of Esquire for 1942.

But that was when we found that some thief, or vandal, liked Petty girl pictures long before we came to search. Out of 12 issues of Esquire, ten of the Petty-type pictures had been snitched.

We started to say Petty girl but now there was a new bug in our soup. For Esquire, it seemed, had used Varga girls, not Petty girls, in 1942. Where do we go from here?

A letter to Esquire, now a bit more sedate than in 1942, brought the response of a gift copy, a calendar reproduction of all the Varga girl pictures for 1942. Gee, had we hit pay dirt? Had she been a Varga girl, rather than a Petty girl?

We had hit another stump, for a quick thumb-through quickly showed that our Memphis Belle picture was not there.

Next, a phone call to Esquire where they put their historian, Tom Robotham, on the line. In my previous letter I had included a picture of the Memphis Belle, showing the girl. With that in hand he soon identified the picture. But another surprise, it was indeed Petty, but from 1941, and had run in the April issue of that year. In 1941 Esquire had used some of Petty's girls and some of Varga's.

Another gallop to the Memphis Public Library.

"Yes, we have Esquire for 1941."

But then the crash. Our vandal had been to 1941 as well. The b------!

Sometimes, it seems the life of a writer or a researcher is meant to be tough.

Next stop, an attorney named Ronald Feldman in New York, custodian for the estate of the late George Petty, artist, painter of leggy girls.

Then, a conversation with Margaret Petty McLeod, daughter of Petty.

"Those original paintings for Esquire have been given to the Spencer Museum of Art at the University of Kansas at Lawrence," she said.

Another phone call to Doug Tillman, director of Spencer Museum. At first he wasn't sure but when he checked, "Yes, the original of that painting is here. Yes, we can make a copy of it for you."

Time to celebrate.

Now, if we could only get our hands on the vandal, or was it thief, who snitched the Petty girls from those library Esquires.

McDill

Hey, We Flew the Belle, Too

It may come as a bit of a surprise for many Memphis Belle fans to learn that dozens of pilots and literally hundreds of crewmen flew B-17 No. 485.

Most devotees of the Belle prefer to believe that the plane was, more or less, the exclusive property of Bob Morgan and the ten men of his crew who flew her back from Europe together.

In fact, at least three other pilots logged their names on the flight log of No. 485 before Lt. Morgan made his first flight on it at Dow Field at Bangor, Maine, on September 3, 1942. When Morgan sat down in the pilot's seat for the first time, the plane had 16 hours on her.

At least four other pilots and at least two other crews flew the Belle in combat over Europe. It was routine that when a pilot and his crew completed their 25 missions, their plane, if still flying, was turned over to new pilots and crews for further missions. Some planes flew 40 or 50 missions, or even more.

This didn't happen to the Belle after the decision was made to send her home for the tour. After the tour had ended, the plane was sent to Spokane, Washington, where from October 8 to December 7 she received a complete overhaul.

It was assumed she would be sent back to the war zone for more combat flying.

Somewhere along the line, Air Force officers changed the signals and decided to send the plane to McDill Field near Tampa, Florida, to be used in training new B-17 crews. By this time, most of the Air Force was switching to B-17Gs, a more advanced plane than the B-17F. But the Belle would do as a training plane. McDill Field would remain her home station until April of 1945.

Then the parade began.

THE MEMPHIS BELLE

When new trainees walked up to No. 485 for the first time, there was that perky and leggy Petty girl on the nose. There was that name, Memphis Belle.

Back in England, in the spring of 1943, Captain Morgan had been nearing the end of his 25 missions. Before he knew that the Memphis Belle would be going home on the tour, he had written his fiancee, Margaret Polk, that he would have the name painted off before he turned the plane over to its next pilot.

He kept the name on, of course, after hearing about the tour. Following the tour, when he and the crew walked away from the plane at Bolling Field at Washington, D.C., the famous name and the Petty girl painting were still on it .

Morgan's engagement to Margaret had been broken by then but the plane and the name were famous and the Air Force may have wanted those decorations to remain on the nose of No. 485.

Possibly someone thought the name had some value to students. It might make them proud, knowing they were flying and training on a famous plane.

The Memphis Belle was assigned as a trainer to the 326th Bomb Group and later to the 815th Bomb Group and the parade of pilots began to show on the plane's logs. At times, there was a new pilot and crew recorded on the log every day.

The names of those pilots include George F. Snyder, W. H. Skaggs, Walter C. Murray, John H. Dietrich, Dean O. Fredrick, J. I. Owens and Joseph P. Hourtal. Many pilots logged only their last names, such as Swana, Elder, Faulkner, McLean, Boswell, Jacobsen, Prince, Castner, Wintersteen, Klunge, Valentine, Davis, Lundsberg, Cline, Masterson, Alexander, Thrift, Brokart, Maxwell, Crawford, Pazalo and Kobel.

The parade of crews and pilots went on for nearly two years, until the war ended.

Flyers who trained on the Belle recognized the fabled plane and proudly remembered their flights on her for years.

Dr. Harry Friedman of Memphis placed a notice in the Eighth Air Force News and in other aviation publications asking for information on the Memphis Belle.

Here came the letters.

William J. Wintersteen of Danville, Pennsylvania, wrote in July of 1981: "I was sent to McDill Field on September 19, 1944, for advanced training and while there I flew the Memphis Belle on three occasions, October 15, October 29 and November 12. I distinctly remember first seeing her and the feeling I had, knowing her brilliant past.

"The Belle was a horror to fly. The throttles were all misaligned. It would have been impossible to fly formation. The supercharger levers were likewise all out of line. Oil was spattered over the nacelles and wings. In spite of all this, I was proud, very proud, to have flown the Queen."

Jim Giamborne, who had been the proud crew chief in England, would groan to hear about those misaligned throttle and supercharger levers.

Robert S. Wardner, of St. Petersburg, Florida, wrote to report that he had flown the Belle from Hendricks Field, near Sebring, Florida.

The Belle was considered a work horse and sometimes was placed on temporary duty to other fields.

Wardner wrote: "Enclosed is a copy of my clearance to fly the Memphis Belle on May 20, 1945. I was a B-17 instructor pilot, and when I spotted the Memphis Belle on the flight line, I flew it that weekend for the pure enjoyment of being able to say I flew that beautiful and historic bird. She was without armament and not entirely clean but mechanically in excellent condition. It was a highlight of my B-17 flying experience."

Apparently someone had adjusted those throttles.

George L. Edgar, of Cincinnati, Ohio, wrote: "I had the honor of flying the Memphis Belle while in training at McDill Field in June of 1944. It was quite an experience to get into the Memphis Belle and look her over. As bombardier I'll never forget sitting up there in the 'spacious' nose, in the padded chair, and taking in the scenery. When our mission was over that afternoon we spent a long time looking over the ship and commenting on the duty she had seen and trying to anticipate what our combat tour would be like."

Considering how many missions the Belle flew out of McDill, with all the young and relatively inexperienced pilots at the controls, it seems a wonder she survived those grueling two years.

One of the pilots who almost lost her was Paul H. Martin, who wrote: "I vividly recall the feeling I had when I learned that the Belle had been assigned to me for a practice bombing mission.

"I also recall the problem we had getting her off the ground when she suddenly lost power as we passed the point of no return. For a moment I thought we would uphold the tradition of 'One-a-day-in-Tampa-Bay,' but we finally coaxed her off the ground.

THE MEMPHIS BELLE

"On another occasion I flew the Belle on a five-hour, 12-plane combat formation flight with full crew. We were told at briefing that there would be times in combat when, after five hours, we would just be reaching the halfway mark. I tried to imagine what it must have been like in the Belle on one of her raids but my imagination left out many things I was soon to experience in combat. I am living proof that the Belle did a great job on my training for I completed my own tour of missions on December 24, 1944."

Apparently the veteran B-17 No. 485 really got around for Robert M. Hosan, of Wilmington, Delaware, wrote about the time in April and May of 1944 when the Belle was on temporary assignment to another Florida airfield, Tyndall Field.

"The Belle was used to carry us future gunners on aerial gunnery practice missions. I distinctly recall being in awe at being able to fly on that great aircraft. At the age of 18 those things really cast a spell on a young aspiring flyer. I can even remember that the pilot was Lt. Ludwig."

Andrew C. Kelleher, of Enfield, Connecticut, remembered another occasion at McDill when he almost lost the Belle.

"I'll never forget my first ride on the Belle," he wrote. "My crew was assigned to the Memphis Belle for some night flying, including touch-and-go landing practice. We made a couple of bomb runs and then came in to do some landings.

"While coming in we lost both radio transmission and our landing lights. We had no way to contact the tower because we didn't even have an Aldis lamp on board. We were a green crew, having flown only a few times, so we were anxious to get back on the ground without killing ourselves or any other crews.

"We could see the field and other planes in the air so we decided to follow one of them in, using his landing lights as a guide, trailing him to the right. We didn't know it but we also were being trailed by another plane.

"The landing was smooth but then we lost the plane we were trailing so we turned off the runway to the right. Our wheels got stuck in the soft dirt, or sand, leaving our tail on the runway. I heard the tower say, 'K for King, OK for touch-and-go.'

"Suddenly the runway lit up and there was K for King coming in. We all bailed out and ran in all directions. The pilot of K for King saw our plane on the runway and by making a fast, low level turn and applying power he just missed our vertical stabilizer by inches. I could almost hear that pilot screaming at us for being in his path.

307

THE MEMPHIS BELLE

"I went tearing across the field to warn the tower, shedding my leather flying jacket as I ran. The WAC tower controller got the message and closed the field while they towed the Belle away.

"As a result of that incident we lost our tail gunner. He had been sitting there in the tail, seeing that other plane trailing us and didn't think it important enough to let us know up front. I could just picture him in combat with a German fighter on our tail.

"We flew the Belle three times after that with no more problems. It intrigued me to see all those autographs on the plane so I added mine. This tale adds nothing to the glory of the Memphis Belle other than that we almost ended its career."

While all this was going on at McDill Field, the war was grinding down to a halt. The Germans surrendered on May 8, 1945, and although the war against Japan would grind on in the Pacific until August 14, the Air Force now found itself with a surplus of B-17s. In the closing months of the war, the brunt of the air bombing war was borne by the newer and bigger B-29s.

The Air Force no longer needed a battered and worn old B-17F called the Memphis Belle, no matter how glorious her past. On July 2, 1945, the Belle was flown to the Air Force Base at Altus, Oklahoma, a sort of gathering point for war planes no longer needed or wanted.

On September 9, 1945, the Belle was placed on storage status and on October 18, 1945, was released to the Reconstruction Finance Corporation, the Federal agency charged with the disposal of sur-plus military property.

It was here that friends of the battered old plane found her and arranged for her to be sold to the City of Memphis as a war memorial.

But that is another story.

Restoration

It Took Such a Long Time

At times, it seemed, it was the Battle of Heartbreak Ridge, that campaign to save the Memphis Belle.

There were, indeed, heartbreaks, defeats, retreats, delays, frustrations, disappointments and failures involved in the battle that lasted more than 40 years before that triumphant day, May 17, 1987, when the Belle, all glowing in new paint and fittings, could be shown to the public, sitting in a new, plastic-domed home on Mud Island in Memphis, Tennessee.

Even in those last months, when the campaign at long last seemed to be headed for success, said Frank Donofrio, the man at the head of the project, "My biggest problem was to keep everyone headed in the same direction."

The long battle began during the summer of 1943, as the Memphis Belle and her crew were making their triumphal tour of the country with the cheers of America ringing out to make heroes of the young flyers. Mayor Walter Chandler of Memphis contacted the War Department and asked if the Belle could be sent to Memphis as a permanent war memorial. The Department said no, the war was still going on and the Belle was a warplane and it was still needed.

The Department first said that after the tour, the plane would be overhauled and sent back to war, with another crew and, perhaps, another name.

However, after it was refurbished at Spokane, Washington, in the fall of 1943, the plane was assigned as a training plane to McDill Field near Tampa, Florida.

Mayor Chandler allowed no time to be wasted, once the war was over. On August 25, 1945, just 11 days after the end of the war in the Pacific, Chandler made his next move to corral the Belle for Memphis.

THE MEMPHIS BELLE

The Belle and her fame were fresh in everyone's mind.

Chandler petitioned the War Department once more to let Memphis have the famous plane. His announced plan was to have a permanent hangar built for the plane at Memphis Municipal Airport, where she could be visited by the public.

Meantime, the Belle had been flown to Altus, Oklahoma, a collecting point for surplus airplanes and, after a few weeks, was declared surplus and turned over to the Reconstruction Finance Corporation, a Federal agency charged with disposal of surplus war goods.

The RFC seemed willing to let Memphis have the plane, but months went by as Chandler continued to write letters, negotiating and working out the details. As usual, the wheels of governmental bureaucracy turned slowly. Even then, certain "gliches" began showing up.

A Civil Aeronautics Administration inspector reported that the Belle was not airworthy enough to fly to Memphis. There was faulty oil pressure on one engine. The emergency hydraulic system seemed to be on the blink. The throttles out of synchronization.

If this had been the big hold-up, it would have been ridiculous. There were, at that time, hundreds of wartime-trained aircraft mechanics who would have been eager to go fix the old plane. And, of course, she could always be dismantled and shipped to Memphis in sections.

Beyond that, if one could believe the stories appearing in the newspapers of the time, the RFC was threatening to throw the Belle in with the other planes being sent to the scrap yards. Would she end up in an aluminum smelter?

Maybe some of this talk was only a bit of a scare tactic to get things moving. In any case, on March 3, 1946, Mayor Chandler, duly stirred to action, announced that he would abandon his campaign by mail and would go to Washington to undertake talks with what was then the War Assets Corporation.

Things now began clicking. A few days later, on March 8, 1946, Mayor Chandler was able to report from Washington that he had purchased the Memphis Belle for the City of Memphis for $350. She had originally cost the U.S. Government $314,109 when delivered by Boeing in 1942. Today a four-engine bomber costs millions.

A well-wisher, who requested to remain anonymous to the public, sent Mayor Chandler a check for $350 so Memphis taxpayers would not have to pay a cent.

THE MEMPHIS BELLE

The next problem was to get the plane to Memphis.

As stories about the final purchase appeared in the newspapers, pilots and crewmen by the dozens began volunteering for the honor of going to Altus and flying the famous plane home. Most were war veterans who had flown this type plane in the war.

In fact, so many volunteered that finally a committee, headed by Downing Pryor, had to be appointed to select the crew. To make as many men as possible happy, the committee called for a command pilot in addition to a pilot.

But how about Colonel Robert K. Morgan, the man who had flown the Belle on her original combat tour in Europe? After all, wasn't he the man who had given the plane its Memphis connection by naming it the Memphis Belle? Without that name and the famed romance that went with it, involving Morgan, there would have been no excuse for bringing the plane to Memphis.

Well, someone finally did bring this up and the designation of a pilot had to start all over again. Mayor Chandler contacted Morgan in Asheville, North Carolina. On June 19, on the third anniversary of the Belle's triumphant return to Memphis to begin the national tour to boost morale and War Bonds, after a telephone conversation with Morgan, Mayor Chandler announced that the original pilot would indeed fly the Belle home on July 2.

Then the gliches continued. Morgan would and then Morgan wouldn't fly the Belle home. The July 2 date was changed. On July 13, 1946, Mayor Chandler was forced to announce that, due to the press of business, Morgan would be unable to make it. Another pilot would have to do it.

It was then announced that Captain Robert E. Little, the man originally picked by the committee, would do the piloting. Little, living in Chicago, had plenty of experience flying B-17s, although his war service had been in the Pacific, rather than Europe. He had flown 73 missions in the Pacific war against Japan and was now a pilot for Southern Airlines, making regular flights to Memphis.

Eventually it did happen. On July 16, Captain Little and his crew boarded an Army C-47 transport plane and flew to Altus. They didn't need a full crew of ten since nobody was needed to man the guns. The guns had been removed, anyway. The crew of seven men who made the trip, other than Little, were all Air Force Reserves. They were Captain R. L. Taylor, navigator; Sergeant Percy Roberts, Jr., flight engineer; Technical Sergeant Charles Crowe, flight engineer; Lieutenant James Gowdy, second navigator;

THE MEMPHIS BELLE

Captain Hamp Morrison, co-pilot, and ARM-2 Stuart Griffin, radio operator.

When the men arrived, they gave the Memphis Belle a flight check. One of the engines wasn't running quite right but new spark plugs and a bit of tinkering fixed that.

On July 17, the Belle took off. There were still some problems, according to aviation editor Robert Gray of Memphis' morning newspaper, the Commercial Appeal, who also made the flight. The plane lifted off the runway handily but then the landing gear refused to retract. The crew men had to use the emergency hand crank.

Then the radio balked, receiving but not sending. At one point in the flight, someone smelled smoke and grabbed a fire extinguisher. It was an overheating generator. Captain Little switched it off and the Belle roared on through the summer sky.

Memphis, here we come.

As Gray put it, Little "greased her in" for a super-smooth landing and the Memphis Belle was - *home at last*.

Some people who were working on a campaign to provide the Belle with a final home, would be using that slogan - *home at last* - in 1987.

In fact, the long battle was only beginning.

For one thing, in the fall of 1946, shortly after the Belle's triumphant return to Memphis the city got a new mayor, Sylvanus Polk. The new mayor probably didn't consider the priorities for the Memphis Belle to be as high as they might have been if Chandler had remained in office.

The new mayor, for example, spoke about the shortage created in building materials during the war. He spoke also of the many pent-up needs of the city, created by nearly four years of war. How could he, he asked, justify spending money and asking for scarce material to house an airplane? People housing came first.

So, as early as November, newspapers were printing stories of how the Belle had been abandoned and sat forlornly, exposed to the weather and to vandals, on a ramp at the Airport. One picture showed upholstery torn by souvenir hunters. "Belle's Gallantry Forgotten, She Rots On Ramp," said a headline in the Commercial Appeal.

"She's sitting at the Airport, weathering away," said another news story.

Stung by the critical news stories, Lieutenant Colonel Lawrence Gilbert of the Fourth Ferrying Command, at the Airport, brought the Belle into one of his hangars but everybody knew this was only a temporary solution.

Robert Gray, the Commercial Appeal's reporter who rode the Memphis Belle on her trip from Altus to Memphis, led the fight in those early years to keep the plight of the Belle before the public.

It was on July 19, 1948, two years after that triumphant flight home from Altus, when expectations had been so high, that a story under Bob Gray's by-line appeared under the headline, "Two More Years of Ignominy Add Dust to Memphis Belle and Shame to Her Owners."

Who were those owners? They could only be the people.

That had been the wish of former Mayor Chandler in returning a donor's check for $350. It had been peanuts, that price, but it was the taxpayers who paid. They owned the plane now.

"Two years have passed but the Memphis Belle today remains a symbol without honor in her own home town," Bob Gray wrote.

She was still in a hangar, supposedly protected, but gathering dust, wrote Gray. He added that, somehow, parts of the plane continued to disappear.

Gray's lament did produce results, although one of the solutions proposed could only bring shudders to true friends of the Belle. The proposal, by an Air Force officer, was to cut off the name, the Petty girl painting and a few key parts, put them in a museum, and use some of the remaining parts for training Air Force personnel.

In reply, Robert Taylor, a Memphis attorney and one of the men who had helped fly the Belle back to Memphis, said it best: "To cut up the Memphis Belle would be sacrilege."

A few citizens stirred into action. A new committee was formed. One new proposal was to find a spot in Overton Park and build a glass enclosure. No decision was made. A cheaper proposal was to give her a coat of clear plastic to protect against the weather.

A Commercial Appeal editorial suggested that the City should find a place and build a shelter. The best the City could do was an offer, from the Park Commission, of a site just north of the Pink Palace Museum in Chickasaw Gardens. Some residents of the area didn't like that. It would draw too many visitors to their quiet, residential area, not to speak of it being an eyesore.

The Park Commission next offered a site in Bellevue Park. By this time, the plane had been moved out of her hangar and now stood on an open ramp at the Airport. The Air Force needed the hangar space.

It was time for the American Legion to get into the act.

The time now was August of 1949. Newspapers called the Memphis Belle a stepchild. Marion Hale, senior vice president of the Memphis American Legion, Post No. 1, announced that the Board of Directors of his post had voted unanimously to adopt the Belle as a Legion project. It proposed to place the Belle on the grounds of the National Guard Armory, facing Central Avenue. The Legion named Roane Waring Jr., to head a committee of six to get some action and for once they got it.

The Legion plan called for an outdoor museum to contain a display of military mementoes with the Memphis Belle as the center piece. It didn't get that far but they did move the Belle.

A picture published in the Commercial Appeal on May 21, 1950, showed the Belle being dismantled. Her wings were off. Then, on May 23, she was towed to the Armory site and hoisted onto a concrete pedestal. Her wings were put back on and her paint was refurbished.

The Legion project was complete. Or was it? For now the vandals took over. Somebody said if they weren't stopped, the vandals would make off with the entire plane, a piece at a time. By October 19, 1951, a chain link fence was erected around the site, topped by barbed wire. The wire slowed the vandals, but if the vandals were determined enough they could get over even that kind of barrier.

And, as the years passed, the weather was taking its toll, too. Aluminum does not rust as steel does. But, when exposed long enough, especially with certain chemical elements in the air, aluminum can corrode. Such corrosion can be treated and, to some degree, retarded but for many of the years the Belle stood there on the pedestal, nothing was being done to retard or prevent corrosion.

Nothing was done in this area for the 27 years - yes, it was that long - that the Memphis Belle perched on her concrete pedestal.

Thousands of Memphians passed that way each day and most became so accustomed to seeing the old plane they seldom gave her a glance. The younger people, born since World War II, hardly knew her name, much less her history. But there were always a few veterans of the military service who would look and feel that tiny twinge of pride at seeing a part of history. A part of their own story was standing there.

THE MEMPHIS BELLE

There would even be some who remembered and would make it a special goal when coming from out of town, to drive down Central and say to their children, "That is the Memphis Belle. She completed 25 bombing missions and was one of the most famous airplanes of World War II." A few, perhaps a bit more knowledgeable, might add a few details they had heard or read about in the newspapers, perhaps the tale of the glorious romance between Margaret Polk and her dashing young pilot, Bob Morgan.

When the crew of the Belle came to Memphis for a reunion in 1961 and 1967, somebody would clean up the old plane, add a bit of paint. The old Petty girl painting and the name, Memphis Belle, along with the swastikas, would be faded and in need of a touch-up.

Newspaper photographers and now the TV men would come out. The crew would line up in front of the plane. There would be a few shots on the evening news. Newspaper writers would crank up a new feature story, recalling and reminding citizens of the old girl's past glories.

Perhaps no one can say for certain how long the Belle might have stood there on her pedestal, waiting. But in 1976 the National Guard forced a new round of activity. The Armory grounds were sold to the nearby Memphis Memorial Stadium. The old plane would have to be moved.

It is time to introduce the man who eventually led the successful effort to get a better home for the Memphis Belle. He is Frank Donofrio. In 1967 he was president of the Mid-South Metal Treating Co.

"I used to drive down Central Avenue on my way to work and I would pass the Memphis Belle," said Donofrio. "Somehow she always intrigued me because I had seen the Belle film during the war. Then, one day in March of 1967, I picked up a copy of Newsweek and read a story under the headline, '50,000 Films for Sale.' It seemed the government was selling off a lot of films, mostly training films, made during the war. I had always been interested in training films because I used them in my business.

"But not all of them were training films. A few of them were documentaries and the Newsweek story was saying that the best of these was a film called the Memphis Belle."

Donofrio has the Newsweek clipping which describes the film as "beautiful, almost impressionistic." He then added, "The film set the style for a decade of documentaries."

Donofrio, his desire whetted by the daily sight of the Belle standing on Central, and now by the high praise of the film, wanted the film so badly that he made a special trip to St. Louis, the Government's film depository, to get it.

Bringing the old 16 mm film home and watching it once more, put the clinchers on the process of making Donofrio a confirmed Memphis Belle fan for life. He would devote a good portion of his life for the next 20 years to something which might simply be called "The Memphis Belle Project."

It started when John Means, a Commercial Appeal writer, heard about Donofrio's trip to St. Louis to obtain what was believed to be the only surviving print of the Memphis Belle movie. Means wrote a news article about it, linking it to Joe Gagliano, a police inspector, who had been a B-17 bombardier at Bassingbourn in the period immediately after the Belle had been sent home in 1943.

Then the 91st Bomb Group Association announced that it had chosen Memphis for its 1967 convention and reunion in July. Colonel Robert K. Morgan would be in Memphis to attend.

One man who attended the meeting was Frank Donofrio, who became an associate member. Dottie Abbott, a Memphis radio personality, began pounding the drums for the Belle. A new committee was formed, perhaps to realize the old dream of former Mayor Walter Chandler to build a permanent home for the Belle.

The committee met in Dottie Abbott's home. Members were Roane Waring, Jr., attorney and former Legion commander, Thomas Williams, city employe, Judge Willard Dixon, Menno Duerksen, Memphis Press-Scimitar reporter, and Donofrio.

Donofrio was elected chairman. He was marked with the sign of the Belle.

For the next few years, Donofrio admits, he was not quite able to provide the spark to get the thing going. In the meantime, the Belle had been painted and refurbished one more time and it did not seem to be urgent.

Until that that day in 1976, when the National Guard began to talk about selling the old Armory grounds and the need to evict the Memphis Belle. Then things started moving again.

Donofrio was contacted by George T. Lewis, Jr., an attorney, and John Emerson, a Shelby County employe, both representing the American Legion which was now trying to crank up a new Memphis Belle project. It was decided that, if the new group was to raise funds as a non-profit organization, it would have to incorporate. Lewis did the legal work. The organization that would eventually create a permanent home for the Belle, the Memphis Belle Memorial Association, was a reality. The date was April 6, 1976.

Donofrio was elected president. Emerson was named vice-president and Lewis, secretary. The first money-raising project was to sell memberships. The drive had limited success, not producing enough to build the new home for the Belle. So, in the spring of 1977, the National Guard served final eviction papers and the new Association was powerless to stop them. The Belle was once more dismantled and, for want of a better place, carted back to the Airport on April 28. It was beginning to go around in circles.

The Association on June 30 held another meeting, kicked Donofrio upstairs by making him permanent chairman, and elected Emerson president. This took place while Donofrio was on a trip to Europe.

Perhaps the intentions were good. Friends of the Belle may have assumed that now things would get done. They didn't. For the next nine years, the best that could be said was that the Memphis Belle Memorial Association did not go out of business. But no major move was put in motion.

"We never had more than $5,000 in the bank at any time," said Donofrio.

However, the advertising agency of Cochran and Sandford gave the Association a blueprint for raising funds.

"If we had followed their advice," said Donofrio, "I believe we could have gotten off the ground."

The right spark was not struck that would make things go.

More was taking place in the area of restoring the plane than in raising funds to build the plane a permanent home. This brings onto center stage the man who, perhaps more than anyone else, carried the ball in getting the old plane back into survival condition - Dr. Harry Friedman.

Dr. Friedman earns his living as a neuro-surgeon at Baptist Memorial Hospital. If someone ran a time check on him, they would almost certainly find that his time devoted to the Memphis Belle would run a close second.

"I must have been about five or six years old when I first saw the Memphis Belle movie at the old Suzore Theater on Jackson," said Friedman. "We just lived a few doors down the street and I spent a lot of time in that old theater. When I was a kid, airplanes were my big passion."

When he was about nine years old, in 1948, his brother Irving was in the Air National Guard at the Airport.

"One day I went out there to see him and the Memphis Belle was standing there," said Dr. Friedman. "My brother let me crawl into her and prowl around. I was in heaven."

He's never been able to get the Belle out of his system since.

Dr. Friedman did not become officially involved in the Belle project until the Association was chartered and he paid his dues and went to work.

His contributions actually began long before that.

"I had been prowling around old aircraft salvage yards for years," she said, "scrounging parts. I had a bomb sight before I ever became connected with the Association."

Afterwards, the parts-collecting work continued in an attempt to replace all the parts of the Belle that had been screwed or pried loose and carried off by vandals during the years.

"I've developed B-17 parts sources all over the U.S.," Friedman said. "I have three in California and others are in Arizona, Illinois, Florida and New York. I bought the bomb sight in New York."

Sometimes, he has found, it pays to scrounge more parts than he needs. He can use them to trade for things he needs when the owner would not consider cash as an incentive. He has even worked three-way trades in which he trades a part to one person who has a part needed by a second person who has a part needed by the Memphis Belle.

Once the campaign got under way to restore the Belle, even the matter of a man's conscience played a part in finding parts. Colonel Morgan, the plane's combat pilot, remembers one such incident.

"One day I got a package in the mail," he said, "and when I opened it, there was the pilot's yoke [steering wheel] for the Memphis Belle, with a note. The writer confessed that one day he and friends had pried some parts off the plane for souvenirs, but now that they were restoring the Belle, his conscience had hurt until he returned the yoke."

One day, one of Dr. Friedman's patients showed up at his office with an old aircraft gauge and gave it to him. He had taken it off the Belle many years ago, as a child, and now wanted to return it so that it could be restored to its rightful place.

As the years went by, Dr. Friedman gradually evolved from one of the troops working on the Belle's restoration to what might be called the restoration coordinator. It was a position he held until that proud day, May 17, 1987, when the new home for the venerable old plane was dedicated on Mud Island. Even after that, said Friedman, "We'll probably never be able to say the job is completely finished. We will never be satisfied until the Belle is just as she was when she flew. We will, in time even have most of the electrical and hydraulic systems on the plane operational. Our restoration work will continue as an ongoing thing."

In the meantime, at one stage of the restoration work, when the Belle was parked near the Vocational Technical School, near the Airport, students at the school worked on the plane for months on end under the direction of their instructor Henry Martin.

During another phase of the restoration, the Belle was parked on the apron near the Air National Guard hangars, and men of the Guard spent hours of their spare time on the Belle project. The man who did more than anyone else, said Friedman, was Master Sergeant Nute Paulk, a full-time Guardsman. The sergeant had been a crew chief for the A-26 flown in Korea by former Shelby County Sheriff Gene Barksdale, who flew combat missions in that war. Later, Paulk remained in the Guard.

"Nute played a major part in all three moves of the Belle that were made in Memphis," said Dr. Friedman, "the first move to the pedestal on Central Avenue in 1950, the return to the Airport in 1977 and the final move to Mud Island in 1987."

The final, successful campaign to provide a permanent home for the Belle got started in 1985 when Dr. Friedman began a correspondence with Colonel Richard C. Uppstrom, director of the U.S. Air Force Museum at Wright-Patterson Air Force Base near Dayton, Ohio. Friedman became acquainted with Uppstrom during his years of research on the Belle and his search for parts.

Uppstrom was dismayed at the years of procrastination by the people of Memphis in providing a proper home for the Belle. Since the city had really done little, if anything, he said, the plane belonged to an Air Force Museum at Wright-Patterson or elsewhere. Anything would be better than more years of rot and neglect.

Uppstrom commented along those lines in letters he wrote to Friedman beginning in June of 1985. The second letter, written November 19, was a bit more blunt:

"I'm beginning to get that gnawing feeling that the citizens of Memphis have no interest in the Belle and, in the long run, the best thing we could do would be to bring her to Wright-Patterson for care at the main Museum."

Barbara Burch, a Commercial Appeal writer, got wind of the Museum's interest. She wrote a story, which appeared under the headline, "Memphis Belle Must Move in or Fly Away." It said Memphians must take concerted action or the Belle would be gone.

"That story did it," said Dr. Friedman. "It got the attention of Mayor Dick Hackett, who called a meeting of Memphis' top business men and told them that a way must be found to keep the Belle in Memphis."

The business leaders proposed that the new home for the Belle be on Mud Island.

A short time later, Jimmy Ogle, director of Mud Island, met with Donofrio and Friedman to present the case for Mud Island, a unique Mississippi River replica park which includes a Mississippi River museum. The park was attracting national attention as something different in the way of spectator entertainment.

"I suppose the main difference in thinking between Emerson and me," said Donofrio, "had been on the type of building we wanted, and the site. He was adamantly opposed to the Mud Island site and he wanted to raise two million dollars to build a permanent, enclosed building. All of which was good if you could do it. But being realistic, I felt that $500,000 was a more practical goal and if the City was willing to give us the Mud Island site, I was willing to settle for that."

In the meantime there was more action from Colonel Uppstrom. In a letter dated February 7, 1986, he had set a deadline. If the newly reorganized Memorial Association could not come up with the means to provide a proper home for the Belle by April 15, he would consider such failure as evidence that Memphis did not have enough interest in the old plane to save her. He would take steps to recover the Belle for the USAF Museum Program.

Directors of the Memphis Belle Memorial Association held another meeting with Memphis business leaders to ask for financial help and to solicit ideas from the business community on projects for raising money.

Three of the men who spoke at that meeting where Ward Archer Jr., an advertising executive, Al Sackett, a retired Naval rear admiral, associated with the Commerical Appeal, and Robert Snowden, a real estate executive. Each offered suggestions - and were promptly asked to put them to work.

Archer, assisted by Sackett, became the chairman of a committee working on local fund-raising projects. Snowden was put in charge of the building committee, which did the actual planning of the building for the plane. It was under Archer's and Sackett's direction that the Association suddenly found itself sponsoring a string of local events such as dances, beauty pageants, exhibitions and what have you. Each reaped dollars.

Mayor Hackett persuaded the Memphis City Council to give $150,000 including the site on Mud Island. Other Memphis business organizations weighed in with smaller gifts. The Commercial Appeal, which had long battled on behalf of the Belle, gave $5,000.

When it became clear that a vigorous new effort was in progress to provide a home for the Memphis Belle in Memphis, Uppstrom extended his deadline to July 31, 1986.

Perhaps this is the place to reveal what took place behind the scenes that lead up to the ultimatum from Colonel Uppstrom. For at the time, Memphians and members of the media did raise the question as to whether the Air Force actually had a right to claim the Memphis Belle.

The U.S. Government had sold thousands of surplus planes when the war was over. Most of them were cut up for scrap and melted down to recover the aluminum. The plane would undoubtedly have been melted down with all the others if Mayor Walter Chandler had not gone to Washington and bought her from $350.

One would assume that the Federal Government had no legal claim on her thereafter.

However, one fact not generally known was that in June of 1977, when the National Guard required the plane to move off the Guard's grounds, the American Legion did not feel that it could continue its custody of the Belle.

The Legion's commander, William T. Jamison, wrote a letter to Air Force officials, saying the Legion "wished to relinquish control of the B-17 bomber known as the Memphis Belle."

Shortly after, Mayor Wyeth Chandler, stepson of former Mayor Walter Chandler, wrote a letter to the same Air Force officials saying: "The City of Memphis wishes to relinquish any claim to the B-17 bomber known as the Memphis Belle. The City does this so that the B-17 can be put on permanent loan to the Memphis Belle Association, Inc., for display in a suitable museum in our city."

Was the the plane then turned over to the Air Force or to the Association? If the Air Force, indeed, believed that Chandler's letter was intended to give the plane back to the Air Force, why did it make no effort at the time to take custody of the Belle? The fact is that nine years passed before Colonel Uppstrom's ultimatum.

A few good lawyers could have had some fun with this sort of situation!

THE MEMPHIS BELLE

Dr. Friedman had this to say: "By the fall of 1985 and the spring of 1986 I was ready to say that if the people of Memphis did not get behind the program to save the Belle, and really take action, I was ready to tell the Air Force to come get her. After all these years, rather than having her continue standing outside and rotting to pieces, I would much rather see her in an Air Force Museum.

Then he added: "I talked to Colonel Uppstrom about it and from these conversations came those letters containing his ultimatum. And if people did not then back that final campaign, they did not deserve the Belle."

Were these letters from Colonel Uppstrom, then, written as a calculated move to spur the City of Memphis and Memphians to action?

Somehow, the whole thing began falling into place.

As the final deadline approached, necessary changes were made, men of influence joined the campaign effort, the media helped, and plenty of plain, ordinary people pitched in.

The Memphis Belle Memorial Association was reorganized. Several members who had fought the battle for a long time, convened a meeting of the board of directors. George T. Lewis, Chancery Court Judge, called for an election of new officers. The old officers had had their chance. It was time to let someone else fight the final battle. Frank Donofrio was restored as president of the Association.

One man who provided a turning point for the new Association was Fred Smith, dynamic president of Federal Express, a major new industry that Smith had created from scratch, providing a nationwide aviation network of overnight package and freight delivery. Smith announced that he was donationg $100,000.

His next contribution was to use his powers of persuasion with Boeing executives in Seattle, Washington.

As Friedman remembers the incident: "Smith was buying some planes from Boeing for his business. He suggested to the Boeing people that they ought to contribute $100,000 to the Memphis Belle project. After all, it was Boeing which had built the plane. They donated the $100,000."

It had not been the first time that Boeing executives had heard about the project. Colonel Emanuel J. Klette, last commander of the 91st Bomb Group, had already approached them and laid the groundwork.

The ABC-TV Network joined the campaign effort by volunteering to do a segment about the Memphis Belle on their popular 20/20 program, which is broadcast nationwide. Hugh Downs showed scenes from the old Memphis Belle film and described the plight of the plane. This brought in hundreds of letters with donations from the show's audience.

Memphians, who had so long waited for something to happen, could hardly believe their ears when on July 31, 1986, they were told that the Memphis Belle Restoration and Museum Fund Drive had gone over the top.

After 40 years, it was indeed hard to believe!

Into the Wild Blue Yonder

It could only have been a sentimental journey, this flight with Colonel Robert K. Morgan at the controls of the B-17 in 1987.

Something to stir the blood of a writer, trying to write the story of the Memphis Belle. I had long ago dreamed of flying on the Memphis Belle.

Sadly, the Belle herself will almost certainly never fly again. For too many years she sat, unprotected from the vandals and the weather. She has been restored, cosmetically, until she looks as good as new as she sits under her new protective plastic cover on Mud Island in Memphis, Tennessee. True, many of her mechanical and electrical components have been rebuilt.

But there are too many wires that have been cut or have corroded, too many switches and connectors no longer dependable. Perhaps even her engines would have to be rebuilt to make them run.

It is, of course, within the realms of possibility to make her once more flyable. After all, men built her and they could build her again, or rebuild her. But the cost, in skilled manpower and parts, would be prohibitive. Many parts, no longer available, might have to be made from scratch.

So, that idea of flying in the Memphis Belle herself will have to remain the impossible dream.

The only other possibility, a substitute, would be to wangle a flight on one of the few, very few, B-17s still flyable in the United States. There are perhaps ten or eleven of them.

The dream of becoming airborne in a B-17 began to become a possibility when the Memphis Belle Memorial Association, in the spring of 1987, reported that they were arranging for as many as possible of the still flyable B-17s to come to Memphis for a grand fly-over as part of the dedication ceremonies for the new home for the Belle on Mud Island on May 17.

Perhaps one of the pilots would let me go up with him.

I felt I would be no ordinary passenger. Long ago, in 1942, as a young reporter for the Memphis Press-Scimitar, I had been assigned by my city editor to write about a plane called the Memphis Belle and the storybook romance of its pilot and his fiancee. As the months went by, I wrote more of them.

On June 19, 1943, when the Belle made her return to Memphis, I was at the airport to meet her. To witness that wild flight of the Belle as she performed for the waiting Memphians, mostly for a girl named Margaret. Perhaps it wasn't really true but I had always felt I was a small part of the Memphis Belle story.

I was working as a press correspondent in Europe and the Middle East during the period after the war when Memphians began fighting to bring the Belle back to her "home town."

When I came back to Memphis I would often drive down Central Avenue and when I passed the Armory gounds I always felt a twinge of pride at the sight of the Memphis Belle sitting on her con-crete pedestal. I would tell my friends and my family, "I played a part in the discovery of the Belle."

For a short time, I served on Frank Donofrio's committee which was trying to find a permanent home for the plane.

In the summer of 1986, as a newly reorganized Memphis Belle Memorial Association started its final drive for funds to give the Belle a decent home, Frank Donofrio suggested that I write a book about the Belle that would tell the real story of a great lady.

When I agreed to do it I knew that, in a sense, at least, it would be a labor of love.

It was during the months of research, reading, interviewing surviving crew members, digging deeper into a story which began to reveal some aspects I had not even known about, that I became even more a part of the Belle.

Together with the pilot and crew members, I began reliving the story, hearing the thunder of the big Wright-Cyclone engines, seeing the vapor trails as they climbed high into the angry skies over German-held Europe, heard the defiant stutter of heavy machine guns as gunners fought to ward off the attacking fighters.

I was seeing, symbolically at least, the wounding of B-17s as they took hits, some of them exploding, some fluttering to earth.

In my reveries I felt the thrust of the trusted engines and rode those sturdy wings that could take so much. I could feel around me just a bit, perhaps, of the atmosphere those men felt in that long-ago time when they flew and fought with the B-17s.

These, then, were the things I was thinking about when I learned that those flyable B-17s would be coming to Memphis.

I asked if any of the pilots bringing B-17s to Memphis had actually flown them in combat in World War II. Yes, I learned, there was one. David C. Tallichet, with Specialty Restaurants of Anaheim, California, who had flown a B-17 on 21 combat missions in the closing months of the war with the 100th Bomb Group.

He would be coming to Memphis with B-17 No. 230604, made by Douglas Aircraft, under contract to Boeing, the first builders of the Flying Fortress.

"We haven't given it a name," he said.

No, it wasn't the plane he flew in the war but one of the later series B-17s. Its major claim to war glory was that it served as a private transport plane for General Glen Barkin in the war in Korea. It had never flown as a combat bomber but it was a B-17.

Dr. Harry Friedman and David White, members of the Memphis Belle Memorial Association, gave me the green light. Said Friedman, "You certainly deserve to go up, if anybody does."

When I arrived at the West Memphis Airport on Saturday, May 16, I discovered that I was about to get an experience I hadn't even hoped for, a flight with none other than Colonel Robert K. Morgan, the original pilot of the Memphis Belle, at the controls.

Colonel Morgan had been having a little dream of his own, his own sentimental journey. The man who had flown so many hours of combat in the skies over Europe, in a time when those pitifully small B-17 formations had been considered guinea pigs, experiments in high altitude daylight bombing, had been nursing a yen to get back into the pilot's seat for many years.

He, too, had been talking to Tallichet. The signal was "Go."

Tallichet climbed into left pilot's seat for the takeoff. Bob Nightingale of Ontario, California, was co-pilot.

As I settled into an improvised jump seat in the compartment just behind the bomb bay and buckled on my seat belt, I looked around at the interior of the big plane. It was easy to see that No. 604 had seen her share of service. She was grease-smeared and battered. It was comforting to remember the countless stories of the B-17 being such a forgiving plane, capable of taking so much abuse and coming back for more.

Remembering times in the days of propeller planes when a stubborn engine didn't want to catch on, it was a comfort to hear how quickly the engines roared when Tallichet hit the starters, one by one. They were signs of good engine maintenance.

The roar was too loud for comfort but a crew member quickly brought a box of earplugs. Then, as Tallichet pushed the throttles, we were out on the runway.

There would be no heavy drag of a load of bombs now and the takeoff run was a short one. The big Hamilton-Standard propellers caught gulps of air and we were airborne over the brown farm fields of Eastern Arkansas. I was indeed flying in one of the famed B-17s.

There were no 1,000-pound bombs in the bomb bay now, waiting to be dropped on enemy targets. No vapor trails followed us, signalling the bitter cold of the upper air where oxygen masks would be required. There were no deadly flak clouds, with jagged hunks of flak slicing through the skin of the plane. There were no stuttering machine guns warding off the enemy fighters and shouts from Johnny Quinlan, in the tail, "There goes another hunk off the tail." But this was as it should be. We didn't need a real war now. We only wanted a few moments to reflect on what had been.

You could look out the side windows at the broad, sturdy wings and watch the whirling arcs of the big propellers. You could listen to the throaty throb of the four big Wright-Cyclone engines and look at the peaceful brown and green countryside below. It was all enough for now.

It was some minutes after takeoff, after a sweep across the broad Mississippi River, over Mud Island where the Memphis Belle now stood in her new home, and back over the Arkansas fields when Tallichet climbed out of the pilot's seat and motioned to Bob Morgan who had been standing behind him.

Morgan could have ridden co-pilot and taken over for a few minutes, but it had always been a matter of pride to Bob that when he had flown the Memphis Belle into battle he had flown in the left seat, first pilot. He flew in the pilot's seat even when he was outranked by the man in the right seat, on those occasions when a commander wanted to experience the true measure of combat missions.

"I never flew the Memphis Belle except as pilot, from the left seat," Morgan remembered.

Bob Morgan was older, heavier of body now than in those days when he had been slim, fit and agile, the wartime pilot of the Belle. It was with a bit of effort that he heaved himself into the "chief's" seat and took over the controls. If there was anything youthful about him now it was in his face. The anticipation of doing what he had done in those long-ago years, working the controls, sensing the response, enjoying the communication between a man and a machine he said was the "best damned airplane ever made."

Someone said they had seen a look like this on Morgan's face the day before when he had climbed into the pilot's seat of the Belle herself, all neat and clean in her new paint, down there on Mud Island. He had sat for long moments, remembering, fingering the controls instinctively, indulging in a bit of nostalgic pride. His lips trembled just a bit, perhaps. In such a moment a mature man could be forgiven for surrendering to emotion.

Today, up in the sky with his hand reaching out to grasp the controls of another B-17, there was again something akin to that other time. Colonel Robert K. Morgan, USAF, Ret., had wanted to do this for a long time. It was a moment of fulfillment.

On this day, Morgan would try none of those crazy antics that had earned for him, back in 1943, the reputation of being one of the wild ones - good but wild. It would be sufficient unto this day to feel the controls, and feel the plane respond to the throttles, the control surfaces on tail and wing and to see that soft countryside floating peacefully past below. It was a moment for remembering, not for violent action.

I, too, as I rode with Bob Morgan that hour, was at peace with myself. I had wanted to do this for a long time. In fact, at one time in 1943, I had been scheduled to ride on the Memphis Belle with Morgan, but a leak in the hydraulic system had cancelled the flight. True, for thrills, this was far short of a blistering ride in a P-51, or a modern jet fighter but it didn't matter. The voices speaking to me now were from an earlier age, another time, when B-17s were queens of the skies.

The only gesture in the direction of a wilder day was one swoop, low over the runway, before we turned and landed. It wasn't one of those wild buzz jobs that Morgan had been noted for in 1943. But for now, in 1987, it would do.

"That was a great feeling," said Bob as he stepped down from B-17 No. 604.

It would not have been proper, at that moment, to ask him to say more.

We had made our sentimental journey into the "Wild Blue Yonder."

The Belle's Last Flight

Perhaps most folks would agree that an airplane must not be allowed the luxury of having a soul.

After all, an airplane is only a machine, made of aluminum, steel, fabric and rubber.

But there are old-time airmen, pilots, men with a long-time association with a single airplane, who would claim that an airplane might have, if not a soul, character.

You would throw your plane into a sharp chandelle, a spiraling dive, a wing-over, listen to the throb of the engines and, in a sense, she would be responding, speaking to you. And you to her. There was a communication of body language, if nothing more. You would like to believe it was more. She was more than a machine then, something alive and a part of you. Your heart throbbing to the tune of the pounding pistons, the bite of the propellers.

Bob Morgan never tried to define his relationship with the Memphis Belle in such terms but it was never hard to determine, from the letters he wrote, from the things he said, the way he flew her, that he had that kind of a relationship with the Memphis Belle.

In a letter to Margaret Polk, his fiancee, he had written from England while on his combat tour, when planes all around him were shot down, "The Memphis Belle will ride the skies safely, always. You can be sure."

In another letter, after returning from one of the toughest raids he and his crew had ever experienced, he wrote, "Your plane wasn't even hit all day and we were attacked more than any of the rest, for the Memphis Belle was in the lead. That makes me very proud to be flying your plane."

It was the language of a brash young pilot with supreme confidence and, dare we say, faith, in his plane. To warrant such faith she would have to embody something just a bit more than an ordinary combination of aluminum and steel.

Even at Bassingbourn in England, as the Memphis Belle neared the end of her 25 missions of combat, other men on the base had spoken of her as a lucky plane. To be truly lucky connotes something a bit more than the ordinary.

329

On those occasions when the Belle was hit, with heavy damage to her right wing and her tail twice shattered by flak, the plane always came home under control.

So, perhaps, we might be allowed to indulge in a bit of fantasy in describing the last flight of the Memphis Belle on September 11, 1986.

Did we say 1986? We did.

There she stood, lashed to the ground outside the Memphis Area Vocational Aviation School at the edge of the Memphis International Airport.

Behind her all those long years of neglect, of being kicked from pillar to post, and sometimes virtually abandoned, exposed to the ravages of the weather and the grasping hands of vandals, who stole parts, cut wires and ripped at her vitals. It had been sheer ignominy for this Boeing Flying Fortress, once a queen of the air, the star of a movie which had won national acclaim, the center of attention on a nationwide tour and even singled out to be honored by the King and Queen of England.

Now, at long last, there was the promise that she would be restored, at least cosmetically, and placed in a museum in a place of honor. In the meantime, for a few more weeks, she would stand there, waiting and dreaming. Can an airplane dream of past glories, of her days high in the blue skies?

Ah, if she could only fly once more. Feel the joy of "lift" once more under her broad, sturdy wings. To fly, to fly. The Memphis Belle was made for flying. But now she stood here, faced with the prospect of never flying again.

True, it was a windy, stormy day, that September afternoon. One of those hot, gusty days when strange things sometimes happen. Did happen.

Airmen, of late, have come to speak of a thing called "wind shear." They are freakish, sudden blasts or whirls of a sidewinder kind of wind that can, and has, wrecked airplanes trying to land.

It was such a gust, perhaps, that was flitting, whirling across the Airport that day. Playing, flirting, with the Memphis Belle.

Does our flight of fancy permit us to suggest that as the wind played in the area of the Belle, the old plane, in her own way, spoke to the wind?

"Dear wind, on whose bosom I flew so many times, please give me a lift. Let me fly. I was meant to soar on the breast of the winds but I haven't been aloft for so many years. Soon that will be impossible. But let me become airborne one more time. Please, dear wind."

And then it happened.

Charles "Chuck" Shelly, an instructor at the school, whose students had been doing some repair work on the old plane, stood there, unbelieving, as it happened. At least 60 of his students also saw it happen. John Steinriede, another instructor, saw it, too.

"We had the Belle staked to the ground with tie-down stakes driven five feet into the ground, about 30 feet from the hangar," said Shelly. "It was a bit stormy and it had started to rain. I decided to close the hangar door.

"I pushed the button and the door was beginning to close when the power went off. The door never came all the way down. I was just standing there, together with my students, when suddenly the Memphis Belle took off.

"Believe me, she was completely off the ground. She had pulled those tie-down stakes right out of the ground. There was a service platform standing between the Belle and the building, at least six or seven feet high. She cleared that platform without even knocking it over."

And then it was over. The Belle landed. Shelly agrees it was not a perfect landing. One of the wings brushed the ground, protruding into the building.

"If that door had closed completely, the wing would have crashed into the door," said Shelly.

As it was, the wing suffered a bit of damage and had to be repaired.

If the Belle had been able to talk she would have probably said, "If only Bob Morgan had been in the pilot's seat, he would have gotten me down safely."

It had all happened in a fleeting moment. A second or two. But the Memphis Belle had gotten her wish. She had flown once more. At least she had been airborne.

Now she was ready, content to be refurbished and transported to her own new home, a glistening plastic dome on Mud Island. To rest quietly amidst her plaques, telling visitors about the glories of her past.

331

For the Past and For the Future

Perhaps Frank Donofrio and the Memphis Belle Memorial Association could be forgiven, after the long, heartbreaking struggle to provide a final home for the Belle, for wanting to make the dedication of that home the most gala of occasions.

There would have to be speeches, banquets, parties, the works. The date selected was a natural, May 17, the anniversary of the day in 1943 when Robert K. Morgan and five members of his crew had completed their designated quota of 25 combat missions.

The theme selected for the big weekend was simply, "Home At Last." The eight surviving members of the crew that had brought the plane home in triumph in 1943 would, of course, be invited. For them, too, it would be a momentous occasion. Like the Memphians who had worked so hard and so long, they also had been waiting a long time for this moment.

Seven of the crew, Bob Morgan, Jim Verinis, Charles Leighton, Bill Winchell, Bob Hanson, Cass Nastal and Harold Loch accepted. It had been hoped that J. P. Quinlan, the feisty tail gunner, would be coming, too, but he had been having health problems, and his doctor advised against it. Norma Scott, widow of Cecil Scott, who had died of a heart attack, would come to represent him. Peggy Evans, sister of bombardier Vince Evans, who died in a plane crash in California in 1980, would represent her brother.

Margaret Polk, the other Memphis belle, would also be there with a place of honor reserved for her.

The Belle herself would have to make her last move, this one from the Airport to Mud Island, a distance of some 10 miles. One plan called for her to be air lifted by one of the Air Force's giant helicopters, but there had been questions of the safety of such a lift. It was finally decided that it would be done by a truck once more, as it had been done on the trips to and from the pedestal on Central, with her wings carefully removed.

The big fly-over of B-17s was arranged, largely through Dr. Friedman. He contacted the owners of the 11 flyable B-17s he had become acquainted with during his years of seeking spare parts for

332

the Belle. They were asked if they could gather in Memphis and fly in formation over Mud Island during the dedication of the Belle's new museum home. Four owners declined because their planes were being repaired or for other reasons. Seven said they could make it.

The seven Flying Fortresses were set to land at the West Memphis Airport, across the Mississippi River, where they would be in a spectacular display open to the public during the weekend. Fly-overs would be held Saturday and Sunday.

Sunday, May 17, was "THE Day." Thousands of Memphis citizens and visitors from out of town jammed the Monorail cars to Mud Island, where the Belle was enthroned in her new museum.

Thousands more walked across the pedestrian bridge to the island or crowded the high river bluffs on the Memphis side from where they could look down on the ceremony.

Under a brilliant May sun, citizens heard the speeches and the introductions of various notables.

Mayor Hackett spoke what was in the hearts of thousands of proud Memphians when he told his listeners about the long fight to save the Belle and how the ceremonies that day were an expression of appreciation to all the men who had fought in World War II.

"The spirit in which they served their country lives on in Memphis," he said.

Perhaps the most eloquent voice to be heard that day was that of Colonel Immanuel J. Klette, last commander of the 91st, who had flown more than 90 combat missions and remembered how the Eighth Bomber Command had grown from those pitiful few of the Memphis Belle's early days to the time, in 1944, when he led a flight of 1,291 bombers.

"When I crossed the border of Germany," he said, "the last of the bombers were still over England, a flight 300 miles long. That 'Mighty Eighth.'"

Gesturing to the Belle behind him in her new dome, he added, "We dedicate her most reverently to future generations whose freedom was made possible by the men of the mighty Eighth Air Force."

Colonel Morgan, too, had his moments of emotion that day. The veteran wartime combat pilot, older now and more mature, found that the events of this day were bringing a lump to his throat. His emotional climax came as Dr. Friedman read the letter from General Ira C. Eaker, who commanded the Eighth Air Force in England during the war. Now 91 and with impaired health, General

Eaker was unable to attend but he sent a letter to Morgan and his crew. It read in part:

"Vivid in my memory is the day, June 6, 1943, almost 44 years ago, when General Devers, Commander of the European Theater, and I bade you farewell at Bovington ... the first Eighth Air Force bomber to be sent home upon the completion of 25 missions ... The Memphis Belle shall remain a living memorial."

Said Morgan later: "Tears came into my eyes when that letter from General Eaker was read. This was a very emotional moment of my life."

Somewhere amidst it all there would come that moment when people in the waiting crowd began shouting, "Here they come!"

They heard the distant thunder of 28 Wright-Cyclone motors, as the largest formation of B-17s seen in America since World War II made its approach. Swooping low over the great river, they came.

It had to be a majestic moment. A prideful moment. Perhaps for some who had waited so many years for this happening, had suffered so many disappointments, this may have been the moment for their own tears of joy. For their own lump in the throat.

Could there be more? There was more. The bomb bay doors of one of the planes opened and down came a shower of flowers and petals, roses, carnations. Thousands and thousands of them. The plane's bombardier had done his work well, for the flowers were falling over the heads of the thousands waiting below. No angry bombs now, only soft petals floating gently to earth as symbols of peace and the fulfillment of a dream. The hope that never again would America be forced to send her sons in warplanes like the Memphis Belle to shower deadly bombs upon other countries.

Almost anyone in the crowd that day could reach up and catch a flower, a petal. It was hard indeed not to feel that tremor of emotion.

As for the Memphis Belle, she sat under the falling petals and the eyes of thousands of cheering citizens, now entitled to her own time of gladsome peace.

The Memphis Belle had indeed come home at last.

These Helped Restore and Relocate The Memphis Bell

164th Tactical Airlift Group
Tennessee Air National Guard

Colonel Charles M. Butler - commander

CMSGT. Nute C. Paulk   MSGT. Donald L. Hawkins

TSGT. Kevin L. Semmendinger   TSGT. Charles B. Love

SSGT. Ricky Way   SSGT. Richard McDowell
                                    (Deceased)

Past Commanders Who Helped
Preserve and Restore the Memphis Belle

Lt. Col. Henry K. Crawler   Lt. Col. Fred G. Hook Jr
Lt. Col. Dewitt Spain   Capt. Alvin Solari
Lt. Col. Ralph F. Newman   Maj. James W. Carter
Col. William M. Johnson   Lt. Col. William B. Smith
Col. Joseph H. Johnson   Col. Alfred B. Cole
Lt. Col. Paul N. Rogers   Lt. Col. David Olinger
Lt. Col. Ivan Oman   Col. William J. McGrath

Blytheville (Arkansas) Air Force Base

97th Field Maintenance Squadron

1Lt Stephen A. Whicker
A1C Todd E. Davis
A1C Tracey L. Crews
SrA William Betit
SrA Michael L. Herndon
TSgt Raymond Figueroa
A1C James Everett
Sgt Michael Whiteside
Sgt Jerry Neal
SSgt Ben Bragg
SSgt Robert Baker
MSgt Wayne E. Miller
Amn Paul C. Wald
MSgt George E. Hoots
A1C Benjamin Kuper
A1C Karen Fiack
Sgt David J. Best
SrA Stephen A. Thompson
SSgt Cash Baptista
A1C Michael Partridge
TSgt Joseph M. Adamski
A1C Bruce Cline
SSgt Michael Hollingsworth
SSgt Stanley T. McCardle

A1C Robert A. George
Amn James D. Dickson
A1C David A. White
A1C Kenneth C. Strabala
SSgt Stephen D. Edwards
Capt James G. Bennett
SSgt Rick Goetz
Sgt Bill Underwood
Sgt John Luttrell
A1C Randy Bick
Sgt Clifton Anthony
SSgt Steve D. Edwards
A1C James R. Redmond
A1C Wayne Shankle
MSgt Norman E. Faith
TSgt Kenneth D. Grossman
Sgt Andrew J. Orsak
A1C Gregory E. Baker
Amn Kenneth Oathout
Sgt Melina Richards
A1C John Wenck
Amn RobertTrudelle
1Lt Arnold J. Gavs
Amn William Miller

These persons and companies donated many personal hours and were helpful in restoring the Memphis Belle and in coordinating the festivities surrounding the opening of the Memphis Belle Pavilion. Thank you so much for your efforts.

Chairman, Plane Restoration
Dr. Harry Friedman

Tennessee Air National Guard Facilities
Colonel Michael Butler

Technical Assistance
M. Sgt. Don Hawkins
CM. Sgt. Nute C. Paulk
Sgt. Kevin Semmemdinger

Provision of Paint
Lowell Patterson, Mid South Paint
Larry Sitzes, Mid South Paint
Glen Workman, DuPont

Painting Equipment
Inn-Ovations

Painting
Leroy Best
Pete Cash
Tom Clark III
Jack Landree
Dan Phillips
James Smith
Wendy Stone
Donald M. Thompson

Nose Art Painting
Joe Giambrone
Phil Starcer

Plane Relocation
Larry Barber
CM. Sgt. Nute C. Paulk
Jim T. Woods

Plane Assembly and Restoration
Don Argall
M. Sgt. Norman Faith
Ron Grasso
Michael L. Herndon
Sonny Higdon
Bill Howell
Henry Martin
Sgt. Jerry Neal
Airman Kenneth Oathout
Airman 1.C. Michael Partridge
Don Santoro
Chuck Shelley
Richard Smith
John Steinreid
1st Lt. Steve Whicker
David White

Dedication Ceremonies
Ward Archer Jr.
Don Argall
Ann Ball
Chelius H. Carter
Marcia Clifton
Frank Donofrio
Dr. Harry Friedman
Ron Grasso
Steve Masler
Laura Reasoner
Nicky Roberts
Lt. Col. David Schilling
Donald M. Thompson

Rose Petals
Professional Florists Association
of Greater Memphis

The Memphis Belle Pavilion
Veteran Docents

C. D. Cash - Navigator/ Bombardier 381 BG
Harold Chrestman - Crew Chief 305 BG
Julian Darlington - Pilot B-24 / co-pilot B-17
D. Q. Darlington - Bombardier 384 BG
Chris Ellis - Pilot B-24
Alvin Fink - 19 BG (Pacific) first group w/ B-17s
Jack Gates - Pilot
William C. Hammers - Pilot
Jim Harrison - 92 BG
J. E. Helms - 8th AF
Willie G. Howell - 305 BG
T. Fred Jenkins - Engineer 92 BG
Ward A. Leap - Pilot B-17 / B-29
Bill Murry - Ball Turret Gunner 457 BG
Kenneth Parker
Jack Perry - Radio Opr. 94 BG
Harold Rudisill
Merle Sarvey - Worked on Belle in 1946 Kelly AFB
Bill Schmidt - POW / WW II
C. W. Shaw - Instructor B-17 / B-29
Paul Simms - Engineer / Top Turret 92 BG
Paul Stillions - Pilot B-25 / 15th AF
James Webb Sr. - B-17 Maintenance
James Webb Jr. - Vietnam Vet / B-17 modeler
Bob Kuehner - Tail Gunner 305 BG
H. Ross Witherspoon - 483 BG
John B. Payne - Tail Gunner 381 BG

The chart on the following two pages shows the missions flown by the Memphis Belle and her crew. It was compiled from military records and from a diary kept by Clarence Winchell, a member of the crew. Thirty missions are listed because there were times when the plane was out of service due to battle damage or mechanical breakdowns and her crew flew missions on other planes. The chart also shows missions on which the Belle was flown by crews other than her regular crew. Some crew members, individually, also flew missions on other planes.

Mission Number	Date	Target Location	Target	Plane	Pilot	Co-Pilot
1.	Nov. 7 1942	Brest, France	Submarine Pens	Memphis Belle	Robert K. Morgan	James Verinis
2.	Nov. 9 1942	St.Nazaire France	Submarine Pens	Memphis Belle	Morgan	Verinis
3.	Nov. 17 1942	St.Nazaire France	Submarine Pens	Memphis Belle	Morgan	Verinis
4.	Dec. 6 1942	Lille France	Locomotive Works	Memphis Belle	Morgan	Verinis
5.	Dec. 20 1942	Romilly s. Seine, Fr.	Air Field	Memphis Belle	Morgan	Verinis
6.	Dec.30 1942	Lorient France	Submarine Pens	Memphis Belle	Verinis	J.S. Jackson
7.	Jan. 3 1943	St.Nazaire France	Submarine Pens	Memphis Belle	Morgan	C.E. Putnam
8.	Jan.13 1943	Lille France	Locomotive Works	Memphis Belle	Morgan	S.J. Wray
9.	Jan. 23 1943	Lorient France	Submarine Pens	Memphis Belle	Morgan	Lt. Col. Lawrence
10.	Feb.4 1943	Emden Germany	Submarine Pens	Jersey Bounce	Morgan	S.J. Wray
11.	Feb. 14 1943	Hamm Germany	Railroad Center	Memphis Belle	Morgan	H.W. Aycock
12.	Feb. 16 1943	St.Nazaire France	Submarine Pens	Memphis Belle	Morgan	Aycock
13.	Feb. 26 1943	Wilhelms- haven,Ger.	Naval Base	Jersey Bounce	Morgan	Aycock
14.	Feb. 27 1943	Brest France	Submarine Pens	Jersey Bounce	Morgan	J.S. Jackson
15.	March 6 1943	Lorient France	Submarine Pens	Memphis Belle	Morgan	Aycock
16.	March 12 1943	Rouen France	Railway Yards	Memphis Belle	Morgan	C.W. Freschauf
17.	March 13 1943	Abbeville France	Air Field	Memphis Belle	Morgan	Freschauf
18.	March 22 1943	Wilhels- haven, Ger	Naval Base	Memphis Belle	Morgan	Freschauf
19.	March 28 1943	Rouen France	Railroad Center	Memphis Belle	Morgan	J.M. Smith
20.	March 31 1943	Rotterdam Holland	Ship Yards	Memphis Belle	H.W. Aycock	Smith
21.	April 5 1943	Antwerp Belgium	Airplane Eng.Wks.	Bad Penny	Morgan	J.H. Miller
22.	April 16 1943	Lorient France	Submarine Pens	Memphis Belle	Morgan	Miller
23.	April 17 1943	Bremen Germany	Airplane Factory	Memphis Belle	Morgan	Miller
24.	May 1 1943	St.Nazaire France	Submarine Pens	Memphis Belle	Morgan	C.E. Debaun
25.	May 4 1943	Antwerp Belgium	Airplane Eng. Wks.	Gr.Speck- led Bird	Morgan	V.A Parker
26.	May 13 1943	Meaulte France	Plane Repair Wk	Memphis Belle	C.L. Anderson	D.F. Gladhart
27.	May 14 1943	Kiel Germany	Shipyards	Memphis Belle	J.H. Miller	V.A. Parker
28.	May 15 1943	Heligoland Germany	Naval Yards	Memphis Belle	Morgan	J. H. Miller
29.	May 17 1943	Lorient France	Submarine Pens	Memphis Belle	Morgan	Haley Aycock
30.	May 19 1943	Kiel Germany	Ship Yards	Memphis Belle	C.L. Anderson	D.F. Gladhart

Navigator	Bombardier	Top Turret	Radio Operator	Waist Gunner	Waist Gunner	Ball Turret	Tail Gunner
Charles Leighton	Vincent Evans	Levi Dillon	Robert Hanson	Clarance Winchell	Harold Loch	Cecil Scott	John Quinlan
Leighton	Evans	Dillon	Hanson	Winchell	Loch	Harvey McNally	Quinlan
Leighton	Evans	Dillon	Hanson	Winchell	Loch	Scott	Quinlan
Leighton	Evans	Eugene Adkins	Hanson	Winchell	Loch	Scott	Quinlan
Leighton	Evans	Dillon	Hanson	Winchell	Loch	Scott	Quinlan
Leighton	Evans	Adkins	Hanson	Winchell	Loch	Scott	Quinlan
Leighton	Evans	Adkins	Hanson	Winchell	Loch	Scott	Quinlan
Leighton	Evans	Adkins	Hanson	Winchell	Loch	Scott	Quinlan
Leighton	Evans	Adkins	Hanson	Winchell	Loch	Scott	Quinlan
Leighton	Evans	Adkins	Hanson	Winchell	Loch	Scott	Quinlan
Leighton	Evans	Harold Loch	Hanson	Winchell	Emerson Miller	Scott	Quinlan
Leighton	Evans	Loch	Hanson	Winchell	Miller	Scott	Quinlan
Leighton	Evans	Loch	Hanson	Winchell	Miller	Scott	Quinlan
J.R. Ehrenberg	A.B. Cornwall	H. Robbins	R.E. Current	N.W. Kirkpatrick	C.B. Pope	R.W. Cole	C.A. Nastal
Leighton	Evans	Loch	Hanson	Winchell	Miller	Scott	Quinlan
Leighton	Evans	Loch	Hanson	Winchell	Miller	Scott	Quinlan
Leighton	Evans	Loch	Hanson	Winchell	Miller	Scott	Quinlan
Leighton	Evans	Loch	Hanson	Winchell	S.J. Spagnolo	Scott	Quinlan
Leighton	Evans	Loch	Hanson	Winchell	Miller	Scott	Quinlan
Leighton	Evans	Loch	Hanson	Winchell	Miller	Scott	Quinlan
Leighton	Evans	Loch	Hanson	Winchell	Miller	Scott	Quinlan
Leighton	Evans	Loch	Hanson	Winchell	Miller	Scott	Quinlan
J.R. Ehrenburg	Evans	L.W. Murray	J. Moore	Winchell	Miller	Scott	W.C. Dager
Leighton	Evans	Loch	Hanson	Winchell	Miller	Scott	Quinlan
W.S. Scovall	E.M. Bruton	H. Robbins	R.E. Current	N.W. Kirkpatrick	J.W. Carse	R.W. Cole	C.A. Nastal
J.R. Ehrenburg	E.M. Bruton	W.D. Spofford	O.L. Stuart	Miller	R.V. Cupp	R.H. McDermott	N.R. Lane
Leighton	Evans	Loch	Hanson	Winchell	Miller	Scott	Quinlan
Raymond Kurtz	Evans	Loch	Hanson	Winchell	Miller	Scott	R.W. Cole
W.S. Scovall	Eugene Adkins	A.B. Cornwall	R.E. Current	J.E. Carse	N.W. Kirkpatrick	R.W. Cole	E.S. Miller

A favorite target for photographers on Memphis Belle national tour: James Verinis and pet named Stuka.   They made many front pages.

"J. P." Quinlan points to what a horseshoe and two good .50s can do.

Bill Winchell, background, backs up crewmate Casimer Nastal.

Scott Miller, left, and Leviticus Dillon when they flew on the Belle.

Gable loved the sights and sounds of London on weekends away from the air wars. Memphis Belle pilot Bob Morgan said Gable was sure to have his pick of the pretties along the Thames when they sometimes visited the capital together.

Harold Lock poses before the familiar star on the side of his Flying Fortress at Bassingbourn.

Ground crew pauses to consider the possibilities. There might be some nice, big fresh eggs lying around in the grass somewhere after this pretty young village lass gets her pretty little band of geese out of the path of the warbirds.

Bombardier Vince Evans, right, discusses how Navigator Bob
Leighton, left, will make his approach to the target for the day.

Robert Hanson shows he's glad to be home from a rough one.

Cecil Scott let's ground crew know he'll do just fine, down below.

Riding the pilot's cockpit with Bob Morgan on all his missions
was some memento of the original Memphis Belle, the girl he
was engaged to marry, Margaret Polk of Memphis. Note the
snapshot he carried of her above his head on this mission.

The shattered tail of this bird makes it appear incapable of flight yet so often they miraculously brought them back this way.

German bullets punched their way through Quinlan's tail.

Old Bill holds up fingers in victory sign in spite of big nose job.

Flying Fortresses came to destory to Nazi war machine - and did.

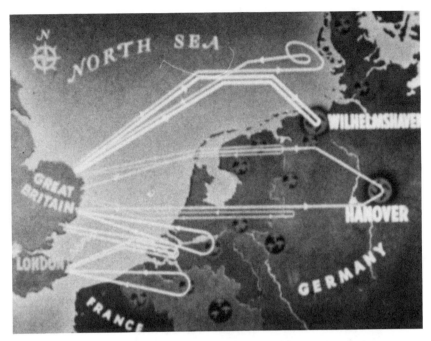

Diversionary feints and path of main attack shown in one day's map.

Priest raises hand in blessing as men pray before flying to war.

Torn apart by the fury of the battle, the Fortress falls with one wing.

Icy vapor trails show interlocking formations giving protection to all.

King and Queen of England visit the crew of the Memphis Belle seen drawn up smartly in a line as their pilot introduces each to the royal couple.

One of the celebrated romances of the age is caught briefly in this
picture as a returning air war hero, Captain Robert K. Morgan, holds
Margaret Polk for whom he named his plane the Memphis Belle.

A grateful nation welcomes the Memphis Belle and lionizes her crew
when the Fortress lands in Washington, first stop on its national tour.

The proud parents of gunner Bill Winchell are thrilled as his returning plane soars with her happy crew through peaceful skies of home.

Flying Fort comes to rest at last, to take off into war clouds no more.

Breaking ground for the permanent home of the Memphis Belle on Mud
Island theme park, on the Mississippi River at Memphis, Tennessee,
were, from left, Colonel Richard C. Uppstrom, Frank Donorfrio nd Dr.
Harry Friedman, all major movers in creating a permanent home for the
Memphis Belle in Memphis.

Arriving outside her new riverside museum home - the Memphis Belle.

Tennessee Air National Guardsmen present the Belle with a new tail cone, providing her a friendly escort as she moves into mature years.

Henry Martin guides Memphis vocational technical education students in school projects that help keep the Memphis Belle at her very best.

Home at last in her own plastic-domed palace, befitting a fabled Queen of the Skies, the Memphis Belle greets visitors daily.

Dignitaries from home and around the world met to celebrate the new home of the Memphis Belle. Mayor Dick Hackett, left, greets Margaret Polk attending with Bob Morgan, the Belle's wartime pilot.

When the bomb bays opened, rose petals instead of bombs rained down on celebrants at the opening of the new museum for the Memphis Belle beside the river. One of the largest peacetime formations of Flying Fortresses gathered from across the nation to join the festivities. It was a thrilling sight!

The Memphis Belle